Winter, 2012

Understanding
and Treating
Pathological
Narcissism

Understanding and Treating **Pathological Narcissism**

EDITED BY

John S. Ogrodniczuk

American Psychological Association

Washington, DC

Published by
American Psychological Association
750 First Street, NE
Washington, DC 20002
www.apa.org

To order
APA Order Department
P.O. Box 92984
Washington, DC 20090-2984
Tel: (800) 374-2721; Direct: (202) 336-5510
Fax: (202) 336-5502; TDD/TTY: (202) 336-6123
Online: www.apa.org/pubs/books
E-mail: order@apa.org

In the U.K., Europe, Africa, and the Middle East, copies may be ordered from
American Psychological Association
3 Henrietta Street
Covent Garden, London
WC2E 8LU England

Typeset in Goudy by Circle Graphics, Inc., Columbia, MD

Printer: United Book Press, Baltimore, MD
Cover Designer: Minker Design, Sarasota, FL

The opinions and statements published are the responsibility of the authors, and such opinions and statements do not necessarily represent the policies of the American Psychological Association.

Library of Congress Cataloging-in-Publication Data

Understanding and treating pathological narcissism / edited by John S. Ogrodniczuk.
    p. cm.
  Includes bibliographical references and index.
  ISBN 978-1-4338-1234-7 — ISBN 1-4338-1234-7 1. Narcissism—Treatment. 2. Personality disorders—Treatment. I. Ogrodniczuk, John S.
  RC553.N36U53 2013
  616.85'854—dc23
                        2012022517

British Library Cataloguing-in-Publication Data

A CIP record is available from the British Library.

Printed in the United States of America
First Edition

DOI: 10.1037/14041-000

CONTENTS

CONTRIBUTORS

Wendy T. Behary, MSW, The Cognitive Therapy Center of New Jersey, Springfield

Rachel Briand-Malenfant, PhD, Université de Montréal, Montréal, Quebec, Canada

Nicole M. Cain, PhD, Long Island University, Brooklyn Campus, Brooklyn, NY

Eve Caligor, MD, New York University School of Medicine, New York, NY

Emilie Descheneaux, Doctoral Candidate, Université de Montréal, Montréal, Quebec, Canada

Diana Diamond, PhD, City University of New York, New York-Presbyterian Hospital, and Weill Cornell Medical College, New York, NY

Eva Dieckmann, MD, University of Freiburg, Freiburg, Baden-Württemberg, Germany

William D. Ellison, MS, The Pennsylvania State University, University Park

Suzy Fox, PhD, Loyola University Chicago, Chicago, IL

Arthur Freeman, PhD, Midwestern University, Downers Grove, IL

Glen O. Gabbard, MD, Baylor College of Medicine, Bellaire, TX

Bridget F. Grant, PhD, National Institute on Alcohol Abuse and Alcoholism, Bethesda, MD

Brin F. S. Grenyer, PhD, University of Wollongong, Wollongong, New South Wales, Australia

Mardi Horowitz, MD, University of California San Francisco

David Kealy, MSW, University of British Columbia, Vancouver, Canada

Otto F. Kernberg, MD, New York-Presbyterian Hospital and Weill Cornell Medical College, New York, NY

Serge Lecours, PhD, Université de Montréal, Montréal, Quebec, Canada

Kenneth N. Levy, PhD, The Pennsylvania State University, University Park

M. David Liberman, PhD, ABPP, Private Practice, Highland Park, IL

Paul S. Links, MD, FRCPC, University of Western Ontario-London, Canada

Andrew F. Luchner, PsyD, University of Central Florida, Orlando

Kevin B. Meehan, PhD, Long Island University, Brooklyn Campus, Brooklyn, NY

John S. Ogrodniczuk, PhD, University of British Columbia, Vancouver, Canada

J. Christopher Perry, MPH, MD, McGill University and Sir Mortimer B. Davis Jewish General Hospital, Montréal, Quebec, Canada

Aaron L. Pincus, PhD, The Pennsylvania State University, University Park

Michelle D. Presniak, PhD, University of Saskatchewan, Saskatoon, Canada

Attila J. Pulay, MD, Semmelweis University, Budapest, Hungary

Eric Russ, PhD, Rush Medical College, Chicago, IL

Jonathan Shedler, PhD, University of Colorado School of Medicine, Aurora

Barry L. Stern, PhD, Columbia University Center for Psychoanalytic Training and Research, New York, NY

Manuel Trujillo, MD, New York University School of Medicine, New York, NY

Frank Yeomans, MD, PhD, New York-Presbyterian Hospital and Weill Cornell Medical College, New York, NY

ACKNOWLEDGMENTS

The genesis of this book is owed to the forward-thinking people at American Psychological Association (APA) Books, especially Susan Reynolds, who recognized a need for such a publication and encouraged its development.

Turning an idea into something real and tangible takes a lot of hard work. This book would not exist were it not for the considerable efforts of the chapter authors. They contributed much time and energy to the careful crafting of their chapters in the service of helping their peers develop a better understanding of pathological narcissism and its treatment. I feel privileged to have benefitted from their experience and wisdom.

In addition to the chapter authors, others had a significant role in this project. The help of my close colleague, David Kealy, was instrumental in the production of this book. Brin Grenyer, another dear colleague, provided sage counsel and helped shape the structure of the book. The patience and encouragement of my family (Jennifer, Mikayla, and Ethan) were crucial for helping this project see the light of day. Finally, I would like to express my gratitude to the anonymous reviewers who provided critical commentary on the initial book outline and the preliminary draft of the book. Their comments were influential in the development of the book's character.

Understanding
and Treating
Pathological
Narcissism

INTRODUCTION

JOHN S. OGRODNICZUK

Warnings of the perils of vanity and self-centeredness can be traced through humanity's history in biblical, mythological, and other types of writings. These writings, perhaps the best-known of which is the Greek myth of Narcissus, have contributed to what, today, we understand as *narcissism*. As suggested by these ancient writings, narcissism refers to self-investment. A moderate degree of self-investment (i.e., healthy or normal narcissism) consists of a reasonable and measured capacity for sustaining positive self-regard. Considered an adaptive and crucial aspect of healthy functioning, this capacity entails a realistic appraisal of one's personal attributes coupled with a capacity for empathy toward others (Stone, 1998). Accordingly, healthy narcissism is required for a sense of personal agency, the pursuit of ambitions, and the preservation or restoration of self-esteem in the face of disappointment or frustration. In contrast,

DOI: 10.1037/14041-019
Understanding and Treating Pathological Narcissism, J. S. Ogrodniczuk (Editor)

3

pathological narcissism "involves significant regulatory deficits and maladaptive strategies to cope with disappointments and threats to a positive self-image" (Pincus & Lukowitsky, 2010, p. 426). In other words, individuals with pathological narcissism lack appropriate mechanisms for the healthy maintenance of positive self-regard.

NARCISSISM: DEFINITION AND THEMES

Both healthy and pathological expressions of narcissism are encompassed within a functional definition of narcissism that was proposed by Stolorow (1975). Narcissism is thus conceived of as any mental activity that serves to "maintain the structural cohesiveness, temporal stability, and positive affective coloring of the self-representation" (Stolorow, 1975, p. 181). Implicit in this view is the notion that narcissism is expressed on a continuum, from healthy and adaptive at one end of the spectrum to pathological and severely maladaptive at the other. Whether narcissism is actually a continuous personality trait and whether a fundamental difference exists between healthy and pathological narcissism continue to be debated in the literature (see Pincus & Lukowitsky, 2010).

Two principal kinds of narcissistic dysfunction, described with varying terminology, have appeared consistently in the literature. Cain, Pincus, and Ansell (2008) distilled the various descriptive labels from the literature into (a) grandiose themes and (b) vulnerable themes. *Grandiose* themes refer to self-inflation, arrogance, and entitlement, all of which reflect intrapsychic regulatory processes such as fantasies of unlimited success and disavowal of negative self-representations. By contrast, *vulnerable* themes refer to feelings of helplessness, suffering, and anxiety regarding threats to the self—feelings that reflect a sense of inadequacy, emptiness, and shame (Kealy & Rasmussen, 2011).

Building on the review by Cain et al. (2008), Pincus and Lukowitsky (2010) further distinguished between types (grandiosity and vulnerability) and expressions (overt and covert) of narcissism. Grandiosity and vulnerability may each be either overtly or covertly expressed. For example, vulnerable themes of fragility and depletion may be predominant and overtly expressed, yet grandiose fantasies may hover covertly in the background. Likewise, overt arrogance can mask covert feelings of inadequacy (Pincus & Lukowitsky, 2010). From this perspective, narcissistic subtypes may be more appropriately considered as states that operate in a dialectical and reciprocal manner. Although many patients might evince one or the other theme much of the time, the contrasting theme remains psychologically salient, albeit unexpressed and not immediately perceptible (Kealy & Rasmussen, 2011).

In this way, a degree of expressive fluctuation between grandiosity and vulnerability is likely for most patients with pathological narcissism, varying in accordance with experiences of success or failure and interpersonal acclaim or rejection (Ronningstam, 2009). For example, an individual who struggles with overt shame and inhibition might reveal previously hidden grandiosity on receiving some encouraging external recognition. Likewise, an individual who is rejected by a friend or romantic partner might experience feelings of profound inferiority and weakness, which may surprise those who thought of him or her as confident and self-assured (Kealy & Ogrodniczuk, 2011). The presence of self-regulatory deficits involving distorted or fluctuating self-esteem has been recommended for the fifth edition of the *Diagnostic and Statistical Manual of Mental Disorders* (*DSM–5;* see http://www.dsm5.org/Pages/Default.aspx) as being more indicative of narcissistic personality disorder than the grandiosity emphasized by the criteria in the fourth edition (text revision) of the *Diagnostic and Statistical Manual of Mental Disorders* (*DSM–V–TR;* American Psychiatric Association, 2000; Ronningstam, 2011b). The changes to the diagnosis of narcissistic personality disorder proposed for *DSM–5* better reflect these self-esteem fluctuations and the compromised interpersonal functioning associated with them.

The self-regulation deficits in pathological narcissism represent a serious form of personality psychopathology and have long been recognized as having a deleterious effect on the individual self and others. Conceptual and clinical reports have linked pathological narcissism with stalled personal accomplishments, superficial relationships, and later-life emptiness and dread (Kernberg, 1984; Kohut, 1968). Pathological narcissism has also been described as underpinning intense rage reactions (Kohut, 1972) and, for some individuals, the descent into severe suicidal states (Ronningstam, Weinberg, & Maltsberger, 2008). Empirical reports have provided further information regarding the problems associated with pathological narcissism. These other areas of pathology include *DSM* Axis I disorders (Bachar, Hadar, & Shalev, 2005), psychiatric distress and functional impairment (Miller, Campbell, & Pilkonis, 2007), interpersonal problems (Dickinson & Pincus, 2003; Ogrodniczuk, Piper, Joyce, Steinberg, & Duggal, 2009), psychopathy (Paulhus & Williams, 2002), depressive tendencies (Kealy, Tsai, & Ogrodniczuk, 2012), impulsivity (Vazire & Funder, 2006), suicidality (Links, Gould, & Ratnayake, 2003), perpetration of child abuse (Wiehe, 2003), and substance abuse (Luhtanen & Crocker, 2005). These findings, taken together with numerous anecdotal reports and social commentaries, substantiate the problematic nature of narcissistic pathology. Adding to the seriousness of pathological narcissism is the widespread notion found throughout the clinical literature that it may be a particularly difficult form of personality pathology to treat.

TREATMENT AND RESEARCH

The topic of treating pathological narcissism generates intense, and at times opposing, reactions from clinicians. These reactions include fear, pessimism, and a sense of therapeutic nihilism but also fascination, hope, and a sense of obligation and responsibility to know more and do more to help patients who present with pathological narcissism. Despite the problems associated with pathological narcissism and the abundant clinical and theoretical literature dealing with the subject, there are no clear, empirically based guidelines for treatment. Psychotherapy, often of long-term duration, is generally considered to be the primary treatment for pathological narcissism. However, no randomized clinical trials of pathological narcissism treatments or naturalistic treatment studies involving patients with pathological narcissism have been reported. This is not to say that patients with narcissistic pathology are not receiving treatment: Narcissistic personality disorder is a consistently represented diagnosis in clinical practice (Morey & Ochoa, 1989; Westen & Arkowitz-Westen, 1998), and one survey reported that 25% of psychotherapy outpatients had this diagnosis (Doidge et al., 2002). Furthermore, the clinical literature abounds with case reports of psychotherapy for narcissistic dysfunction, and patients with pathological narcissism have been included in studies of transdiagnostic personality disorder treatment (e.g., Ogrodniczuk et al., 2009). General practice guidelines for working with narcissistic patients (e.g., Kealy & Ogrodniczuk, 2012; Ronningstam, 2011a) are helpful, but they are limited by the absence of empirical findings to ground recommendations.

The limited research regarding the treatment of pathological narcissism is a significant concern, and it is perhaps surprising given the amount of attention paid to narcissism in the clinical literature. In addition, mental health services have increasingly prioritized clinical research and evidence-based practice, yet the treatment of pathological narcissism has thus far received little attention. Paradoxically, this evidence-based climate—implemented to promote patient safety, treatment efficacy, and quality control—may place patients with pathological narcissism at risk of being excluded from treatment because policymakers may be reluctant to fund treatments that lack an empirical basis. Most of the literature on the treatment of pathological narcissism is theory driven and organized according to different schools of thought usually aligned with the seminal works of Kohut (1971) and Kernberg (1984). Using empirical research to establish consistent treatment guidelines would thus appear to be highly desirable, to promote optimal outcomes and to reduce iatrogenic effects among a patient group that is often labeled "difficult to treat." I hope this book stimulates efforts to study the effectiveness of different approaches to treating pathological narcissism.

SCOPE OF THE BOOK

Understanding and Treating Pathological Narcissism is intended to provide an overview of important issues related to the psychotherapeutic treatment of patients with this debilitating condition. The book draws on the knowledge of highly skilled, well-respected contributors who are at the forefront of clinical and empirical advances in the field, and the concise chapters provide an introduction to various topics that are relevant to the treatment of patients with pathological narcissism. This point deserves emphasis: This book should not be perceived as a comprehensive treatment guide or definitive textbook on pathological narcissism, but rather as a synopsis of key issues that provides the reader with a basic grounding. The complexity of pathological narcissism cannot be addressed comprehensively in the space of a series of short chapters. That being said, the unique focus and the breadth of topics covered herein should make this book a useful clinical reference.

Chapter 1 provides an historical overview of the construct of narcissism and thus offers context and background necessary for the remainder of the book. The ancient Greek myth of Narcissus, from which the term *narcissism* is derived, illustrates the distorted self-perception and interpersonal impact associated with narcissism. Although several versions of the myth exist, they share the common element of tragic self-absorption. The variety of potential interpretations can be thought of as reflecting the plurality of theoretical positions on narcissistic pathology, explored throughout the development of psychoanalytic theory and, more recently, personality and social psychology.

The chapters in Part II (Diagnosis and Assessment) address how to recognize pathological narcissism, a critical exercise for detecting patients in need and informing treatment choices. Part II begins with a review of conceptual and empirical work concerning the phenomenology of pathological narcissism, focusing on discussion of narcissistic subtypes (Chapter 2). Subsequent chapters then address diagnosis through the lens of the *DSM* (Chapter 3) and the more comprehensive *Psychodynamic Diagnostic Manual* (PDM Task Force, 2006; Chapter 4). Complementing these chapters is a discussion of case formulation using the configurational analysis method (Chapter 5). Finally, the recently developed Pathological Narcissism Inventory (Pincus et al., 2009) is featured (Chapter 6) because it represents a promising method for detailed assessment of pathological features related to different narcissistic subtypes.

Part III (Clinical Features of Pathological Narcissism) focuses on how pathological narcissism presents in patients. Although the empirical literature on pathological narcissism in clinical samples is somewhat sparse, the chapters contained in this section represent some of the more contemporary empirical efforts in the clinical field. By considering topics such as prototypical interpersonal behaviors (Chapter 7), affect regulation and mentalization in pathological narcissism (Chapter 8), and common intrapsychic conflicts and defenses (Chapter 9) in narcissistic patients, readers can develop a greater appreciation of issues that patients with pathological narcissism contend with. Suicidality is addressed (Chapter 10) because it represents a frequent and serious concern when dealing with narcissistic patients. Co-occurring psychiatric disorders that narcissistic patients present with are reviewed (Chapter 11).

Part IV (Treatment Considerations and Approaches) begins with a consideration of fundamental issues that psychotherapists should attend to, regardless of the theoretical model they follow. These include managing countertransference (Chapter 12), which is universally accepted as a critical issue in the treatment of narcissistic patients, and maintaining therapeutic boundaries (Chapter 13). The rest of the chapters provide an overview of several contemporary psychotherapeutic approaches, with specific reference to treating pathological narcissism. These chapters do not purport to be a primary source for developing a deep and sophisticated understanding of any one treatment approach for pathological narcissism. Rather, each chapter identifies the core features of narcissism that the treatment approach focuses on and explains how a particular treatment technique may apply to the core problems of narcissism. Part IV includes descriptions of treatments based on the seminal works of Kernberg (Chapter 14) and Kohut (Chapter 15), regarded by many to be the most theoretically well-developed approaches to treatment for pathological narcissism. Although it is generally considered that long-term therapy is necessary when working with patients suffering from pathological narcissism, the application of short-term treatments, such as short-term dynamic psychotherapy (Chapter 16), to core problems of narcissism may be possible. An integrated treatment that blends features of object relations and cognitive theory, called schema therapy, is described in Chapter 17. The book ends with a description of a cognitive therapy approach to treating pathological narcissism (Chapter 18), notable for its emphasis on helping patients accommodate to their narcissistic tendencies rather than addressing the core issues that underlie pathological narcissistic behavior.

CONCLUSION

Mental health clinicians are likely to routinely encounter patients with narcissistic problems. Although the term *narcissist* is commonly used pejoratively, patients with pathological narcissism face very real suffering and impairment. For this reason, clinicians need to be alert to pathological narcissism in practice settings and, where appropriate, seek to ameliorate it.

However, narcissism is considered difficult to comprehend, let alone to remedy. Clinicians who seek to learn more about pathological narcissism have access to an extensive literature that, for many, can seem overwhelming. Less available, however, is a succinct yet comprehensive overview of literature relating to the treatment of pathological narcissism, the absence of which is a significant obstacle to providing effective care to patients who suffer from its debilitating effects. It is my hope that this book, which attempts to help fill this void in the literature, will assist clinicians in developing a better appreciation of the complexities of pathological narcissism and the strategies that can be used to treat it.

REFERENCES

American Psychiatric Association. (2000). *Diagnostic and statistical manual of mental disorders* (4th ed., text rev.). Washington, DC: Author.

American Psychiatric Association. (2011). Personality disorders. In *DSM-5: The future of psychiatric diagnosis*. Retrieved from http://www.dsm5.org/proposedrevision/pages/personalitydisorders.aspx

Bachar, E., Hadar, H., & Shalev, A. Y. (2005). Narcissistic vulnerability and the development of PTSD: A prospective study. *Journal of Nervous and Mental Disease, 193,* 762–765. doi:10.1097/01.nmd.0000185874.31672.a5

Cain, N. M., Pincus, A. L., & Ansell, E. B. (2008). Narcissism at the crossroads: Phenotypic description of pathological narcissism across clinical theory, social/personality psychology, and psychiatric diagnosis. *Clinical Psychology Review, 28,* 638–656. doi:10.1016/j.cpr.2007.09.006

Dickinson, K. A., & Pincus, A. L. (2003). Interpersonal analysis of grandiose and vulnerable narcissism. *Journal of Personality Disorders, 17,* 188–207. doi:10.1521/pedi.17.3.188.22146

Doidge, N., Simon, B., Brauer, L., Grant, D., First, M., Brunshaw, J., . . . Mosher, P. (2002). Psychoanalytic patients in the U.S., Canada, and Australia: I. *DSM–III–R* disorders, indications, previous treatment, medications, and length of treatment. *Journal of the American Psychoanalytic Association, 50,* 575–614. doi: 10.1177/00030651020500021201

Kealy, D., & Ogrodniczuk, J. S. (2011). Narcissistic interpersonal problems in clinical practice. *Harvard Review of Psychiatry, 19,* 290–301. doi:10.3109/10673229.2011.632604

Kealy, D., & Ogrodniczuk, J. S. (2012). Pathological narcissism: A frontline guide. *Practice, 24,* 161–174.

Kealy, D., & Rasmussen, B. (2011). Veiled and vulnerable: The other side of grandiose narcissism. *Clinical Social Work Journal.* Advance online publication. doi:10.1007/s10615-011-0370-1

Kealy, D., Tsai, M., & Ogrodniczuk, J. S. (2012). Depressive tendencies and pathological narcissism among psychiatric outpatients. *Psychiatry Research*, *196*, 157–159.

Kernberg, O. F. (1984). *Severe personality disorders: Psychotherapeutic strategies*. New Haven, CT: Yale University Press.

Kohut, H. (1968). The psychoanalytic treatment of Narcissistic Personality Disorders: Outline of a systematic approach. *The Psychoanalytic Study of the Child*, *23*, 86–113.

Kohut, H. (1971). *The analysis of the self*. Chicago, IL: University of Chicago Press.

Kohut, H. (1972). Thoughts on narcissism and narcissistic rage. *The Psychoanalytic Study of the Child*, *27*, 360–400.

Links, P. S., Gould, B., & Ratnayake, R. (2003). Assessing suicidal youth with antisocial, borderline, and narcissistic personality disorder. *Canadian Journal of Psychiatry*, *48*, 301–310.

Luhtanen, R. K., & Crocker, J. (2005). Alcohol use in college students: Effects of level of self-esteem, narcissism, and contingencies of self-worth. *Psychology of Addictive Behaviors*, *19*, 99–103. doi:10.1037/0893-164X.19.1.99

Miller, J. D., Campbell, W. K., & Pilkonis, P. A. (2007). Narcissistic personality disorder: Relations with distress and functional impairment. *Comprehensive Psychiatry*, *48*, 170–177. doi:10.1016/j.comppsych.2006.10.003

Morey, L. C., & Ochoa, E. S. (1989). An investigation of adherence to diagnostic criteria: Clinical diagnosis of the *DSM–III* personality disorders. *Journal of Personality Disorders*, *3*, 180–192. doi:10.1521/pedi.1989.3.3.180

Ogrodniczuk, J. S., Piper, W. E., Joyce, A. S., Steinberg, P. I., & Duggal, S. (2009). Interpersonal problems associated with narcissism among psychiatric outpatients. *Journal of Psychiatric Research*, *43*, 837–842. doi:10.1016/j.jpsychires.2008.12.005

Paulhus, D. L., & Williams, K. M. (2002). The dark triad of personality: Narcissism, Machiavellianism, and psychopathy. *Journal of Research in Personality*, *36*, 556–563. doi:10.1016/S0092-6566(02)00505-6

PDM Task Force. (2006). Psychodynamic Diagnostic Manual, In *Personality patterns and disorders* (pp. 15–64). Silver Spring, MD: Alliance of Psychoanalytic Organizations.

Pincus, A. L., Ansell, E. B., Pimentel, C. A., Cain, N. M., Wright, A. G., & Levy, K. N. (2009). Initial construction and validation of the Pathological Narcissism Inventory. *Psychological Assessment*, *21*, 365–379. doi:10.1037/a0016530

Pincus, A. L., & Lukowitsky, M. R. (2010). Pathological narcissism and narcissistic personality disorder. *Annual Review of Clinical Psychology*, *6*, 421–446. doi:10.1146/annurev.clinpsy.121208.131215

Ronningstam, E. (2009). Narcissistic personality disorder: Facing DSM–V. *Psychiatric Annals*, *39*, 111–121. doi:10.3928/00485713-20090301-09

Ronningstam, E. (2011a). Narcissistic personality disorder: A clinical perspective. *Journal of Psychiatric Practice, 17*, 89–99. doi:10.1097/01.pra.0000396060. 67150.40

Ronningstam, E. (2011b). Narcissistic personality disorder in *DSM–V*: In support of retaining a significant diagnosis. *Journal of Personality Disorders, 25*, 248–259.

Ronningstam, E., Weinberg, I., & Maltsberger, J. T. (2008). Eleven deaths of Mr. K: Contributing factors to suicide in narcissistic personalities. *Psychiatry: Interpersonal and Biological Processes, 71*, 169–182.

Stone, M. (1998). Normal narcissism: An etiological and ethological perspective. In E. Ronningstam (Ed.), *Disorders of narcissism: Diagnostic, clinical, and empirical implications* (pp. 7–28). Washington, DC: American Psychiatric Association.

Stolorow, R. D. (1975). Toward a functional definition of narcissism. *The International Journal of Psychoanalysis, 56*, 179–185.

Vazire, S., & Funder, D. C. (2006). Impulsivity and the self-defeating behavior of narcissists. *Personality and Social Psychology Review, 10*, 154–165. doi:10.1207/ s15327957pspr1002_4

Westen, D., & Arkowitz-Westen, L. (1998). Limitations of Axis II in diagnosing personality pathology in clinical practice. *The American Journal of Psychiatry, 155*, 1767–1771.

Wiehe, V. R. (2003). Empathy and narcissism in a sample of child abuse perpetrators and a comparison sample of foster parents. *Child Abuse & Neglect, 27*, 541–555. doi:10.1016/S0145-2134(03)00034-6

I

INTRODUCTION TO NARCISSISM

1

HISTORICAL OVERVIEW OF PATHOLOGICAL NARCISSISM

BRIN F. S. GRENYER

Pathological narcissism has long exerted an important hold on the imagination. Mythological, biblical, and other religious writings and doctrines have included sanctions against vanity and warnings about choosing self-love over the love of others and society. These dangers, long discussed in stories, paintings, and plays, have found a modern form in the presentation of a particular kind of personality style, narcissistic personality disorder, in psychology and psychiatry.

The purpose of this overview is to demonstrate how contemporary views on pathological narcissism and its treatment can be enhanced through understanding the history of the concept. Understanding the historical roots of narcissism brings more clearly to light the contemporary implications of narcissism and the current debates and advances in the field (Ronningstam, 2009). I begin with the original Greek myth and then discuss the psychological literature up until 1979, which marks the publication of the narcissistic

DOI: 10.1037/14041-001
Understanding and Treating Pathological Narcissism, J. S. Ogrodniczuk (Editor)
Copyright © 2013 by the American Psychological Association. All rights reserved.

personality inventory (Raskin & Hall, 1979), followed 1 year later by the inclusion of narcissism as a personality disorder (*Diagnostic and Statistical Manual of Mental Disorders*, 3rd ed.; *DSM–III*; American Psychiatric Association, 1980). Considerable clinical, experimental, and theoretical work on narcissism has been undertaken since then (Cain, Pincus & Ansell, 2008).

THE ANCIENT GREEK MYTH OF NARCISSUS

The term *narcissism* evolved from the ancient Greek myth of Narcissus, a young, beautiful boy who rejects the love of others as unworthy and falls in love with his own reflection in water. The longer he stares at his own image, the more he is driven by both passion and heartache, and over time he dies in this state of despair. The ancient Greek story has been told in various versions by ancient writers, and each ends in tragedy. In the earliest known version (which dates to around 50 BCE and is attributed to Virgil's tutor, Parthenius of Nicaea), a spurned male suitor persuades a god to make the self-obsessed but beautiful Narcissus stare at his image forever. This drives Narcissus to commit suicide; he collapses in a pool of blood (Keys, 2004). This early version whereby Narcissus commits suicide was later also adopted by Conon, a mythographer and contemporary of Ovid in his Narrations number 24 (Conon, 25 BCE/1738). In the version by Ovid (AD 8/1717), Narcissus melts and withers away from heartbreak. In another version by Pausanias (AD 143–176; Habicht, 1985), written some 100 years after Ovid, Narcissus falls in love with his identical twin sister and has a sexual relationship with her. When she dies, he pretends to see her reflection in the water to recall his love of her. Each version includes an erotic component—for Parthenius it is spurned homosexual love, for Ovid it is self-love and the nymph Echo's unrequited love for Narcissus, and for Pausanias it is intrafamilial incest. The version that is the best known, with the broadest appeal, and also the longest with the most developed plot, belongs to Ovid.

Ovid's version (AD 8/1717) is written in the hexameter epic narrative poem style. Narcissus comes upon a perfectly clear pool of water that has not been disturbed by any animal or leaves and, being thirsty, lies down to drink. He falls in love with the reflection and tries to embrace and kiss the beautiful boy he sees, disturbing the water. At first, he does not recognize the image in the lake as his own ("Nor knew, fond youth! it was himself he lov'd"). This unrequited love leads him to neglect sleep and food, and he is gradually tortured by the person in the water, calling for him: "My lips to his, he fondly bends to mine. / Hear, gentle youth, and pity my complaint, / Come from thy well, thou fair inhabitant"—until he has insight—"It is my self I love, my self I see; / The gay delusion is a part of me." Prior to these events, the seer Teiresias had prophesied that "Narcissus will live to a ripe old age, provided that he never knows himself" (Graves, 1955, p. 286). Narcissus's mother was a beautiful nymph who had attracted the attentions of the River god Cephisus. It is perhaps prophetic, therefore, that Narcissus's own fate be bound up with water.

The poem is in Book 3 of the *Metamorphoses*, a collection of 15 books in which the heroes are variously transformed into such things as animals, star constellations, trees, rocks, and flowers (Ovid, AD 8/1717). Narcissus's recognition of himself in the water is his downfall; he withers away in a pool of blood and is transformed into a white narcissus flower (an iris lily). At the time, balm distilled from this flower was used in temples. Derived from the plant was "narcissus oil," a narcotic. In fact, the word *narcotic* derives from the name "narc-issus." It is telling that the myth of Narcissus can also be understood as a tale about the effects of narcotics in terms of narcissistic bliss, that is, a euphoria of love and happiness bound up in a singular self-state (in drug abuse the state is that of the addict who is high on the substance). The word *narcissus* derives from the Greek word for sleep or numbness. It is therefore not surprising that 2,000 years later, modern analytic theories refer to drug abuse as a narcissistic disorder (Wurmser, 1974).

THE ANCIENT GREEK NYMPH ECHO

The tragedy of Narcissus provides a powerful narrative for modern psychological theories on the dangers and consequences of an unhealthy preoccupation with the self as love object. Thus, the roots of pathological narcissism as an important clinical diagnosis can be traced back to stories told at the beginning of civilization. Often overlooked in considerations of narcissism and the Greek myth is the important role played by the nymph Echo in the Ovid version. In the final scenes of the story, Narcissus and Echo are joined together in a tragic coupling. Echo, a lively and beautiful nymph, is punished for talking too much, in that by her love of talking and telling long stories she distracted the jealous Hera (Juno) from catching her husband, Zeus (Jupiter), consorting with other mountain nymphs. Echo is condemned to repeat the last words of what she hears others say: "She long'd her hidden passion to reveal, /And tell her pains, but had not words to tell: / She can't begin, but waits for the rebound, / To catch his voice, and to return the sound." In the final scene Echo, caught in an obsessive love of Narcissus, is unable to connect with him in her love, and he in turn rejects her for his own image. Thus wounded, Echo spends the rest of her days obsessed by both her love of Narcissus and his rejection of her and is only able to communicate with the words of others, not her own.

The significance of Echo to the story is that both she and Narcissus suffer in ways familiar today to our thinking about pathological narcissistic subtypes (Cain et al., 2008; Gabbard, 1989; see also Chapter 2, this volume). Narcissus, in love with his own unattainable image, represents the grandiose, oblivious subtype of narcissistic disorder. Echo, in her destructive obsessive love of another whose words she can only repeat, represents the fused hyper-vigilant narcissist, who can only live through another:

> She answer'd sadly to the lover's moan, / Sigh'd back his sighs, and groan'd to ev'ry groan: / "Ah youth! Belov'd in vain," Narcissus cries; / "Ah youth! Belov'd in vain," the nymph replies. / "Farewel," says he; the parting sound scarce fell / From his faint lips, but she reply'd, "farewel." / Then on th' wholsome earth he gasping lyes, / 'Till death shuts up those self-admiring eyes (Ovid, 8 AD/1717)

Common to both Narcissus and Echo was the incapacity for healthy love and the escape from this in obsession with the self or with another. In this way, the early myths of Narcissus and Echo form early case studies in pathological narcissism, probably told, like most of the Greek myths, to illustrate and educate listeners and readers in the spectrum of human motives and behaviors.

TRANSFORMATION OF THE GREEK MYTH INTO A PERSONALITY TYPE

Since this powerful narrative was first told, Western civilization has found inspiration in art, drama, and poetry for retelling this story. For example, Milton (1667) in *Paradise Lost* cleverly pictures the process of coming across the reflection, and it bending and weaving along with the movements:

> As I bent down to look, just opposite / A Shape within the watry gleam appeerd / Bending to look on me, I started back, / It started back, but pleasd I soon returnd, / Pleasd, it returnd as soon with answering looks / Of sympathie and love, there I had fixt / Mine eyes till now, and pin'd with vain desire.

Notable paintings include *Narcissus* by Caravaggio (1597–1599, Galleria Nazionale d'Arte Antica, Rome). Over time, painters turned their attention to more public manifestations of narcissism, particularly paintings of beautiful women entranced at their mirror, often with death symbols warning against this unhealthy obsession (the sin of vanity).

Up until the end of the 19th century, references to Narcissus were connected to the Greek mythological story. Havelock Ellis (1898) was the first to evoke the Greek myth in psychological writings. Paul Näcke (1851–1913), a Russian-born German psychiatrist and director of an asylum at Colditz, Saxony, is first credited with introducing the term *narcissism* into psychiatry in 1899 in a study of sexual perversions, particularly excessive masturbation (Näcke, 1899). In this way, the instance of the Greek story of a young boy was generalized into a commonly recognized trait. A year before, Havelock Ellis, who was actively studying and writing on sexual matters, referred to excessive love as *narcissus-like* if it develops a self-love component. In fact, Näcke translated Ellis's paper into German, adding the "ism" to create the term *narcissism*. Ellis's (1898) paper described the case of women who become lost in self-admiration (symbolized by the mirror), which "appears to exist by itself, to the exclusion of any attraction for other persons" (p. 290). By 1927, Ellis had developed and summarized these views into a more complete paper on "the conception of narcissism," which he regarded as *autoeroticism*, or the self-absorption of sexual emotion into self-admiration. Ellis considered this to be a particular issue most likely found in young women as their consciousness of beauty develops, and indeed he considered the Greek god Narcissus to be quite feminine in characteristics in his youthfulness. It is interesting to speculate that the feminine components of Narcissus may have increased the attraction of Echo, in that they may have had a mirroring narcissistic reflection of her own beauty. Ellis's contribution beyond these conceptions is to further the pathological aspects of our understanding of narcissism. He extended this discussion into group psychology, explaining how "national narcissism" (patriotism and the hatred of foreigners) forms along similar lines. Similarly, "specific narcissism" glorifies humanity and mankind in triumphal narratives that contain narcissistic themes.

Ellis considered pathological narcissism to be a feature of specific persons, not a universal condition. Similarly, in 1911 Otto Rank published the first monograph on narcissism emphasising the self-love and vanity aspects of the personality type. Rank discussed the phenomenon whereby a particular female can allow herself to love only after she has first established that her suitor loves her. Ellis, Rank, and Näcke confined their views to individuals or groups of individuals. These early uses of the term *narcissism* were illustrative in that it was used to describe behaviors of specific people. All that changed in 1914 with the publication of the highly significant and important paper "On Narcissism" (Freud, 1914/1957). Freud took the term and developed within it a thorough analysis of the possible causes of narcissism, the developmental aspects, its positive and potentially adaptive components, and negative components or effects. Within this paper, then, Freud introduced a sophisticated analysis of the underlying issues of the relationship between the self and others and of self-love and other-love.

FREUD'S ANALYSIS OF NARCISSISM

Freud (1914/1957) began "On Narcissism" by differentiating his views from his predecessors. He rejected the argument that masturbation or autoeroticism is necessarily related to the psychological term *narcissism;* he considered narcissism to be related to the development of the sense of self. Similarly, Freud differentiated narcissism from its more extreme form of megalomania, with the latter having more to do with omnipotent power and delusions of grandeur. He described narcissism as "libido that has been withdrawn from the external world has been directed to the ego and thus gives rise to an attitude which may be called narcissism" (p. 75). Freud did not pass judgement on self-love (or narcissism) in comparison with other-love (or anaclitic attachment based); his focus was on understanding these processes and choices and their consequences for mental health. Self-love can be both healthy and unhealthy:

> A strong egoism is a protection against falling ill, but in the last resort we must begin to love in order not to fall ill, and we are bound to fall ill if, in consequence of frustration, we are unable to love. (p. 85)

Developmentally, it is healthy for young children to have self-love, especially as conveyed through the behaviors of parents, who provide the conditions for primary narcissism in their selfless care and admiration of their child. The development of healthy self-esteem (or ego) requires a degree of narcissism.

Freud extended this discussion by introducing not only self-love but also the need for love from others as confirming this narcissism. What is clear, therefore, is how such conditions can be heightened when people are themselves beautiful and charming, as was the Greek god Narcissus, with such processes applying equally to both males and females. Freud then considered both sides of these issues: first, the case of the narcissistic person who receives the confirming love of another and then, the effect on the loving other, who has to renounce some of their own narcissism in loving the other. In the case of mutual love, narcissistic and anaclitic processes are shared in equal measure:

> The effect of dependence upon the loved object is to lower that feeling: a person in love is humble. A person who loves has, so to speak, forfeited a part of his narcissism, and it can only be replaced by his being loved. In all these respects self-regard seems to remain related to the narcissistic element in love. (p. 98)

In this analysis, Freud extended the understanding of narcissism by providing a more comprehensive context by which the processes can be both adaptive and pathological and an explanation for how these bear critically on the fate of love-relations with others. Freud also introduced possible variants associated with narcissism: (a) loving oneself in the present; (b) loving what one once was; (c) loving what one hopes to become; or (d) loving someone who was once part of oneself. The echo subtype (which Freud terms the anaclitic attachment type) is preoccupied with feeding and protecting the overvalued other (p. 89).

Freud's development of the theory of these interpersonal processes helps us understand further the Greek myth. Narcissus invests his entire libido in himself, and Echo invests all her libido in Narcissus. She is therefore left empty (literally to disappear into the forest as a hollow voice), and he is left tortured and unwell, without the capacity to enter into a relationship with the thing he loves because it has no sustaining mutuality. In his conclusion, Freud hinted at a deeper analysis of narcissism, in relation to not only interpersonal relationships but also the broader impact on society, which in turn became the foundation for his later concepts of the superego and ego-ideal.

FURTHER DEVELOPMENT OF PATHOLOGICAL NARCISSISTIC SUBTYPES: 1926–1979

Many writers further developed the conceptualization of narcissism after Freud (Teicholz, 1978). A few examples are given. Clarke (1926) progressed the discussion of how to undertake psychotherapy with highly narcissistic patients when the ordinary transference neurosis does not operate. Reich (1933/1949) further developed the discussion of a particular type of male narcissism, characterized by arrogant and sadistic features that can be found in certain leaders, perhaps influenced by the emergence of hard-line military dictators in World War II. Fenichel (1945) extended this discussion to outline the vulnerabilities behind such personality types. Balint (1960) rejected the idea of a primary narcissism but developed a theory focussing on another component—the fate of libidinal impulses. For Balint, the individual is born in a state of intense relatedness to the environment biologically and libidinally. The trauma of birth accelerates the separation between individual and environment. Within these developments, love can become variously invested. Balint introduced the term *oncophilic* to describe the "echo" love relation, the overvaluation of love into another person and the consequent intense dependence on them. By contrast, the *philobatic* subtype describes the "narcissus" investment of love into the self, along the lines, described by Reich and Fenichel, of a loner with indifferent, deceitful, and untrustworthy characteristics.

Hendrick made a significant advance on the understanding of narcissism; his work was based on Freud's initial theoretical developments, the work of Murray (1964), and the earlier work of Balint and colleagues. Hendrick

(1964) expanded the interpersonal understanding of narcissistic relations, to further describe the "Echo" component, whereby a person with a very immature ego invests his or her libido wholly in another person and becomes dependent on that person for libidinal gratification. This person becomes the "ego ideal" just as Narcissus was the ideal for Echo. Hendrick deepened this discussion by referring to developmental processes. It is normal for a prepubescent child to invest love in another person (e.g., the parent), but in normal development that process is then displaced onto multiple others. The arrest of this process creates an unhealthy dependence on the idealized other. This dependence is then highly fragile and reliant on the consistency of the other to maintain the person's mental health. The death or loss of the idealized other creates a crisis whereby the person risks regressing to more primitive unsociable narcissism with its attendant psychopathology. Thus, when Narcissus dies, Echo is destroyed. Hendrick's discussion advances further our understanding of the fragility of the ego when the process sustaining it, in this case the idealization of another, is taken away.

Freud first introduced the relationship between narcissism and a healthy superego, but it was Kohut who further developed Freud's and Hendrick's ideas. Kohut (1966) extended the discussion into the function of narcissistic attitudes as both learning and growth extending opportunities. Narcissism through primary identifications with the mother and her struggles, and the healthy strivings in her life, presents new ideas of narcissistic processes as having a positive force if they move beyond primitive self-admiration. Similarly, he focused on the therapeutic situation, arguing that transforming narcissism into more healthy forms that serve society is preferable to simply trying to replace it with an alternative love object. In this way, he depathologized narcissistic processes and presented the emergence of the idealizing libido as a maturational step in development. In treatment, both idealizing and mirroring transferences can be present and can be transformed to assist the patient's progress.

Kohut (1966) discussed the healthy processes of idealization of parents at a critical stage in the child's development and explained how these processes provide a sense of security in the face of challenging developmental milestones. Kohut then moved on to discuss how the superego, the internalization of parental values, becomes established only when the narcissistic identification and idealisation of the parents diminishes, as the child disperses his or her identifications across a wider number of objects and internalized parental security. For healthy development to proceed, parents must also play a role in moderating their child's grandiosity. First, parents must support the grandiosity in order to enhance esteem. When positive self-regard has been internalized, they then need to qualify the grandiosity over time to develop maturity in the child. Failure to manage this process can lead to a developmental arrest at the grandiose stage. At this arrested stage, there is an ongoing dependence on others to bolster the grandiosity. Therefore, the development of the narcissistic self is a maturational step.

For Kohut, premature interference with this maturational process may lead to narcissistic vulnerability, as the grandiose fantasy becomes repressed and inaccessible to modification. The person most likely to experience shame is the ambitious person who has a poorly integrated grandiose self-concept and an incapacity to empathize with the narcissism of others. The development of healthy narcissism, bound up in super-ego processes, becomes associated with self-esteem in the face of success, a healthy enjoyment of activities, and shame in the face of disappointments and failures. Creativity, empathy, capacity to contemplate impermanence, sense of humor, and wisdom are healthy transformations of narcissism, in that they moderate successes and failures in the interests of maintaining a healthy self-esteem. Kohut (1966) illustrated how dynamic these processes are. As an example, he cited the artist who alternates between productivity and satisfaction to a conviction that the work has no value. Humor and wisdom are seen as ways of mastering narcissistic demands and delusions, and thus Kohut (1971, 1977) moved his discussion into existential areas.

Kernberg (1970, 1972) explored the more extreme forms of narcissism, at the malignant antisocial or psychopathic level, and his explanation of these processes differed from that of Kohut. Kernberg referred to Freud's introduction of self-love and other-love and explained how psychopathology develops and manifests within this sphere. First, in its extreme form, narcissistic patients in psychotherapy are unable to experience the therapist as separate from themselves; rather, they see the therapist as an extension of themselves. Second, the independence of the therapist is resisted by patients' devaluation, spoiling, and depreciation of the therapist. It is critical that the therapist undo these attempts. Because insecurity and inferiority underlie grandiosity, the experience of a separate therapist may induce paranoia, suspiciousness, hatred, and envy. Over time, as differentiation is reinforced within the safety of therapy, the patient may experience guilt and despair for treating the therapist in such a way. Thus it is clear that in pathological narcissism, the ideal self, ideal object, and actual self become fused. In other words, the ego and superego, self and internalized values, are so insecure and unstable that they become fused into a grandiose self that projects unacceptable features into others. Kernberg's contribution to this development of ideas is the uncovering of the therapeutic implications of extreme narcissism and his discovery that underneath insecurity may be a rage and aggression expressed toward others (and sometimes the self). Thus, Kernberg (1975) brought into focus the primitive conflicting and splitting forces of aggression and libido, frustration and gratification, bad and good, as they are in Kleinian British object relations theory (Klein, 1952; Mendez, Fine, & Guntrip, 1976).

There is an extensive literature on the differences between Kohut and Kernberg's views (Adler, 1986). It is possible that their work describes different subtypes of narcissism, possibly emerging in part from the different settings they collected their data. Kohut discussed in particular a "merger self-object transference" that may align more with the role of Echo. In contrast, Kernberg discussed the "self-sufficient transference," which may be more like the role of Narcissus. Both authors emphasized the difficulties for the therapist in managing these patients: Both the Echo and Narcissus types can stir up in the therapist difficulties with tolerating boredom in the therapy, managing idealization by the patient, and handling aggression and devaluation by the patient.

Returning to Freud, what is clear is that the Narcissus and Echo processes are best understood within the bounds of the patient's seeming choices on how to tolerate insecurities, and therefore both types of behaviors may be present in the same patient at different times. Such issues bear upon the development of the concept of narcissism, since these debates began in the 1970s and 1980s (Cain et al., 2008). The emergence of new tools and measures has emphasized the importance of considering dimensional understandings rather than just categorical differences. In this way, the ancient Greek story of Narcissus and Echo may be less about actual persons than different psychological processes. Nevertheless, it is remarkable that such ancient myths continue to hold an important place in our understanding of contemporary psychology.

REFERENCES

Adler, G. (1986). Psychotherapy of the narcissistic personality disorder patient: Two contrasting approaches. *The American Journal of Psychiatry, 143,* 430–436.

American Psychiatric Association. (1980). *Diagnostic and statistical manual of mental disorders* (3rd ed.). Washington, DC: Author.

Balint, M. (1960). Primary narcissism and primary love. *The Psychoanalytic Quarterly, 29,* 6–43.

Cain, N. M., Pincus, A. L., & Ansell, E. B. (2008). Narcissism at the crossroads: Phenotypic description of pathological narcissism across clinical theory, social/ personality psychology, and psychiatric diagnosis. *Clinical Psychology Review, 28,* 638–656. doi:10.1016/j.cpr.2007.09.006

Clarke, L. P. (1926). The phantasy method of analyzing narcissistic neurosis. *Psychoanalytic Review, 13,* 225–232.

Conon (1738). *Bibliotheque de Photius: 186 Recits de Conon* (A. Gedoyn, Trans.). Paris, France: Histoire de l'Academie Royale des inscriptions et belles letteres.

Retrieved from http://remacle.org/bloodwolf/erudits/photius/conon.htm (Original work 25 BCE)

Ellis, H. (1898). Auto-erotism: A psychological study. *Alienist and Neurologist, 19,* 260–299.

Ellis, H. (1927). The conception of narcissism. *Psychoanalytic Review, 14,* 129–153.

Fenichel, O. (1945). *The psychoanalytic theory of neurosis.* New York, NY: Norton.

Freud, S. (1957). On narcissism. In J. Strachey (Ed. & Trans.), *The standard edition of the complete psychological works of Sigmund Freud* (Vol. 14, pp. 66–102). London, England: Hogarth Press. (Original work published 1914)

Gabbard, G. O. (1989). Two subtypes of narcissistic personality disorder. *Bulletin of the Menninger Clinic, 53,* 527–532.

Graves, R. (1955). *The Greek myths.* Harmondsworth, England: Penguin.

Habicht, C. (1985). *Pausanias' guide to Ancient Greece.* Berkeley: University of California Press.

Hendrick, I. (1964). Narcissism and the prepuberty ego ideal. *Journal of the American Psychoanalytic Association, 12,* 522–528. doi:10.1177/000306516401200305

Kernberg, O. F. (1970). Factors in the psychoanalytic treatment of narcissistic personalities. *Journal of the American Psychoanalytic Association, 18,* 51–85. doi:10.1177/000306517001800103

Kernberg, O. F. (1975). *Borderline conditions and pathological narcissism.* New York, NY: Jason Aronson.

Keys, D. (2004). The ugly end of Narcissus. *BBC History Magazine, 5*(5), 9.

Klein, M. (1952). The origins of transference. *The International Journal of Psychoanalysis, 33,* 433–438.

Kohut, H. (1966). Forms and transformations of narcissism. *Journal of the American Psychoanalytic Association, 14,* 243–272. doi:10.1177/000306516601400201

Kohut, H. (1971). *The analysis of the self.* New York, NY: International Universities Press.

Kohut, H. (1972). Thoughts on narcissism and narcissistic rage. *The Psychoanalytic Study of the Child, 27,* 360–400.

Kohut, H. (1977). *The restoration of the self.* New York, NY: International Universities Press.

Mendez, A. M., Fine, H. J., & Guntrip, H. (1976). A short history of the British school of object relations and ego psychology. *Bulletin of the Menninger Clinic, 40.* 357–382.

Milton, J. (1667). *Paradise lost.* Retrieved from http://www.literature.org/authors/milton-john/paradise-lost/chapter-04.html

Murray, J. M. (1964). Narcissism and the ego ideal. *Journal of the American Psychoanalytic Association, 12,* 477–511. doi:10.1177/000306516401200302

Näcke, P. (1899). Die sexuellen perversitäten in der irrenanstalt [The sexual perversions in the mental hospital]. *Psychiatriche en Neurologische Bladen, 3,* 122–149.

Ovid. (1717). *Metamorphoses* (Book 3; Sir Samuel Garth and John Dryden, Trans.). (Original work published 8 AD) Retrieved from http://classics.mit.edu//Ovid/metam.html.

Rank, O. (1911). A contribution to narcissism [Ein beitrag zum narzissismus]. *Jahrbush fur Psychoanalytische und Psychopathologische Forschungen, 3*, 401–426.

Raskin, R. N., & Hall, C. S. (1979). A narcissistic personality inventory. *Psychological Reports, 45*, 590. doi:10.2466/pr0.1979.45.2.590

Reich, W. (1949). *Character analysis* (3rd ed.; T. P. Wolfe, Trans.). New York, NY: Orgone Institute Press. (Original work published 1933)

Ronningstam, E. (2009). Narcissistic personality disorder. In P. H. Blaney & T. Millon (Eds.), *Oxford textbook of psychopathology* (2nd ed., pp. 752–771). New York, NY: Oxford University Press.

Teicholz, J. G. (1978). A selective review of the psychoanalytic literature on theoretical conceptualisations of narcissism. *Journal of the American Psychoanalytic Association, 26*, 831–861.

Wurmser, L. (1974). Psychoanalytic considerations of the etiology of compulsive drug use. *Journal of the American Psychoanalytic Association, 22*, 820–843. doi:10.1177/000306517402200407

II

DIAGNOSIS AND
ASSESSMENT

2

DEFINING NARCISSISTIC SUBTYPES

ERIC RUSS AND JONATHAN SHEDLER

Despite its severity and stability (Blais, Hilsenroth, & Castlebury, 1997; Perry & Perry, 2004), narcissistic personality disorder (NPD) is one of the least-studied personality disorders. The available research focuses on narcissism as a unitary disorder, but a recent body of research has emerged on subtypes of narcissism. We begin this chapter with a description of the evolution of the diagnosis of narcissism and the limitations of the current approach. We explain why attention to subtypes of NPD deepens our understanding of the diagnosis. Finally, we describe a program of research to identify empirically derived and clinically useful subtypes of NPD.

DOI: 10.1037/14041-002
Understanding and Treating Pathological Narcissism, J. S. Ogrodniczuk (Editor)

DEVELOPMENT OF THE CURRENT NPD CRITERIA

The manner in which NPD is conceptualized has a significant impact on research and treatment. The approach we take to describing NPD influences the questions we ask to assess the disorder and the way we design our treatments and measure therapeutic change. Given these high stakes, it may be helpful to consider ways to improve current diagnostic criteria. A more detailed understanding of the empirical literature on NPD can help improve the new diagnostic system for personality disorders that will be presented in the fifth edition of the *Diagnostic and Statistical Manual of Mental Disorders* (*DSM–5*; American Psychiatric Association, 2011; Shedler et al., 2010). Before we discuss how we think the current system can be improved, we briefly describe the evolution of the diagnosis of narcissism over time. (For a more thorough description, see Chapter 1 in this volume.)

Freud (1914) first developed the concept of narcissism almost a century ago. He described narcissistic self-love as a normal part of the development of a sense of self, which could become pathological if this normal developmental process was disrupted.

The major theoretical advances in the concept of narcissism occurred in the 1960s and 1970s with the clinical theories of Heinz Kohut (1971) and Otto Kernberg (1975). Although both considered narcissism to be a disorder of self-esteem regulation, they disagreed about developmental trajectories and etiology. Kohut conceptualized narcissistic patients as developmentally arrested in a normal stage of infantile narcissism. He argued that over the course of normal development, before the development of conscience, a child is entirely self-focused. Normally, an empathic caregiver provides recognition and validation ("mirroring"), which helps the child develop both the capacity for self-esteem regulation and a functioning conscience (by internalizing parental standards). Failure to help the child regulate self-esteem leaves the child prone to swings in self-evaluation and particularly to a grandiosity that reflects a deficit in internalized regulatory functions (Kohut, 1966, 1971).

In contrast, Kernberg's (1998) theory emphasized a disruption in representations of self and others caused by parents who are at once both cold and rejecting and admiring. According to Kernberg, narcissistic individuals maintain a sense of self by locating "good" in themselves and projecting "bad" outward. Both their views of themselves and their ego ideal or ideal self are grandiose; they create standards for the self that are impossible to reach and hence they need to distort their self-representations in a correspondingly grandiose direction. Projection of "bad" attributes onto others, according to Kernberg, leads narcissistic individuals to devalue others and may result in explosive rage at others (Kernberg, 1975, 1989, 1998).

Whether narcissistic rage is diagnostic, and if so, what elicits it, are open questions. Morrison argued (1983, 1999) that the rage sometimes seen in NPD patients is actually preceded by a moment of (usually unconscious) shame. This shame is psychologically overwhelming and is instead defended against by excessive pride (grandiosity). Some NPD patients do not seem to experience much shame and might be motivated more by pride than shame (Campbell, Foster, & Brunell, 2004). It is possible that Kernberg's description more closely fits those motivated by shame, whereas Kohut's description fits those motivated by pride. In fact, Kernberg and Kohut may have been describing two qualitatively different types of narcissistic patients (Gabbard, 1998; McWilliams, 1994).

Millon (1969, 1998) led the transition of clinical formulations by psychoanalytic theorists into the formalized criteria for NPD in the third edition of the *Diagnostic and Statistical Manual of Mental Disorders* (*DSM–III*; American Psychiatric Association, 1980; see Chapter 3, this volume, for a historical account of NPD in the *DSM*). These criteria largely stayed the same in the third revised edition of the *DSM* (*DSM–III–R*; American Psychiatric Association, 1987), although the approach to diagnosing NPD, as in the rest of the diagnostic manual, shifted from a mixed polythetic–monothetic system to a purely polythetic system (i.e., instead of requiring several criteria related to grandiosity plus two among a list of interpersonal criteria, the selection of five of nine criteria from a single list was sufficient). The *DSM–III* and *DSM–III–R* criteria describe a person with a grandiose sense of self-importance and preoccupation with fantasies of unlimited success. The narcissist described in the *DSM–III* and *DSM–III–R* lacks empathy and experiences feelings of rage, shame, or humiliation when criticized.

Although this initial formulation provided a common set of criteria for research, it was not empirically derived, and the NPD diagnosis showed significant diagnostic overlap with other personality disorders (Gunderson, Ronningstam, & Smith, 1995). Ronningstam and Gunderson (1990) sought to address this diagnostic overlap by investigating which criteria best differentiated NPD patients from other patient groups. They developed the Diagnostic Interview for Narcissism (Gunderson & Ronningstam, 1987; Gunderson, Ronningstam, & Bodkin, 1990) to evaluate the *DSM–III–R* criteria. Their results indicated that statements about grandiosity, interpersonal relations (e.g., exploitiveness), and high or low achievement were highly discriminating of NPD (Ronningstam & Gunderson, 1989). Largely as a result of this study, the fourth edition of the *DSM* (*DSM–IV*; American Psychiatric Association, 1994) added the criterion "shows arrogant, haughty behaviors or attitudes" and eliminated the criterion "reacts to criticism with feelings of rage, shame or humiliation." Ronningstam and Gunderson (1990) noted that the patients they interviewed still possessed these reactive characteristics;

however, the characteristics did not discriminate narcissists from other patients. The decision to delete a characteristic feature of the disorder might reduce comorbidity, but it raises thorny questions about whether doing so omits important elements of the construct and presents a clinically inaccurate, or at least incomplete, portrait.

The evolution of NPD criteria from clinical descriptions to largely behavioral symptoms reduced comorbidity but sheds little light on underlying personality processes that tend to be the target of effective treatments. Additionally, the current system of choosing five of nine criteria allows for a heterogeneous presentation of the disorder with 126 possible symptom combinations to meet criteria and the possibility that two people diagnosed with NPD may overlap on only one symptom. Overall, the transition from early clinical conceptualizations to the current *DSM* diagnosis has led to the construction of *DSM* criteria for NPD that both allows for substantial heterogeneity and underemphasizes aspects of personality and internal functioning that are central to the disorder.

To illustrate the limitations of the current diagnostic criteria, we describe here a study from our group that suggests a broader conceptualization of NPD. Westen and Shedler (1999b) asked a random national sample of psychologists and psychiatrists to provide descriptions of a patient with a given personality disorder using a psychometric instrument designed for use by clinically experienced observers, the Shedler-Westen Assessment Procedure 200 (SWAP-200; Westen & Shedler, 1999b). The SWAP-200 is a personality assessment instrument that asks informants to sort 200 statements about personality according to their descriptiveness, from least descriptive to most descriptive. (SWAP-200 software is available for download at http://www.SWAPassessment.org.) We focus here on the results for NPD ($n = 40$).

SWAP-200 items that had the highest mean ratings across NPD patients included *DSM–IV* criteria but also additional interpersonal and intrapersonal criteria, including an item written to reflect the criterion deleted from *DSM–IV* ("Reacts to criticism with feelings of rage, shame or humiliation") as well as "Tends to be angry or hostile (whether consciously or unconsciously)," "Tends to blame others for own failures and shortcomings," "Tends to be controlling," "Tends to be critical of others," "Tends to get into power struggles," "Tends to be competitive with others," and "Tends to feel misunderstood, mistreated, or victimized" (Westen & Shedler, 1999a). Additionally, the investigators used Q-factor analysis to derive diagnoses independent of *DSM* criteria. (*Q-factor analysis* is an inverted factor analysis in which people rather than items are factored and hence grouped together, yielding diagnostic configurations.) An empirically derived NPD diagnosis emerged, which once again included the *DSM–IV* criteria but also included several additional items, many of which (as was the case with the empirical description of NPD patients as defined in *DSM–IV*) were more central to the construct quantita-tively than many *DSM–IV* criteria: "Reacts to criticism with feelings of rage, shame or humiliation" "Tends to be competitive," "Lacks close friendships," "Expects self to be perfect," "Tends to be self-critical," "Appears afraid of commitment to a long-term love relationship," and "Seeks to be the cen-ter of attention" (Westen & Shedler, 1999b). These aspects of narcissistic personality could be included in future iterations of the diagnostic manual. However, improving the diagnostic criteria in this way does not fully address the problem of heterogeneity—that is, the existence of distinct personality subtypes within the diagnosis of NPD.

NARCISSISTIC SUBTYPES

An emerging literature from several research groups supports the clini-cal hypothesis that two distinct types of narcissism exist: grandiose and vul-nerable (Dickinson & Pincus, 2003; Gabbard, 1989, 1998; Gersten, 1991; Pincus & Lukowitsky, 2010; Pincus, Lukowitsky, & Wright, 2010; Revik, 2001; Smolewska & Dion, 2005; Wink, 1991). The *grandiose* subtype can be described as "grandiose, arrogant, entitled, exploitative, and envious"; the *vulnerable* subtype is characterized as "overly self-inhibited and modest but harboring underlying grandiose expectations for oneself and others" (Dick-inson & Pincus, 2003, pp. 188–189). Criterion validity of these subtypes has been suggested by research comparing subtypes on various measures indepen-dent of those used for subtyping. For example, the vulnerable subtype tends to report insecure attachment styles by self-report, whereas the grandiose subtype reports a more secure attachment style (Dickinson & Pincus, 2003; Smolewska & Dion, 2005). Though highly suggestive, a significant limitation of such studies is their heavy reliance on self-report questionnaires. In fact, it seems unlikely that either subtype has secure attachment relationships, given the interpersonal characteristics attributed to narcissists by observers (Klonsky, Oltmanns, & Turkheimer, 2002).

In fact, almost all previous subtyping approaches have to rely on self-report measures of narcissism, either scales of self-report personality question-naires such as the Minnesota Multiphasic Personality Inventory or narcissism questionnaires such as the Narcissistic Personality Inventory. However, studies comparing self-report to other-report suggest that narcissistic individuals do not provide accurate self-descriptions (Klonsky, Oltmanns, & Turkheimer, 2002), suggesting the need for alternative methods. Indeed, the notion of studying NPD by relying on the self-descriptions of narcissistic individuals (for whom lack of insight and distorted self-perceptions are diagnostic) is inherently problematic.

Research from our group offers an alternative to relying on self-reports. We describe here a follow-up to the SWAP-200 study just described. Using an updated version of the SWAP-200 instrument, we developed empirically derived NPD subtypes that describe variations in NPD presentation commonly seen in clinical practice. This approach has the advantage of making diagnosis more clinically meaningful without sacrificing the important empirical gains made over the past 20 years.

As part of a larger National Institute of Mental Health–funded study examining personality pathology, a national sample of clinicians reported on a randomly selected patient. Clinicians completed the Shedler-Westen Assessment Procedure-II (SWAP-II). The SWAP-II is the latest version of the SWAP-200, which has been used in a number of taxonomic studies (Shedler & Westen, 2004a, 2004b; Westen & Shedler, 1999a, 1999b).

The SWAP-II item set subsumes Axis II criteria included in *DSM–III* and *DSM–IV*. Additionally, it incorporates selected Axis I criteria relevant to personality (e.g., anxiety, depression), personality constructs described in the clinical and research literatures over the past 50 years, and clinical observations from pilot studies. The original SWAP-200 item set was the product of a 7-year iterative item revision process; similarly, the SWAP-II was revised to accommodate new findings, clarify existing item content, and minimize item redundancy. A growing body of research supports the validity and reliability of the adult and adolescent versions of the SWAP-II in predicting a wide range of external criteria, such as suicide attempts, history of psychiatric hospitalizations, ratings of adaptive functioning, interview diagnoses, and developmental and family history variables (e.g., Westen & Muderrisoglu, 2003, 2006; Westen & Shedler, 1999a; Westen, Shedler, Durrett, Glass, & Martens, 2003; Westen & Weinberger, 2004).

We selected patients from the larger data set diagnosed with NPD ($N = 101$) and applied Q-factor analysis to their SWAP profiles. Q-factor analysis is computationally identical to conventional factor analysis except that people rather than items are factored and hence grouped together. We retained three Q-factors interpretable as subtypes (see Exhibit 2.1; for further methodological detail, see Russ, Shedler, Bradley, & Westen, 2008). Each subtype showed distinct patterns of correlations with external criterion variables. These included comorbidity with Axis I and Axis II disorders, measures of adaptive functioning, and etiological variables. Additionally, the subtypes showed low to moderate correlations ($r = -.01–.35$) with each other. Taken together, this suggests that we have identified three distinct subtypes of narcissists, although we do not assume that these subtypes are categorical. Because the aggregation of data over 100 individuals (necessary for reliability) minimizes individual

EXHIBIT 2.1
Q-Factors: Subtypes of Narcissism

Q-Factor 1: Grandiose/Malignant Narcissist

Has an exaggerated sense of self-importance (e.g., feels special, superior, grand, or envied).

Appears to feel privileged and entitled; expects preferential treatment.

Has little empathy; seems unable or unwilling to understand or respond to others' needs or feelings.

Tends to blame own failures or shortcomings on other people or circumstances; attributes his/her difficulties to external factors rather than accepting responsibility for own conduct or choices.

Tends to be critical of others.

Tends to be controlling.

Tends to have extreme reactions to perceived slights or criticism (e.g., may react with rage, humiliation, etc.).

Has little psychological insight into own motives, behavior, etc.

Tends to get into power struggles.

Tends to be angry or hostile (whether consciously or unconsciously).

Takes advantage of others; has little investment in moral values (e.g., puts own needs first, uses or exploits people with little regard for their feelings or welfare, etc.).

Tends to be dismissive, haughty, or arrogant.

Tends to seek power or influence over others (whether in beneficial or destructive ways).

Tends to hold grudges; may dwell on insults or slights for long periods.

Tends to be manipulative.

Tends to feel misunderstood, mistreated, or victimized.

Is prone to intense anger, out of proportion to the situation at hand (e.g., has rage episodes).

Experiences little or no remorse for harm or injury caused to others.

Q-Factor 2: Fragile Narcissist

Tends to feel unhappy, depressed, or despondent.

Tends to be critical of others.

Has an exaggerated sense of self-importance (e.g., feels special, superior, grand, or envied).

Tends to be angry or hostile (whether consciously or unconsciously).

Tends to feel anxious.

Tends to feel envious.

Is prone to painful feelings of emptiness (e.g., may feel lost, bereft, abjectly alone even in the presence of others, etc.).

Tends to fear s/he will be rejected or abandoned.

Tends to be competitive with others (whether consciously or unconsciously).

Tends to have extreme reactions to perceived slights or criticism (e.g., may react with rage, humiliation, etc.).

Tends to feel misunderstood, mistreated, or victimized.

Lacks close friendships and relationships.

Tends to ruminate; may dwell on problems, replay conversations in his/her mind, become preoccupied with thoughts about what could have been, etc.

Is articulate; can express self well in words.

Tends to feel like an outcast or outsider.

Appears to feel privileged and entitled; expects preferential treatment.

(continues)

EXHIBIT 2.1
Q-Factors: Subtypes of Narcissism   *(Continued)*

Tends to feel s/he is inadequate, inferior, or a failure.

Is self-critical; sets unrealistically high standards for self and is intolerant of own human defects.

Q-Factor 3: High Functioning/Exhibitionistic Narcissist

Has an exaggerated sense of self-importance (e.g., feels special, superior, grand, or envied).

Is articulate; can express self well in words.

Appears to feel privileged and entitled; expects preferential treatment.

Enjoys challenges; takes pleasure in accomplishing things.

Tends to be energetic and outgoing.

Tends to be competitive with others (whether consciously or unconsciously).

Seeks to be the center of attention.

Is able to use his/her talents, abilities, and energy effectively and productively.

Seems to treat others primarily as an audience to witness own importance, brilliance, beauty, etc.

Tends to seek power or influence over others (whether in beneficial or destructive ways).

Is able to assert him/herself effectively and appropriately when necessary.

Tends to be controlling.

Finds meaning and satisfaction in the pursuit of long-term goals and ambitions.

Has fantasies of unlimited success, power, beauty, talent, brilliance, etc.

Tends to be critical of others.

Appears comfortable and at ease in social situations.

Has a good sense of humor.

Tends to be sexually seductive or provocative (e.g., may be inappropriately flirtatious, preoccupied with sexual conquest, prone to "lead people on," etc.)

differences, we suggest that these subtypes be conceptualized as prototypes that any individual NPD patient may fit to a greater or lesser degree. The descriptions of the three subtypes that follow are based on the SWAP-II items that make up the subtype as well relevant external criterion variables.

We labeled the first subtype *grandiose/malignant narcissism*. This subtype is similar to the grandiose type found in previous research but with the important difference that the grandiosity appears to be more elemental and less defensive. Grandiose/malignant narcissistic individuals lack empathy, externalize blame, and react harshly when criticized. This subtype represents an aggressive narcissistic style with a seething anger or rage, interpersonal manipulativeness, an exaggerated sense of self-importance, and feelings of privilege. Individuals with this condition tend not to experience underlying feelings of inadequacy or to be prone to negative affect states other than anger. They have little insight into their own behavior and tend to blame others for their problems. This differs from some previous descriptions, which have described grandiose narcissistic individuals as merely being more successful at covering their inadequacy. Grandiose/malignant narcissists shares features with individuals with antisocial personality disorder and paranoid personality disorder and also tend to have comorbid substance use disorders. This subtype is characterized by externalizing behaviors such as fighting or being the perpetrator in an abusive relationship. Finally, the grandiose/malignant subtype is the most likely to have displayed externalizing behavior as a child, including setting fires and torturing animals.

The second subtype, labeled *fragile narcissism*, is similar to the vulnerable type found in previous research (Pincus & Lukowitsky, 2010). Fragile narcissists feel both grandiose and inadequate, suggesting an alternation of representations of self, defensive grandiosity, or a grandiosity that emerges under threat. These grandiose self-representations seem to aid in averting feelings of inadequacy, smallness, anxiety, and loneliness. They want to feel important and privileged, and when the defense is operating effectively, they do. However, when the defense fails, they have a powerful current of negative affect that brings out feelings of inadequacy, often accompanied by rage. Fragile narcissists shares features with individuals with borderline personality disorder, avoidant personality disorder, and dependent personality disorder. Compared with the other narcissism subtypes, people in this subtype had the worst adaptive functioning; they had the most difficulty in work settings and in interpersonal relationships.

We labeled the third subtype *high functioning/exhibitionistic narcissism*, reflecting the fact that individuals with high loadings on this Q-factor are grandiose, self-centered, and competitive and feel entitled, but they also have a number of healthy characteristics; they are articulate, energetic, interpersonally comfortable, and achievement oriented. The high functioning/exhibitionistic narcissist is not well represented in previous research literature but is well represented in the clinical literature (e.g., Westen, 1990). Patients who match this subtype have an exaggerated sense of self-importance and feelings of privilege but are also articulate, energetic, and outgoing. They tend to show surprisingly good adaptive functioning relative to the other subtypes, and their narcissism motivates them to succeed. As expected, people in this subtype, although not free from pathology, tend to do reasonably well in their lives.

One question frequently raised about person-centered (typological or prototypal) approaches to diagnosis is the extent to which they can be reduced to their constituent traits. The subtypes identified here differed considerably in their trait profiles. Grandiose/malignant narcissism was strongly associated with most of the NPD traits we identified, particularly the Psychopathy and Hostility factors. Fragile narcissism was moderately associated with the Psychopathy and Emotional Reactivity factors and negatively associated with the Hostility factor. These associations suggest the importance of assessing and understanding narcissistic features across the personality disorders, particularly Cluster B. High functioning narcissism was strongly associated with the Grandiosity factor, suggesting the relatively "pure" grandiosity of this group. However, careful examination of the subtypes in terms of their underlying trait structure does not suggest a ready reproducibility of the subtypes from the traits. Rather, they seem to provide different levels of analysis, with the subtypes identifying distinct, clinically meaningful constellations, with grandiose/malignant narcissism on the border with psychopathy, fragile narcissism describing a kind of defensive retreat into grandiosity, and high functioning narcissism associated with a less limited capacity to love and work.

IMPLICATIONS FOR TREATMENT

In addition to phenomenological differences, it is likely that these subtypes would respond differently to psychotherapy and potentially to medication. As part of the study described in the preceding section, we also collected exploratory treatment data, asking clinicians to rate the effectiveness of their treatment with each patient. Clinicians reported that grandiose/malignant narcissistic patients were the least responsive to treatment. Given the features of this subtype, such patients are likely to be difficult to work with. Because they lack the vulnerability of the other subtypes, grandiose/malignant narcissistic patients are likely to have little motivation to seek out or work in psychotherapy. They would be more likely to attempt to manipulate their clinician or attempt to establish dominance in the room. Fragile narcissistic patients may be better suited for psychotherapy. They would likely benefit from interventions focused on acknowledging both sides of their fundamental narcissistic conflict, grandiose feelings and the underlying vulnerability that drives them. Because fragile narcissist patients may be less aware of their vulnerability, they may require the clinician's help to tolerate feelings of vulnerability without resorting to grandiosity or devaluation of others. Finally, high functioning/exhibitionistic narcissistic patients might benefit from an interpretive, insight-oriented approach to help them become more aware of their narcissistic defenses and increase the potential for meaningful relationships. (Issues of transference and countertransference are explored in more detail in Chapter 12, this volume.)

CASE VIGNETTES

In this section, we describe case vignettes to better illustrate these distinctions. Patient identities have been disguised to maintain confidentiality.

A Grandiose/Malignant Narcissist Patient

M. is a 46-year-old divorced man with an Axis I diagnosis of alcohol abuse. He is in his 12th month of treatment at a residential treatment facility. M. has a history of arrests for fighting and domestic violence and has difficulty holding a job because of interpersonal conflicts in the workplace. M.'s parents, who were alcoholic, divorced when M. was 3 years old, and M. was raised by a succession of relatives. On the SWAP-II, M. is described as self-important, privileged, entitled, arrogant, lacking empathy, and disdainful of others. He appears to believe that conventional rules of conduct do not apply to him. He seeks to be the center of attention, treats others primarily as an audience, and appears to believe that he should associate only with people who are high-status or otherwise "special." He is prone to intense anger and blames others for his difficulties. M.'s clinician described therapy as completely ineffective to date.

A Fragile Narcissist Patient

F. is a 34-year-old married man with an Axis I diagnosis of major depressive disorder, who has been treated for 9 months in a private practice setting. He comes from an upper middle class background, holds a master's degree in his field, and has been continuously employed. F.'s parents divorced when he was 14 years old. As described by the SWAP-II, F. presents with a mix of seemingly contradictory attributes, with features of grandiosity coexisting with feelings of inadequacy and vulnerability. F. has an exaggerated sense of self-importance and appears to feel privileged and entitled. He expects preferential treatment and has fantasies of unlimited success, power, beauty, talent, and brilliance. For example, he spends much of his day imagining what he would do and say to his coworkers if he was in charge of his company. He lacks empathy and seems unable or unwilling to understand or respond to others' needs or feelings unless they coincide with his own. F. also feels unhappy, depressed, and despondent, and he finds little pleasure or satisfaction in life's activities. Interpersonally, F. tends to be critical of others, angry, hostile, oppositional, or contrary. He tends to hold grudges and to have conflicts with authority figures. At the same time, F. feels envious of others; tends to feel misunderstood, mistreated, or victimized; and tends to feel helpless and powerless. F.'s clinician rated therapy as somewhat effective to date.

A High Functioning/Exhibitionistic Narcissist Patient

E. is a 58-year-old man, currently separated, who has been treated for 16 months in a private practice setting. He has Axis I diagnoses of anxiety disorder no other symptom and adjustment disorder. He is employed and working to his full potential. As described by the SWAP-II, E. is psychologically insightful, tends to be energetic and outgoing, appears comfortable and at ease in social situations, is articulate, and has a good sense of humor. However, E. also has an exaggerated sense of self-importance. He appears to feel privileged and entitled and expects preferential treatment. He seeks to be the center of attention, expresses emotion in exaggerated and theatrical ways, and seems to treat others primarily as an audience to witness his own importance, brilliance, beauty, and so on. E. is also highly self-critical; he sets unrealistically high standards for himself and is intolerant of his own defects. He tends to feel envious of others and competitive with others, and he can be dismissive, haughty, or arrogant. E.'s clinician rated therapy as mostly effective.

DISCUSSION

Our approach to subtyping narcissistic personality using the SWAP-II has several advantages over prior approaches. By recruiting through a national practice network, we were able to gather data on a large number of patients diagnosed with NPD. Additionally, the use of quantified clinical judgment gives this approach several advantages over previous research. Most important, it allowed us to avoid the problem of relying on narcissistic individuals to report their own symptoms, which they generally cannot do. In addition, clinical and social psychological theory and research on narcissism have largely occurred in separate literatures, and the methodological approach described above allowed us to cross some of those boundaries.

Although the subtypes discussed above were developed from empirical, theory-blind research, they correspond well with the subtypes of narcissistic personality described in the *Psychodynamic Diagnostic Manual* (*PDM*; PDM Task Force, 2006; see Chapter 4, this volume). The PDM describes "arrogant/entitled" and "depressed/depleted" variants of narcissism, which roughly correspond to our grandiose/malignant and fragile types, respectively. The PDM also captures our high functioning/exhibitionistic type by noting that each personality disorder has a less disturbed variant that may be considered a personality *pattern* or *style* rather than a "disorder."

Finally, the research discussed above suggests the construct of narcissism may be a more complex construct than portrayed by *DSM–IV*. In addition to improving the current diagnostic criteria, it may be helpful for future editions of the manual to describe the grandiose/malignant, fragile, and high functioning/exhibitionistic subtypes of NPD. These subtypes reflect a more nuanced, empirically derived understanding of NPD that may help bridge the gap between empirically and clinically derived concepts of narcissistic pathology.

REFERENCES

American Psychiatric Association. (1980). *Diagnostic and statistical manual of mental disorders* (3rd ed.). Washington, DC: Author.

American Psychiatric Association. (1987). *Diagnostic and statistical manual of mental disorders* (3rd ed., Rev.). Washington, DC: Author.

American Psychiatric Association. (1994). *Diagnostic and statistical manual of mental disorders* (4th ed.). Washington, DC: Author.

American Psychiatric Association. (2011). Personality disorders. Retrieved from http://www.dsm5.org/proposedrevision/pages/personalitydisorders.aspx

Blais, M. A., Hilsenroth, M. J., & Castlebury, F. D. (1997). Content validity of the DSM–IV borderline and narcissistic personality disorder criteria sets. *Comprehensive Psychiatry, 38*, 31–37. doi:10.1016/S0010-440X(97)90050-X

Campbell, W., Foster, J. D., & Brunell, A. B. (2004). Running from shame or reveling in pride? Narcissism and the regulation of self-conscious emotions. *Psychological Inquiry, 15*, 150–153.

Dickinson, K. A., & Pincus, A. L. (2003). Interpersonal analysis of grandiose and vulnerable narcissism. *Journal of Personality Disorders, 17*, 188–207. doi:10.1521/pedi.17.3.188.22146

Freud, S. (1914). On narcissism: An introduction. In J. Strachey (Ed. & Trans.), *The standard edition of the complete psychological works of Sigmund Freud, 14*, 111–140.

Gabbard, G. O. (1989). Two subtypes of narcissistic personality disorder. *Bulletin of the Menninger Clinic, 53*, 527–532.

Gabbard, G. O. (1998). Transference and countertransference in the treatment of narcissistic patients. In E. Ronningstam (Ed.), *Disorders of narcissism: Diagnostic, clinical, and empirical implications* (pp. 125–145). Washington, DC: American Psychiatric Press.

Gersten, S. P. (1991). Narcissistic personality disorder consists of two subtypes. *Psychiatric Times, 8*, 25–26.

Gunderson, J. G., & Ronningstam, E. (1987). *The diagnostic interview for narcissism.* Belmont, MA: McLean Hospital.

Gunderson, J. G., Ronningstam, E., & Bodkin, A. (1990). The diagnostic interview for narcissistic patients. *Archives of General Psychiatry, 47*, 676–680. doi:10.1001/archpsyc.1990.01810190076011

Gunderson, J. G., Ronningstam, E., & Smith, L. E. (1995). Narcissistic personality disorder. In J. Livesley (Ed.), *The DSM–IV personality disorders* (pp. 201–212). New York, NY: Guilford Press.

Kernberg, O. F. (1975). *Borderline conditions and pathological narcissism.* New York, NY: Jason Aronson.

Kernberg, O. F. (1989). An ego psychology object relations theory of the structure and treatment of pathological narcissism: An overview. *Psychiatric Clinics of North America, 12*, 723–729.

Kernberg, O. F. (1998). Pathological narcissism and narcissistic personality disorder: Theoretical background and diagnostic classification. In E. Ronningstam (Ed.), *Disorders of narcissism: Diagnostic, clinical, and empirical implications* (pp. 29–51). Washington, DC: American Psychiatric Press.

Klonsky, E. D., Oltmanns, T. F., & Turkheimer, E. (2002). Informant-reports of personality disorder: Relation to self-reports and future research directions. *Clinical Psychology: Science and Practice, 9*, 300–311. doi:10.1093/clipsy.9.3.300

Kohut, H. (1966). Forms and transformations of narcissism. *Journal of the American Psychoanalytic Association, 14*, 243–272. doi:10.1177/000306516601400201

Kohut, H. (1971). *The analysis of the self.* New York, NY: International Universities Press.

McWilliams, N. (1994). *Psychoanalytic diagnosis.* New York, NY: Guilford Press.

Millon, T. (1969). *Modern psychopathology: A biosocial approach to maladaptive learning and functioning.* Philadelphia, PA: Saunders.

Millon, T. (1998). DSM narcissistic personality disorder. In E. F. Ronningstam (Ed.), *Disorders of narcissism: Diagnostic, clinical, and empirical implications* (pp. 75–101). Washington, DC: American Psychiatric Press.

Morrison, A. P. (1983). Shame, ideal self, and narcissism. *Contemporary Psychoanalysis, 19*, 295–318.

Morrison, A. P. (1999). Shame, on either side of defense. *Contemporary Psychoanalysis, 35*, 91–105.

PDM Task Force. (Ed.). (2006). *Psychodynamic diagnostic manual.* Silver Spring, MD: Alliance of Psychoanalytic Organizations.

Perry, J. D. C., & Perry, J. C. (2004). Conflicts, defenses and the stability of narcissistic personality features. *Psychiatry: Interpersonal and Biological Processes, 67*, 310–330.

Pincus, A. L., & Lukowitsky, M. R. (2010). Pathological narcissism and narcissistic personality disorder. *Annual Review of Clinical Psychology, 6*, 421–446. doi:10.1146/annurev.clinpsy.121208.131215

Pincus, A. L., Lukowitsky, M. R., & Wright, A. G. C. (2010). The interpersonal nexus of personality and psychopathology. In T. Millon, R. F. Krueger, & E. Simonsen (Eds.), *Contemporary directions in psychopathology: Scientific foundations of the DSM–V and ICD–11* (pp. 523–552). New York, NY: Guilford Press.

Revik, J. O. (2001). Overt and covert narcissism: Turning points and mutative elements in two psychotherapies. *British Journal of Psychotherapy, 17*, 435–447. doi:10.1111/j.1752-0118.2001.tb00608.x

Ronningstam, E., & Gunderson, J. (1989). Descriptive studies on narcissistic personality disorder. *Psychiatric Clinics of North America, 12*, 585–601.

Ronningstam, E., & Gunderson, J. (1990). Identifying criteria for narcissistic personality disorder. *The American Journal of Psychiatry, 147*, 918–922.

Russ, E., Shedler, J., Bradley, R., & Westen, D. (2008). Refining the narcissistic diagnosis: Defining criteria, subtypes, and endophenotypes. *The American Journal of Psychiatry, 165*, 1473–1481. doi:10.1176/appi.ajp.2008.07030376

Shedler, J., Beck, A., Fonagy, P., Gabbard, G. O., Gunderson, J., & Kernberg, O. (2010). Personality disorders in DSM–5. *The American Journal of Psychiatry, 167*, 1026–1028. doi:10.1176/appi.ajp.2010.10050746

Shedler, J., & Westen, D. (2004a). Dimensions of personality pathology: An alternative to the five-factor model. *The American Journal of Psychiatry, 161*, 1743–1754. doi:10.1176/appi.ajp.161.10.1743

Shedler, J., & Westen, D. (2004b). Refining personality disorder diagnoses: Integrating science and practice. *The American Journal of Psychiatry, 161*, 1350–1365. doi:10.1176/appi.ajp.161.8.1350

Smolewska, K., & Dion, K. L. (2005). Narcissism and adult attachment: A multivariate approach. *Self and Identity, 4*, 59–68. doi:10.1080/13576500444000218

Westen, D. (1990). The relations among narcissism, egocentrism, self-concept, and self-esteem: Experimental, clinical and theoretical considerations. *Psychoanalysis and Contemporary Thought, 13*, 183–239.

Westen, D., & Muderrisoglu, S. (2003). Reliability and validity of personality disorder assessment using a systematic clinical interview: Evaluating an alternative to structured interviews. *Journal of Personality Disorders, 17*, 351–369. doi:10.1521/pedi.17.4.351.23967

Westen, D., & Muderrisoglu, S. (2006). Clinical assessment of pathological personality traits. *The American Journal of Psychiatry, 163*, 1285–1287. doi:10.1176/appi.ajp.163.7.1285

Westen, D., & Shedler, J. (1999a). Revising and assessing Axis II. Part 1: Developing a clinically and empirically valid assessment method. *The American Journal of Psychiatry, 156*, 258–272.

Westen, D., & Shedler, J. (1999b). Revising and assessing Axis II. Part 2: Toward an empirically based and clinically useful classification of personality disorders. *The American Journal of Psychiatry, 156*, 273–285.

Westen, D., Shedler, J., Durrett, C., Glass, S., & Martens, A. (2003). Personality diagnosis in adolescence: DSM–IV axis II diagnoses and an empirically derived alternative. *The American Journal of Psychiatry, 160*, 952–966. doi:10.1176/appi.ajp.160.5.952

Westen, D., & Weinberger, J. (2004). When clinical description becomes statistical prediction. *American Psychologist, 59*, 595–613. doi:10.1037/0003-066X.59.7.595

Wink, P. (1991). Two faces of narcissism. *Journal of Personality and Social Psychology, 61*, 590–597. doi:10.1037/0022-3514.61.4.590

3

NARCISSISM IN THE *DSM*

KENNETH N. LEVY, KEVIN B. MEEHAN, NICOLE M. CAIN,
AND WILLIAM D. ELLISON

In the last few decades interest in narcissism has grown, both within academia and in the popular media. Despite this interest, the status of narcissism as a diagnosis has been threatened by proposed changes to the *Diagnostic and Statistical Manual of Mental Disorders* (4th ed., text rev.; *DSM–IV–TR*; American Psychiatric Association, 2000). First, we discuss the influences for inclusion of narcissism in the third edition of the *Diagnostic and Statistical Manual of Mental Disorders* (*DSM–III*; American Psychiatric Association, 1980), including the increasing clinical interest generated by the Kernberg–Kohut debates as well as contributions from social psychological research. We then discuss the evolution of the diagnosis through *DSM–III*, the third revised edition of the *Diagnostic and Statistical Manual of Mental Disorders* (*DSM–III–R*; American Psychiatric Association, 1987), and *DSM–IV–TR* and the influences for these changes. We describe more recent research identifying aspects of narcissism not currently captured by the fourth edition

DOI: 10.1037/14041-003
Understanding and Treating Pathological Narcissism, J. S. Ogrodniczuk (Editor)

(*DSM–IV*; American Psychiatric Association, 1994). Next, we briefly introduce alternate systems for categorizing narcissism, such as the *International Classification of Diseases* (10th ed.; *ICD-10*; World Health Organization, 1992); behavioral approaches; and the *Psychodynamic Diagnostic Manual* (*PDM*; Psychodynamic Diagnostic Manual Task Force), which is expanded on in Chapter 4, this volume. We conclude with a discussion of the proposed changes for *DSM–5* (American Psychiatric Association, 2011b), including the rationale for and critique of these changes.

A BRIEF HISTORY OF THE *DSM*

In 1935, the American Psychiatric Association developed a diagnostic system based on Kraepelin's (1899/1990, 1913/1971, 1913/1976) influential textbooks. This systematic approach to mental disorders was based on case studies and was less relevant for acute conditions, thus leading hospitals to develop their own systems, which were often discordant and created communication difficulties. The first edition of the *DSM* (American Psychiatric Association, 1953), an effort to standardize the diagnostic systems, was a glossary describing 108 diagnostic categories based on Adolf Meyer's developmental psychobiologic views, many of which were described as reactions to environmental conditions that could result in emotional problems. The second edition (*DSM–II*; American Psychiatric Association, 1968) specified 182 different disorders and distinguished between neurotic and psychotic disorders. Except for the description of neuroses, which were strongly influenced by psychodynamic thought, *DSM–II* did not provide a theoretical framework for understanding nonorganic mental disorders; it was based on the best clinical judgment of a committee of experts and its consultants (Widiger, Frances, Pincus, Davis, & First, 1991). Narcissism or narcissistic personality disorder (NPD) was not an official diagnosis in either the first or the second edition of the manual.

Beginning around 1970, clinical investigators in the United States began to feel increasing dissatisfaction with the imprecision of psychiatric diagnostic criteria. This culminated in the publication of *DSM–III* in 1980, which provided a detailed lexicon or taxonomy that established common definitions of various psychopathological states that now enabled investigators and clinicians to have greater consistency (reliability) in their diagnoses.

DSM–III attempted to establish a "multiaxial, theoretically neutral system" that placed a wide range of descriptive symptoms into 265 separate categories or disorders. In attempts "to resolve various diagnostic issues, the task force relied, as much as possible, on research evidence relevant to various kinds of diagnostic validity" (American Psychiatric Association, 1980, p. 3). Concepts of reliability and validity from the psychometric tradition within psychology were influential in shaping the organization of *DSM–III*. Extensive field trials were conducted to deal with unacceptable levels of reliability (Spitzer & Fleiss, 1974). Because of the lack of sufficient research, however, the committee deliberations were often "unstructured" and "many decisions continued to be based primarily on the best clinical judgment and experience of the committee members" (Widiger et al., 1991, p. 281). The task force attempted to remain theoretically neutral in its deliberations so as to create an atheoretical nomenclature that could be used broadly by clinicians of various orientations.

The *DSM–III* task force used primarily descriptive symptom criteria to create a multiaxial diagnostic classification system, separating personality disorders (Axis II) from clinical syndromes (Axis I). The classificatory system was *polythetic* (Millon, 1991), meaning that not all symptoms or diagnostic criteria for a given disorder were necessary for making a diagnosis. Thus, the classificatory system created prototypic descriptions of particular disorders on the basis of a cluster of symptoms, and these became the concrete signs of discrete categories. Because there were "many instances in which the criteria were not entirely clear, were inconsistent across categories, or were even contradictory" (American Psychiatric Association, 1987, p. xvii), the American Psychiatric Association revised *DSM–III* in 1987 (*DSM–III–R*); field trials were used to establish concurrent and descriptive validity of "clinicians' diagnoses . . . rather than simply [addressing] . . . the reliability of the diagnoses" (Widiger et al., 1991, p. 282).

CLINICAL MODELS OF THE CONCEPT OF NARCISSISM

NPD was first introduced into the official diagnostic system with *DSM–III*, owing to the widespread use of the concept by clinicians and the writings of Kernberg, Kohut, and Millon. Kernberg (1967) and Kohut's (1968) writings on narcissism were, in part, a reaction to increased clinical interest in treating these patients. Their papers, in turn, stimulated increased clinical interest in the concept. However, these clinical trends also paralleled trends in critical social theory (Adorno, 1967; Lasch, 1979; Marcuse, 1955; Wolfe, 1977) as well as the identification of narcissism as a personality factor in a number of social psychological studies (Block, 1971; Eysenck & Eysenck, 1975; Murray, 1938; Raskin & Hall, 1979; see also Frances, 1980).

In Kernberg's (1975, 1984) view, narcissism develops as a consequence of parental rejection, devaluation, and an emotionally invalidating environment. The child copes with parents who are inconsistent in their investment or who relate only in order to satisfy their own needs by defensively withdrawing and forming a pathologically grandiose self-representation. By combining aspects of the real self with fantasized aspects of what the child wants to be, as well as fantasized aspects of an ideal, loving parent, the grandiose self serves as an internal refuge from the harsh and depriving environment. The negative self-representation of the child is disavowed and not integrated into the grandiose representation, which is the seat of agency from which the narcissist operates. This split-off unacceptable self-representation can be seen in the emptiness, chronic hunger for admiration and excitement, and shame that also characterize the narcissist's experience (Akhtar & Thomson, 1982).

In contrast, Kohut (1971, 1977) viewed pathological narcissism as a normal developmental process gone awry. For Kohut, childhood grandiosity is normal and can be understood as a process by which the child attempts to identify with and become like his idealized parental figures by taking on attributes of perceived competence and power. In normal development this early grandiose self becomes modulated and eventually contributes to an integrated sense of self, with realistic ambitions and goals. However, if not properly modulated, what follows is the failure of the grandiose self to be integrated into the individual's whole personality. Others are taken as extensions of the self (Kohut's term is *selfobject*) and are relied upon to regulate one's self-esteem and anxieties regarding a stable identity. Because narcissistic individuals are unable to sufficiently manage the normal fluctuations of daily life and its affective correlates, other people are unwittingly relegated to roles of providing internal regulation for them (by way of unconditional support, admiration, and total empathic attunement), the same way a parent would provide internal regulation for a young child.

In contrast to Kernberg and Kohut, Millon (1981) articulated an evolution-based social learning theory of narcissism. Millon (1981) postulated that narcissism develops not as a response to parental devaluation but rather as a consequence of parental overvaluation. According to Millon (1981), as a child the narcissistic individual is treated as a special person, given much attention, and led by parents to believe that he or she is perfect. Millon (1981) contended that such unrealistic overvaluation leads to self-illusions that "cannot be sustained in the outer world" (p. 165). According to Millon, firstborn and only children are more vulnerable to narcissism because they tend to receive an abundance of attention and special treatment. However, the evidence is mixed regarding birth order, and there is no evidence that only-child status is related to narcissism.

INTRODUCTION OF NARCISSISM TO THE *DSM–III*

A committee of psychiatrists and psychologists developed the *DSM–III* definition of NPD and its criteria by consensus from a summary of the pre-1978 literature, without the benefit of empirical evaluation by clinical study groups. The criteria represented amalgamations of the theoretical and clinical work of Kernberg, Kohut, and Millon, with "expert" input (see Frances, 1980, for a description). *DSM–III* criteria for NPD included the following characteristics:

1. a grandiose sense of self-importance or uniqueness;
2. preoccupation with fantasies of unlimited success, power, brilliance, beauty, or ideal love;
3. exhibitionism (seeking of constant attention and admiration); and
4. cool indifference or marked feelings of rage, inferiority, shame, humiliation, or emptiness in response to criticism, indifference to others, or defeat.

At least two of the following disturbances in interpersonal relationships were required for the diagnosis:

1. entitlement (expectations of special favors);
2. interpersonal exploitativeness;
3. alternations between extreme overidealization and devaluation in relationships; or
4. lack of empathy.

A number of the *DSM–III* NPD criteria (e.g., cool indifference or marked feelings of rage, inferiority, shame, humiliation, or emptiness in response to criticism; indifference to others or defeat; and vacillation between idealization and devaluation) captured both the dynamic and defensive nature of narcissism proposed by the early psychoanalytic writers as well as Kernberg and Kohut's later writings. In addition, the description of NPD noted that "frequently the sense of self-importance alternates with feelings of special unworthiness" (p. 315) and "self-esteem is often fragile; the individual may be preoccupied with how well he or she is doing and how well he or she is regarded by others" (American Psychiatric Association, 1980, p. 316). As Cain, Pincus, and Ansell (2008) noted, the criteria in *DSM–III*, although not explicit, "assumed an underlying insecurity that was often, but not always, compensated for by overt grandiose behaviors" (p. 647).

The criteria for NPD in *DSM–III–R* (American Psychiatric Association, 1987) followed the criteria for *DSM–III* rather closely. However, the disorder was changed from a mixed polythetic–monothetic category to an entirely polythetic one. The interpersonal criteria, which had originally included four parts (entitlement, exploitativeness, alternating between idealization and devaluation, and lack of empathy), were reduced to three parts, with "alternating between idealization and devaluation" eliminated. The criterion that included both grandiosity and uniqueness was split into two separate criteria, and a criterion addressing preoccupation with feelings of envy was added. These changes resulted in a greater emphasis on grandiose themes and criteria (Cain et al., 2008; Gunderson, Links, & Reich, 1991; Gunderson, Ronningstam, & Smith, 1995). Additionally, Morey (1988), in a survey of 170 clinicians reporting on 291 patients, found that the changes in criteria and cutoff points between *DSM–III* and *DSM–III–R* resulted in a 350% increase in the number of patients meeting criteria for NPD (from 6% to 22%). However, it is unclear from epidemiological studies whether these criterion changes resulted in noticeable increases in the diagnosis of NPD in the community.

The *DSM–IV* task force made a number of further changes to the criteria for NPD to better differentiate it from other disorders with which it showed high comorbidity (see Cain et al., 2008). Thus, because the criterion reflecting negative reactions to criticism, as written, did not adequately differentiate NPD from paranoid and borderline personality disorders, it was dropped. The lack of empathy criterion was revised to increase discrimination of NPD from the lack of remorse exhibited in antisocial personality disorder. Furthermore, the envy criterion was revised based on findings that NPD patients frequently infer that others are envious of them. The committee also added the criterion of arrogant, haughty behaviors or attitudes. The current *DSM–IV* criteria for NPD include the following characteristics:

1. grandiose sense of self-importance;
2. a preoccupation with fantasies of unlimited power, success, brilliance, beauty, or ideal love;
3. belief that he or she is "special" or unique and can only be understood by, and should associate with, other special or high status people or institutions;
4. requiring excessive admiration;
5. a sense of entitlement;
6. interpersonal exploitativeness;
7. lack of empathy;
8. envy of others or belief that others are envious of him or her; and
9. arrogant, haughty behaviors or attitudes.

FINDINGS RELATED TO *DSM–IV* CRITERIA

Although many of the changes to NPD criteria from *DSM–III* to *DSM–III–R* and *DSM–IV* were the result of increased attention to empirical findings, Cain et al. (2008) noted that many findings relating to underlying vulnerable themes continued to be neglected, and others have stressed this idea as well (Levy, Reynoso, Wasserman, & Clarkin, 2007). Using Q-factor analysis for patients who met criteria for NPD, Russ, Shedler, Bradley and Westen (2008) identified three subtypes: grandiose/malignant, fragile, and high functioning/exhibitionistic (see also Chapter 2, this volume). Russ et al. described grandiose narcissistic patients as angry, interpersonally manipulative, and lacking empathy and remorse; their grandiosity was viewed as primary rather than defensive or compensatory. In contrast, fragile narcissistic patients demonstrate grandiosity under threat (defensive grandiosity) and experience feelings of inadequacy and anxiety indicating that they vacillate between superiority and inferiority. High functioning narcissistic patients are grandiose, competitive, attention seeking, and sexually provocative, and they tend to show adaptive functioning and use their narcissistic traits to succeed. Thus, it appears that distinct subtypes of narcissistic patients may exist even within *DSM–IV* NPD, including narcissistic patients characterized by vulnerable concerns that are not captured by the criterion set.

Other aspects of the phenomenology of narcissism not reflected in *DSM–IV* have been identified as well. Westen and Shedler (1999) surveyed a large group of experienced psychiatrists and psychologists of varying clinical orientations regarding the personality characteristics of patients with varying personality disorders, including NPD. Using factor analytic procedures to derive an empirical profile, they found that narcissistic patients as described by clinicians appear to be more controlling, more likely to get into power struggles, and more competitive than *DSM–IV* suggests. Together, these studies suggest that the revision to the NPD criterion set for *DSM–IV* may have sacrificed the true phenomenological nature of the disorder in an effort to avoid overlap with other diagnoses.

COMPARISON OF NARCISSISM IN THE *DSM* WITH NARCISSISM IN OTHER SYSTEMS

In addition to the *DSM* criteria, several other diagnostic models have been proposed in the literature for conceptualizing NPD. Kernberg (1975, 1984) and Akhtar and Thomson (1982) have provided the most systematic conception of NPD from a psychoanalytic standpoint, and Beck and Freeman (1990) proposed the most systematic cognitive conception. Furthermore, a number of authors have described assessing and diagnosing personality disorders from a radical behavioral framework (e.g., Koerner, Kohlenberg, & Parker, 1996; Nelson-Gray & Farmer, 1999). Other classification systems have been developed that categorize NPD in notable ways, including the *ICD-10* (World Health Organization, 1992) and more recently, the

Psychodynamic Diagnostic Manual (PDM; Psychodynamic Diagnostic Manual Task Force, 2006).

Beck and Freeman (1990) proposed that diagnosing and assessing personality disorders be based on the assumption that each personality disorder can be classified by unique cognitive distortions and maladaptive core and conditional beliefs. These cognitive contents are inferred on the basis of patients' behaviors. Beck and Freeman listed the following examples of the narcissistic individual's core beliefs: "Since I am special, I deserve special dispensations, privileges, and prerogatives"; "I am superior to others, and they should acknowledge this"; and "I'm above the rule" (pp. 50–51). Nelson-Gray, Huprich, Kissling, and Ketchum (2004) examined the relationship between specific dysfunctional thought patterns (or beliefs) and personality disorder. Although specific dysfunctional thought patterns were generally related to corresponding personality disorders, most thought patterns lacked specificity. For example, in addition to narcissistic thought pattern scores, histrionic, avoidant, dependent, paranoid and obsessive–compulsive thought pattern scores were also significantly related to NPD scores (and histrionic thought pattern was the most highly correlated scale with a NPD diagnosis).

Young (1994) developed a schema-focused approach to the treatment of personality disorders by hypothesizing that personality disorders are the result of one of 18 early maladaptive schemas. Young and Flanagan (1998) suggested that those with NPD are characterized by three core maladaptive schemas (entitlement, emotional deprivation, and defectiveness) and a number of secondary schemas (e.g., approval seeking, subjugation, mistrust, avoidance) that are clustered into separate aspects of the self (special self, vulnerable child, and self-soother), which all alternate in reaction to changes and events in the environment. Young (1994) developed a measure to assess which schemas are present or active. However, to date there has not been any research examining the validity of this model.

From a radical behavioral framework, Koerner et al. (1996) described a functional analytic assessment procedure in which, in addition to patients' reports of their behaviors toward others, the therapist's private reactions and feelings are central to diagnosis. They noted that if a therapist feels demeaned and belittled, the patient may have features of NPD. It is interesting to note that the approach advocated by these authors is very similar to traditional psychoanalytic approaches, in which clinicians are encouraged to improve their diagnostic accuracy by focusing on their own countertransference responses to patients (Kernberg, 1975).

From a psychoanalytic conception, Kernberg (1975, 1984) classified narcissism along a dimension of severity, from normal to pathological, and identified three levels of pathological narcissism: high-, middle-, and low-functioning groups. At the highest level, patients are able to achieve the admiration necessary to gratify their grandiose needs. These patients may function successfully during their lifetime but are susceptible to breakdowns with advancing age as their grandiose desires go unfulfilled. At the middle level, patients present with a grandiose sense of self and have little interest in true intimacy. At the lowest level, patients present with comorbid border-line personality traits. These patients' sense of self is generally more diffuse and less stable; they frequently vacillate between pathological grandiosity and suicidality. In addition, Kernberg (1975, 1984) identified an NPD subtype known as malignant narcissism. Patients with this disorder are not only char-acterized by typical NPD symptoms but also display antisocial behaviors, tend toward paranoid features, and take pleasure in aggression and sadism toward others. They are thought to be at high risk for suicide, despite the absence of depression, because suicide for these patients is thought to represent sadistic control over others, a dismissal of a denigrated world, or a display of mastery over death. Despite the richness of Kernberg's descriptions, to date there has been no direct research on malignant narcissism.

More recently, in response to growing dissatisfaction with the DSM approach within the psychodynamic community, a task force was created by the major psychoanalytic organizations that developed a diagnostic manual integrating descriptions of internal dimensions and external manifestations of disorders (Psychodynamic Diagnostic Manual Task Force, 2006). The PDM has adopted two of the aforementioned conceptual distinctions in its approach to classifying NPD. First, the PDM explicitly states that patients with NPD should be characterized according to level of severity. Like Kern-berg, the PDM describes narcissistic pathology on a continuum from neurotic to more severely disturbed personality pathology. On the neurotic end of the continuum, individuals may have strong needs for admiration but may be socially adept and successful enough to function in social and occupational environments and receive some degree of the sought admiration; deeper inti-macy may be more difficult to achieve. At lower levels, the deficient capacity for intimacy may interfere significantly with social and occupational func-tioning, whereas the lowest level of pathology parallels Kernberg's descrip-tion of malignant narcissism. Second, the PDM distinguishes between an arrogant/entitled type, which parallels the description of grandiose narcis-sism, and a depressed/depleted type, which parallels the description of vulner-able narcissism. Whereas the arrogant/entitled type is more closely aligned with the DSM description of NPD, including overtly haughty, entitled, and devaluing behaviors, the depressed/depleted type characterizes individuals who are quietly envious of and wounded by the success of others, with whom they nonetheless may try to ingratiate themselves.

In contrast to the clinically rich description of narcissistic pathology in the PDM, the ICD-10 (World Health Organization, 1992) does not specifically define the characteristics of NPD. This diagnosis is not one of the eight main personality disorders, but instead is classified in the category "Other Specific Personality Disorders," and thus no specific criteria are articulated. In the *ICD-10* system, to meet criteria for NPD the individual must meet none of the specifications for the main personality disorders (i.e., paranoid, schizoid, dissocial [antisocial], emotionally unstable [borderline], histrionic, anankastic [obsessive–compulsive], anxious [avoidant], and dependent). Given that NPD has been found to have problematically high overlap with other Axis II disorders, most notably antisocial, histrionic, borderline, and passive-aggressive personality disorders (see Levy et al., 2007), with comorbidity rates often exceeding 50%, the NPD diagnosis is therefore of limited use in the *ICD-10* system.

PROPOSED CHANGES FOR NPD IN *DSM–5*: RATIONALE AND CRITIQUES

Initial proposals from the American Psychiatric Association's Personality Disorders Work Group indicated that NPD would be deleted as a personality type from *DSM–5*, along with four other *DSM–IV* disorders (Skodol, Bender, Morey, et al., 2011; Skodol, Clark, Bender, et al., 2011), because of low prevalence and insufficient research as compared with other retained disorders. Rather than represent NPD as a diagnosis in its own right, characteristics of pathological narcissism and NPD were to be captured through dimensional ratings of five personality disorder types (antisocial, avoidant, borderline, obsessive–compulsive, and schizotypal); six higher order personality trait domains (negative emotionality, introversion, antagonism, disinhibition, compulsivity, and schizotypy); levels of self and interpersonal functioning; and failures in adaptive functioning. This system was intended to provide a multidimensional profile of personality types and traits, pathology, and level of functioning. The work group argued that these proposed revisions would reduce the excessive comorbidity among personality disorders, provide official recognition that many forms of personality pathology occur on a continuum, and replace the unstable behavioral personality disorders criteria with personality traits that are more stable over time, thus providing a richer and more clinically useful portrayal of personality pathology and narcissistic functioning.

After the publication of the work group's proposal, however, several critiques emerged among the scientific community regarding both the hybrid model for assessing personality pathology in general and the exclusion of NPD as a personality type. Many found the proposed hybrid model to be cumbersome and potentially difficult for clinicians to use with its combined prototype matching and personality trait dimensional rating scales (Pilkonis,

Hallquist, Morse, & Stepp, 2011; Shedler et al., 2010). Samuel, Lynam, Widiger, and Ball (2011) noted that the trait domains for assessing narcissism were quite limited; whereas the *DSM–IV* personality disorders retained as "types" in *DSM–5* were described by nine to 11 separate trait dimensions, the disorders proposed for deletion were described by far fewer, and in the case of NPD, one of the four traits proposed was simply the name of the disorder itself (narcissism). Miller, Widiger, and Campbell (2010) argued that essential traits in conceptualizing narcissism, such as maladaptive extraversion, maladaptive agreeableness, and maladaptively low neuroticism, had been excluded. Furthermore, several theorists and researchers argued that broadening the NPD criteria to include items reflective of narcissistic vulnerability, competitiveness, and hostility would significantly reduce its overlap with other personality disorders (Cain et al., 2008; Levy et al., 2007; Ronningstam, 2009, 2010; Russ et al., 2008). Widiger (2011) contended that although *DSM–IV* NPD has a low prevalence rate and is poorly researched compared with the other disorders slated for retention, a large body of research on the broader construct of narcissism and its importance for diverse outcomes (e.g., Bushman & Baumeister, 1998; Miller, Campbell, & Pilkonis, 2007; Ogrodniczuk, Piper, Joyce, Steinberg, & Duggal, 2009; Pincus et al., 2009) was omitted as well as its higher prevalence in clinical practice than the current *DSM–IV* criteria capture.

Responding to these criticisms, the Personality Disorders Work Group (American Psychiatric Association, 2011b) offered a significant revision of the hybrid model for assessing personality pathology in general, as well as the re-inclusion of narcissism as a personality disorder. The proposed criteria integrate many of the aforementioned suggestions, with some notable exceptions. First, the assessment of personality disorders has been streamlined considerably; patients are now rated in two major domains of impairment in personality (i.e., self and interpersonal) functioning and pathological personality traits. In the case of NPD, impairments in self-functioning would be indicated by problems related to identity and self-direction. Whereas impairment in identity may include an inflated view of the self, unlike the *DSM–IV* the proposed model also captures vacillations in self-esteem that include a deflated view of the self, thus allowing for both narcissistic grandiosity and vulnerability (Cain et al., 2008; Levy et al., 2007; Miller et al., 2010; Ronningstam, 2009, 2010). The proposed criteria also note that "emotion regulation mirrors fluctuations in self-esteem," thus recognizing the internal regulatory function (as opposed to simply the outward appearance) of these extreme self-appraisals.

Impairment in self-functioning related to self-direction includes and integrates aspects of *DSM–IV* criteria, such as the unreasonably high expectations of oneself and others and a sense of entitlement leading to lower expectations for oneself as compared with others. Furthermore, whereas the *DSM–IV* notes that individuals with NPD demand recognition for their accomplishments, the proposed model goes one step further in noting how the need for such approval acts as a motivation for subsequent goal choices. One area not sufficiently captured by this impairment as it is presently defined, but noted by Ronningstam (2010), is the intense aggression that can be directed toward oneself in the form of self-criticism for perceived failures, as well as the intense aggression that can be directed toward others who do not meet these high standards. Another omission in this proposed domain, implied but not explicitly identified, is the trait-level maladaptive perfectionism often associated with this deficit in self-functioning (Ronningstam, 2010).

In terms of impairments in interpersonal functioning, the deficits in empathy described in the current proposal are consistent with the *DSM–IV* criteria. However, unlike the *DSM–IV*, the proposed model omits any reference to envy (i.e., feeling envious of others, as well as assuming others are envious of oneself). Ronningstam (2010) noted that empathic failures may not just be related to self-centeredness but may also be due to the affective dysregulation and subsequent retaliatory behaviors that may occur when feelings of envy, shame, and humiliation are elicited in relational contexts.

Impairment in interpersonal functioning related to intimacy reflects the *DSM–IV* description of the exploitativeness often observed in the relationships of individuals with NPD. However, the proposed model goes one step further in implying that relationships may be used instrumentally not just for external or secondary gain but also for internal regulation. There is an emphasis on the fact that not only does self-esteem vacillate and therefore needs to be regulated (rather than self-esteem simply being too high) but that individuals with NPD also look for external regulation of self-esteem in the context of relationships.

The proposed criteria for NPD also include the pathological trait facet of antagonism, as indicated by pathological grandiosity and attention seeking. As previously noted, the proposed model's definition of grandiosity goes beyond the *DSM–IV* emphasis on overt displays of entitlement to include a more covert expression of this trait, though there is still a primary emphasis on outward displays of haughty and condescending behaviors. Pathological attention seeking reflects the *DSM–IV* criteria of need for excessive admiration. However, Ronningstam (2010) noted that individuals with NPD may also be characterized by pathological avoidance of attention by others. Although narcissistic individuals may desperately seek attention for behaviors that validate a positive self-appraisal, they may also desperately avoid attention out of fear of receiving feedback that may validate a negative self-appraisal. Attention seeking as it is currently defined may not be able to adequately assess the maladaptive extraversion trait facets of dominance, excitement seeking, and behavioral activation and approach that are a part of narcissistic grandiosity. Extraversion-related traits have been found to mediate the relationship between narcissism and several behavioral problems such as aggression and excessive risk-taking (Miller & Campbell, 2010). Furthermore, the proposed traits might not adequately capture the trait-level maladaptive agreeableness and maladaptively low neuroticism identified by Miller and colleagues.

In addition to evaluating the domains of impairment in personality functioning and pathological personality traits, the proposed *DSM–5* criteria also include an assessment of severity that places pathology on a continuum from healthy (no impairment or mild impairment) to pathological (moderate to severe impairment). The Levels of Personality Functioning Scale (American Psychiatric Association, 2011a) evaluates the degree of impairment in both self (i.e., identity and self-direction) and interpersonal (i.e. empathy and intimacy) functioning. Such assessment is consistent with both Kernberg's model and the PDM in that it allows for the disorder to be placed on a continuum from higher functioning to more severely disturbed personality pathology. Perhaps most important, this scale focuses on internal dimensions of functioning, as opposed to the *DSM–IV* Global Assessment of Functioning (GAF) Scale (Endicott, Spitzer, Fleiss, & Cohen, 1976), which primarily focuses on external functioning. This distinction is particularly important for evaluating NPD, because individuals with NPD may be "successful" in work by achieving a high status (e.g., in business or politics) and yet have malignant features characterized by a deficit in empathic relatedness to others. Whereas such individuals could receive a high GAF score, they could be rated as having more severe impairment on the Levels of Personality Functioning Scale.

CONCLUSION

Although the concept of narcissism has a long and rich history, it was not included in the *DSM* system until 1980, with the appearance of *DSM–III*. Its inclusion followed a confluence of factors, including increased clinical interest in narcissism based on the writings of Kohut (1971, 1977) and Kernberg (1975, 1984), factor-analytic and social-personality psychology research from academia (Block, 1971; Eysenck & Eysenck, 1975; Harder, 1979; Raskin & Hall, 1979; see also Frances, 1980), and increased societal awareness as a result of trends in critical social theory (Adorno, 1967; Lasch, 1979; Marcuse, 1955; Wolfe, 1977). *DSM–III–R* and *DSM–IV* brought modifications to both the approach (from a mixed polythetic–monothetic category to an entirely polythetic one) and criterion sets (e.g., the elimination of a criterion regarding the alternating between extremes and the addition of a criterion about pre-occupation with feelings of envy). These modifications seem to have solved some problems but created others. A number of these changes were designed to increase the concept's specificity and reduce comorbidity. However, doing so resulted in greater emphasis on the grandiose aspects of narcissism and less on the vulnerable aspects of narcissism as well as the dynamic of vacillating between these two narcissistic states. Ultimately, the changes in *DSM–III–R* and *DSM–IV* may have resulted in the *DSM* failing to capture the intended clinical phenomena (Cain et al., 2008; Levy et al., 2007). NPD is currently included among the six proposed major personality types for *DSM–5* and is described by other elements of the proposed model (level of personality functioning, general personality dysfunction, and personality traits). Research is needed to examine how well narcissistic functioning is captured through the use of this hybrid model.

REFERENCES

Adorno, T. (1967). Sociology and psychology. *New Left Review, 46,* 67–80.

Akhtar, S., & Thomson, J. A. (1982). Overview: Narcissistic personality disorder. *American Journal of Psychiatry, 139,* 12–20.

American Psychiatric Association. (1953). *Diagnostic and statistical manual of mental disorders.* Washington, DC: Author.

American Psychiatric Association. (1968). *Diagnostic and statistical manual of mental disorders* (2nd ed.). Washington, DC: Author.

American Psychiatric Association. (1980). *Diagnostic and statistical manual of mental disorders* (3rd ed.). Washington, DC: Author.

American Psychiatric Association. (1987). *Diagnostic and statistical manual of mental disorders* (3rd ed., rev.). Washington, DC: Author.

American Psychiatric Association. (1994). *Diagnostic and statistical manual of mental disorders* (4th ed.). Washington, DC: Author.

American Psychiatric Association. (2000). *Diagnostic and statistical manual of mental disorders* (4th ed., text rev.). Washington, DC: Author.

American Psychiatric Association. (2011a). *Levels of personality functioning.* Retrieved from http://www.dsm5.org/proposedrevisions/pages/proposedrevision.aspx?rid=468

American Psychiatric Association. (2011b). *Personality disorders.* Retrieved from http://www.dsm5.org/proposedrevision/pages/personalitydisorders.aspx

Beck, A. T., & Freeman, A. (1990). *Cognitive therapy of personality disorders.* New York, NY: Guilford Press.

Block, J. (1971). *Lives through time.* Berkeley, CA: Bancroft Books.

Bushman, B. J., & Baumeister, R. F. (1998). Threatened egotism, narcissism, self-esteem, and direct and displaced aggression: Does self-love or self-hate lead to violence? *Journal of Personality and Social Psychology, 75*, 219–229. doi:10.1037/0022-3514.75.1.219

Cain, N. M., Pincus, A. L., & Ansell, E. B. (2008). Narcissism at the crossroads: Phenotypic description of pathological narcissism across clinical theory, social/personality psychology, and psychiatric diagnosis. *Clinical Psychology Review, 28*, 638–656. doi:10.1016/j.cpr.2007.09.006

Endicott, J., Spitzer, R. L., Fleiss, J. L., Cohen, J. (1976). The global assessment scale. A procedure for measuring overall severity of psychiatric disturbance. *Archives of General Psychiatry, 33*, 766–771.

Eysenck, H. J., & Eysenck, S. B. J. (1975). *Eysenck Personality Questionnaire manual*. San Diego, CA: Educational Testing Service.

Frances, A. J. (1980). The *DSM–III* personality disorder section: A commentary. *The American Journal of Psychiatry, 137*, 1050–1054.

Gunderson, J. G., Links, P. A., & Reich, J. H. (1991). Competing models of personality disorders. *Journal of Personality Disorders, 5*, 60–68.

Gunderson, J. G., Ronningstam, E., & Smith, L. E. (1995). Narcissistic personality disorder. In W. J. Livesley (Ed.), *The DSM–IV personality disorders* (pp. 201–212). New York, NY: Guilford Press.

Harder, D.W. (1979). The assessment of ambitious-narcissistic character style with three projective tests: The Early Memories, TAT, and Rorschach. *Journal of Personality Assessment, 43*(1), 23–32.

Kernberg, O. (1967). Borderline personality organization. *Journal of the American Psychoanalytic Association, 15*, 641–685. doi:10.1177/000306516701500309

Kernberg, O. (1975). *Borderline conditions and pathological narcissism*. New York, NY: Jason Aronson.

Kernberg, O. (1984). *Severe personality disorders: Psychotherapeutic strategies*. New Haven, CT: Yale University Press.

Koerner, K., Kohlenberg, R. J., & Parker, C. R. (1996). Diagnosis of personality disorder: A radical behavioral alternative. *Journal of Consulting and Clinical Psychology, 64*, 1169–1176. doi:10.1037/0022-006X.64.6.1169

Kohut, H. (1968). The psychoanalytic treatment of narcissistic personality disorders: Outline of a systematic approach. *The Psychoanalytic Study of the Child, 23*, 86–113.

Kohut, H. (1971). *The analysis of the self*. New York, NY: International Universities Press.

Kohut, H. (1977). *The restoration of the self*. New York, NY: International Universities Press.

Kraepelin, E. (1899). *Psychiatrie: ein Lehrbuch für Studirende und Aertze* (6th ed.). Leipzig, Germany: Barth Verlag. (Reprinted as *Psychiatry: A textbook for students and physicians*, by J. M. Quen, Ed., and H. Metoiu & S. Ayed, Trans., 1990, Canton, MA: Science History.)

Kraepelin, E. (1913). *Psychiatrie: ein Lehrbuch für Studierende und Ärzte*. Leipzig, Germany: Barth. (Reprinted in part as *Manic–depressive insanity and paranoia* by G. M. Robertson, Ed., and R. M. Barclay, Trans., 1971, Huntington, NY: Robert E. Kreiger; and in part as *Dementia praecox and paraphrenia* by G. M. Robertson, Ed., and R. M. Barclay, Trans., 1976, Huntington, NY: Robert E. Kreiger.)

Lasch, C. (1979). *The culture of narcissism: American life in an age of diminishing expectations*. New York, NY: Warner Books.

Levy, K. N., Reynoso, J., Wasserman, R. H., & Clarkin, J. F. (2007). Narcissistic personality disorder. In W. O'Donohue, K. A. Fowler, & S. O. Lilienfeld (Eds.), *Personality disorders: Toward the DSM–V* (pp. 233–277). Thousand Oaks, CA: Sage.

Marcuse, H. (1955). *Eros and civilization*. New York, NY: Vintage Books.

Miller, J. D., & Campbell, W. K. (2010). The case for using research on trait narcissism as a building block for understanding narcissistic personality disorder. *Personality Disorders: Theory, Research, and Treatment, 1*, 180–191. doi:10.1037/a0018229

Miller, J. D., Campbell, W. K., & Pilkonis, P. A. (2007). Narcissistic personality disorder: Relations with distress and functional impairment. *Comprehensive Psychiatry, 48*, 170–177. doi:10.1016/j.comppsych.2006.10.003

Miller, J. D., Widiger, T. A., & Campbell, W. K. (2010). Narcissistic personality disorder and the DSM-V. *Journal of Abnormal Psychology, 119*, 640–649. doi:10.1037/a0019529

Millon, T. (1981). *Disorders of personality: DSM–III Axis I*. New York, NY: Wiley.

Millon, T. (1991). Classification in psychopathology: Rationale, alternatives, and standards. *Journal of Abnormal Psychology, 100*, 245–261. doi:10.1037/0021-843X.100.3.245

Morey, L. C. (1988). Personality disorders in *DSM–III* and *DSM–III–R*: Convergence, coverage, and internal consistency. *American Journal of Psychiatry, 145*, 573–577.

Morf, C., & Rhodewalt, F. (2001). Unraveling the paradoxes of narcissism: A dynamic self-regulatory processing model. *Psychological Inquiry, 12*, 177–196. doi:10.1207/S15327965PLI1204_1

Murray, H. A. (1938). *Explorations in personality*. New York, NY: Oxford University Press.

Nelson-Gray, R. O., & Farmer, R. F. (1999). Behavioral assessment of personality disorders. *Behaviour Research and Therapy, 37*, 347–368. doi:10.1016/S0005-7967(98)00142-9

Nelson-Gray, R. O., Huprich, S. K., Kissling, G. E., & Ketchum, K. (2004). A preliminary examination of Beck's cognitive theory of personality disorders in undergraduate analogues. *Personality and Individual Differences, 36*, 219–233. doi:10.1016/S0191-8869(03)00081-3

Ogrodniczuk, J. S., Piper, W. E., Joyce, A. S., Steinberg, P. I., & Duggal, S. (2009). Interpersonal problems associated with narcissism among psychiatric outpatients. *Journal of Psychiatric Research, 43,* 837–842. doi:10.1016/j.jpsychires.2008.12.005

Pilkonis, P. A., Hallquist, M. N., Morse, J. Q., & Stepp, S. D. (2011). Striking the (im)proper balance between scientific advances and clinical utility: Commentary on the DSM–5 proposal for personality disorders. *Personality Disorders: Theory, Research, and Treatment, 2,* 68–82. doi:10.1037/a0022226

Pincus, A. L., Ansell, E. B., Pimentel, C. A., Cain, N. M., Wright, A. G., & Levy, K. N. (2009). Initial construction and validation of the Pathological Narcissism Inventory. *Psychological Assessment, 21,* 365–379. doi:10.1037/a0016530

Psychodynamic Diagnostic Manual Task Force. (2006). *Psychodynamic diagnostic manual.* Silver Spring, MD: Alliance of Psychoanalytic Organizations.

Raskin, R. N., & Hall, C. S. (1979). A narcissistic personality inventory. *Psychological Reports, 45,* 590. doi:10.2466/pr0.1979.45.2.590

Ronningstam, E. (2009). Narcissistic personality disorder: Facing DSM–V. *Psychiatric Annals, 39,* 111–121. doi:10.3928/00485713-20090301-09

Ronningstam, E. (2010). Narcissistic personality disorder: A current review. *Current Psychiatry Reports, 12,* 68–75. doi:10.1007/s11920-009-0084-z

Russ, E., Shedler, J., Bradley, R., & Westen, D. (2008). Refining the construct of narcissistic personality disorder: Diagnostic criteria and subtypes. *The American Journal of Psychiatry, 165,* 1473–1481. doi:10.1176/appi.ajp.2008.07030376

Samuel, D. B., Lynam, D. R., Widiger, T. A., & Ball, S. A. (2011). An expert consensus approach to relating the proposed DSM-5 types and traits. *Personality Disorders: Theory, Research, and Treatment.* Advance online publication. doi:10.1037/a0023787

Shedler, J., Beck, A., Fonagy, P., Gabbard, G. O., Gunderson, J., Kernberg, O., . . . Westen, D. (2010). Commentary: Personality disorders in DSM–V. *The American Journal of Psychiatry, 167,* 1026–1028. doi:10.1176/appi.ajp.2010.10050746

Skodol, A. E., Bender, D. S., Morey, L. C., Clark, L. A., Oldham, J. M., Alarcon, R. D., . . . Siever, L. J. (2011). Personality disorder types proposed for DSM–5. *Journal of Personality Disorders, 25,* 136–169. doi:10.1521/pedi.2011.25.2.136

Skodol, A. E., Bender, D. S., Oldham, J. M., Clark, L. A., Morey, L. C., Verheul, R., . . . Siever, L. J. (2011). Proposed changes in personality and personality disorder assessment and diagnosis for DSM–5: Part II. Clinical application. *Personality Disorders: Theory, Research, and Treatment, 2,* 23–40. doi:10.1037/a0021892

Skodol, A. E., Clark, L. A., Bender, D. S., Krueger, R. F., Morey, L. C., Verheul, R., . . . Oldham, J. M. (2011). Proposed changes in personality and personality disorder assessment and diagnosis for DSM–5: Part I. Description and rationale. *Personality Disorders: Theory, Research, and Treatment, 2,* 4–22. doi:10.1037/a0021891

Spitzer, R. L., & Fleiss, J. L. (1974). A re-analysis of the reliability of psychiatric diagnosis. *British Journal of Psychiatry, 125,* 341–347. doi:10.1192/bjp.125.4.341

Westen, D., & Shedler, J. (1999). Revising and assessing Axis II: Part II. Toward an empirically based and clinically useful classification of personality disorders. *The American Journal of Psychiatry, 156*, 273–285.

Widiger, T. A. (2011). A shaky future for personality disorders. *Personality Disorders: Theory, Research, and Treatment, 2*, 54–67. doi:10.1037/a0021855

Widiger, T. A., Frances, A. J., Pincus, H. A., Davis, W. W., & First, M. B. (1991). Toward an empirical classification for the *DSM–IV*. *Journal of Abnormal Psychology, 100*, 280–288. doi:10.1037/0021-843X.100.3.280

Wolfe, T. (1977). The "me" decade and the third great awakening. In *Mauve gloves & madmen, clutter & vine* (pp. 126–167). New York, NY: Bantam.

World Health Organization. (1992). *The ICD-10 classification of mental and behavioural disorders: Clinical descriptions and diagnostic guidelines*. Geneva, Switzerland: Author.

Young, J., & Flanagan, C. (1998). Schema-focused therapy for narcissistic patients. In E. Ronningstam (Ed.), *Disorders of narcissism: Diagnostic, clinical, and empirical implications* (pp. 239–267). Washington, DC: American Psychiatric Association.

Young, J. E. (1994). Cognitive therapy for personality disorders: A schema-focused approach. *Practitioner's resource series*. Sarasota, FL: Professional Resource Press.

4

NARCISSISM IN THE *PSYCHODYNAMIC DIAGNOSTIC MANUAL*

EVE CALIGOR

One of the strengths of the psychodynamic tradition is the emphasis it places on evaluating and treating personality pathology. Contemporary psychodynamic approaches to the diagnosis of personality disorders typically combine assessment of personality traits, or personality style, with evaluation of certain key psychological functions that underlie healthy and pathological personality functioning. This approach is described and used in the "Personality Patterns and Disorders" section of the *Psychodynamic Diagnostic Manual* (*PDM*; PDM Task Force, 2006); it is summarized in this chapter.

DOI: 10.1037/14041-004
Understanding and Treating Pathological Narcissism, J. S. Ogrodniczuk (Editor)

Clinical Illustration

Mr. B. (the patient's identity has been disguised to maintain confidentiality) is a 38-year-old married, unemployed lawyer seen in consultation with a complaint of "problems with work." Though the interview initially focused on his recent difficulty finding a job in a challenging economic environment, it emerged that Mr. B. had been fired from a series of jobs since graduating law school 10 years earlier. When employed, he quickly became bored with his work and as a result often failed to complete projects and missed deadlines. He also had a history of falsifying time sheets and frequently calling in sick. He felt that his behavior was justified—he was underpaid and as a result entitled to take extra time and money as he was able. He had most recently worked as a paralegal, a job he found demeaning, and had been fired 6 months earlier in the setting of an argument with his supervisor, whom he described as a "pompous fool." In discussing his difficulty finding work, Mr. B. repeatedly complained about "the suits" walking around out there making "wads of money" and feeling themselves to be "superior." Mr. B. described himself as alternating between feeling smarter than everyone and like a "dumb loser." He demonstrated no feeling for his wife and explained that he stayed in the marriage because of the financial support she provided. He told the consultant that even though his wife was very beautiful and he had originally seen her as the most wonderful woman he had ever met, he had lost sexual interest in her early in the marriage, and he periodically visited prostitutes. When asked to describe his wife he responded that she was "too serious and boring" and could say little more. He complained of feeling empty, bored, and restless. He wanted the consultant to tell him how to feel less dysphoric and anxious and how to have a more stable sense of himself as exceptional. At the end of an hour-long interview, the consultant found himself with only a vague and superficial sense of Mr. B. and an even more shadowy image of his wife. The consultant felt overwhelmed with the intractability of Mr. B.'s difficulties and was concerned that Mr. B. had little genuine motivation for treatment.

Mr. B. has a narcissistic personality disorder (NPD) and a borderline level of personality organization. This diagnosis can provide a great deal of information about him, including the nature and severity of his pathology, his prognosis, and his central anxieties and vulnerabilities. This diagnosis can also be used to guide treatment planning and to anticipate difficulties likely to emerge in treatment, as well as reactions a treating clinician is likely to experience in relation to Mr. B.

Personality and Personality Pathology

Personality refers to the relatively stable ways of thinking, feeling, behaving, and relating to others (described as personality traits) that characterize an individual's experience and behavior. Personality also includes the individual's moral values and ideals. In the normal personality, personality traits are not extreme and they are flexibly activated in different settings, allowing for adaptation to external demands and to internal needs. In contrast, in the setting of personality pathology, personality traits are more extreme, and they are rigid, which is to say that they are automatically and repeatedly activated, even in settings in which they are maladaptive. When rigidity of personality functioning becomes sufficiently extreme to cause clinically significant distress or failure of adaptation, the condition is called a *personality disorder*.

Descriptive and Structural Assessment

When assessing personality pathology, evaluation of personality traits enables the clinician to make a descriptive diagnosis of a particular personality disorder. The descriptive features of a personality disorder include personality traits, which can be observed by a third party (e.g., a sense of entitlement, shyness), along with characteristic, rigidly fixed internal experiences (e.g., recurrent grandiose fantasies, chronic self-doubt) that can be reported by the individual. The descriptive approach to diagnosing personality pathology is the approach taken in the *Diagnostic and Statistical Manual of Mental Disorders* (4th ed., text rev.; *DSM–IV–TR*; American Psychiatric Association, 2000). Each of the 11 *DSM–IV–TR* personality disorders is defined by a constellation of personality traits that tend to cluster together; the diagnosis of a particular personality disorder is made when the patient endorses a specified number of the traits that characterize that disorder. A descriptive diagnosis enables the clinician to anticipate central anxieties that organize the patient's internal experience and interpersonal behavior and that are likely to emerge in the early phases of treatment.

A psychodynamic evaluation of personality pathology couples assessment of descriptive features of personality pathology with evaluation of core psychological functions or capacities (often referred to as *structures* in the psychoanalytic literature) that organize both normal personality functioning and personality pathology. Structural assessment provides essential information about the nature of personality functioning and the severity of pathology and can be used to guide treatment planning.

The psychodynamic structural approach to classifying personality pathology was originally developed by Otto Kernberg (Kernberg & Caligor, 2005), and the approach presented in this chapter is an elaboration of Kernberg's original formulations. Kernberg has focused in particular on the psychological functions of identity (sense of self and sense of others), defensive operations (characteristic ways of coping with external stressors and internal anxieties), and reality testing (capacity to distinguish internal from external reality) to classify personality pathology. Based on evaluation of identity formation, defenses, and reality testing, the personality disorders can be characterized on a dimension of severity, ranging from neurotic personality organization at the healthiest end of the personality disorders, through high borderline personality organization to, at the most severe end of the spectrum, low borderline personality organization.[1] The relationship between this classification of personality pathology and the *DSM–IV–TR* (American Psychiatric Association, 2000) personality disorders is represented in Figure 4.1.[2] The figure illustrates that each of the 11 personality disorders listed in the manual is associated with a range of severity of psychopathology.

The neurotic personality disorders are characterized by fully consolidated identity, corresponding with an integrated, realistic, complex, and stable experience of self and others. Personality rigidity, often limited to a particular area of difficulty, reflects the impact of repression-based[3] defenses on psychological functioning and interferes with optimal coping and adaptation. The neurotic personality also makes use of more adaptive, mature defenses,[4] and reality testing is intact and stable. Borderline level of personality organization (BPO) is characterized by pathology of identity formation, corresponding with superficial, extreme, black-and-white, and often unstable, caricaturelike experiences of the self and others. Personality rigidity is severe and global. In BPO, identity pathology is associated with the predominance of maladaptive, lower level, or splitting-based defenses,[5] and reality testing can at times be compromised in the setting of stress or anxiety. The borderline group is divided into high BPO and the more severe low BPO. Moving from high BPO to low BPO, manifestations of identity pathology, the predominance of lower level defenses, and vulnerability of reality testing all become more extreme. In addition, low BPO

---

[1]There is a distinction between the *DSM–IV–TR* borderline personality disorder and BPO. Borderline personality disorder is a specific personality disorder, diagnosed on the basis of a constellation of descriptive features. BPO is a much broader category based on structural features, as described here; it subsumes *DSM–IV–TR* borderline personality disorder, as well as all of the severe personality disorders.
[2]The classification of "three levels of personality organization" is in fact dimensional rather than categorical. In other words, there is no abrupt cutoff between the neurotic and high borderline levels of personality organization or between the high and low borderline levels of personality organization; rather, they exist on a continuum.
[3]Repression-based defenses include reaction formation, displacement, isolation of affect, intellectualization, neurotic projection, and repression proper.
[4]Mature or "healthy" defenses include suppression, anticipation, altruism, humor, and sublimation.
[5]Lower level or splitting-based defenses include idealization, devaluation, projective identification, omnipotence, denial, and splitting proper.

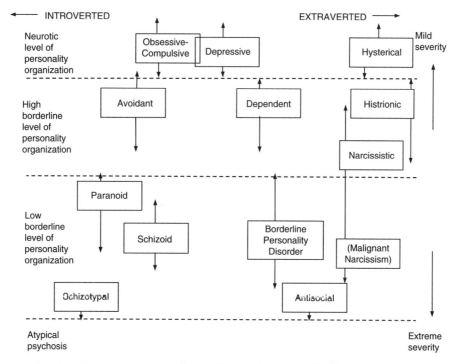

Figure 4.1. Severity ranges for each *DSM–IV–TR* personality disorder. Disorders are presented from the mildest (top of the page) to the extremely severe (bottom of the page). Vertical arrows indicate ranges of severity. *DSM–IV–TR = Diagnostic and Statistical Manual of Mental Disorders* (4th ed., text rev.).

is characterized by significant pathology of moral functioning, an inability to form stable or meaningful relationships, and the dominance of aggression in affective experience (see Table 4.1).

Mr. B., introduced at the beginning of this chapter, can be seen to have a personality that is organized at a low borderline level. His sense of self is characterized by instability and a lack of depth; he defines himself in relation to others, as either superior or inferior, "the best" or "the worst." Mr. B.'s view of his wife is similarly unstable and extreme; originally "the most wonderful," she is currently someone he devalues. His experience of her is superficial and vague ("too serious and boring"), similar to his view of the people he worked with as "fools" and "suits"; even when pressed he was unable to provide a three-dimensional description of anyone in his world. Mr. B.'s defensive style relies heavily on the lower level defenses of idealization and devaluation (e.g., his wife, his boss), as well as lower level projection (his sense that the "suits" are out to humiliate him). As far as we know, Mr. B.'s reality testing is, for the most part, intact. He is severely impaired in

TABLE 4.1
Structural Approach to Classification of Personality Pathology

Psychological function	Personality organization			
	Normal	Neurotic	High borderline	Low borderline
Personality rigidity	None	Mild–moderate	Extreme	Very extreme
Identity	Consolidated	Consolidated	Mild–moderate pathology	Severe pathology
Dominant defensive functioning	Mature	Repression-based	Splitting-based and repression-based	Splitting-based
Reality testing	Intact; stable	Intact; stable	Intact	Intact (transient psychotic states)
Object relations	Deep; mutual	Deep; mutual	Some mutual	Need fulfilling
Moral functioning	Internalized; flexible	Internalized; rigid	Inconsistent	Pathology
Affects	Complex; well modulated	Complex; well modulated	Poorly integrated; poorly modulated and unstable	Crude; extremely poorly modulated and unstable

his capacity to form meaningful relations with others; he is overtly exploitative of his wife and seems to demonstrate no genuine attachment to her, while at the same time describing her as his closest relation. Pathology in moral functioning is expressed in Mr. B.'s lack of guilt and rationalizations about falsifying time sheets, as well as his financially exploiting his wife and lying to her about using prostitutes.

The authors of the "Personality Patterns and Disorders" section of the *PDM* (PDM Task Force, 2006) elaborated on Kernberg's formulation, identifying seven dimensions of psychological functioning that can be used to characterize severity of personality pathology and to make a structural assessment of personality functioning (the psychoanalytic term for each function described is in parentheses):

- the capacity to view the self and others in complex, stable, and accurate ways (identity);
- the capacity to maintain intimate, stable, and satisfying relationships (object relations);

- the capacity to experience in self and perceive in others the full range of age-expected affects (affect tolerance);
- the capacity to regulate impulses and affects in ways that foster adaptation and satisfaction, with flexibility in using defenses or coping strategies (affect regulation);
- the capacity to function according to a consistent and mature moral sensibility (superego integration, ideal self-concept, ego ideal);
- the capacity to appreciate, if not necessarily to conform to, conventional notions of what is realistic (reality testing); and
- the capacity to respond to stress resourcefully and to recover from painful events without undue difficulty (ego strength and resilience).

The normal personality is characterized by all of these capacities. The individual who is organized at a neurotic level has most of these capacities to a significant degree, although one or two areas (often broad affective experience or satisfaction in relationships) may be somewhat compromised. Individuals who are organized at a borderline level have significant pathology in the first four capacities outlined, and those in the low borderline range have greater pathology across Dimensions 1 through 4 in addition to pathology of moral functioning and variable reality testing.

Implications for Treatment

Structural assessment and diagnosis have implications for treatment planning and enable the clinician to anticipate problems likely to emerge in the treatment of particular groups of patients. Individuals organized at a neurotic level have an excellent prognosis in general and do well in relatively unstructured dynamic therapies. Clinicians typically find that patients who are organized at a neurotic level are easy to understand and easy to empathize with. Individuals organized at a high BPO may do poorly in unstructured treatments but have a very positive prognosis in more structured psychodynamic therapies. They may appear to be organized at a neurotic level at first glance, but they are far more likely than neurotic patients to quickly elicit strong emotional reactions in their therapists. Individuals in the low borderline range have a more guarded prognosis and typically behave in destructive and self-destructive ways in relation to a clinician. These individuals require treatments specially tailored to address their psychopathology (see, e.g., Chapters 14 and 15 of this volume) and are best treated by clinicians specially trained to manage the very powerful and often unpleasant emotional reactions that low borderline patients routinely elicit in those who treat them.

PDM APPROACH TO EVALUATING AND DIAGNOSING NPD

Within a contemporary psychodynamic frame of reference, the diagnosis of NPD includes a broad spectrum of patients with very different, often seemingly contradictory, presentations and very different clinical needs. In fact, on the dimension of severity, NPD includes the broadest range of psychopathology of all the personality disorders (Figure 4.1). There are, however, core structural and descriptive features that characterize the narcissistic personality at all levels of severity.

Structural Features of NPD: Identity, Defenses, and Reality Testing

From a structural perspective, at the core of NPD is pathology of identity formation or pathology of the self. As a result, all patients with the diagnosis of NPD are seen to be organized at a borderline level of personality organization (Kernberg & Caligor, 2005). However, NPD includes patients who fall across the entire borderline spectrum, ranging from the bottom of the low borderline level of personality organization through the healthiest range of the high borderline spectrum. The broad and inclusive approach to the diagnosis of NPD that we describe is to be distinguished from the *Diagnostic and Statistical Manual of Mental Disorders* (4th ed.; *DSM–IV*; American Psychiatric Association, 1994) classification described in Chapter 3, this volume; the *DSM* classification describes a relatively homogenous and highly disturbed group falling at the more pathological end of the narcissistic spectrum.

At the healthiest end of the narcissistic spectrum, patients may, on initial presentation, appear to have normal identity consolidation and thus to fall in the neurotic range of personality organization. These individuals are typically socially appropriate, often professionally and socially successful, charming, and even charismatic. Stable relationships may be maintained, although always characterized by some degree of superficiality, an underlying quid pro quo orientation, and a lack of intimacy. In contrast, at the more pathological end of the spectrum NPD is one of the most severe personality disorders, falling in the low borderline range of personality organization. Patients in this group, sometimes referred to as suffering from *malignant narcissism*, present with an unstable and grossly distorted sense of self and of others, extremely disturbed relationships marked by frank exploitation and sadism, and severe pathology of moral functioning characterized by antisocial behavior. At the most severe end of the spectrum is NPD, comorbid with antisocial personality disorder or psychopathy.

Identity formation is evaluated by exploring the individual's experience of self and of significant others. In the narcissistic spectrum, identity pathology has a particular presentation that, to some degree, distinguishes NPD from other personality disorders of comparable severity. For example, in contrast to borderline personality disorder, where clinicians typically see unstable, unrealistic, superficial, polarized and contradictory experiences of self as well as of others, patients with NPD have a relatively stable experience of self, and at the healthier end of the spectrum they may appear to be relatively well integrated. This apparent integration of the sense of self is in marked contrast with the view of significant others, which is characteristically vague, caricature-like, and markedly superficial. For example, a woman with NPD might provide what she views as an adequate description of her husband by saying "He is tall, a workaholic, has a bad temper, and drinks too much." When asked to describe a significant other, individuals with NPD, even those who are high functioning, are typically unable to provide a description of sufficient subtlety or depth to enable the examiner to develop a three-dimensional view of the person being described.

Although the most striking manifestation of identity pathology in NPD is the marked lack of depth in the experience of others, on careful evaluation one can identify more subtle pathology in the sense of self as well. In NPD, self-experience, even if relatively stable, is superficial; it is based on comparison with others, or on recent achievements or failures, rather than on a truly integrated, internalized sense of self. This superficiality in the sense of self often leads to feelings of being "chameleonlike" or incomplete, and it leaves the narcissistic individual poorly equipped to weather disappointments or setbacks. In NPD, as identity pathology becomes more severe, overt pathology in the sense of self as well as in the sense of others emerges; self experience is characterized by idealized and, alternatively, devalued views of the self, which are extreme, unrealistic, and often unstable.

Individuals with NPD rely on a wide spectrum of defenses, including both lower level, splitting-based, and at the healthier end of the spectrum, repression-based defenses. Across the spectrum of severity, the splitting-based defenses of idealization and devaluation are central to psychological functioning. These defenses lead to polarized, extreme, and often unstable views of others and often of the self as well. For example, a man may initially experience a woman he is dating as literally the most wonderful woman he has even known, and then several weeks or even days later, perhaps in the setting of frustration or disappointment, experience her, equally concretely, as totally uninteresting and lacking any redeeming features. In NPD, idealization and devaluation, coupled with omnipotence, denial, and rationalization, function together to protect against feelings of inferiority and inadequacy, vulnerability, envy, and shame. At the more severe end of the severity spectrum, individuals rely predominantly on these and other lower level defenses such as splitting and projective identification. In contrast, in healthier narcissistic individuals we see a defensive style characterized by a combination of splitting-based defenses and higher level, repression-based defenses, such as reaction formation, intellectualization, isolation of affect, and repression proper.

In NPD, reality testing is intact and stable. However, there is a caveat to this statement. As narcissistic pathology becomes severe, reliance on omnipotence becomes more extreme. In this setting, the individual's experience becomes "Because I want or need or believe it to be so, it is." This kind of thinking can lead to apparent breaches in reality testing. For example, a scientist may claim that he did all of the work leading up to a particular publication, when in fact his graduate student had initiated the project and done the bulk of the work. In the setting of NPD, it can be difficult to be sure whether the scientist is lying or whether he truly believes that the work is his own, because he wants it to be.

Descriptive Features of NPD

Although there are many different presentations of NPD, there are core descriptive features shared by all individuals with narcissistic pathology: pathological self-esteem maintenance; pathology of interpersonal relations; and painful subjective states characterized by feelings of emptiness, meaninglessness, or boredom.

Pathological Self-Esteem Maintenance

Regardless of the particular presentation or severity of psychopathology, pathology of self-esteem maintenance is the cardinal descriptive feature of NPD. All individuals with NPD have profound problems with self-esteem and spend great amounts of time evaluating their status relative to others. To feel good about themselves, they need to feel special and superior, and because they lack an internalized sense of being "good enough," they require constant confirmation of their superiority in the form of admiration, elevated status, wealth, power, beauty, and success. Similarly, individuals with NPD generally affiliate themselves only with those they perceive to be of higher status, as a way to feel more important or special by association; devaluing others is another way to feel superior. When the narcissistic individual succeeds in extracting confirmation of being special and superior, he or she feels an internal elation, often behaves in a grandiose manner, and treats others (perceived to be of lower status) with contempt. When the environment fails to fuel the individual's grandiosity, narcissistic individuals typically feel depressed, shamed, painfully envious of, and devaluing toward those they perceive as obtaining the supplies that they lack. Because their sense of self and self-worth is so fragile and dependent on external supplies, individuals with NPD are excessively sensitive to criticism or slights.

Arrogant/Entitled Subtype. Many individuals with NPD have a predominantly grandiose and arrogant style, labeled Arrogant/Entitled (PDM Task Force, 2006); this subtype includes individuals who have been described in the literature as "oblivious" (Gabbard, 1989), "thick-skinned" (Rosenfeld, 1987), or "overt" (Akhtar, 1989) narcissists. People in this group are overtly grandiose, feel entitled to special treatment, and are either perplexed or enraged (or both) when they do not receive it. They devalue most other people and typically strike observers as vain, manipulative, and self-involved; alternatively, they may seem charismatic and commanding. Other individuals in this group are more overtly unstable and oscillate, depending on circumstances, between two contradictory and discrete self states: feeling grandiose and expansive on the one hand and depleted, depressed, and shamed on the other.

Depressed/Depleted Subtype. A group of individuals with NPD fall into the *Depressed/Depleted* (PDM Task Force, 2006) subtype; they do not present with overt grandiosity but rather are overly diffident and often painfully shy. (This subtype is not included in any version of the *DSM*.) Individuals in this group, often misdiagnosed as depressive, masochistic, or avoidant, are described in the literature as "thin-skinned" (Rosenfeld 1987), "hypervigiliant" (Gabbard, 1989), or "covert" (Cooper & Ronningstam, 1992) narcissists. People in this group experience themselves as deficient or damaged and want to know how to be "normal" or to have what more fortunate people have. These individuals are highly self-critical, easily slighted or wounded, and suffer from chronic feelings of envy in relation to others, whom they regard as superior. However, underneath their conscious inferiority and preoccupations with others, they harbor grandiose fantasies and views of themselves, feel entitled to special treatment, and are highly preoccupied with themselves.

Pathology of Interpersonal Relations

Pathology of interpersonal relations is another descriptive anchor shared by all individuals with NPD. At the healthiest end of the narcissistic spectrum, these features may be both subtle and covert; as pathology becomes more severe, views of relationships and interpersonal functioning become increasingly pathological. However, across the spectrum of severity, individuals with NPD lack a capacity for genuine intimacy and mutual dependency, and they have limited ability to value the needs of others independent of their own needs. Relationships are superficial and are seen as a means to an end, either to advance a particular purpose or to enhance self-esteem. The interpersonal relations of the individual with NPD are characterized by a lack of genuine interest in the other person as an individual, beyond the status, power, narcissistic supplies, and need fulfillment associated with the relationship. In all relationships there is a consciously considered sense of "what I get out of it" and "what I give," with attention to "who gets more." More disturbed individuals are overtly exploitative or parasitic, openly using others to meet their own needs with no sense of wrongdoing and then discarding them when they are no longer useful. Individuals at the healthier end of the narcissistic spectrum may be vulnerable to feeling exploited themselves or may be quietly detached while remaining attentive to what each person brings to the relationship.

"Lack of empathy" is often included in criteria for NPD, and it is important to define exactly what is meant by *empathy*; empathy involves both the ability to perceive the inner psychological states of others as well as the capacity to identify with and feel the feelings and needs of other people. Some oblivious narcissistic individuals have deficits in both areas; however, other narcissistic individuals may be highly astute when it comes to perceiving the internal experience of others. In particular, they may be highly attuned to the vulnerabilities of others but lack the concern or genuine interest that might accompany awareness of another person's inner state and instead use their understanding of others in a self-serving fashion.

Painful Subjective States

Individuals with NPD are vulnerable to painful subjective states characterized by feelings of emptiness, meaninglessness, and boredom. When grandiosity is fueled, these feelings can be temporarily avoided; the recurrent need for external confirmation described above can function to ward off negative affect states. However, when external supplies are not provided, the individual may be flooded with painful feelings of emptiness and meaninglessness. At the healthier end of the spectrum, individuals with NPD may throw themselves into work; when they work on something that they view as special and important and meet with success, feelings of elation may replace emptiness and boredom. However, the emotional benefits of success are short-lived, and as soon as the pace slows, feelings of restlessness and boredom quickly return. Some individuals with NPD use the promise of a new relationship in the same way, turning to the thrill of pursuit and promise of conquest or of connection with an idealized other to feel (temporarily) engaged and alive. Still others turn to substances to avoid intolerable internal states. The internal states characteristic of NPD are linked to a characteristic inability to make emotional investments in depth. The individual with NPD typically displays a lack of deeper commitments to specific values or ideals, which often come and go, along with a poorly developed capacity to make lasting investments in a profession, relationship, hobby, or intellectual interest, beyond the wish to obtain narcissistic supplies. A scholar may work hard to attain public recognition but become bored with his subject matter; an administrator may seek power and money but have no interest in actually making a system work;

an entrepreneur may obsessively build a business but abruptly lose interest when it no longer promises to be a dramatic success. The lack of genuine pleasure or capacity for in-depth and sustained emotional, intellectual, or spiritual investments, and the sense of meaninglessness or emptiness that commonly accompanies this deficit, can be painful to witness.

Associated Features

Pathology of moral functioning is often, though not universally, associated with NPD. As a result, careful assessment for a history of illegal or unethical behavior should always be part of the clinical evaluation of the patient with NPD. In individuals with NPD who are organized at a low borderline level, severe pathology of moral functioning is coupled with ego-syntonic exploitation of others. Unethical and illegal behaviors are typically executed in the setting of feelings of entitlement and a lack of a sense of wrongdoing. These individuals may become involved in violent crime as well as nonviolent criminal behavior. In those with NPD organized at a high borderline level, moral pathology is often covert (e.g., a visibly ethical individual who proves to be involved in some kind of dishonest activity, much to everyone's surprise). Common presentations include everything from plagiarism, to infidelity, to white collar crime. Highly successful people who violate professional ethics are often narcissistic; examples include financiers who become involved in "insider trading" or medical researchers whose financial interests lead them to falsify scientific work. The typical pattern involves rationalizing behavior the individual with NPD understands to be unethical or illegal. Somatization and hypochondria are also commonly associated with NPD, as is substance abuse. These individuals move away from threatening or painful aspects of emotional experience and instead become preoccupied with physical complaints or fears of illness, or turn to psychoactive substances, to mitigate painful internal states.

Assessment

To make a diagnosis of NPD, one must establish (a) that the patient has a personality disorder, (b) that the patient meets the structural criteria for borderline level of personality organization in general and NPD in particular, and (c) that the patient endorses the core descriptive features of NPD.[6]

---

[6]The Structured Interview of Personality Organization (STIPO; Clarkin, Caligor, Stern, & Kernberg, 2004) is a semi-structured interview that evaluates personality organization. Though developed as a research tool, the STIPO provides examples of specific questions that can be used in a clinical setting to evaluate identity formation, defensive operations, quality of relationships, and moral functioning. The STIPO can be found at http://psinstitute.org/pdf/Structured.Interview-of-Personality-Organization.pdf

To diagnose a personality disorder, it is necessary to demonstrate that personality pathology is of sufficient severity to cause either impairment of functioning or significant distress. In the course of evaluation, we focus in particular on how the individual functions interpersonally, at work, and in his or her leisure time. Evaluation of relationships includes exploring the quality of hierarchical and peer relationships as well as intimate and romantic bonds. How stable, conflict-ridden, or stormy are these relationships? Are they meaningful to the patient, and have they been sustained across time? Are they a source of pleasure and satisfaction or of frustration and disappointment? Evaluation of functioning at work or school includes assessment of how well the individual is performing given his or her abilities and training, whether there have been recurrent areas of difficulty, and the degree to which he or she enjoys and obtains satisfaction from work. Evaluation of leisure activities, including hobbies, interests, and the capacity to enjoy recreational pursuits, rounds out the evaluator's picture of the patient's personality functioning. A comprehensive assessment of personality functioning involves asking the patient to illustrate with specific examples his or her responses to the evaluator's questions, with the goal of developing a clear and consistent picture of how the patient functions in each of these domains.

After it is established that a patient has a personality disorder, the next step is to evaluate personality organization. Structural criteria for the diagnosis of NPD include pathology of identity formation and the presence of prominent splitting-based defenses, in particular, idealization and devaluation. To evaluate identity formation, it is useful to begin by asking patients to identify two people who are important to them. The next step is to ask the patient to describe each of these people in sufficient detail to enable the evaluator to get a clear and three-dimensional picture of who the significant other is as an individual. If the patient provides a string of adjectives, it can be helpful to point this out and ask for greater detail. If the patient provides descriptors of only a single valence, either all positive or all negative, this too can be pointed out. Throughout this process the evaluator is assessing whether the patient has a view of significant others that is complex and well differentiated, involving subtlety and shades of gray, consistent with fully integrated identity and neurotic level of personality organization, or whether descriptions of significant others are two-dimensional, superficial or vague, black-and-white and lacking subtlety, consistent with identity pathology and a borderline level of personality organization. This line of inquiry can be followed by asking the patient to paint a picture of himself or herself in a similar fashion. Most people find it more difficult to describe themselves than to describe a significant other, but individuals with normally consolidated identity are able with effort to provide a complex, multifaceted, and realistic picture of themselves, whereas those with identity pathology are typically unable to do so.

To assess the role of splitting-based defenses in a patient's defensive organization, clinicians focus primarily on the impact that these defenses have on subjective experience. To evaluate the role of splitting-based defenses overall, it is often useful to ask patients whether they tend to see things in black-and-white terms, whether their experience of others (or of themselves) can seem discontinuous or can shift suddenly or dramatically, whether they find it difficult to accurately infer the internal experience of others, and whether they tend to ignore or deny important realities in their lives that are painful or frightening. To evaluate more specifically the impact of idealization and devaluation on psychological experience, one can ask patients whether they have noticed that they can think highly of someone and then suddenly lose interest or think poorly of them, whether they find that they can attach great value to something one day and quickly lose interest, and whether they tend to admire people or things from a distance but find they appear very differently up close.

If a patient proves to have evidence of identity pathology characterized by a vague or superficial view of significant others in conjunction with prominent splitting-based defenses, in particular, idealization and devaluation, it is time to turn to evaluation of the descriptive features of NPD. To diagnose NPD at the healthier end of the spectrum, clinicians focus in particular on the assessment of the quality of the patient's relationships. In this process, it is helpful to ask patients whether they tend to see relationships in terms of what each person is getting out of the relationship and who is getting more, whether they have ever formed a relationship with someone because the person has wealth or status or might be useful to the patient, and whether they have cut people off abruptly because the other person disappointed them or did not give them what they wanted. With patients at the more severe end of the borderline spectrum, we also evaluate how overtly exploitative and/or sadistic they are in their relationships and their attitude toward these behaviors. When evaluating narcissistic pathology, we also explore the quality and stability of self-esteem maintenance, for example by asking patients whether they tend to spend a lot of time comparing themselves with others, seeing themselves as more successful or attractive or fortunate, or perhaps as less so. To make the diagnosis of NPD, it is also useful to inquire about feelings of emptiness or boredom, especially in the setting of quiet or unstructured time. Moral functioning should always be evaluated when NPD is in the differential diagnosis. One can begin by asking patients if there are times when they have deliberately deceived others, for example, twisted the facts to make themselves look more successful or attractive to someone else or to get something they want. This line of inquiry can be followed by questions about specific moral transgressions, including a history of lying, infidelity, tax evasion, plagiarism, questionable business practices, and overt problems with the law.

Countertransference

Individuals with NPD typically elicit strong emotional reactions from clinicians. Devaluing and overtly grandiose patients typically generate feelings of hostility, whereas healthier and more successful narcissistic patients may induce feelings of inadequacy or envy. In contrast, the patient with NPD who relies heavily on idealization can leave a clinician feeling special and admired, at least at initial contact. Thin-skinned narcissistic individuals may present as painfully fragile, leading the clinician to bend over backwards not to injure them. Regardless of their initial reactions, over time, most clinicians find themselves feeling bored by the patient with NPD. The narcissistic individual's self-preoccupation and lack of interest in anything the clinician might say or have to offer tend to generate feelings of disinterest, detachment, and demoralization at best, and hostility and contempt for the patient at worst. Clinicians can, to some degree, contain such negative feelings toward the patient with NPD by remaining mindful of the feelings of inadequacy, vulnerability, and paranoia that underlie the narcissistic individual's grandiosity and self-preoccupation.

CONCLUSION

NPD has many presentations and can be associated with pathology across a broad spectrum of severity. The clinician's capacity to identify and to comprehensively evaluate the individual with NPD rests on an understanding of the core structural and descriptive features of the disorder reviewed in this chapter. Comprehensive assessment of structural and descriptive features of narcissistic personality pathology is crucial for appropriate treatment planning.

REFERENCES

Akhtar, S. (1989). Narcissistic personality disorder: Descriptive features and differential diagnosis. *The Psychiatric Clinics of North America, 12,* 505–529.

American Psychiatric Association. (1994). *Diagnostic and statistical manual of mental disorders* (4th ed.). Washington, DC: Author.

American Psychiatric Association. (2000). *Diagnostic and statistical manual of mental disorders* (4th ed., text rev.). Washington, DC: Author.

Clarkin, J. F., Caligor, E., Stern, B. L., & Kernberg, O. F. (2004). *The Structured Interview of Personality Organization (STIPO)*. New York, NY: Personality Disorders Institute, Weill Cornell Medical College of Cornell University. Retrieved from http://psinstitute.org/pdf/Structured-Interview-of-Personality-Organization.pdf

Cooper, A., & Ronningstam, E. (1992). Narcissist personality disorder. In A. Tasman & M. Riba, (Eds.), *American Psychiatric Press review of psychiatry* (Vol. 11, pp. 527–532). Washington, DC: American Psychiatric Press.

Gabbard, G. O. (1989). Two sub-types of narcissistic personality disorder. *Bulletin of the Menninger Clinic, 53*, 527–532.

Kernberg, O. F., & Caligor, E. (2005). A psychoanalytic theory of personality disorders. In M. Lenzenweger & J. F. Clarkin (Eds.), *Major theories of personality disorder* (2nd ed., pp. 114–156). New York, NY: Guilford Press.

PDM Task Force. (2006). *Psychodynamic diagnostic manual, personality patterns and disorders* (pp. 15–64). Silver Spring, MD: Alliance of Psychoanalytic Organizations.

Rosenfeld, H. (1987). Afterthought: Changing theories and changing techniques in psychoanalysis. In *Impasse and interpretation* (pp. 265–279). London, England: Tavistock.

5

PROTOTYPICAL FORMULATION OF PATHOLOGICAL NARCISSISM

MARDI HOROWITZ

The promise of the *Diagnostic and Statistical Manual of Mental Disorders* (American Psychiatric Association, 1994) is that empirically based criteria can provide a sensitive and specific prototype of psychopathology for a variety of mental disorders. Such a promise falls far from being fulfilled in the case of narcissistic personality disorder (NPD). This being so, an alternative approach that formulates a prototypical case of narcissistic vulnerability may provide maximum aid to clinicians to more accurately evaluate the characterological configuration of patients who might have NPD.

In this chapter, I present a prototypical formulation of pathological narcissism that is based on a series of steps in accordance with the configurational analysis method (Horowitz, 1987, 2005). In my discussion, I do not follow the definition of NPD in the fourth edition of the *Diagnostic and Statistical Manual of Mental Disorders* (DSM–IV; American Psychiatric Association, 1994), although I contributed to it. Instead, I focus on an appreciation of the

DOI: 10.1037/14041-005
Understanding and Treating Pathological Narcissism, J. S. Ogrodniczuk (Editor)

less structured reality of the clinician's dyadic encounter with a narcissistic patient. I start at the surface of presenting problems, review various states of mind of a symptomatic quality, and then focus on schemata of self and others that organize state cycles. With further investigation, perhaps elements of this approach can be used as new diagnostic criteria (Ronningstam, 2009; Russ et al, 2008).

PHENOMENA

The prototypical person with pathological narcissism overly attends to sources of either praise or blame in the interpersonal field (Horowitz, 1981, 2009; Kernberg, 1975, 2009; Kohut, 1972, 1977). There may be intrusive experiences of feeling blamed, as well as omissions in which realistic fault goes unnoticed. People or environmental stimuli that might enhance the self-concept are selectively taken in, whereas attempts are made to pay attention to (but also minimize or rebut) sources of information that might lower self-esteem.

As a corollary, errors in recollection of events are significant phenomena: Negative acts of self may be omitted or rationalized. The patient may significantly alter the facts of a prior session as recalled by the clinician. In these cases, clinicians should strive to be tactful to avoid communicating an accusatory tone about changes in facts.

When attributes of "who was who" in a transaction are reported, there is often a dislocation of traits between self and other. Characteristics of the patient that might seem mean, foolish, weak, selfish, inconsiderate, or grandiose are especially dislocated from the self and often attributed to another person. It follows that positive ideas, acts, or attributes of the other person are sometimes incorporated as if they were traits or actions of the self. This phenomenon of inaccurate portrayal of personal attributes is not delusional, as in psychotic states, but rather a sliding away from truth in order to render a more positive self-image.

Individuals with narcissistic character organization emphasize associations leading to enhancement of their self-image. Choices that might involve recognizing that the self is not sufficiently skilled to embark on a plan of action may be totally omitted from a conscious sequence of associations. Consideration of the needs of others may also be absent from the stream of associations. These phenomena strengthen the underlying narcissistic character structure through supporting grandiosity.

It follows that such patients seem to others as if they sometimes forgive themselves much too easily. Instead of repairing problems they have caused, they may fantasize about illusory resolutions in the future. Rather than accepting realistic limits, they may continue to pursue vain attempts toward perfection. The narcissistic person may have high ambitions but neglect to think through a specific plan in order to accomplish any of these goals. Instead, there is a fantasylike demand that, with scant effort, one suddenly ascends to the target. The result is a feeling of entitlement and an expectation of always getting the best, being first, and avoiding pain.

Any perceived talents are grasped onto and expanded upon to advance the excessive estimation of self. Tribute from others is constantly expected, yet the narcissistic person may also markedly underestimate peers. Sometimes the ruthless thrust toward self-enhancement is concealed by pseudohumility and suavity (the essential coolness of a pseudowarmth).

But the lack of concern for others is usually eventually recognized. In due course, the other person learns that he or she is being used or exploited or is disliked. As the attachment is spoiled, the narcissistic person has to befriend a new acquaintance in an attempt to gratify his or her narcissistic needs. Alternatively, he or she may bribe or blackmail the other to stay committed. In that case, it is common for the other to feel bored and restless, as the affection or loyalty is only feigned.

Given such an impoverishment of interpersonal relationships, lack of creative success, or absence of compensatory thrill-seeking or pleasure, the narcissistic person cannot maintain grandiosity. Instead, he or she is increasingly vulnerable to shame, panic, helplessness, or depression as life progresses without genuine support from admiring others. With a loss of cohesiveness in the self-concept because of lack of admiration and empathy from others, such persons may develop hypochondriasis, depersonalization, or self-destructiveness. Feelings of envy, rage, paranoia, and outrageous demands on others often develop when a narcissistic individual is subjected to the stress of degradation, including the inevitable stress of aging and declining physical appearance and function.

Talented, wealthy, or exceptionally good-looking persons driven by narcissistic personality traits often display such charisma that they can continue to take on new relationships as old relationships fracture and perish. Social climbing is often a common feature, but the narcissistic person may also cling to acquaintances that can be relied on to provide a positive reflection. When the narcissistic person feels truly powerful, he or she may discard or depreciate persons who are no longer of use in bolstering his or her self-image.

In the less talented narcissistic individual, an idealized other may be selected as a self-proxy. The weaker narcissist clings to the idealized other in order to obtain positive reflection and avoid shame. (Kohut, 1972) described interpersonal patterns in terms of mirror, idealizing, and twinship patterns of transference.

STATES OF MIND AND STATE CYCLES

A few notable states of mind are prominent in the prototypical narcissistic personality, including the state of self-righteous rage (Horowitz, 1981; Kohut, 1972). Entry into a state of self-righteous rage may be fairly explosive and sudden, as a person rapidly switches from a composed state into suddenly becoming hostile toward others. The trigger to this explosion is often the interpretation of an interpersonal encounter as involving some kind of insult.

Others often see this state of self-righteous rage as an exaggerated response because of the level of violence that it contains. Whether manifested physically or verbally, the aggressive response exceeds the usual social standards of acceptable behavior. Despite the socially unacceptable nature of the reaction, the individual feels justified in disparaging or even harming the other while in the self-righteous rage state.

This kind of towering rage can be considered narcissistic because of two important features. One is the inflated grandiosity assumed during the state. This kind of grandiosity aims to defend against an inferior, bad, or damaged self-concept. The second narcissistic feature in such rages is that others are assigned subhuman status. This is why the state is sometimes called *blind hatred*. The person flying into such rages does not recognize that other persons have a right to exist or that they have ever been good or kind to the self. There is a readiness to injure others on the grounds that they are destructive monsters who have no right to survive. This describes an extreme form, but many of these features can be recognized in more moderate representations of self-righteous rage states.

Another shading of anger may be found in the state of *chronic embitterment*. In this state, the person carries a chip on his or her shoulder and dares other people to knock it off. There may be blustery-outgoing or sullen-withdrawing forms of chronic embitterment. In comparison with indignant rage states, the hostility is subdued. Its source is an internal dialogue in which the self is being unfairly abused by others or by fate.

Whereas self-righteous rage and chronic embitterment may be fairly evident to observers and perhaps even to the individual who experiences them, there is a more confusing state that also contains angry emotions. This is a *mixed state* in which anger is intermingled with shame and anxiety. The person is unclear about which negative emotions he or she is feeling and their cause. Shame develops in response to exposing aspects of the self, including the irrational acts of anger, whereas fear can arise in response to losing control over one's anger or over further degradations to the self, which in turn can lead to further shame.

The fear present in the mixed state may become clearer as it is heightened and purified to the point of panic in what might be called a *chaotic state*. It is during these states that fear of flying apart, losing bodily integrity, or fragmenting one's identity may become especially prominent. There can be a progression from hypochondriasis, to identity diffusion sensations, to a panicky dread of immediate death.

At the opposite end of the spectrum of psychic arousal is an unexcited state of numb, apathetic dullness. The self is enfeebled and without hope of restoration. The person entering a *leaden apathetic state* has, in a way, decided to hibernate. Of interest, this state of mind also occurs prominently during some denial phases of mourning, in which the loss of a relationship has undermined self-security, contributing to inhibition of grief in order to avoid the perceived intolerable quality of such emotional pain.

A *state cycle* may be an aspect of a repetitive, maladaptive pattern of relating. The harm of being rejected may lead to embittered states; when someone can be blamed the state may shift to indignant rage, and when that seems inappropriate, the mixed state may occur.

The range of states that exemplify different types of angry colorations (self-righteous rage, mixed state, and chronic embitterment) can be matched with an analogous series of positive states of mind. In forming the positive states, the self-concept has been bolstered, perhaps by fantasy, illusions of entitlement, restoration of self-objects, or personal accomplishment. A state of exhilaration, characterized by grand ebullience and charm, is the opposite polarity of the negative state of self-righteous rage. The negative affective mixed state of shame, rage, and fear may be related to a positive but mixed state in which there is some fear of failure together with exhilaration at potential success. There may be excitement as a result of self-elevation through sexual or creative prowess, mixed with fear that the self-enhancing actions will not meet expectations. Thus, there may be a quality of anxious impatience that mars an otherwise exciting experience. The chronic embitterment state would be analogous to a chronic hankering for attention state, a semi-positive state of being ever tuned toward social sources of praise.

Themes of success, failure, and blame are often highly emotional. The idea of public humiliation is a frequent, recurrent theme for narcissistic individuals. The person may persist in overvaluing the self in order to reduce the threat. The person may lie in an attempt to avoid acknowledging the painful reality and then further exacerbate the situation in which the exposure of lying may induce shame. Although the "ground rules" of psychotherapy emphasize honesty, this process occurs in the treatment room as well.

Because some memories are wounding to the self, they may be compartmentalized. Dissociation may occur, so that there is a fragmented sense of continuity of self over time. This can lead to a vicious cycle, as this kind of fragmentation reduces coherence in overall self-organization (Stolorow & Lachman, 1980). In other words, inferior views of self are held too far apart from superior views of self, and more importantly, from realistically competent views of self (Rothstein, 1984; Wurmser, 1981). The person cannot mitigate a specific personal shortcoming through recalling more positive memories, because of the dissociation of experiences.

The low tolerance for certain affects, especially shame, is worth noting again. Having experienced humiliation or embarrassment, the narcissistic person may take an unusually long time to restore positive self-regard. When activated, his or her feelings of shame may have a slow rate of dissolution. Paradoxically, the person then is very demanding of a return to a more hedonic state and feels entitled to it at all costs.

In terms of normal anger, expressing hostility has an interpersonal purpose, which is to get the other person to come through or to back off. The right degree of hostility is used to accomplish this aim. In a person conflicted about anger themes, there is usually an avoidance of expressing such emotions. The anticipated consequences are that the other person will be strong and retaliatory or weak and harmed by the hostility. The self will then have to experience fear of retaliation, shame over being judged by others as being too harmful, or guilt that the other person has been hurt. In the narcissistic person, anger is not well-targeted or even clearly localized in the self. There is rage "in the air," and any object may become the target.

The rage in the narcissistic individual arises in part from the potential sense of damage to or enfeeblement of the self. The aim is destruction of the other in a more total form rather than a limited goal. As such, there is more danger in the anger because there is no plan for what may happen, or what, if any, self-governance might control the degree of expressed anger.

Similarly, in terms of shame, a person without narcissistic features prefers to defer and hide from the social criticism resulting from a shameful action or failure to act. For idiosyncratic and irrational reasons, the narcissistic person sees acceptable acts as if they were shameful. The self as constituted is shameful not only because of a specific act or failure to act; the indefinite unstructured threat of social disgrace makes this affect harder to tolerate because it exists in a sense of identity. Defenses such as reversal to anger become imperative and more pathologic in implementation.

SCHEMATA OF SELF AND OTHERS

Some patients with pathological narcissism initially present with symptoms of anxiety and depression, but it later becomes apparent that they are experiencing major problems either with the self-righteous rage state, the ensuing mixed shame/rage/fear state, or with extreme efforts to ward off both states. I focus in this section on a three-party role-relationship model that is useful in understanding transitions into and out of the self-righteous rage state.

The role of each party can be prototypically viewed as hero, monster, and critic. The role of the critic is to admire the hero and loathe the monster. The use of the extreme label of *monster* is appropriate given that this person is often the target of hostility beyond what might be directed at humans. An abundance of modern television shows and movies use such monster roles to permit destructive behaviors in heroes, and we the audience are the critics. If the hero is all good (loves dogs, is nice to old people, smiles at children) and the monster is bad (kills animals, rapes daughters, tortures children), we applaud and cheer the violence that destroys the monster.

Viewing others as monsters is a dissociative defense in which the human qualities of a person are forgotten while in this state organized by role schemata. This defense allows the person to maintain the illusion that the critic is wholly admiring the hero and utterly loathing the monster. There can be no guilt, fear, or shame over hostility in this state. The anger is an enjoyable energy, a thrill. It is only after transitioning from this state that the person may be aware of shame or remorse for his or her actions during the state.

The term *hero* is useful for the role of the self-righteous one because it also exemplifies the grand sense of entitlement and singularity of the self-concept when in this state. The hero is strong and feels powerful; thus, the weak schemata of self that have led to leaden, dull states are more easily dissociated from self-organization.

As mentioned, the hostility in the role-relationship model is exciting because the hero expects to receive praise and admiration from the critic for expressing these hostile feelings toward the monster. The hero feels entitled to sadistic gratification as well as exhibitionistic gratification over the dehumanized other. The grandeur of the self is heightened by the pleasure of merger with the powerful critic, an aspect of Kohut's mirroring, idealizing, and twinship relationship patterns.

Were the critic suddenly to pity the monster and despise the violence of the hero, there would then be a sudden state transition from self-righteous rage to a mixed state of shame, rage, and anxiety. This is what occurs in the state cycling patterns of some persons with pathological narcissism. The hero is embarrassed by the critic for changing allegiances, feeling ashamed under the eyes of the critic, and is anxious that the self is now vulnerable to punishment or retaliation for the expressed hostility.

In my description of self-righteous rages I assumed a schema for self as strong, hence the hero role. A similar set of psychodynamics can occur with the self schematized as weak, organizing a state of mind that Parkin (1980) called *masochistic enthrallment*. In this role-relationship model involving the weak self, another person is in the role of the hero. The self is a subordinate attached to the hero. As a dynamic duo they attack the monster. Seeing the monster as evil, bad, brutal, dirty, or ugly allows these traits to be disowned from what otherwise might be a defective self-concept. The attributes are now located in someone else, and the self and the hero are justified in attacking the bad object. The self may take a beating or carry out "bad orders," but guilt and shame are avoided because the hero and the critic are merged. If the self believes that he or she is obeying the hero's requests to "Do it" and "Follow my orders," the actions of the self, however destructive, are defined as good.

Through externalization of all bad traits and idealization of the hero, the self can attach and have an idealizing transference. The self is elevated over the monster, who is bad, and can thus safely feel hauteur and contempt, as well as disgust and rage. Guilt, shame, or fear of retaliation may come later with transition to some other state.

The grandiose self-schemata and related role-relationship models that characterize much of the behavioral pathology of the narcissistically disturbed personality may have a defensive function: They ward off states of mind organized by self-schemata of being weak, bad, damaged, or incomplete without having to rely on using another person as an extension of the self. These weaker self-schemata tend to emerge in some states, and the person then becomes symptomatic in terms of feeling worried over identity, obsessed with shame themes, compulsive about achieving self-restorative operations, or progressively more anxiety ridden.

TECHNICAL IMPLICATIONS
FOR PSYCHOTHERAPY TREATMENT

For many patients with narcissistic psychopathology, clinicians find that therapy proceeds in overlapping phases. The first phase aims to establish a secure therapeutic alliance in order to increase the patient's sense of being safely contained. By establishing a secure alliance, the clinician can help the patient improve his or her deployment of attention in order to realize the capacity to govern his or her own states of mind.

As the patient's sense of empathic understanding within a secure treatment relationship increases, he or she becomes more empathic as a self-reviewing or reflecting self toward the patient's own sense of identity, using newly acquired skills of reflective conscious awareness. Self-criticism gains a new, softer judgment through identification with the therapist's restraint in making harsh evaluations. This leads to improvement in stabilization of working states and reduction in problematic and dreaded states of mind that tend to include undermodulated shame, fear, and rage.

The growing sense of empathy overlaps with what could be considered a second phase of therapy. During this second phase, the therapist increases use of techniques to help the patient modify habitual defensive avoidances, such as automatic tendencies toward externalization of blame and segregations of meaning attributions that, in effect, lead to dissociation of various self-other beliefs. As the second phase progresses, there may be illumination, using enhanced reflective self-awareness, of how these attributions may be enacted in emergent transference states of mind.

These remarks so far involve a relatively here-and-now focus by the therapist on what is happening in the treatment situation and in current outside relationships. In the third phase, which overlaps with the first two, the past as a source of dysfunctional beliefs, attitudes, and role relationship models may be considered, as a further amplification of self-understanding. In other words, associations related to states of self-disgust or fragmentation lead to work in which identity itself is gradually consolidated with a new narrative of the story of life thus far.

State Stabilization

The states that are dreaded are usually layered, and a less dreaded one can even be used defensively to avoid an even more dreaded one. A multiple state labeling approach can help clarify this for a patient. A patient might dread entering into a flaming rage because it tends to lead to relationship ruptures, yet he or she might also find it valuable to learn that the strength felt during a rage might serve as a defensive maladaptation by warding off the threat of states of mind characterized by self-enfeeblement. Enfeeblement states, or mixed states of anger/fear/shame emotions, are still preferable in the patient's intuitive or unconscious expectations to potential states of chaos in self-identity.

In a positive therapeutic alliance, the therapist protects against destructive states, including the harmful chaotic state related to a lapse in self-coherence and thus the absence of a comprehensive personal identity. The therapist can help the patient recognize the feared state by naming it and identifying triggers for potential entry into the state. When these triggers are detected, the patient can learn through therapy to implement constructive self-soothing and self-restorative methods; for example, listening to music rather than seeking a more dangerous escape through violence, promiscuity, or substance abuse. This often confusing medley of anger, fear, and shame can then be "unpacked" and better understood through uncovering the attitudes about self and relationships with others that arouse these emotional qualities. In this example, the therapist can learn more through empathic listening to the music as well as to the words of what happens in the therapy room. The patient can learn to identify with such an attitude, become more aware of the mind within, and gain a self-reflective capacity that is more intelligent and less harshly self-judgmental.

Metabolism of Shame

With enhanced communicative frankness and self-listening, the patient's increasing ability to stay with difficult topics can allow the therapeutic pair to conduct a dose-by-dose desensitization to experiences of embarrassment. Shame is accepted as part of the human predicament rather than a catastrophic feeling that the soul is being murdered by negative emotion. That is, even situations involving failure and relationship ruptures are seen as unpleasant yet tolerable, rather than searing self-decomposing experiences. This approach leads to new topics related to self-strengthening, such as how to improve one's skills to ensure that short-term goals become more aligned with long-term life achievement goals.

Confrontation of Reality-Distorting Defenses

When a positive therapeutic alliance is established and the patient perceives the therapist to be an empathic, motivated expert, the therapist can tactfully highlight the patient's distortions of reality. Together, therapist and patient can examine the patient's unconscious attitudes. This can lead toward a "rewrite" of the patient's life narrative: Prior memories and fantasies are reappraised at a more mature level.

Often, this process involves reprioritizing what is of value to the self and putting these values into words. For example, it might be the case that the patient begins to consider that emotional relationships of mutuality (as currently felt with the therapist) are more meaningful and hold more value than accumulating wealth, property, and other external achievements.

These techniques aim to increase self-coherence and avoid maladaptive ways of self-strengthening. The patient often still craves and attempts to elicit positive feedback from the therapist and is willing to idealize the therapist in return. This can become a trap that may need to be identified in order to complete treatment. The therapist should seek to clarify the patient's irrational beliefs and unconscious conceits in favor of a more realistic appraisal of what is happening.

Reformation of Self-Organization

In the later phases of therapy, issues of self-conceptualizations and roles of relationship with others are addressed as enduring schematizing functions. Because externalization of blame may have been prominent in one's mental life for many years, clarification of what happened and who did what to whom tends to be repeated and gradually deepened into present-day interpretations and newly informed understandings of past memories. The goal is a realistic view of the present and the future. This can lead to feelings of remorse for instances where harm (emotionally, mentally, or physically) has been done to others.

Therapeutic tactics involve helping the patient increase self-observation through a higher level of reflective awareness of what is being thought and felt and what is intended and expected. Increased observation of the feelings of others and their likely attitudes and motives is also encouraged. Ambivalence is clarified and identified as a part of everyday life, leading toward increased tolerance of interpersonal frustrations.

Gradually, the patient's automatic defensive dissociation using grandiose and enfeebled self-concepts is reduced. Self-coherence increases as the patient learns to accept more ambivalence in self-judgments as a normal part of mature, adult life. Some of this is learned through identification. The therapist can set a good example for the patient through maintaining truthful personal boundaries and a positive but realistic regard for the patient and by acknowledging errors or lapses in his or her understanding of what is transpiring in the therapeutic process.

CONCLUSION

The phenomenology of individuals with pathological narcissism has been discussed in three categories: phenomena (i.e. signs and symptoms), recurrent distressing states of mind, and recurrent maladaptive views of self and others. Although no one person perfectly fits the prototype described, the overall gestalt can help the clinician recognize variations in individual cases and formulate the case in order to clarify where to direct attention in treatment.

Treatment may benefit from attention to emotional self-governance in situations that usually activate embarrassment, rage, and rationalizations for decisions based on entitlement attitudes. The therapist would be wise to ensure that interpretations and comments are tactful, which will strengthen the therapeutic alliance as the patient learns that clarifications of reality are not meant as insults. Learning capacities for empathy, reevaluation, and compassion for others leads towards greater realistic self-esteem and social respect.

REFERENCES

American Psychiatric Association. (1994). *Diagnostic and statistical manual of mental disorders* (4th ed.). Washington, DC: Author.

Horowitz, M. J. (1981). Self-righteous rage and the attribution of blame. *Archives of General Psychiatry, 38*, 1233–1238. doi:10.1001/archpsyc.1981.01780360049004

Horowitz, M. J. (1987). *States of mind: Configurational analysis of individual personality* (2nd ed.). New York, NY: Plenum Press.

Horowitz, M. J. (2005). *Understanding psychotherapy change: A practical guide to configurational analysis.* Washington, DC: American Psychological Association. doi:10.1037/11083-000

Horowitz, M. J. (2009). Clinical phenomenology of narcissistic pathology. *Psychiatric Annals, 39*, 124–128. doi:10.3928/00485713-20090301-06

Horowitz, M. J., & Arthur, R. J. (1988). Narcissistic rage in leaders: The intersection of individual dynamics and group process. *International Journal of Social Psychiatry, 34*, 135–141. doi:10.1177/002076408803400208

Kernberg, O. (1975). *Borderline conditions and pathological narcissism.* New York, NY: Jason Aronson.

Kernberg, O. (2009). Narcissistic personality disorders. *Psychiatric Annals, 39*, 105–167. doi:10.3928/00485713-20090301-04

Kohut, H. (1972). Thoughts on narcissism and narcissistic rage. *The Psychoanalytic Study of the Child, 27*, 360–400.

Kohut, H. (1977). *The restoration of the self.* New York, NY: International Universities Press.

Parkin, A. (1980). On masochistic enthrallment: A contribution to the study of moral masochism. *The International Journal of Psychoanalysis, 61*, 307–314.

Ronningstam, E. (2009). Narcissistic personality disorder: Facing *DSM–V. Psychiatric Annals, 39*, 111–121. doi:10.3928/00485713-20090301-09

Rothstein, A. (1984). The fear of humiliation. *Journal of the American Psychoanalytic Association, 32*, 99–116. doi:10.1177/000306518403200107

Russ, E., Shedler, J., Bradley, R., & Westen, D. (2008). Refining the construct of narcissistic personality disorder: Diagnostic criteria and subtypes. *The American Journal of Psychiatry, 165*, 1473–1481. doi:10.1176/appi.ajp.2008.07030376

Stolorow, R. D., & Lachmann, F. M. (1980). *The psychoanalysis of developmental arrests.* New York, NY: International Universities Press.

Wurmser, L. (1981). *The mask of shame.* Baltimore, MD: Johns Hopkins Press.

6

THE PATHOLOGICAL NARCISSISM INVENTORY

AARON L. PINCUS

Despite its longevity and importance as a psychological construct, narcissism and the associated narcissistic personality disorder (NPD) have been inconsistently defined and measured across disciplines (Cain, Pincus, & Ansell, 2008; Miller & Campbell, 2008). Several recent reviews have highlighted the issues associated with integrating the empirical and clinical literature on narcissistic pathology (e.g., Levy, Reynoso, Wasserman, & Clarkin, 2007; Pincus & Lukowitsky, 2010; Ronningstam, 2005a, 2005b). Divergences in phenotypic and taxonomic models of pathological narcissism, especially inconsistencies between a century of clinical conceptualizations and NPD criteria in the *Diagnostic and Statistical Manual of Mental Disorders* (4th ed., text rev.; *DSM–IV–TR*; American Psychiatric Association, 2000), have led to major construct definition and criterion problems that weaken the cumulative research base and obfuscate the accurate assessment of narcissistic pathology (Pincus, 2011; Pincus & Lukowitsky, 2010). With each successive edition of the manual, criteria for NPD have become increasingly narrow in scope;

DOI: 10.1037/14041-006
Understanding and Treating Pathological Narcissism, J. S. Ogrodniczuk (Editor)

currently they capture predominantly grandiose themes of the disorder (Cain et al., 2008) while eliminating many of the clinically meaningful characteristics associated with impaired self and emotion regulation (e.g., shameful reactivity or humiliation in response to narcissistic injury, alternating states of idealization and devaluation). These are now described in the "Associated Features and Disorders" section where clinicians are also cautioned that patients may not outwardly exhibit such vulnerable characteristics.

However, if one moves beyond the manual's definition of NPD, reviews of the clinical, psychiatric, and social and personality psychology literature clearly paint a broader portrait of pathological narcissism encompassing two phenotypic themes of dysfunction, narcissistic grandiosity and narcissistic vulnerability (Cain et al., 2008; Dickinson & Pincus, 2003; Miller, Hoffman, et al., 2011; Pincus & Lukowitsky, 2010; Pincus & Roche, 2011). The lack of sufficient vulnerable NPD criteria in the *DSM–IV* (American Psychiatric Association, 1994) is now a common criticism (Gabbard, 2009; Miller, Widiger, & Campbell, 2010; Ronningstam, 2009). The overly narrow construct definition of pathological narcissism found in *DSM–IV–TR* NPD limits its clinical validity and utility because therapists and diagnosticians may be more likely to see narcissistic patients when they are in a vulnerable self-state (Kealy & Rasmussen, 2012; Pincus et al., 2009). Thus, a clinician relying solely on *DSM–IV* NPD diagnostic criteria may not recognize pathological narcissism in a presenting patient. The Pathological Narcissism Inventory (PNI; Pincus et al., 2009) was recently developed with these concerns in mind. It is a multidimensional measure of pathological narcissism that assesses both overt and covert expressions of narcissistic grandiosity and narcissistic vulnerability.

DEFINITION AND PHENOTYPIC DESCRIPTION
OF PATHOLOGICAL NARCISSISM UNDERLYING THE PNI

I begin with a contemporary definition of narcissism that provides the foundation for understanding its diverse phenomenology and facilitates integration and synthesis across disciplines. I propose that *narcissism* be defined as one's capacity to maintain a relatively positive self-image through a variety of self-regulation, affect-regulation, and interpersonal processes and that it underlies individuals' needs for validation and admiration, as well as the motivation to overtly and covertly seek out self-enhancement experiences from the social environment (Pincus et al., 2009; Pincus & Roche, 2011). In basing the definition of narcissism on the individual's needs, motives, and regulatory capacities, I explicitly distinguish between what narcissism is (i.e., underlying psychological structures and processes) and how it is expressed in thought, feeling, and behavior. It is important to recognize the difference between a definition of psychopathology and the description of individual differences in its phenomenological expression (Pincus, Lukowitsky, & Wright, 2010; Pincus & Wright, 2010), and it is the latter of the two that is typically assessed by self-report scales, diagnostic interview questions, and DSM personality disorder criteria (Pincus, 2005a, 2005b, 2011; Widiger, 1991).

I believe the fundamental dysfunction associated with pathological narcissism is related to intense needs for validation and admiration that energize the person to seek out self-enhancement experiences. Such needs and motives are normal aspects of personality, but they become pathological when they are extreme and coupled with impaired regulatory capacities. It is normal for individuals to strive to see themselves in a positive light and to seek experiences of self-enhancement (e.g., Hepper, Gramzow, & Sedikides, 2010), such as successful achievements and competitive victories (Conroy, Elliot, & Thrash, 2009). Most individuals can manage these needs effectively, seek out their gratification in acceptable ways and contexts, and regulate self-esteem, negative emotion, and interpersonal behavior when disappointments are experienced. In contrast, pathological narcissism involves impairment in the ability to manage and satisfy needs for validation and admiration, such that self-enhancement becomes an overriding goal in nearly all situations and may be sought in maladaptive ways and in inappropriate contexts. This heightens sensitivity to the daily ups and downs of life and relationships (McCullough, Emmons, Kilpatrick, & Mooney, 2003; Zeigler-Hill, Myers, & Clark, 2010) and impairs regulation of self-esteem, emotion, and behavior. This definition of pathological narcissism, unlike NPD, encompasses narcissistic grandiosity and narcissistic vulnerability.

Narcissistic Grandiosity and Narcissistic Vulnerability

To the layperson, the construct of narcissism is most often associated with arrogant, conceited, and domineering attitudes and behaviors (Buss & Chiodo, 1991), which are captured by the term *narcissistic grandiosity*. This accurately identifies some common expressions of maladaptive self-enhancement associated with pathological narcissism. However, the definition of narcissism underlying the PNI combines maladaptive self-enhancement with regulatory impairments leading to self, emotional, and behavioral dysregulation in response to ego threats or self-enhancement failures. This *narcissistic vulnerability* is reflected in experiences of anger, envy, aggression, helplessness, emptiness, low self-esteem, shame, social avoidance, and even suicidality (Akhtar, 2003; Dickinson & Pincus, 2003; Kohut & Wolf, 1978; Pincus et al., 2009; Ronningstam, 2005a). A comprehensive hierarchical model of pathological narcissism is presented in Figure 6.1. Evidence for the two phenotypic themes of narcissistic grandiosity and narcissistic vulnerability come from clinical theory, psychiatric diagnosis, and social and personality

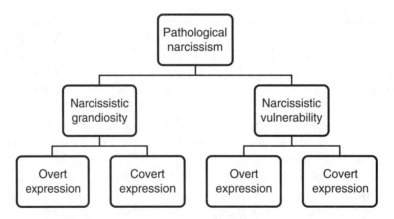

Figure 6.1. The hierarchical structure of pathological narcissism. From "Pathological Narcissism and Narcissistic Personality Disorder," by A. L. Pincus and M. R. Lukowitsky, 2010, *Annual Review of Clinical Psychology, 6,* p. 431. Copyright 2010 by Annual Reviews. Reprinted with permission.

psychology (Cain et al., 2008; Pincus & Roche, 2011); and in recent years, recognition of both grandiose and vulnerable themes of narcissistic dysfunction has increasingly become the norm (e.g., Horowitz, 2009; Kernberg, 2009; Ronningstam, 2009; Russ, Shedler, Bradley, & Westen, 2008). Narcissistic grandiosity involves intensely felt needs for validation and admiration, giving rise to urgent motives to seek out self-enhancement experiences. When this dominates the personality, the individual is concomitantly vulnerable to increased sensitivity to ego threat and subsequent self, emotion, and behavioral dysregulation (i.e. narcissistic vulnerability).

Overt and Covert Narcissism

The distinctions among overt and covert expressions of pathological narcissism are found in both clinical (e.g. Revik, 2001) and social and personality (e.g., Otway & Vignoles, 2006) psychology. Unfortunately, overt expressions of narcissism are often incorrectly associated exclusively with grandiosity and covert expressions of narcissism exclusively with vulnerability. These linkages are inaccurate, as is the view that overt and covert narcissism are distinct types or phenotypes. *DSM* NPD criteria, items on various self-reports, interviews, and rating instruments assessing pathological narcissism, and most certainly clinical conceptualizations of all forms of personality pathology include a mix of overt elements (behaviors, expressed attitudes and emotions) and covert experiences (cognitions, private feelings, motives, needs; e.g., McGlashan et al., 2005). In Figure 6.1, the distinction between overt and covert expressions of narcissism is secondary to phenotypic variation in grandiosity and vulnerability, and there is no empirical evidence that distinct overt and covert types of narcissism exist (Pincus & Lukowitsky, 2010).

Clinical Examples

Clinical experience with narcissistic patients indicates they virtually always exhibit both covert and overt grandiosity and covert and overt vulnerability. An example of overt grandiosity involved a narcissistic patient who routinely threatened people who parked in his apartment's assigned parking space and even called his therapist to report that he planned to buy a gun and shoot the next person he found parked there. It is important to note that the patient did not own a car and did not drive. In contrast, narcissistic grandiosity can also be expressed covertly as reflected in criteria such as grandiose fantasies. A notable clinical example of covert grandiosity involved a narcissistic patient who, at midlife, was unemployed, socially isolated, and lived in his parents' basement. The patient spent most of his days fantasizing about being the loved and admired head of his own philanthropic organization while concurrently lacking any motivation or effort to address his current social, occupational, and psychological deficits. Narcissistic vulnerability can also be expressed overtly and covertly. Overt vulnerability includes angry dysregulation and suicidal reactions to narcissistic injury. One narcissistic patient became so distraught after hearing that his trust fund had been exhausted that he made a strategic suicide attempt (overdose) timed such that his mother would find him unconscious when she arrived for their weekly shopping trip. Finally, covert vulnerability includes shame, social withdrawal, and devaluation of the self in reaction to unmet idealized expectations. For example, one narcissistic patient who did not make a positive impression and elicit admiration from new neighbors became depressed and ashamed, punishing himself by not eating for days. These instances are drawn from different psychotherapies. Over the course of treatment, each of these patients exhibited instances of grandiosity and vulnerability expressed both overtly and covertly.

THE PNI

Most existing instruments assessing pathological narcissism are based on *DSM* NPD criteria and are thus limited to assessment of narcissistic grandiosity. The scope of most narcissism scales, from omnibus instruments assessing pathological traits such as the Schedule for Nonadaptive and Adaptive Personality (Simms & Clark, 2006) and the Dimensional Assessment of Personality Pathology (Livesley, 2006), to measures of normal narcissistic traits such as the Narcissistic Personality Inventory (Raskin & Hall, 1981), are similarly limited. The Hypersenstive Narcissism Scale (Hendin & Cheek, 1997) does appear to assess narcissistic vulnerability, but it provides only a single global score. The PNI was constructed to assess self- and informant-reported individual differences in overt and covert expression of narcissistic grandiosity and narcissistic vulnerability that have been identified across disciplines (Pincus et al., 2009).[1] This fills a niche in clinical assessment as the only multidimensional inventory that measures seven clinically meaningful facets of pathological narcissism and generates scores for both grandiosity and vulnerability.

Initial Construction

A test construction team that included clinical faculty and graduate students, psychotherapists, and psychology undergraduates examined the theoretical and empirical literature on pathological narcissism to understand how it has been conceptualized and operationalized across disciplines, generating a comprehensive review (Cain et al., 2008). Additionally, psychotherapists working with patients who exhibit narcissistic personality pathology gave case presentations and reviewed tapes of sessions that characterized core aspects of pathological narcissism. This comprehensive review of the literature and the discussion of clinical cases culminated in the identification of seven target dimensions encompassing grandiose and vulnerable aspects of pathological narcissism. The hypothesized dimensions of narcissistic vulnerability were Contingent Self-Esteem, Entitlement Rage, Devaluing of Others and Needs for Others, and Narcissistic Social Avoidance. The hypothesized dimensions of narcissistic grandiosity were Exploitativeness, Grandiose Fantasies, and Self-Sacrificing Self-Enhancement. The test construction team generated an initial pool of 131 items tapping these seven factors. Several iterative empirical processes, including factor analyses on a sample of 796 young adults, reduced the item pool to seven factors, assessed by 52 items, which corresponded well to a priori expectations. This seven-factor structure was then validated using confirmatory factor analysis in a large independent sample of 2,801 young adults (Pincus et al., 2009).

The PNI Scales and Higher Order Factors

The PNI has 52 items tapping seven scales that reliably (αs typically range from .80 to .93) assess facets of narcissistic grandiosity and narcissistic vulnerability. Scales assessing grandiosity include Exploitativeness (EXP,

---

[1]Requests for a PNI assessment packet can be sent to the author at alp6@psu.edu.

five items), reflecting a manipulative interpersonal orientation; Grandiose Fantasy (GF, seven items), reflecting engagement in compensatory fantasies of gaining success, admiration, and recognition; and Self-Sacrificing Self-Enhancement (SSSE, six items), reflecting the use of purportedly altruistic acts to support an inflated self-image. Scales assessing vulnerability include Contingent Self-Esteem (CSE, 12 items), reflecting a significantly fluctuating experience of self-esteem and acknowledgement of dysregulation in the absence of external sources of admiration and recognition; Hiding the Self (HS, seven items), reflecting an unwillingness to show others faults and needs; Devaluing (DEV, seven items), reflecting disinterest in others who do not provide needed admiration and shame over needing recognition from disappointing others; and Entitlement Rage (ER, eight items), reflecting angry affects when entitled expectations are not met. Some PNI scales exhibit modest gender differences in scores, but these differences are quite small.

Using confirmatory factor analysis, Wright, Lukowitsky, Pincus, and Conroy (2010) demonstrated that the seven PNI scales load on two correlated higher order factors of grandiosity (EXP, GF, SSSE) and vulnerability (CSE, HS, DEV, ER). The Narcissistic Grandiosity factor is characterized by self-serving beliefs and self-enhancement strategies (e.g., "I like to have friends who rely on me because it makes me feel important" [SSSE]; "I often fantasize about being recognized for my accomplishments" [GF]; "I can make anyone believe anything I want them to" [EXP]), whereas the Narcissistic Vulnerability factor is characterized by susceptibility to self and emotional dysregulation (e.g., low self-esteem, shame, anger, anxiety) when narcissistic needs are not met (e.g., "It irritates me when people don't notice how good a person I am" [ER]; "It's hard for me to feel good about myself unless I know other people admire me" [CSE]; "When others don't meet my expectations, I often feel ashamed about what I wanted" [DEV]; "When others get a glimpse of my needs, I feel anxious and ashamed" [HS]). A notable feature of the PNI's higher order factor structure is that the item content for both narcissistic grandiosity and narcissistic vulnerability spans overt and covert expressions of narcissism. Grandiose and vulnerable expressions of narcissism each can be overt (e.g., "I try to show what a good person I am though my sacrifices" [SSSE]; "It's important to show people I can do it on my own, even if I have some doubts inside" [HS]) or covert (e.g., "I often fantasize about performing heroic deeds" [GF]; "I often find myself envying others' accomplishments" [CSE]). Additionally, the positive correlation between the higher order PNI factors suggests that narcissistic grandiosity and narcissistic vulnerability are separable but keenly interrelated with each other.

Using multigroup factor analytic methods appropriate for second-order factor models, Wright et al. (2010) also demonstrated that the higher order structure of the PNI was measurement invariant across genders. In this study, invariance was achieved at all levels (i.e. configural, factorial of first and second-order, disturbances, second-order variances and covariance, and intercept). Thus, the PNI can be confidently used to assess pathological narcissism in both men and women.

Scoring the PNI in Practice

Because of the variability in scale length, mean item endorsement scores are used instead of sums for easy comparison across scales. The first-order factor scores are highly correlated with their respective mean scale scores (range of $rs = .95-.99$). The second-order factor scores also are highly correlated with their respective mean scale scores for Narcissistic Grandiosity ($r = .86$) and Narcissistic Vulnerability ($r = .97$). Thus, it is appropriate for practicing clinicians to use the mean scale scores for ease of calculation. Scale and factor descriptions are summarized in Exhibit 6.1, and current

EXHIBIT 6.1
Pathological Narcissism Inventory Scales and Factors

Narcissistic Vulnerability	*Self-enhancement failures and disappointment of entitled expectations trigger significant self and emotional dysregulation.*
Contingent Self-Esteem (CSE)	Self-esteem is experienced as fluctuating. Self and emotional dysregulation arise in the absence of external sources of admiration and recognition.
Hiding the Self (HS)	Dependency feels weak and shameful. Conceals needs and concerns from others. Disclosure of imperfections evokes anxiety and is avoided.
Devaluing (DEV)	Disinterested in and avoidance of others who do not provide needed admiration. (Devaluing of Others)
	Shame and self-rebuke over needing recognition from others in the first place. (Devaluing of Self)
Entitlement Rage (ER)	Becomes angry when entitled expectations of self and others are not met.
Narcissistic Grandiosity	*Engages in maladaptive and compensatory self-enhancement strategies and holds self-serving beliefs.*
Exploitativeness (EXP)	Is manipulative and self-centered in interpersonal relationships.
Grandiose Fantasy (GF)	Is preoccupied with being powerful or achieving great things. Frequently engages in compensatory fantasies of receiving desired respect, admiration, and recognition from others.
Self-Sacrificing Self-Enhancement (SSSE)	Uses purportedly altruistic acts to support an inflated sense of self. Provides instrumental or emotional support to others, but concurrently harbors contempt for those being helped and secretly experiences the relationship as reflecting their own specialness, superiority, and moral goodness.

TABLE 6.1
Student and Clinical Norms for the PNI

PNI Scale	Students (n = 2,801)		Outpatients (n = 62)		
	M	SD	M	SD	t
Continent Self-Esteem	2.00	1.11	2.51	1.22	3.57***
Hiding the Self	2.53	0.99	2.99	1.26	3.60***
Devaluing	1.41	0.96	2.34	1.15	7.45***
Entitlement Rage	1.99	1.02	2.40	1.05	3.10**
Exploitativeness	2.27	1.08	1.92	1.06	2.50*
Grandiose Fantasy	2.87	1.15	2.66	1.31	1.42
Self-Sacrificing Self-Enhancement	2.86	0.91	2.92	1.02	0.51
Narcissistic Grandiosity	2.89	0.66	2.47	0.87	3.60***
Narcissistic Vulnerability	2.13	0.74	2.42	0.83	3.02**
PNI Total	2.23	0.75	2.43	0.72	2.08*

Note. PNI = Pathological Narcissism Inventory (Pincus et al., 2009).
*$p < .05$. **$p < .01$. ***$p < .001$.

norms in student and outpatient samples are provided in Table 6.1. Patients score significantly higher than students on the PNI total score, narcissistic vulnerability, and all of its facets. In this comparison, students score significantly higher on narcissistic grandiosity and EXP. This is likely because of the clinical sample's composition, which is very small, 84% female, and oversampled for borderline personality disorder features. A larger general clinical sample with greater gender equity will probably shift the results for narcissistic grandiosity.

VALIDITY

Like all instruments, validation of the PNI is an ongoing process; here I briefly review the emerging correlational and experimental literature. Grandiosity and vulnerability as assessed by the PNI exhibit convergent and divergent patterns of relationships across important clinical domains, providing preliminary support for their construct validity. For brevity, I emphasize data on narcissistic grandiosity and narcissistic vulnerability rather than PNI subscales.

Personality Traits

Grandiosity and vulnerability exhibit distinct and substantively meaningful patterns of correlations across narcissistic and impulsive traits, and omnibus models of general personality. Grandiosity exhibits modest positive correlations with the Narcissistic Personality Inventory total score, all inventory subscales, and measures of psychological entitlement. In contrast, Vulnerability is only positively correlated with measures of psychological entitlement (Ackerman et al., 2011; Pincus et al., 2009). Regarding impulsivity, Grandiosity correlated positively with "positive urgency" (positive affect-based impulsivity) and "sensation seeking," whereas Vulnerability was positively correlated with both "positive urgency" and "negative urgency" (negative affect-based impulsivity; Miller, Dir, et al., 2010). With regard to the five-factor model, Grandiosity is negatively correlated with Neuroticism and Agreeableness and positively correlated with Extraversion (N-, A-, E+); similarly, Vulnerability is negatively correlated with Agreeableness, but it is positively correlated with Neuroticism and negatively correlated with Extraversion (N+, A-, E-; Miller, Dir, et al., 2010). Similar patterns are found in relation to the HEXACO personality model with the notable addition that both Grandiosity and Vulnerability are related to low Honesty-Humility (Bresin & Gordon, 2011). These varied trait associations suggest that narcissistic individuals (at least pathological narcissists) are not merely "disagreeable extraverts" (Miller, Gaughan, Pryor, Kamen, & Campbell, 2009; Paulhus, 2001).

Psychopathology and Externalizing Problems

Grandiosity and vulnerability exhibit distinct and substantively meaningful patterns of correlations across measures of psychopathological symptoms in both normal and clinical samples. Ellison, Levy, Cain, and Pincus (2009) found that Grandiosity is significantly associated with presenting patients' initial scores for mania and violence and that Vulnerability significantly predicted presenting patients' initial scores for depression, psychosis, and sleep disturbance. In a student sample, Miller, Dir, et al. (2010) found that Vulnerability exhibited significant correlations with anxiety, depression, hostility, interpersonal sensitivity, paranoid ideation, and global distress. In contrast, Grandiosity only exhibited a significant negative correlation with interpersonal sensitivity. Using a sample of undergraduates, Tritt, Ryder, Ring, and Pincus (2010) found that Vulnerability was positively related to depressive and anxious temperaments and negatively related to the extraverted, energetic hyperthymic temperament. In contrast, Grandiosity was strongly positively correlated with hyperthymic temperament. In a clinical sample, both Grandiosity and Vulnerability were related to depressive tendencies (Kealy, Tsai, & Ogrodniczuk, 2012). Grandiosity and Vulnerability were also associated with borderline personality pathology in student samples (Miller, Dir, et al., 2010; Pincus et al., 2009). In a clinical sample, Pincus et al. (2009) found that both Grandiosity and Vulnerability predicted suicide attempts, but, consistent with Miller, Dir, et al. (2010), only Vulnerability predicted parasuicidal behaviors. Importantly, the SSSE Scale appears to be consistent predictor of homicidal ideation and violence (Ellison et al., 2009; Pincus et al., 2009). Only Grandiosity significantly predicted criminal behavior and gambling (Miller, Dir, et al., 2010), and Vulnerability uniquely interacted with child sexual abuse to predict overt and cyber stalking in men (Ménard & Pincus, 2012).

Emotions and Self-Esteem

Narcissistic Grandiosity and Vulnerability exhibit distinct associations with measures of self-esteem, self-conscious emotions, and core affect. Vulnerability is negatively associated with self-esteem, whereas Grandiosity is positively associated with self-esteem (Maxwell, Donnellan, Hopwood, & Ackerman, 2011; Miller, Dir, et al., 2010; Pincus et al., 2009). Vulnerability is positively correlated with shame and hubris, negatively correlated with authentic pride, and unrelated to guilt. In contrast, Grandiosity is positively related to guilt and unrelated to pride and shame (Pincus, Conroy, Hyde, & Ram, 2010). Vulnerability is positively correlated with negative affectivity and envy and negatively correlated with positive affectivity; Grandiosity is only positively correlated with positive affectivity (Krizan & Johar, 2012; Miller, Dir, et al., 2010). Finally, high levels of pathological narcissism predicted strong experimental effects for the implicit priming of self-importance (Fetterman & Robinson, 2010).

Attachment, Parenting, and Early Maladaptive Schemas

Miller, Dir, et al. (2010) found that Vulnerability was associated with attachment anxiety and avoidance, recalling parents as cold and psychologically intrusive, and reporting a history of emotional, verbal, physical, and sexual abuse. Grandiosity was unrelated to these variables. Zeigler-Hill, Green, Arnau, Sisemore, and Myers (2011) examined the distinctions between Grandiosity and Vulnerability regarding early maladaptive schemas. They found that both Grandiosity and Vulnerability correlated positively with the Mistrust and Abandonment schema domains reflecting beliefs that others will abuse, manipulate, or leave them. Grandiosity was also correlated positively with the Entitlement schema domain and negatively correlated with the Defectiveness schema domain reflecting belief that the self is perfect and should be able to do or have whatever it wants. Vulnerability was positively correlated with the Subjugation, Unrelenting Standards, and Emotional Inhibition, and negatively correlated with the Dependence schema domains, reflecting beliefs in unrealistically high standards in a world of important others where emotional expression and interpersonal dependency have negative consequences.

Interpersonal Functioning

Interpersonal problems in NPD, which is limited in scope to grandiosity, reflect a narrow range of vindictive, domineering, and intrusive behaviors (Ogrodniczuk, Piper, Joyce, Steinberg, & Duggal, 2009). Pincus et al. (2009) showed that the PNI Grandiosity scales (EXP, GF, SSE) were associated with a similar range of interpersonal problems and that PNI Vulnerability scales were also associated with vindictive (DEV, ER) interpersonal problems as well as exhibiting unique associations with exploitable (CSE) and avoidant (HS) interpersonal problems. Similarly, PNI subscales were meaningfully associated with a variety of interpersonal sensitivities (i.e. being bothered by others' interpersonal behaviors; Hopwood et al., 2011). In a series of studies examining pathological narcissism and response to ego threat (Besser & Priel, 2010; Besser & Zeigler-Hill, 2010), Grandiosity was associated with significant increases in anger and negative affect in response to achievement failures but not in response to interpersonal rejection. In contrast, Vulnerability was associated with significant increases in anger and negative affect mainly in response to interpersonal rejection. Additionally, these effects were further affected by their public or private status; Grandiosity was particularly associated with public ego threats, and Vulnerability was particularly associated with private ego threats.

Psychotherapy

In the only study examining the PNI and psychotherapy, Pincus et al. (2009) found that Grandiosity was negatively correlated with treatment use (telephone-based crisis services, partial hospitalizations, inpatient admissions, taking medications) and positively correlated with outpatient therapy no-shows. Vulnerability was positively correlated with use of telephone-based crisis services, inpatient admissions, and outpatient therapy sessions attended and cancelled. Consistent with the findings of Ogrodniczuk et al. (2009), narcissistic grandiosity was negatively related to treatment use. Using the PNI, we also see that narcissistic vulnerability was positively associated with treatment use, supporting the view that narcissistic patients are more likely to present for services when they are in a vulnerable self-state (Pincus et al., 2009). Finally, both novice and expert clinicians were able to predict a priori PNI associations with established indices of normal personality traits, psychopathology and clinical concerns, and pathological personality traits (Thomas, Wright, Lukowitsky, Donnellan, & Hopwood, 2012). The authors concluded there was substantial evidence for the criterion validity and clinical utility of the PNI.

FUTURE DEVELOPMENT

Because the PNI is new, many additional steps must be taken to evaluate its validity and clinical utility. Although adequate student norms exist, clinical norms based on a large heterogeneous patient sample are urgently needed. Further work investigating the PNI's associations with other personality disorders is also needed, including the criteria and pathological traits proposed for the fifth edition of the *Diagnostic and Statistical Manual of Mental Disorders* (*DSM–5*; American Psychiatric Association, 2011). The PNI was developed to be used as a self- or informant report, although only preliminary work on informant-rated data has been completed. Future investigations of pathological narcissism's effects on psychotherapy process and outcome, as well as the PNI's sensitivity to change in treatment, should be undertaken. Other important research areas include examinations of the temporal dynamics of grandiosity and vulnerability within patients, potential social triggers of narcissistic dysregulation, and the development of specific interventions informed by a contemporary understanding of narcissistic dysfunction. The PNI is a new multidimensional measure of pathological narcissism that has a growing body of evidence supporting its validity and clinical utility. It fills a niche in the assessment of pathological narcissism as the only instrument based on clinical phenomenology constructed to explicitly assess both narcissistic grandiosity and narcissistic vulnerability. This aligns it well with the proposed *DSM-5* NPD criteria. The PNI is currently being translated into several languages, including French, German, Chinese, Japanese, Italian, Greek, Hebrew, and Polish, and cross-cultural research on pathological narcissism is beginning. Clinicians and researchers seeking to avoid the construct definition and criterion problems associated with *DSM–IV* (American Psychiatric Association, 1994) NPD criteria and DSM-based measures will find the PNI easy to use and appropriate for gathering self- and informant reports of pathological narcissism in both clinical and nonclinical populations.

REFERENCES

Ackerman, R. A., Witt, E. A., Donnellan, M. B., Trzesniewski, K. H., Robins, R. W., & Kashy, D. A. (2011). What does the Narcissistic Personality Inventory really measure? *Assessment, 18,* 67–87. doi:10.1177/1073191110382845

Akhtar, S. (2003). *New clinical realms.* London, England: Jason Aronson.

American Psychiatric Association. (1994). *Diagnostic and statistical manual of mental disorders* (4th ed.). Washington, DC: Author.

American Psychiatric Association. (2000). *Diagnostic and statistical manual of mental disorders* (4th ed., text rev.). Washington, DC: Author.

American Psychiatric Association. (2011). *Personality disorders*. Retrieved from http://www.dsm5.org/proposedrevision/pages/personalitydisorders.aspx

Besser, A., & Priel, B. (2010). Grandiose narcissism versus vulnerable narcissism in threatening situations: Emotional reactions to achievement failure and interpersonal rejection. *Journal of Social and Clinical Psychology, 29*, 874–902. doi:10.1521/jscp.2010.29.8.874

Besser, A., & Zeigler-Hill, V. (2010). The influence of pathological narcissism on emotional and motivational responses to negative events: The roles of visibility and concern about humiliation. *Journal of Research in Personality, 44*, 520–534. doi:10.1016/j.jrp.2010.06.006

Bresin, K., & Gordon, K. H. (2011). Characterizing pathological narcissism in terms of the HEXACO model of personality. *Journal of Psychopathology and Behavioral Assessment, 33*, 228–235. doi:10.1007/s10862-010-9210-9

Buss, D. M., & Chiodo, L. M. (1991). Narcissistic acts in everyday life. *Journal of Personality, 59*, 179–215. doi:10.1111/j.1467-6494.1991.tb00773.x

Cain, N. M., Pincus, A. L., & Ansell, E. B. (2008). Narcissism at the crossroads: Phenotypic description of pathological narcissism across clinical theory, social/personality psychology, and psychiatric diagnosis. *Clinical Psychology Review, 28*, 638–656. doi:10.1016/j.cpr.2007.09.006

Conroy, D. E., Elliot, A. J., & Thrash, T. M. (2009). Achievement motivation. In M. R. Leary & R. H. Hoyle (Eds.), *Handbook of individual differences in social behavior* (pp. 382–399). New York, NY: Guilford Press.

Dickinson, K. A., & Pincus, A. L. (2003). Interpersonal analysis of grandiose and vulnerable narcissism. *Journal of Personality Disorders, 17*, 188–207. doi:10.1521/pedi.17.3.188.22146

Ellison, W., Levy, K. N., Cain, N. M., & Pincus, A. L. (2009, November). *The impact of client narcissism on psychotherapy course and outcome*. Paper presented at the mid-Atlantic regional meeting of the Society for Psychotherapy Research, Philadelphia, PA.

Fetterman, A. K., & Robinson, M. B. (2010). Contingent self-importance among pathological narcissists: Evidence from an implicit priming task. *Journal of Research in Personality, 44*, 691–697. doi:10.1016/j.jrp.2010.09.002

Gabbard, G. O. (2009). Transference and countertransference: Developments in the treatment of narcissistic personality disorder. *Psychiatric Annals, 39*, 129–136. doi:10.3928/00485713-20090301-03

Hendin, H. M., & Cheek, J. M. (1997). Assessing hypersensitive narcissism: A reexamination of Murray's Narcissism Scale. *Journal of Research in Personality, 31*, 588–599. doi:10.1006/jrpe.1997.2204

Hepper, E. G., Gramzow, R. H., & Sedikides, C. (2010). Individual differences in self-enhancement and self-protection strategies: An integrative analysis. *Journal of Personality, 78*, 781–814. doi:10.1111/j.1467-6494.2010.00633.x

Hopwood, C. J., Ansell, E. A., Pincus, A. L., Wright, A. G. C., Lukowitsky, M. R., & Roche, M. J. (2011). The circumplex structure of interpersonal sensitivities. *Journal of Personality, 79*, 707–740. doi:10.1111/j.1467-6494.2011.00696.x

Horowitz, M. (2009). Clinical phenomenology of narcissistic pathology. *Psychiatric Annals, 39*, 124–128. doi:10.3928/00485713-20090301-06

Kealy, D., & Rasmussen, B. (2012). Veiled and vulnerable: The other side of grandiose narcissism. *Clinical Social Work Journal, 40*, 356–365. doi:10.1007/s10615-011-0370-1

Kealy, D., Tsai, M., & Ogrodniczuk, J. S. (2012). Depressive tendencies and pathological narcissism among psychiatric outpatients. *Psychiatry Research, 196*, 157–159. doi:10.1016/j.psychres.2011.08.023

Kernberg, O. F. (2009). Narcissistic personality disorders: Part 1. *Psychiatric Annals, 39*, 105–107. doi:10.3928/00485713-20090301-04

Kohut, H., & Wolf, E. S. (1978). The disorders of the self and their treatment: An outline. *The International Journal of Psychoanalysis, 59*, 413–425.

Krizan, Z., & Johar, O. (2012). Envy divides the two faces of narcissism. *Journal of Personality.* Advance online publication. doi:10.1111/j.1467-6494.2012.00767.x

Levy, K. N., Reynoso, J. S., Wasserman, R. H., & Clarkin, J. F. (2007). Narcissistic personality disorder. In W. O'Donohue, K. A. Fowler, & S. O. Lilienfeld (Eds.), *Personality disorders: Toward the DSM–V* (pp. 233–277). Thousand Oaks, CA: Sage.

Livesley, W. J. (2006). The dimensional assessment of personality pathology (DAPP) approach to personality disorder. In S. Strack (Ed.), *Differentiating normal and abnormal personality* (2nd ed., pp. 401–429). New York, NY: Springer.

Maxwell, K., Donnellan, M. B., Hopwood, C. J., & Ackerman, R. A. (2011). The two faces of Narcissus? An empirical comparison of the Narcissistic Personality Inventory and the Pathological Narcissism Inventory. *Personality and Individual Differences, 50*, 577–582. doi:10.1016/j.paid.2010.11.031

McCullough, M. E., Emmons, R. A., Kilpatrick, S. D., & Mooney, C. N. (2003). Narcissists as "victims": The role of narcissism in the perception of transgressions. *Personality and Social Psychology Bulletin, 29*, 885–893. doi:10.1177/0146167203029007007

McGlashan, T. H., Grilo, C. M., Sanislow, C. A., Ralevski, E., Morey, L. C., Gunderson, J. G., . . . Pagano, M. (2005). Two-year prevalence and stability of individual DSM–IV criteria for schizotypal, borderline, avoidant, and obsessive–compulsive personality disorders: Toward a hybrid model of Axis II disorders. *The American Journal of Psychiatry, 162*, 883–889. doi:10.1176/appi.ajp.162.5.883

Ménard, K. S., & Pincus, A. L. (2012). Predicting overt and cyber stalking perpetration by male and female college students. *Journal of Interpersonal Violence, 27*, 2183–2207. doi: 10.1177/0886260511432144

Miller, J. D., & Campbell, W. K. (2008). Comparing clinical and social-personality conceptualizations of narcissism. *Journal of Personality, 76*, 449–476. doi:10.1111/j.1467-6494.2008.00492.x

Miller, J. D., Dir, A., Gentile, B., Wilson, L., Pryor, L. R., & Campbell, W. K. (2010). Searching for a vulnerable dark triad: Comparing factor 2 psychopathy, vulnerable narcissism, and borderline personality disorder. *Journal of Personality, 78*, 1529–1564. doi:10.1111/j.1467-6494.2010.00660.x

Miller, J. D., Gaughan, E. T., Pryor, L. R., Kamen, C., & Campbell, W. K. (2009). Is research using the NPI relevant for understanding narcissistic personality disorder? *Journal of Research in Personality, 43*, 482–488. doi:10.1016/j.jrp.2009.02.001

Miller, J. D., Hoffman, B. J., Gaughan, E. T., Gentile, B., Maples, J., & Campbell, W. K. (2011). Grandiose and vulnerable narcissism: A nomological network analysis. *Journal of Personality, 79*, 1013–1042. doi:10.1111/j.1467-6494.2010.00711.x

Miller, J. D., Widiger, T. A., & Campbell, W. K. (2010). Narcissistic personality disorder and the DSM–V. *Journal of Abnormal Psychology, 119*, 640–649. doi:10.1037/a0019529

Ogrodniczuk, J. S., Piper, W. E., Joyce, A. S., Steinberg, P. I., & Duggal, S. (2009). Interpersonal problems associated with narcissism among psychiatric outpatients. *Journal of Psychiatric Research, 43*, 837–842. doi:10.1016/j.jpsychires.2008.12.005

Otway, L. J., & Vignoles, V. L. (2006). Narcissism and childhood recollections: A quantitative test of psychoanalytic predictions. *Personality and Social Psychology Bulletin, 32*, 104–116. doi:10.1177/0146167205279907

Paulhus, D. L. (2001). Normal narcissism: Two minimalist accounts. *Psychological Inquiry, 12*, 228–230.

Pincus, A. L. (2005a). A contemporary integrative interpersonal theory of personality disorders. In J. Clarkin & M. Lenzenweger (Eds.), *Major theories of personality disorder* (2nd ed., pp. 282–331). New York, NY: Guilford Press.

Pincus, A. L. (2005b). The interpersonal nexus of personality disorders. In S. Strack (Ed.), *Handbook of personology and psychopathology* (pp. 120–139). New York, NY: Wiley.

Pincus, A. L. (2011). Some comments on nomology, diagnostic process, and narcissistic personality disorder in the DSM–5 proposal for personality and personality disorders. *Personality Disorders: Theory, Research, and Treatment, 2*, 41–53. doi:10.1037/a0021191

Pincus, A. L., Ansell, E. B., Pimentel, C. A., Cain, N. M., Wright, A. G., & Levy, K. N. (2009). Initial construction and validation of the Pathological Narcissism Inventory. *Psychological Assessment, 21*, 365–379. doi:10.1037/a0016530

Pincus, A. L., Conroy, D. E., Hyde, A. L., & Ram, N. (2010, May). *Pathological narcissism and the dynamics of self-conscious emotions*. Paper presented at the annual meeting of the Association for Psychological Science, Boston, MA.

Pincus, A. L., & Lukowitsky, M. R. (2010). Pathological narcissism and narcissistic personality disorder. *Annual Review of Clinical Psychology, 6*, 421–446. doi:10.1146/annurev.clinpsy.121208.131215

Pincus, A. L., Lukowitsky, M. R., & Wright, A. G. C. (2010). The interpersonal nexus of personality and psychopathology. In T. Millon, R. Kreuger, & E. Simonsen (Eds.), *Contemporary directions in psychopathology: Scientific foundations for DSM–V and ICD–11* (pp. 523–552). New York, NY: Guilford Press.

Pincus, A. L., & Roche, M. J. (2011). Narcissistic grandiosity and narcissistic vulnerability. In W. K. Campbell & J. D. Miller (Eds.), *Handbook of narcissism and narcissistic personality disorders* (pp. 31–40). Hoboken, NJ: Wiley.

Pincus, A. L., & Wright, A. G. C. (2010). Interpersonal diagnosis of psychopathology. In L. M. Horowitz & S. Strack (Eds.), *Handbook of interpersonal psychology* (pp. 359–381). Hoboken, NJ: Wiley.

Raskin, R., & Hall, C. S. (1981). The Narcissistic Personality Inventory: Alternate form reliability and further evidence of construct validity. *Journal of Personality Assessment, 45*, 159–162. doi:10.1207/s15327752jpa4502_10

Ronningstam, F. (2005a). *Identifying and understanding the narcissistic personality.* New York, NY: Oxford.

Ronningstam, E. (2005b). Narcissistic personality disorder: A review. In M. Maj, H. S. Akiskal, J. E. Mezzich, & A. Okasha (Eds.), *Evidence and experience in psychiatry. Vol. 8. Personality disorders* (pp. 277–327). New York, NY: Wiley.

Ronningstam, E. F. (2009). Narcissistic personality disorder: Facing DSM–V. *Psychiatric Annals, 39*, 111–121. doi:10.3928/00485713-20090301-09

Revik, J. O. (2001). Overt and covert narcissism: Turning points and mutative elements in two psychotherapies. *British Journal of Psychotherapy, 17*, 435–447. doi:10.1111/j.1752-0118.2001.tb00608.x

Russ, E., Shedler, J., Bradley, R., & Westen, D. (2008). Refining the construct of narcissistic personality disorder: Diagnostic criteria and subtypes. *The American Journal of Psychiatry, 165*, 1473–1481. doi:10.1176/appi.ajp.2008.07030376

Simms, L. J., & Clark, L. A. (2006). The schedule for nonadaptive and adaptive personality (SNAP): A dimensional measure of traits relevant to personality and personality pathology. In S. Strack (Ed.), *Differentiating normal and abnormal personality* (2nd ed., pp. 431–450). New York, NY: Springer.

Thomas, K. M., Wright, A. G. C., Lukowitsky, M. R., Donnellan, M. B., & Hopwood, C. J. (2012). Evidence for the criterion validity and clinical utility of the Pathological Narcissism Inventory. *Assessment, 19*, 135–145. doi:10.1177/1073191112436664

Tritt, S. M., Ryder, A. G., Ring, A. J., & Pincus, A. L. (2010). Pathological narcissism and the depressive temperament. *Journal of Affective Disorders, 122*, 280–284. doi:10.1016/j.jad.2009.09.006

Widiger, T. A. (1991). Definition, diagnosis, and differentiation. *Journal of Personality Disorders, 5*, 42–51. doi:10.1521/pedi.1991.5.1.42

Wright, A. G. C., Lukowitsky, M. R., Pincus, A. L., & Conroy, D. E. (2010). The higher-order factor structure and gender invariance of the Pathological Narcissism Inventory. *Assessment, 17*, 467–483. doi:10.1177/1073191110373227

Zeigler-Hill, V., Green, B. A., Arnau, R. C., Sisemore, T. B., & Myers, E. M. (2011). Trouble ahead, trouble behind: Narcissism and early maladaptive schemas. *Journal of Behavior Therapy and Experimental Psychiatry, 42*, 96–103. doi:10.1016/j.jbtep.2010.07.004

Zeigler-Hill, V., Myers, E. M., & Clark, C. B. (2010). Narcissism and self-esteem reactivity: The role of negative achievement events. *Journal of Research in Personality, 44*, 285–292. doi:10.1016/j.jrp.2010.02.005

III

CLINICAL FEATURES OF PATHOLOGICAL NARCISSISM

7

INTERPERSONAL PROBLEMS OF NARCISSISTIC PATIENTS

JOHN S. OGRODNICZUK AND DAVID KEALY

The term *narcissism* commonly evokes the notion of rapt self-involvement rather than a palette of interpersonal interactions. Such narcissistic self-involvement is generally appreciated as having an effect on others. However, knowledge of specific interpersonal behaviors associated with pathological narcissism is not yet widely considered in routine clinical practice. Although clinicians providing general mental health care frequently recognize their patients' interpersonal problems, they may overlook the potential narcissistic function of these behaviors. Certain interpersonal patterns may be indicative of a narcissistic disorder that has yet to be diagnosed. On the other hand, patients clinically identified as suffering from pathological narcissism may obscure, at least initially, the nature and depth of their interpersonal difficulties. Narcissistic pathology is deeply entangled with interpersonal problems, and the nature of narcissism decreases the likelihood of these issues being openly reported on. Narcissistic patients may avoid discussing

DOI: 10.1037/14041-007
Understanding and Treating Pathological Narcissism, J. S. Ogrodniczuk (Editor)

aspects of their psychopathology (e.g., problematic interpersonal behaviors) in an effort to avoid scrutiny and criticism. Alternatively, narcissistic patients might be so oblivious to the effects of their behaviors on others that they simply neglect to report on potentially significant interpersonal problems. Furthermore, the clinician's efforts to explore the patient's role in interpersonal scenarios can evoke either a cantankerous or dismissive response, rather than reflective concern. Getting to know the patient with pathological narcissism therefore involves becoming familiar with a range of interpersonal difficulties, perhaps more so than with any other disorder.

The hand-in-hand nature of interpersonal dysfunction and pathological narcissism is reflected in the clinical aphorism that narcissistic individuals are not necessarily identified by how they feel, but according to how they make others feel. This includes treatment providers; patients who present as arrogant, entitled, and dismissive can leave clinicians feeling befuddled, angry, insulted, and helpless. Such feelings, and the intertwined narcissism and interpersonal dysfunction that engender them, constitute a significant part of the diagnostic and treatment planning process. Recognizing and treating pathological narcissism and its interpersonal dysfunction is extremely important. Although they might appear haughty or indifferent, those with narcissistic problems may suffer tremendously in terms of their core identity, self-esteem regulation, and dysphoric affects. This is particularly so if their actual abilities or achievements are widely out of step with their fantasies and expectations. Narcissistic individuals' interpersonal dysfunction may contribute not only to their own unhappiness but also to difficulties in the lives of their loved ones. Moreover, difficulties interacting with others place narcissistic patients at risk for significant disruptions in their career, social, and family-life trajectories. Stinson et al. (2008) found that substance use, mood, and anxiety disorders are highly comorbid with narcissistic personality disorder. Often it is one of these comorbid conditions that prompts the patient with pathological narcissism to seek treatment. However, Axis I disorders tend to respond poorly to treatment when personality disorders are comorbid (Newton-Howes, Tyrer, & Johnson, 2006). For many patients, addressing narcissistic dysfunction is therefore necessary to obtain relief from other conditions.

This chapter focuses on the interpersonal difficulties associated with narcissistic pathology. In our experience, pathological narcissism as a diagnostic formulation is underrepresented in mental health and outpatient clinic practice, and as such, potential links between problematic interpersonal behaviors and narcissistic dysfunction are often overlooked. We describe the various interpersonal problems associated with narcissistic pathology in order to identify signs of pathological narcissism where it might not otherwise be suspected and to assist with understanding such phenomena when encountered in the treatment situation. Each problem area is illustrated with a case example; patient identities have been disguised to maintain confidentiality.

INTERPERSONAL PROBLEMS AND PATHOLOGICAL NARCISSISM

Our descriptions are based on the behaviors portrayed by the Inventory of Interpersonal Problems (Horowitz, Rosenberg, Baer, Ureno, & Villasenor, 1988), a widely used instrument designed to assess problems in interpersonal interactions, and on interpersonal theory. We discuss these interpersonal problems as they relate to vulnerable and grandiose features of pathological narcissism (see Exhibit 7.1). It is important to bear in mind that narcissistic vulnerability and grandiosity (as discussed in Chapter 2, this volume) are likely to oscillate or occur simultaneously in an individual patient; therefore, the interpersonal problems discussed under the respective subtypes are best regarded as potentials. Indeed, clinicians can probably expect to encounter mixtures of these interpersonal problems in any given patient with narcissistic tendencies. Their delineation is nonetheless useful for heuristic and diagnostic purposes. Consideration of these interpersonal problems as potentially part of an overall narcissistic disorder can cue the clinician to the underlying pathology. Furthermore, because treatment (and especially psychotherapy) necessitates an interpersonal situation, narcissistic interpersonal problems are inevitably brought directly into the treatment relationship. Understanding these interactional behaviors, which may be reflected in transference and countertransference patterns, is therefore useful in navigating what can sometimes be difficult treatment encounters.

Grandiose Narcissism

Much of the literature has focused on the grandiose type of pathological narcissism. The following descriptions of interpersonal problems are based not only on characterizations of the interpersonal behavior of grandiose narcissistic patients found within the clinical literature but also on the findings of recent studies that have examined the associations between narcissism and interpersonal dysfunction in different samples. These studies (Dickinson &

EXHIBIT 7.1
Interpersonal Problems Associated With Narcissistic Subtypes

Grandiose	Vulnerable
▪ Dominance	▪ Coldness
▪ Vindictiveness	▪ Social avoidance
▪ Intrusiveness	▪ Exploitability

Pincus, 2003; Miller, Campbell, & Pilkonis, 2007; Ogrodniczuk, Piper, Joyce, Steinberg, & Duggal, 2009; Pincus et al., 2009; Pincus & Wiggins, 1990) have found that the interpersonal style of grandiose narcissistic patients is generally characterized by domineering, vindictive, and intrusive behavior. We discuss each of these behaviors in turn.

Dominance

Individuals with narcissistic personality disorder may feel a strong need to exert control over others. This is particularly evident among patients who exhibit grandiose narcissistic trends (Dickinson & Pincus, 2003; Ogrodniczuk et al., 2009). Domineering behavior may take the form of explicit demands for others to obey or conform to the individual's idiosyncratic standards. For example, family members may be forced into complying with strict rules of conduct, having to seek special authority for any kind of exceptional request; one patient of ours insisted that his wife obtain his approval when selecting which outfit to wear each day. In workplace settings, domineering behavior may take the form of a "my way or the highway" kind of attitude when dealing with subordinates or peers: The person's demands are to be followed simply because that is what is desired, without regard for reason or due process. The control exerted in this kind of narcissistic functioning reveals an absence of empathy for those on the receiving end of such behavior. The feelings of others are simply disregarded as the person with narcissistic dysfunction ruthlessly pursues his own agenda. When eventually confronted with the disgruntled reactions of others, dominant narcissistic individuals may be truly surprised, if not indignant, that their efforts have not been appreciated. Dominant behavior is also a blatant expression of grandiosity: They believe that their specialness entitles them to call the shots. However, an additional message is sent out in this kind of interacting: that others are feeble and incapable. In this way, social dominance may reflect a behavioral manifestation of defensive projection: Intolerable self-states associated with weakness are continually assigned to others as the narcissistic individual maintains an authoritative self-representation.

Clinical Example

Mr. C. insisted that his laundry be stored in a separate hamper from other family members' laundry while waiting to be washed, lest any stains spread to his clothes. If his children forgot this rule, he would erupt in fury. In group therapy, he demanded that he be allowed to show up late each session; he argued that his lateness was legitimate because his job was more important than those of other group members.

Although domineering individuals may initially impress others as being confident, take-charge types, those close to them eventually tire of being treated as though they are incompetent or invisible. In the treatment setting, dominance may also be expressed explicitly through demands for the therapist to provide special modifications to accommodate the patient. For example, the patient may insist on a special fee or individualized appointment time arrangements. In group therapy, the patient might clamor for a personal exemption to one of the group rules or norms and may even initially convince group members that this should be provided.

A more surreptitious form of dominance can also enter the treatment in the form of a "sounding board" transference pattern (Gabbard, 2009), in which the patient barely allows the therapist to get a word in edgewise. Although the patient may initially appear to be adhering to the principle of free association, it becomes clear after a while that he or she has little interest in what the therapist might be thinking or feeling, and his or her verbal output serves to control the therapist. The clinician, then, may have feelings of anger, boredom, or disengagement (Gabbard, 2009). The therapist's counter-transference feelings of being excluded may be similar to the feelings of other people in the patient's life, providing a window into his or her interpersonal dynamics with others. This can be further linked to the patient's object relations: He or she might have developed a way of controlling and excluding the effects of intrusive early caregivers and now habitually seeks to prevent an anticipated similar experience. Alternatively, such countertransference feelings could reflect dissociated aspects of the patient's self experience, perhaps related to a disavowed past as a narcissistic object of the parents. In other words, the therapist's feelings of being shut out may represent an identification with an early object relations configuration involving the patient's exclusion—a painful sense of shame for needing more of a parent's attention than was available.

Vindictiveness

Vindictive interpersonal behavior among narcissistic individuals often presents as suspicious, vengeful conduct fueled by envy and resentment. In an acute, activated state this may take the form of narcissistic rage (Wolf, 1988), where the individual feels compelled to enact vengeance to redress what he or she experiences as an intolerable injury to self-esteem. For example, one patient explained that he had to get in the last word if anyone insulted him in any way; anything less than a compensatory strike toward the offending party would be experienced as a soul-crushing humiliation. The envy and shame evoked by the other person being in any kind of "one-up" position might for some narcissistic individuals feel completely unbearable. Shame and envy are closely linked: The experience of an unrequited need or desire can evoke painful feelings of inferiority, particularly when such need concerns an interpersonal response such as affirmation or admiration. Narcissistic individuals may find it difficult to tolerate another person's possession of an attribute or capacity that they lack. Vindictiveness pertains to shame and envy as a powerful defense against these difficult affect states. Some patients may have a sense of vindictiveness always at the ready, living out a chronic narcissistic rage (Ornstein, 1993/2006). Vindictive responses may take the form of persistent, if sometimes subtle, devaluation as a preemptive guard against envy. In order not to long for another person's possessions or attributes (which would leave the narcissistic patient feeling hungry and weak), they may psychologically spoil whatever is coveted by devaluing it. One patient in group therapy would consistently find ways of offering backhanded compliments to each group member; no one—articulate speakers, successful professionals, parents with children—had anything he would wish for. The more explosive variant of acute, narcissistic rage may also manifest in therapy, as, for example, the patient storms out of the session after unleashing a torrent of verbal abuse onto the therapist.

Clinical Example

Ms. D., a public service administrator, was preoccupied with feelings of resentment toward one of her subordinates, whom she felt was always trying to upstage her. The fact that her junior associate seemed competent and intelligent was bothersome to no end. Vigilant monitoring of this employee's performance for any sign of weakness began to dominate her work: She felt certain that he was indeed a fraud. In group therapy, she seemed to sulk whenever another member received attention or positive feedback from the group. In time it was revealed that, once outside the building after group sessions, Ms. D. would gather some of the members together to disparage the therapist.

Some patients with narcissistic tendencies seem to enter the consulting room with a vindictive agenda, ready to immediately assign fault to the therapist for a host of perceived faults or injuries that have befallen the patient in the past. Such patients may have felt other care providers to have been incompetent and may unconsciously seek to punish the current clinician for the perceived or real deficiencies of others. They may approach the consultation in a "guns blazing" manner that masks the vulnerable affects associated with having been disappointed by others. This stance may represent a simultaneous disavowal of having been hurt and a preemptive effort at avoiding further pain by becoming the one who hurts. This defensive maneuver is thus enacted through verbal devaluation of the therapist or actual sabotaging of treatment efforts. Indeed, it is conceivable that vindictive interpersonal processes might account for part of the substantial treatment drop-out among narcissistic patients. By unilaterally terminating therapy, the patient may be enacting a vindictive fantasy against the therapist, either for perceived wrongdoings or for anticipated disappointments.

Other patients might bring vindictive behavior into the clinical situation more gradually in the form of insidious devaluation of the therapist, subtly expressing the belief that the therapist is somehow incompetent or inferior. Gabbard (2009) elaborated on the contemptuous transference pattern encountered with some narcissistic patients and the consequent countertransference challenges faced by clinicians. As Gabbard noted, contemptuous transference often comprises a defensive effort against envy of what the therapist is perceived to possess, including the capacity to be helpful to the patient. Vindictive behaviors might also emerge in the wake of what the patient experiences as devaluation by the therapist. For some narcissistic patients, even well-meaning interventions may be felt to be insulting or belittling. A strike back might be deemed necessary by the patient in order to restore a stable sense of self. One group therapy patient of ours felt so exposed and humiliated by any intervention, whether interpretive or the setting of basic group norms, that denigration of the group therapists seemed to become the focus of his attention in therapy. His vindictive efforts escalated to the point of sabotaging his treatment. Kernberg (1984, 2007) described patients with malignant narcissism whose self-esteem seems to be enhanced through the expression of aggression, including the sadistic defeat of the therapist. Severe vindictiveness in the form of malignant features combined with antisocial traits could present a contraindication for treatment.

Intrusiveness

Intrusive interpersonal behavior often involves exhibitionistic displays that encroach on other people's personal space. A feature of the grandiose side of the narcissistic spectrum, intrusiveness may comprise behaviors intended to cultivate a sense of superiority or to elicit admiration from others. Although the exhibitionistic behavior may demonstrate legitimate talents or skills, its deployment may be consistently ill-timed and lacking in consideration for how others might actually experience it. For example, one woman, an able singer, felt compelled to sing aloud at her daughter's music recitals, oblivious to her daughter's embarrassment at being upstaged. Intrusive behavior can also consist of insistence on one's specialness. Frequent name dropping of important people with whom the individual had a minor connection is one such example. Seemingly casual hints of one's specialness might be woven into conversations, or activities might just happen to be routinely organized around the individual to garner admiration. Individuals with this intrusive pattern may also show a disregard for personal boundaries, feel free to offer unsolicited wisdom to others, or take for themselves what they feel entitled to. The intrusive narcissistic individual is likely to fail to appreciate that his or her behavior can engender superficiality and distance in relations with others, rather than admiration and affection.

Clinical Example

Mr. E. had a history of being terminated from jobs, despite an impressive sales record. He felt that his colleagues could not handle that he was "the best in the business" and had him fired out of spite. He later acknowledged that female colleagues had complained about his habit of flirtatious advances and sexual innuendo. He consulted with a female therapist about his reaction to the latest rejection. At times during the sessions, he seemed to focus on describing his various accomplishments. At other times, Mr. E. would visually scan the therapist's body, ask personal questions, and make inappropriate attempts at humor (e.g., "What's your husband like? I bet you wear the pants in the family").

Intrusive behavior may be one of the more persistent interpersonal patterns of narcissistic patients. For patients who completed an 18-week psychiatric day treatment program, intrusiveness was the only interpersonal domain to not show a significant change by the end of treatment (Ogrodniczuk et al., 2009). Group therapy presents a range of opportunities for narcissistic patients to act out intrusive and exhibitionistic behavior. They might begin the session with a long-winded, dramatic tale of their latest exploits, oblivious to the pressing needs of other members to explore issues of conflict and distress. When other group members do speak about some kind of personal tragedy, intrusive patients may shift the focus onto themselves with over-the-top tears of "sympathy." They might proffer unsolicited hugs to members and invite them to call after the session, ignoring the boundaries and norms set up by group leaders, who seem callous compared to the fervent altruism displayed by these patients. Boundaries may be likewise blurred in the individual treatment setting; patients may prefer to treat the clinician more like a friend than a therapist. Their priority in therapy may shift from exploration to cultivating admiration as they regale the therapist with examples of their accomplishments. Such a pattern may underscore patients' disavowed longing for the therapist's love and approval. Similarly, a profound curiosity and inquiry into the therapist's life can also denote such yearnings while shifting focus away from patients' weaknesses as they present themselves in more of a "friend" role.

Vulnerable Narcissism

Most standardized assessments of narcissism have emphasized the grandiose variant described in the *Diagnostic and Statistical Manual of Mental Disorders* (4th ed.; text rev.; *DSM–IV–TR*; American Psychiatric Association, 2000). Consequently, there is a lack of empirical data from clinical patients regarding the interpersonal problems associated with vulnerable narcissism. This could contribute to an underestimation of the relational and behavioral sequelae of this narcissistic subtype. The comparatively less dramatic nature of vulnerable narcissistic interpersonal behaviors can also potentially obscure their identification as markers of significant psychopathology. A key difference with the vulnerable subtype is a tendency to feel a high degree of distress regarding their interpersonal relationships, whereas grandiose narcissistic individuals typically are not overly concerned about this issue (Dickinson & Pincus, 2003). Using the newly developed Pathological Narcissism Inventory (see Chapter 6, this volume), which assesses aspects of vulnerable narcissism, Pincus et al. (2009) found that vulnerable narcissism was associated with cold, avoidant, and exploitable interpersonal behaviors. Further empirical research is required to clarify the associations between vulnerable narcissism and these problematic interactional patterns.

Coldness

Some patients with a vulnerable form of narcissism may be most recognizable in terms of what they lack: genuine emotional warmth. Because of feelings of inner emptiness, envy, or anxiety regarding relationships, these patients can tend to be distant and aloof. Their coldness may function as a form of disavowal of normative needs for closeness. Yet, at the same time, they may hold a covert attitude of entitlement with regard to receiving love and admiration. Although vulnerable narcissistic individuals report high interpersonal distress (Dickinson & Pincus, 2003), their defenses often lead them to attribute an external causality for this. For example, one patient felt wounded whenever his wife did not show her appreciation of him, while at the same time denying the importance of her appraisal. He manifested an aloof stance toward her, reflecting a denial of his vulnerability, thereby construing his wife as the needy, weakened partner.

> ### Clinical Example
>
> Ms. F. complained of a staid marriage and lackluster social interactions. She had no idea about causes of these problems. In her therapy, she showed a tendency to march in and out of the consulting room with almost no greeting to the therapist. She sat rigidly with minimal eye contact. Over time the therapist felt disengaged and frequently flirted with the wish to terminate the therapy prematurely.

In the treatment situation, lack of interpersonal warmth may be revealed in the patient's nonverbal behavior. Patients may be capable of verbalizing thoughts, feelings, and issues to work on in therapy, but their demeanor may be aloof. Some patients with this interpersonal style might have difficulty with eye contact and with the normative friendly gestures of social interaction. Other such patients may be capable of these ordinary and customary social behaviors but may strongly resist the "real relationship" (Greenson, 1972) aspect of the treatment situation. They may view the therapist as simply "doing a job" rather than being capable of genuine warmth. Attempts to explore the transference relationship may yield the response, "What relationship?" In this sense, interpersonal coldness may manifest a variant of the sounding-board transference pattern, although without the self-aggrandizing quality. The therapy situation may be construed unilaterally as a service—akin to visiting the laundromat—rather than as a relational experience. This is often reflective of an incapacity to depend on others, defending against deeply walled-off yearnings for love and merger, the emergence of which could be perceived by the patient as dangerous or destabilizing (Kernberg, 1984). For the therapist, prolonged exposure to this kind of coldness in the consulting room can lead to a fatigued countertransference characterized by boredom and feelings of futility, perhaps following failed attempts at enlivening the therapeutic encounter through various interventions.

Social Avoidance

Socially avoidant behavior consists of cautious, inhibited, and limited interactions with others. Often this includes actual retreat from social interactions. Dickinson and Pincus (2003) found that in reflecting self-conscious concerns about being approved of by others, narcissistic social avoidance shares some overlap with avoidant personality features. However, they noted that whereas (nonnarcissistic) avoidant individuals fear lack of acceptance, vulnerable narcissistic individuals fear lack of admiration and narcissistic supply. In this sense, narcissistic avoidant behavior may forestall severe dysphoria or "fragmentation" (Kohut & Wolf, 1978) entailed in the disappointment of enti-tled interpersonal expectations. Social gatherings may be experienced as arenas for potentially humiliating encounters. For example, going to a parent–teacher interview could leave the patient in a dysphoric tailspin for days if the teacher did not recognize the child's talents (which may be experienced as direct reflec-tions of the parent). Anticipating such encounters can evoke feelings of undue stress. Ironically, by vigilantly steeling themselves against potential insults, frag-ile narcissistic individuals risk creating a self-fulfilling prophecy where social rigidity and unease actually elicit subtle rejecting behaviors from others.

Clinical Example

Mr. G., director of a health care facility, maintained a "closed door policy" at work. He sought to limit his interactions with subordinates as much as possible, lest they say anything negative to him. Any criticism was felt as a massive exposure of his weakness, following which he would ruminate for several days on how he could buttress himself against further attacks. He was frequently absent from group therapy, often following a session in which he received feedback from a group member.

Gabbard (2009) described the phenomenon of fear of humiliation as a central transference pattern in psychotherapy with vulnerable narcissistic patients. Where such patients try to avoid social interactions that carry the potential for humiliation, they may experience therapy as a profound expo-sure of their inadequacy and shame. The very act of being a patient is felt as a signal of a serious personal defect. Consequently, the transference associated with social avoidance may revolve around the patient's sense of embarrass-ment or personal injury. This can be manifest in a vigilant stance toward the therapist, scanning for potentially shaming words or actions. Clarifying comments and interpretations, for example, may be perceived by the patient as intolerable insults that seem to "rub it in" that the therapist and patient are not on an equal playing field. Kohut (1968) developed the construct of the mirror transference through discovering that certain narcissistic patients could not tolerate anything beyond a verbal reflection of essentially what they had just said: Anything more seemed intrusive and enraging to the patient, presumably because it activated narcissistic shame and envy.

Exploitability

The exploitable domain refers to difficulty expressing anger toward others and readiness to go along with others' wishes. Therefore, a sense of being taken advantage of is often a feature of this interpersonal domain. In discussing the vulnerable subtype of narcissistic personality disorder, Cooper (1988/2006, 1998) has emphasized the presence of masochism in contrast with many of the *DSM* diagnostic markers for the disorder, noting that the vulnerable narcissist "is more exploited than exploiter" (Cooper, 1998, p. 70). Enacting the role of a suffering individual allows for a secret and paradoxical exploitation of social relatedness: deriving a sense of specialness out of relentless "doing for" others without reward.

Cooper noted that this form of narcissistic masochism entails self-defeating interpersonal interactions in order to maintain complex fantasies related to both grandiosity and weakness. Persistent interpersonal defeat—unconsciously "arranged"—provides a covert, defensive extraction of satisfaction from being mistreated. This form of interpersonal dysfunction may be particularly difficult to assess and explore, in part because of patient indignation ("Why am I always being picked on?") combined with a strong need to consciously regard their actions as wholly altruistic. After having described their efforts at helping others, however, they may then complain that other people seem to "use" or take advantage of their kindness. For some patients, this type of interpersonal scenario may become a recurring theme, representing a self-regulatory compromise between seeking admiration (and thus not true attunement to others' needs) and holding on to a sense of injustice (Campbell & Baumeister, 2006).

Clinical Example

Ms. H. served on her church's planning committee, led their fund-raising campaigns, and taught Sunday school. She complained bitterly to the therapist about being "roped into" too many responsibilities and expressed the conviction that no one recognized the burden involved in "going along" with these requests. In therapy, she maintained an exceedingly agreeable stance toward the therapist, almost never indicating the slightest irritation. During the course of a session, the therapist offered a kind remark. The patient replied, with genuine anger, "You're too damn nice. Sometimes I wish you'd just slap me across the face and tell me straight up what I should do."

Exploitable interpersonal dysfunction may be difficult to discern in the treatment situation, at least initially. This has to do with the desirability of agreeable behavior, reflecting an ordinary facilitative transference (Freud, 1912) considered important for a working alliance. In time, however, it may become clear that although the patient describes one scenario of interpersonal set-back after another, the patient construes the therapy relationship as being somehow pristine and immune to such disappointment. Attempts to explore latent allusions to even mild, expectable negative transference material may be flatly rebuffed. Kohut (1968) described and conceptualized the idealized transference as a developmentally derived phenomenon that requires preservation in psychotherapy (at least for a sufficient period of time) rather than interpretation. In describing the narcissistic—masochistic character style, Cooper (1998) emphasized that idealizing and excessively agreeable transference patterns may serve to conceal rage and to set up the therapy as a large, eventual disappointment. In line with Kohut's observations, countertransference can potentially take the form of extreme discomfort at being the object of idealization. In group therapy, the patient with exploitable features might behave as a model of pleasantness and cooperation in the group, only to secretly relish when another group member lambasts the therapist for some perceived wrongdoing. Alternatively, exploitable patients in group treatment might describe themselves as carrying the weight of all the other members' problems; their experience of intense caring for others leads them to feel inhibited in being able to personally benefit from the therapy.

CONCLUSION

Pathological narcissism and maladaptive interpersonal behaviors are intertwining problems for mental health clinicians to confront in clinical practice. A broad conceptualization of pathological narcissism includes both grandiose and vulnerable subtypes. These may oscillate within any given patient according to narcissistic self-regulation needs, with each subtype or theme carrying a potential for different forms of interpersonal dysfunction. Particular interpersonal difficulties are different for each patient; here we outlined some of the core behavior problems associated with narcissistic pathology. Clinicians must be aware of the ways in which these behaviors may be carried into treatment situations.

REFERENCES

American Psychiatric Association. (2000). *Diagnostic and statistical manual of mental disorders* (4th ed.; text rev.). Washington, DC: Author.

Campbell, W. K., & Baumeister, R. F. (2006). Narcissistic personality disorder. In J. Fisher & W. O'Donohue (Eds.), *Practitioner's guide to evidence-based psychotherapy* (pp. 423–431). New York, NY: Springer. doi:10.1007/978-0-387-28370-8_42

Cooper, A. M. (1998). Further developments in the clinical diagnosis of narcissistic personality disorder. In E. Ronningstam (Ed.), *Disorders of narcissism: Diagnostic, clinical, and empirical implications* (pp. 53–74). Washington, DC: American Psychiatric Association.

Cooper, A. M. (2006). The narcissistic–masochistic character. In A. Cooper (Ed.), *Contemporary psychoanalysis in America: Leading analysts present their work* (pp. 111–132). Arlington, VA: American Psychiatric Publishing. (Original work published 1988)

Dickinson, K. A., & Pincus, A. L. (2003). Interpersonal analysis of grandiose and vulnerable narcissism. *Journal of Personality Disorders, 17*, 188–207. doi:10.1521/pedi.17.3.188.22146

Freud, S. (1912). The dynamics of transference. In J. Strachey (Ed. & Trans.), *The standard edition of the complete psychological works of Sigmund Freud* (Vol. 12, pp. 97–108). London, England: Hogarth Press.

Gabbard, G. O. (2009). Transference and countertransference: Developments in the treatment of narcissistic personality disorder. *Psychiatric Annals, 39*, 129–136. doi:10.3928/00485713-20090301-03

Greenson, R. R. (1972). Beyond transference and interpretation. *The International Journal of Psychoanalysis, 53*, 213–217.

Horowitz, L. M., Rosenberg, S. E., Baer, B. A., Ureno, G., & Villasenor, V. S. (1988). Inventory of Interpersonal Problems: Psychometric properties and clinical applications. *Journal of Consulting and Clinical Psychology, 56*, 885–892. doi:10.1037/0022-006X.56.6.885

Kernberg, O. F. (1984). *Severe personality disorders: Psychotherapeutic strategies.* New Haven, CT: Yale University Press.

Kernberg, O. F. (2007). The almost untreatable narcissistic patient. *Journal of the American Psychoanalytic Association, 55*, 503–539.

Kohut, H. (1968). The psychoanalytic treatment of narcissistic personality disorders: Outline of a systematic approach. *Psychoanalytic Study of the Child, 23*, 86–113.

Kohut, H., & Wolf, E. S. (1978). The disorders of the self and their treatment: An outline. *The International Journal of Psychoanalysis, 59*, 413–425.

Miller, J. D., Campbell, W. K., & Pilkonis, P. A. (2007). Narcissistic personality disorder: Relations with distress and functional impairment. *Comprehensive Psychiatry, 48*, 170–177. doi:10.1016/j.comppsych.2006.10.003

Newton-Howes, G., Tyrer, P., & Johnson, T. (2006). Personality disorder and the outcome of depression: Meta-analysis of published studies. *British Journal of Psychiatry, 188*, 13–20. doi:10.1192/bjp.188.1.13

Ogrodniczuk, J. S., Piper, W. E., Joyce, A. S., Steinberg, P. I., & Duggal, S. (2009). Interpersonal problems associated with narcissism among psychiatric outpatients. *Journal of Psychiatric Research, 43*, 837–842. doi:10.1016/j.jpsychires.2008.12.005

Ornstein, P. H. (2006). Chronic rage from the underground: Reflections on its structure and treatment. In A. Cooper (Ed.), *Contemporary psychoanalysis in America: Leading analysts present their work* (pp. 449–464). Arlington, VA: American Psychiatric Publishing. (Original work published 1993)

Pincus, A. L., Ansell, E. B., Pimental, C. A., Cain, N. M., Wright, A. G. C., & Levy, K. N. (2009). Initial construction and validation of the Pathological Narcissism Inventory. *Psychological Assessment, 21*, 365–379. doi:10.1037/a0016530

Pincus, A. L., & Wiggins, J. S. (1990). Interpersonal problems and conceptions of personality disorders. *Journal of Personality Disorders, 4*, 342–352. doi:10.1521/pedi.1990.4.4.342

Stinson, F. S., Dawson, D. A., Goldstein, R. B., Chou, S. P., Huang, B., Smith, S. M., . . . Grant, B. F. (2008). Prevalence, correlates, disability, and comorbidity of DSM–IV narcissistic personality disorder: Results from the Wave 2 National Epidemiologic Survey on Alcohol and Related Conditions. *Journal of Clinical Psychiatry, 69*, 1033–1045.

Wolf, E. S. (1988). *Treating the self: Elements of clinical self psychology.* New York, NY: Guilford Press.

8

AFFECT REGULATION AND MENTALIZATION IN NARCISSISTIC PERSONALITY DISORDER

SERGE LECOURS, RACHEL BRIAND-MALENFANT, AND EMILIE DESCHENEAUX

Pathological narcissism is a complex, multifaceted phenomenon that encompasses a wide range of levels of functioning (Pincus & Lukowitsky, 2010; Ronningstam, 2009). Patients diagnosed with a narcissistic personality disorder (NPD) are a subset of narcissistic individuals presenting themselves as grandiose and arrogant. In this chapter, we examine an aspect of the psychological functioning of this group of patients that has been somewhat neglected in clinical writings and research, namely, affect regulation and mentalization. We think that a closer look at some nondeclarative mechanisms of affect regulation might shed some light on phenomena that arise in the psychological treatment of patients with NPD.

In a nutshell, our affect regulation–based model integrates a psychoanalytic conceptualization of mentalization, emotion theory, and a neurocognitive understanding of memory. It posits that early experiences of helplessness and denigration lead to feelings of shame that are concretely experienced and too painful to bear because of their traumatic nature. The

DOI: 10.1037/14041-008
Understanding and Treating Pathological Narcissism, J. S. Ogrodniczuk (Editor)

narcissistic solution to the regulation of these experiences is to build an inflated impression of self-worth in order to avoid unmentalized feelings of inadequacy as well as internalized self-denigrating attacks. Moreover, in an attempt to circumvent future potential interpersonal experiences of humiliation, learned action-based denigrating relational patterns are actively adopted and maintained in relationships with others. We propose that any successful psychotherapy facilitates mentalization and improved emotion regulation by modifying the proceduralized narcissistic coping solutions through a convergence of means: the exposure to painful affective states, their increased tolerance, and the extinction of narcissistic coping mechanisms; the instauration and maintenance of an empathic and benevolent interpersonal ambiance, which help create new interpersonal and intrapersonal procedures; and the labeling and articulation of emotional experience, which increase the capacity to differentiate painful mental states and inhibit compensatory strategies for emotional regulation. The rest of the chapter "unpacks" the main elements of this dense summary and draws more explicit implications for the psychotherapy of NPD.

HOW CAN PATHOLOGICAL NARCISSISM BE UNDERSTOOD IN TERMS OF AFFECT REGULATION AND MENTALIZATION?

In the *Diagnostic and Statistical Manual of Mental Disorders* (4th ed., text rev.; *DSM–IV–TR*; American Psychiatric Association, 2000), the NPD represents a prototype of pathological narcissism. Grandiosity is the essential feature of the disorder (Gunderson, Ronningstam, & Smith, 1995), and it clearly underlies more than half the diagnostic criteria (grandiose sense of self, fantasies of unlimited success, belief in specialness, requirement of admiration, sense of entitlement). Another important feature is a type of interpersonal antagonism expressed through callousness and denigration (exploitativeness, lack of empathy, envy, and arrogance). In extreme forms, such as in malignant narcissism (Kernberg, 1984; Ronningstam, 2009), this antagonism can reach levels found in antisocial personalities. Although it is somewhat secondary in the NPD description, this antagonistic feature might be underestimated in the *DSM* definitions of NPD (Westen & Shedler, 1999).

Grandiosity and Arrogance

We consider two important features of NPD, grandiosity and arrogance, to be broad regulatory measures aiming at countering intense feelings of helplessness and shame, one mostly intrapersonal (inflated sense of self-worth) and the other mainly interpersonal (denigration of others). The intrapersonal–interpersonal distinction is obviously relative because grandiose exhibitionism and entitlement, for instance, can easily have an interpersonal impact (Pincus & Lukowitsky, 2010), but it brings some clarity to our presentation. Throughout this chapter, we focus on the grandiose version of the NPD. Other "shyer" or more vulnerable presentations of pathological narcissism have been described. Because pathological narcissism is currently conceptualized as manifesting both grandiosity and vulnerability in oscillation (Ronningstam, 2009), our discussion of the core vulnerability of NPD and its narcissistic regulatory solutions should be relevant to all forms of pathological narcissism.

Affect Regulation and Mentalization

We maintain that affect regulation is not restricted to mood regulation. Because affect is generally defined as an inclusive category for a variety of valenced (pleasant–unpleasant) motivational experiences, including emotion, mood, and drive, affect regulation has a wider application than mood regulation. In NPD, affect regulation also subsumes the regulation of shame. Our basic assumption is familiar to researchers and clinicians: Grandiosity and arrogance are strategies for "bypassing" helplessness and shame. However, our perspective on affect regulation differs by emphasizing the role of nonsymbolic mental contents and processes and their mentalization. We define *mentalization* as the transformation of an affect's core somatic and behavioral components (forming its basic action tendency) through the intervention of a combination of mechanisms, including nonsymbolic relational processes and symbolic operations such as representation and symbolization (Lecours, 2007; Lecours & Bouchard, 1997). At its lowest level of mentalization, an affect is experienced as a bodily event with no significant subjective meaning. With further processing, it can be known as a concrete psychological phenomenon, felt as "real" and intolerably painful, needing thus to be dealt with urgently. When an affect is well mentalized, it is tolerated, felt, and owned as a subjective experience; it has a symbolic "as-if" quality and can be reflected on or metacognitively elaborated (Fonagy, Gergely, Jurist, & Target, 2002; Lecours & Bouchard, 1997; Semerari et al., 2003). In another highly compatible vernacular, nonsymbolic or unmentalized aspects of affect regulation can be construed as governed by nondeclarative memory processes and structures (Lecours, 2007). We thus reformulate some well-known hypotheses about NPD in terms of emotional memory (classical conditioning), proceduralized attempts to regulate it (through thoughts or actions), and interpersonal ways of being, again involving emotional and procedural memory.

Nondeclarative Memory Systems

We begin with a refresher on nondeclarative memory systems. Classical conditioning, or emotional memory, and procedural memory are two forms of nondeclarative memory, that is, a memory that cannot be consciously "declared" (as opposed to forms memory that can become conscious such as autobiographical or semantic memory). *Classical conditioning* is an associative memory in which, as in the famous Pavlovian experiment, a neutral sensory perception (bell) is associated with another sensory stimulus (food), which spontaneously evokes a somatic (or emotional) response (salivation); after pairing the two stimuli, the neutral stimulus becomes capable of unconsciously triggering the somatic response (the bell triggers salivation). *Procedural memory* is the nonconscious memory of how to do things (e.g., how to ride a bicycle). With practice, sequences of actions can be executed automatically, without the intervention of a conscious recall of the required steps. Other nondeclarative memory systems exist, but these two are the most relevant to psychotherapy (Davis, 2001).

Contrasting Models of Mentalization

Our model of mentalization differs from Fonagy et al.'s (2002) conceptualization of mentalizing and reflective functioning in many ways. Our model was initially inspired by early French psychoanalytic contributions on mentalization, which put emphasis on the transformation of affective-drive somatic derivatives through the acquisition and organization of mental representations (Luquet, 2002; Marty, 1991), whereas Fonagy's model posits the acquisition of a theory of mind through the development of cognitive abilities facilitated by a secure attachment context. Consequently, and more importantly, we see the formal characteristics of the different types of unmentalized experiences as stemming from the properties of the memory systems interacting to shape an affective response and not as a return to modes of thinking anterior to the acquisition of the fully developed mentalization ability. For instance, Fonagy understands psychic equivalence observed in adults as such a retrogression. Psychic equivalence, characterized by a mind–world isomorphism making subjective experiences feel too real and alternative perspectives rare or nonexistent (Bateman & Fonagy, 2006), is for us the consequence of the activation of emotional memory networks in their sensorimotor form, triggered with the felt urgency and actuality typical of high arousal conditioned emotional memory (e.g., the absolute conviction of the imminence of danger in the triggering of a phobic response).

This difference of focus brings about differences in the conceptualization of change. Since emotional and procedural memory systems are impermeable to direct verbal–symbolic action because of their heterogeneity, we see the modification of nondeclarative structures in personality disordered patients as occurring principally through nondeclarative mechanisms, as opposed to Bateman and Fonagy's (2009) mentalization-based treatment, which "aims to strengthen patient's capacity to understand their own and other's mental states in attachment context" (p. 1355) in order to address multiple issues related to affect regulation. However, although Bateman and Fonagy (2009) concentrated their therapeutic efforts on improving what they called *explicit mentalization* (declarative components of mentalization), their actual treatment also offers many avenues for the strengthening of what they referred to as *implicit mentalization* (nondeclarative components of mentalization). For instance, basic mentalizing techniques such as "stop, listen, look" or "stop, rewind, explore" exercise the patient to pay closer attention to and explore his or her way of thinking about mental states and emotions, which unavoidably end up modifying patients' (procedural) ways of acting (here, focusing attention, act curious, explore) toward their own or others' emotions (Bateman & Fonagy, 2006). In addition, other general relational factors (e.g., offering support, empathy) produce changes in nondeclarative structures in mentalization-based treatment.

WHAT IS PATHOLOGICAL NARCISSISM TRYING TO AVOID OR COMPENSATE?

Research on the etiology of NPD is remarkably scant. As is the case for all major mental disorders, the "making" of a clinically significant NPD involves the interaction of temperamental factors, problematic developmental-attachment issues, and early adverse or traumatic interpersonal events. We concentrate on the shaping of affect regulation and mentalization, clearly at the intersection of the etiological factors enumerated above, in order to provide a fresh look at the construction of the intrasubjective and intersubjective regulatory strategies of NPD patients.

Shame and Helplessness

Shame is often presumed to be the central affect of narcissistic pathologies (Broucek, 1982; Morrison, 1986; Wurmser, 1981). In its fully developed form, shame is the painful feeling of having one's self exposed to the disapproving eye of another. At optimal "doses," shame has an adaptive value: It reinforces social cohesion through conformity to shared ideals, or it fuels motivation to change (Izard, 1991). However, shame can also have a disorganizing impact on the self when it occurs too early during development (when the self is vulnerable and highly impressible), too frequently (e.g., chronic or systematic devaluation), or too intensely (e.g., in abuse). It has been suggested that, prior to the emergence of shame proper (i.e., 12 to 18 months of age: Lewis, 1982), when negative affects are undifferentiated, a traumatic event can lead to a profound state of distressed helplessness, constituting a precursor to shame (Krystal, 2000). A perceived failure to initiate, maintain, or extend a desired emotional engagement with a caregiver has also been seen as provoking an early form of shame response (Broucek, 1997). Hence, the aspect of self functioning that is disrupted by shame varies according to the level of development achieved when self-thwarting occurs. For instance, systematic shaming of a child's elated exhibitionistic bursts at Mahler's practicing period (Schore, 2003), when language development has not yet occurred, is more injurious to the future adult's self organization and self-esteem than, say, a boy being ridiculed whenever he puts on a precocious "manly" attitude during his oedipal phase. Common to all experiences of shame is a painful feeling or displaying of a lack of competence, efficacy, adequacy, or agency. However, a range in the severity or pathology of shame experiences is postulated (Ciccone & Ferrant, 2009): from a shame about being or existing (Roussillon, 1999; Wurmser, 1997), based on a primary state of helplessness, to a shame about more mature self-states, such as one's virility in the example given above, with corollary levels of self-fragmentation and depletion. For the rest of the chapter, we use the term *shame* in reference to all forms of shame and its less differentiated precursors. As for NPD, shame is thought to emerge from the earlier experiences of helplessness and intersubjective inefficacy, resulting in a more borderline level or identity-defining feeling of inadequacy (e.g., "What is my value as a human being?"), in contrast to later experiences of shame, at the heart of more neurotic narcissistic preoccupations, where, for instance, doubts about one's sexual powers take the forefront (e.g., "What is my level of desirability as a man?").

Nondeclarative Aspects of Shame

Overwhelming experiences of shame are intolerable for the child. Just as intense fear can lead to a posttraumatic stress disorder, intense shame can have a traumatic impact. These disorganizing forms of shame are essentially registered as nondeclarative, classically conditioned emotional memory (for a discussion of traumatic fear, see LeDoux, 1996). Classically conditioned emotions are encoded in a richly embodied form (the amygdala-hypophysis connection with rapid and direct stimulation of motor activity and somatic activation), and they are tightly associated with the sensory information that is perceived during the emotional event. This bodily connection, because of its sensorimotor nature, is thus basically unmentalized. The conditioned sensory information acts as a trigger to the full conditioned emotional reaction.

LeDoux (1996) argued that this conditioned memory, linking sensory data to emotional activation, is indelible. Emotional reactivity is reduced, not by "forgetting," but by an active inhibitory process named extinction: When the conditioned stimulus is presented but not followed by the initial consequence, the emotional response is reduced. To illustrate, if a child is ridiculed when he expresses sadness, thus provoking shame, the experience of sadness is associated with shame. If this shaming is systematic, the child learns to not show sadness; in effect, he becomes phobic of sadness (McCullough et al., 2003). If, however, the child shows sadness and this expression is no longer followed by denigration, the fear of suffering shame is reduced and the avoidance of sadness is extinguished. NPD patients essentially become phobic of whatever behavior has been shamed or treated as weak in order to avoid the intolerable shame-related affects. Whenever the shame-inducing stimulus is presented to the individual, the shame response is triggered and avoided.

In addition to learning to associate sensory data to an emotional reaction, the individual also learns how to act with himself and with shame-arousing others. The classical psychoanalytic formulation of such a process is the internalization of the relationship in the form of self and object representations. The unattuned and denigrating relationship is learned as a whole through observation and is encoded into behavior patterns. That is, while children are shamed, they learn how to shame themselves and others. This embodied observational learning, which probably operates through the intervention of mirror neurons (Gallese, 2009), is compatible with object relations formulations: An individual can at times act the role of the victim and at other times the role of the aggressor. However, what is not sufficiently acknowledged in these models is the procedural and action-based nature of the learning. Thus, using his early interpersonal interactions as models, the NPD patient learns to scorn and criticize himself and others. These actions, often mental actions that manifest themselves as self-derogatory internal remarks, are learned as ways of being with oneself and others, and they are associated with the shame-provoking stimulus. NPD patients harshly condemn themselves for having been needy or vulnerable, for instance, but at other times they are the ones denigrating others for being needy or vulnerable. These learned reactions of affect phobia and of denigrating vulnerability "on sight," either in oneself or in others, are very likely important contributing factors to the lack of empathy found in NPD patients.

HOW ARE THE NARCISSISTIC COPING SOLUTIONS FORGED?

Early experiences of abuse, misattunement, and denigration can elicit very painful states of shame-related affects. The avoidance of these unmentalized affects is requisite to the survival of the child's sense of self-integration.

Psychoanalytic models have described a range of defense mechanisms used by NPD patients for warding off a profound sense of inadequacy: splitting, dissociation, and the creation of a grandiose self. These mechanisms can be reformulated in terms of nondeclarative, mental procedures that can be associated with shame-inducing interpersonal situations and automatically triggered in order to avoid the anticipated painful affect (Gillett, 1996; Westen & Gabbard, 2002a). Are they regulatory or defense mechanisms? The difference is a question of conceptual emphasis: Although defense mechanisms can be conceived as unconscious affect regulation mechanisms, to call them "defense" mechanisms implies the operation of a protective agency such as ego or self. The bottom line is that these strategies serve the function of avoiding unbearable shame. Thus, grandiosity can become an automatically activated affective structure to suppress self-depletion, that is, the pleasurable elation-saturated fantasy of omnipotence can be recruited to cover up the profound pain of unmentalized shame. In other words, NPD patients grow "addicted" to omnipotence as a coping solution for the regulation of shame. The more pervasive the state of shame, the more exaggerated and chronic becomes the attempt to undo the experience of self fragmentation.

Arrogance can also become proceduralized as a means to establish a dominant relationship with others, as a kind of "preventive strike" against the chance of being humiliated or domineered. "Offense is the best defense," the NPD patient might say. Arrogance is modeled from early abuse, with a turning of passivity into activity, a taking control over, and undoing of, intolerable helplessness in the presence of an overbearing figure. Psychoanalytic formulations have designated this mechanism as identification to the aggressor.

Grandiosity as a way of being (acting with self and others) can also be learned through reinforcement. Mitchell (1988) showed that grandiosity can become a type of relational engagement, based on early significant relationships that value narcissistic involvement. For example, grandiosity is reinforced as an essential mode of interacting with a grandiose parent insisting on being mirrored by his child's accomplishments. Here, not being grandiose would mean risking being abandoned and thus being faced with unbearable affects.

Thus, to regulate self-depletion, a series of mental and behavioral actions can become registered as procedural memory. All interpersonal encounters evoking "vulnerable" feelings such as dependence, neediness, envy, inferiority, or helplessness activate the narcissistic "defense" or regulatory solution. When these regulatory mechanisms are not successful in creating the impression of mastery, superiority, or competence, the unarticulated deflated self affect is experienced in a vague depressive affect, which explains why grandiosity can be unstable and can oscillate with depression, as reality inevitably contradicts the narcissistic illusion of perfection.

HOW CAN NONDECLARATIVE REGULATORY SOLUTIONS BE REDUCED OR MODIFIED?

Having recognized the issues of shame regulation described above, one might wonder how they differ from mainstream psychoanalytic formulations of NPD pathology (self-structure, object relations). Differences emerge when the properties of nondeclarative memory structures and processes are fully taken into account and their implications for the psychological treatment of NPD made more explicit.

Some psychoanalysts have begun addressing the contribution of nondeclarative memory systems to theories of change (Boston Change Process Study Group, 2007; Davis, 2001; Fosshage, 2005; Westen & Gabbard, 2002a, 2002b). As a heuristic shortcut, one can associate relational curative factors to nondeclarative memory systems and self-awareness to declarative systems. Some have discussed the fundamental heterogeneity of nondeclarative and declarative memory systems (see Fosshage, 2005): They operate independently, in parallel, and are governed by different cerebral structures. One very important implication for psychotherapy is that declarative processes cannot directly modify nondeclarative structures. In other words, interpretation cannot directly alter emotional-associative or procedural structures. Think of how phobias are resistant to the awareness of their irrationality or how one cannot learn not to overly slice a tennis backhand just by knowing that it is not appropriate. How the declarative and nondeclarative systems are precisely related is still open to speculation.

How, then, can we modify nondeclarative structures in psychotherapy? Essentially through nondeclarative mechanisms. Self-awareness can temporarily inhibit a nondeclarative sequence, but it cannot directly modify it. Again, think of the momentary relief and freedom from the automaticity of unconscious process that is provided by a meaningful interpretation; the change does not last and the psychoanalytic theory of technique informs us that it has to be "worked through" by further interpretive work. This inhibitory interaction has been documented by McClelland in his work on implicit and self-attributed (explicit) motives (McClelland, Koestner, & Weinberg, 1989). Implicit (nondeclarative) motives are the "default" guiding forces, they motivate spontaneous and automatic behavior, but when an explicit (declarative) motive is activated, the latter dominates motivation as long as it is present in working memory. When it leaves conscious awareness, implicit motives take back the lead. Again, to illustrate, the overly sliced backhand is operative in a live tennis match. However, if we remind ourselves to bring the racquet down and use an upward swing, the slice is suspended and replaced with a flat or top-spin backhand. When play resumes and the instructions for a good backhand fall out of awareness, the heavy slice returns. However, declarative systems do matter; the following section explains how self-awareness can contribute to the creation of new nondeclarative structures.

Changing Nondeclarative Narcissistic Structures

We suggest that three broad "fronts" have to be addressed simultaneously for an optimal reduction of nondeclarative narcissistic regulatory strategies.

Building Affect Tolerance

Tolerance for shame and vulnerable emotions has to be increased. This essentially occurs through the extinction of the shame and fear-of-shame responses through classical learning mechanisms. Extinction is achieved through the patient's repeated exposure to shame and vulnerable self-states. Exposure is a ubiquitous phenomenon in successful psychotherapy, whatever the therapist's theoretical persuasion. An active, empathic, and compassionate exploration of the patient's painful emotional states progressively and "silently" builds the capacity to tolerate vulnerable affects.

Reducing Self-Denigrating and Creating Benevolent Procedures

Procedural ways of denigrating self and others have to be inhibited, and benevolent ways of being with self and others have to be created. These changes usually take place in the "internalization" of a more empathic and compassionate relationship. In other words, new ways of interacting with self and others are created, and they eventually dominate at the end of a success-ful treatment.

The transformation of emotional memory and procedural knowledge takes time because new structures can be created only through direct exposure or practice. In addition, maladaptive structures do not disappear, so new permissive structures have to be built over them, and they have to eventually predominate if they are to guide experience and behavior. This is especially true of NPD individuals who have been systematically devalued over the years, thus having thoroughly rehearsed their pathological strategies for avoiding shame.

Expanding Self-Awareness

Self-awareness has to be expanded. Essentially, the creation of more complex declarative meaning networks builds an increasingly efficient and constant inhibitory effect on automatically triggered nondeclarative (emo-tional and procedural) systems. For instance, if an NPD patient learns that he wrongly anticipates being ridiculed for showing sadness, even with his partner who welcomes such reactions, he eventually becomes able to suspend his tendency to mock sadness long enough to expose himself to being sad without being scorned. Self-knowledge can thus contribute to the creation of new more adaptive nondeclarative structures; in this case, more tolerance of sadness and a more assertive attitude toward the expression of sadness.

Implications for the Psychological Treatment of NPD

When considering the process of psychotherapy with NPD patients more specifically, the following considerations can usefully guide therapeutic interventions. The general goal of psychotherapy with NPD patients, in terms of affect regulation and mentalization, is to help patients increase their tolerance of shame so that they can further mentalize it. Two factors impede the realization of this objective: the painfully traumatic and unmentalized nature of shame-related affects, forcing their avoidance; and the regulatory procedures created to ward off these affects (grandiosity and arrogance). These two factors are intertwined and can be regarded as the two sides of the same coin: Shame is "too hot to handle" and so has to be avoided; the encapsulation (dissociation, splitting) of shame hampers its mentalization. That is why we feel that the building of shame tolerance has to be worked on concurrently with the reduction of the narcissistic procedures. However, the suspension of narcissistic regulatory mechanisms requires sufficiently robust declarative resources (executive functions, ego strength) so as to achieve a truly inhibitory effect on procedural structures.

Primacy of Nondeclarative Curative Factors

Because affect intolerance, grandiosity, and arrogance are based on nondeclarative structures and mechanisms, and because declarative structures for affect regulation are usually weak in these patients, we think that therapeutic efforts should place more attention on nondeclarative relational factors in the psychotherapy of severely unmentalized pathologies such as NPD, especially at the beginning of treatment when affect tolerance is at its lowest. The mentalization of nondeclarative structures is usually achieved in psychotherapy through the concurrent action of bottom-up processes (working on nondeclarative structures to facilitate the use of declarative mechanisms) and top-down processes (using declarative mechanisms to reduce nondeclarative structures). With severe personality disordered patients, the first kind of processes has to be preponderant. Otherwise, without sufficient affect tolerance, interventions aiming at increasing self-awareness are experienced as threatening the patient's fragile sense of self (either by opening the door to painfully unmentalized affects and the consequent self-fragmentation, or by being concretely misread as critical or denigrating remarks by the therapist). Thus, we suggest that interpretations have to be preceded by a "preparatory work" on nondeclarative structures for NPD patients. Again, this is not a new idea (see, e.g., Bernstein, 2010), but its formulation in terms of declarative and nondeclarative mechanisms is. By contrast, neurotic patients, because of their robust declarative resources and the less severely pathological and less prevailing nondeclarative structures, would benefit more from an emphasis on top–down processes in psychotherapy (Lecours, 2007).

Examples of Relational Ways of Changing Nondeclarative Structures

Here are only a few examples of how the relationship with the therapist acts on nondeclarative structures. In these instances, (inter)action matters more than content in the therapeutic exchange. First, the therapist's manifest openness to and explicit empathy toward vulnerable affects serves as a model for the patient: The therapist values vulnerability, which serves as the basis for a more accepting attitude toward such affects by the patient. The therapist's tendency not to shame patients when they reveal emotions provides experiences of extinction of fear of being shamed. Their ability to acknowledge their own empathic failures and their willingness to repair them also allow for the building of trusting representations of others, again, by extinction of fear of rejection and the creation of more positive emotional associations between the expression of hurt and an open and benevolent receptivity from other. Using affirmative interventions, such as validation (Killingmo, 1995) or signs of appreciation and admiration, the therapist helps create new validating procedures. When therapists "survive" and work to repair the bond after their patients' narcissistic rage (Ornstein, 2009), they facilitate extinction of fear of being dismissed and help build a more accepting attitude toward hurt and anger.

Nondeclarative Effects of Declarative Interventions

NPD patients have been found to present low levels of metacognition (Dimaggio et al., 2007; Nicolò, Carcione, Semerari, & Dimaggio, 2007). In our opinion, the lack of self-awareness and reflective functioning observed in NPD patients rests on affect intolerance. This nondeclarative foundation of self-awareness explains why self-knowledge is so difficult to bring about: Affects are terrifying (the affect phobia and unmentalized nature of emotional memory) and subjected to active internal self-denigrating attacks ("I'm so stupid for being so weak"). In addition to their contribution to self-awareness, interventions aiming at improving the identification, labeling, and understanding of affective states have also a mentalizing impact through nondeclarative mechanisms. The nondeclarative ingredients of verbal interventions are especially consequential in early phases of treatment. For example, a therapist observing that a patient must have felt hurt by his boss's critical remark is doing many things in addition to transmitting declarative information about the patient's emotions: By focusing the patient's attention on feeling hurt, he is arousing this emotional state in him (thus creating an opportunity for exposure); he is not denigrating the vulnerable affect (extinction of fear of being ridiculed); quite the contrary, he is showing interest in his feeling hurt (modeling an accepting attitude towards negative emotions); and he is normalizing and validating the emotion (gratifying a previously thwarted self-need, thus reducing hurt and the need for avoiding pain). All these nonverbal components of verbal interventions combine to create new nondeclarative structures, more tolerant of shame-related affects.

Impact of Declarative Mechanisms on Nondeclarative Structures

The communication of symbolic contents about affects builds declarative structures in many ways. Using the last example, we see that by singling out shame, the therapist is contributing to its differentiation from other negative affects; he is suggesting a causal model for shame, such as being the result of a critical comment; this causal model reduces anxiety about shame by making it predictable; he contributes to a more coherent and complex view of self ("I tend to feel humiliated by critical remarks"); he is implicitly suggesting that the patient has experienced an emotion, that is, "only an emotion" and not an actual humiliating attack (not the reliving of the original traumatic shameful abuse, thus permitting an "as-if," symbolic stance toward emotions and increased metacognition); this symbolized emotion can serve as a signal to the self (Krystal, 1988). All these verbal–symbolic components of verbal interventions conjoin to form a larger, more complex, and differentiated declarative network, which becomes increasingly apt at inhibiting nondeclarative structures and putting symbolic structures to the fore of mental life, thus reducing automaticity in favor of more deliberate and self-serving goals.

CONCLUSION: RELATIONSHIP TO KOHUT'S AND KERNBERG'S APPROACH

We have argued that affect dysregulation in NPD patients rests essentially on unmentalized nondeclarative structures. We have proposed principally nondeclarative therapeutic solutions to the reduction of grandiosity and arrogance: furthering affect tolerance through exposure and extinction and the creation of new intra- and interpersonal, more accepting, procedures. Verbal interventions also create nondeclarative structures by their interactive or relational impact. The symbolic content of interventions, while building declarative networks, cannot directly modify or create nondeclarative structures. However, it can potentiate the creation of nondeclarative structures by momentarily inhibiting unfavorable nondeclarative procedures. As we see it, the nondeclarative processes and structures are modified, even though not always explicitly in terms of theory of technique, by all successful therapeutic approaches to NPD.

Kohut's approach to the treatment of NPD, as we understand it, is in tune with the nondeclarative emphasis of our argument. The process he called *transmuting internalization* (Kohut, 1984) is conceivably what we have referred to as the construction of nondeclarative structures through interpersonal (or intersubjective) transactions. Kernberg's (1984) therapeutic model of NPD, on the other hand, proposes the systematic interpretation of the grandiose self, which amounts to a treatment strategy principally based on declarative mechanisms. Thus, on paper, this approach seems to minimize the contribution of nondeclarative factors in the curative impact of psychotherapy. Now, in practice, the many years needed for the exploration of the defensive function of the grandiose self give many occasions for the "silent" exposure to and extinction of shame and the "internalization" by the patient of a more benevolent attitude toward his self and, thus, a strengthening of affect tolerance. This first "working through" part of the treatment is, in our opinion, at least as much a learning of new nondeclarative ways of being with self and others as an enterprise in "knowing" what grandiosity is about.

One might wonder: If every therapist eventually influences nondeclarative structures, sometimes even without being aware of it, why insist on their importance in the treatment of NPD? Because we feel these nondeclarative structures are at the heart of NPD patients' character organization. Their nondeclarative nature is precisely what makes them so resistant to change. Clearly, we are not submitting yet another "brand" of psychotherapy for NPD. Rather, we underline factors that we think are determinative in any successful treatment of NPD, whatever its theoretical persuasion. We hope we have made the reader more aware of the importance of taking into account the nature of nondeclarative structures and mechanisms. We also hope we have shown how clinicians can optimize the impact of their interventions for the modification of the unmentalized components of grandiosity and arrogance in patients with NPD.

REFERENCES

American Psychiatric Association. (2000). *Diagnostic and statistical manual of mental disorders* (4th ed., text rev.). Washington, DC: Author.

Bateman, A., & Fonagy, P. (2006). *Mentalization-based treatment for borderline personality disorder: A practical guide*. Oxford, England: Oxford University Press.

Bateman, A., & Fonagy, P. (2009). Randomized controlled trial of outpatient mentalization-based treatment versus structured clinical management for borderline personality disorder. *The American Journal of Psychiatry, 166,* 1355–1364. doi:10.1176/appi.ajp.2009.09040539

Bernstein, S. B. (2010). Treatment preparatory to psychoanalysis: A reconsideration after twenty-five years. *Journal of the American Psychoanalytic Association, 58*(1), 27–57. doi:10.1177/0003065110361251

Boston Change Process Study Group. (2007). The foundational level of psychodynamic meaning: Implicit process in relation to conflict, defense and the dynamic unconscious. *The International Journal of Psychoanalysis, 88,* 843–860. doi:10.1516/T2T4-0X02-6H21-5475

Broucek, F. J. (1982). Shame and its relationship to early narcissistic development. *The International Journal of Psychoanalysis, 63,* 369–378.

Broucek, F. J. (1997). Shame: Early developmental issues. In M. R. Lansky & A. P. Morrison (Eds.), *The widening scope of shame* (pp. 41–62). Hillsdale, NJ: Analytic Press.

Ciccone, A., & Ferrant, A. (2009). *Honte, culpabilité et traumatisme* [Shame, culpability, and trauma]. Paris, France: Dunod.

Davis, J. T. (2001). Revising psychoanalytic interpretations of the past: An examination of declarative and non-declarative memory processes. *The International Journal of Psychoanalysis, 82,* 449–462. doi:10.1516/0AHF-QTGK-V7WK-VQWB

Dimaggio, G., Procacci, M., Nicolò, G., Popolo, R., Semerari, A., Carcione, A., & Lysaker, P. H. (2007). Poor metacognition in narcissistic and avoidant disorders: Four psychotherapy patients analysed using the metacognition assessment scale. *Clinical Psychology & Psychotherapy, 14,* 386–401. doi:10.1002/cpp.541

Fonagy, P., Gergely, G., Jurist, E., & Target, M. (2002). *Affect regulation, mentalization and the development of the self.* New York, NY: Other Press.

Fosshage, J. L. (2005). The explicit and implicit domains in psychoanalytic change. *Psychoanalytic Inquiry, 25,* 516–539. doi:10.2513/s07351690pi2504_7

Gallese, V. (2009). Mirror neurons, embodied simulation, and the neural basis of social identification. *Psychoanalytic Dialogues, 19,* 519–536. doi:10.1080/10481880903231910

Gillett, E. (1996). Learning theory and intrapsychic conflict. *The International Journal of Psychoanalysis, 77,* 689–707.

Gunderson, J. G., Ronningstam, E. F., & Smith, L. E. (1995). Narcissistic personality disorder. In W. J. Livesley (Ed.), *The DSM–IV personality disorders* (pp. 201–212). New York, NY: Guilford Press.

Izard, C. E. (1991). *The psychology of emotions.* New York, NY: Plenum Press.

Kernberg, O. F. (1984). *Severe personality disorders: Psychotherapeutic strategies.* New Haven, CT: Yale University Press.

Killingmo, B. (1995). Affirmation in psychoanalysis. *The International Journal of Psychoanalysis, 76,* 503–518.

Kohut, H. (1984). *How does analysis cure?* Chicago, IL: University of Chicago Press.

Krystal, H. (1988). *Integration and self-healing: Affects, trauma, alexithymia.* Hillsdale, NJ: Analytic Press.

Krystal, H. (2000). Affect regulation and narcissism: Trauma, alexithymia, and psycho-somatic illness in narcissistic patients. In E. F. Ronningstam (Ed.), *Disorders of narcissism: Diagnostic, clinical, and empirical implications* (pp. 299–325). Northvale, NJ: Jason Aronson.

Lecours, S. (2007). Supportive interventions and non symbolic mental functioning. *The International Journal of Psychoanalysis, 88,* 895–915. doi:10.1516/U7GK-3G8H-1532-2152

Lecours, S., & Bouchard, M.-A. (1997). Dimensions of mentalisation: Outlining levels of psychic transformation. *The International Journal of Psychoanalysis, 78,* 855–875.

LeDoux, J. E. (1996). *The emotional brain.* New York, NY: Touchstone.

Lewis, M. (1982). Origins of self-knowledge and individual differences in early self-recognition. In J. Suls (Ed.), *Psychological perspectives on the self* (Vol. 1, pp. 55–78). Hillsdale, NJ: Erlbaum.

Luquet, P. (2002). *Les niveaux de pensée* [The levels of thought]. Paris, France: Presses Universitaires de France.

Marty, P. (1991). *Mentalisation et psychosomatique* [Mentalization and psycho-somatics]. Paris, France: Laboratoire Delagrange.

McClelland, D. C., Koestner, R., & Weinberg, J. (1989). How do self-attributed and implicit motives differ? *Psychological Review, 96,* 690–702. doi:10.1037/0033-295X.96.4.690

McCullough, L., Kuhn, N., Andrews, S., Kaplan, A., Wolf, J., & Hurley, C. L. (2003). *Treating affect phobia.* New York, NY: Guilford Press.

Mitchell, S. A. (1988). *Relational concepts in psychoanalysis: An integration.* Cambridge, MA: Harvard University Press.

Morrison, A. P. (1986). *Essential papers on narcissism.* New York, NY: New York University Press.

Nicolò, G., Carcione, A., Semerari, A., & Dimaggio, G. (2007). Reaching the covert, fragile side of patients: The case of narcissistic personality disorder. *Journal of Clinical Psychology, 63,* 141–152. doi:10.1002/jclp.20337

Ornstein, P. H. (2009). "Chronic rage from underground": The treatment of a patient with a severe narcissistic disorder. *Psychiatric Annals, 39*(3), 137–143. doi:10.3928/00485713-20090301-07

Pincus, A. L., & Lukowitsky, M. R. (2010). Pathological narcissism and narcis-sistic personality disorder. *Annual Review of Clinical Psychology, 6,* 421–446. doi:10.1146/annurev.clinpsy.121208.131215

Ronningstam, E. F. (2009). Narcissistic personality disorder: Facing DSM–V. *Psychiatric Annals, 39*(3), 111–121. doi:10.3928/00485713-20090301-09

Roussillon, R. (1999). *Agonie, clivage et symbolisation* [Agony, splitting and symbolization]. Paris, France: Presses Universitaires de France.

Schore, A. N. (2003). *Affect regulation and the repair of the self*. New York, NY: Norton.

Semerari, A., Carcione, A., Dimaggio, G., Falcone, M., Nicolò, G., Procacci, M., & Alleva, G. (2003). How to evaluate metacognitive functioning in psychotherapy? The metacognitive assessment scale and its applications. *Clinical Psychology & Psychotherapy, 10*, 238–261. doi:10.1002/cpp.362

Westen, D., & Gabbard, G. O. (2002a). Developments in cognitive neuroscience: I. Conflict, compromise, and connectionism. *Journal of the American Psychoanalytic Association, 50*(1), 53–98. doi:10.1177/00030651020500011501

Westen, D., & Gabbard, G. O. (2002b). Developments in cognitive neuroscience: II. Implications for theories of transference. *Journal of the American Psychoanalytic Association, 50*(1), 99–134. doi:10.1177/00030651020500011601

Westen, D., & Shedler, J. (1999). Revising and assessing axis II. Part I: Developing a clinically and empirically valid assessment method. *The American Journal of Psychiatry, 156*, 258–272.

Wurmser, L. (1981). *The mask of shame*. Baltimore, MD: Johns Hopkins Press.

Wurmser, L. (1997). The shame about existing: A comment about the analysis of "moral" masochism. In M. R. Lansky & A. P. Morrison (Eds.), *The widening scope of shame* (pp. 367–382). Hillsdale, NJ: Analytic Press.

9

CONFLICTS AND DEFENSES IN NARCISSISTIC PERSONALITY DISORDER

J. CHRISTOPHER PERRY AND MICHELLE D. PRESNIAK

There is a rich tradition in the psychodynamic literature surrounding the origins, characterologic dynamics, and psychodynamic treatment of narcissistic personality disorder (NPD) that includes but transcends simple description (see Perry & Perry, 1996). This chapter focuses on two cornerstones of the psychoanalytic perspective on character: conflict and defense. We begin with a review of some of the relevant theoretical and empirical literature concerning conflicts and defenses associated with NPD. We end the chapter with a clinical case that demonstrates the moment-to-moment interplay of these conflicts and related defenses in a selection from a dynamic psychotherapy session. Together, these materials should enable the reader to understand the relevance of conflicts and defenses from the theoretical level down through empirical findings, ending with a demonstration of how they operate together in real life.

DOI: 10.1037/14041-009
Understanding and Treating Pathological Narcissism, J. S. Ogrodniczuk (Editor)
Copyright © 2013 by the American Psychological Association. All rights reserved.

CONFLICTS IN NPD

From the earliest psychoanalytic writing about defenses and unacceptable ideas (Freud 1894/1962), psychoanalytic psychology has posited that conflict plays a central role in psychopathology. At a fundamental level, individuals have a continuous task of expressing their motives (wishes and fears) in a way that adapts to both the internal and external environments. Originally, intrapsychic conflict was viewed as arising when circumstances trigger incompatible motives originating from different psychic structures (e.g., id, ego, superego). For instance, a salient wish, conflicting with a strict prohibition of the wish, results in a sense of threat (i.e., signal anxiety), which the ego then responds to with defensive actions (Freud, 1826/1959). The ego keeps the conflict out of awareness, thereby reducing the sense of threat, while temporarily allowing partial expression of some motives while denying others. The result leads to either symptom formation or compromise formations. Over time the concept of intrapsychic conflict has been broadened to include ideas that certain conflicts are specific to phases of development or that certain motives and defenses are associated with specific object representations that, in turn, affect the individual's interpersonal relationship patterns. As conflict is internal and partly or wholly unconscious, in the end, we can only infer conflict indirectly through what can be observed as anomalies or disturbances. From a measurement perspective, we consider a psychodynamic conflict as a pattern of motives, attitudes, beliefs, and other cognitions, characteristic interpersonal behaviors, object representations, and ways of handling affects that predispose the individual to having difficulty coping with certain stressors. The conflict, developed over time and embedded in the individual's personality, gives a particular pathogenic meaning to certain internal and external life stressors. In this view, stressful life events do not directly lead to the development of symptoms; rather, particular life events have a stressful meaning in part because the conflict gives it that meaning. Together, stressor and conflict function somewhat like a lock and key, which, mediated by defense mechanisms, lead to the onset of a symptom pattern, such as depression, anxiety, or impulsive behavior, or to attempts to avoid awareness of something related to the conflict. This view has evolved from ego psychology, but it also incorporates aspects of object relational and self psychology. This section summarizes findings about specific conflicts associated with NPD and narcissistic pathology.

The following findings were gathered from two studies, both using the Psychodynamic Conflict Rating Scales (PCRS; Perry, 2006). The PCRS assess 14 conflicts, along with 14 companion scales that reflect healthy adaptation to each conflict (Perry, 1990, 1997, 2006; Perry & Cooper, 1986). Each conflict reflects the scores of a series of 8 to 15 items, which are low-inferential statements of some affective, behavioral, or cognitive facets of the conflict. There are seven focal and seven global scales, roughly synonymous with pre-oedipal and oedipal level conflicts.

The first study consisted of 55 individuals taken from a larger ($N = 124$) naturalistic study of individuals with borderline, schizotypal, and antisocial personality disorders compared with bipolar type II affective disorder. NPD was not one of the disorders in the inclusion criteria for the study, with the result that every person with NPD had at least one other study diagnosis. Diagnostic scoring of NPD was made directly in the intake Guided Clinical Interview for the second phase of subject collection ($n = 33$), but by rating videotaped dynamic interviews of individuals gathered in the first phase ($n = 92$; NPD diagnosis $k_w = .47$; NPD continuous score $I_R = .56$). Diagnoses and ratings of conflict were made independently and blinded to one another by different, experienced, clinician raters; for interrater reliability of an early version of the PCRS, mean intraclass $R = .59$ for conflict pattern identification (Perry & Cooper, 1986) and .61 intraclass R for the 14 continuous pathological scales (Perry & Perry, 2004).

The second study also consisted of 55 individuals taken from a larger ($N = 226$) naturalistic study of individuals entering residential treatment at the Austen Riggs Center (Stockbridge, Massachusetts) for treatment of refractory disorders. In the whole study group, 17 (8%) had NPD and 41 (18%) had significant narcissistic traits. Resources allowed only 55 to be rated.

In a report comparing both studies (Perry, 2009), the following six conflicts were found to be associated with the degree of narcissistic features in one or both samples. Each conflict is described below in descending order of the magnitude of the association.

- *Rejection of others*, perhaps the most central conflict in NPD, reflects disturbances in the regulation of self-esteem and affect and the experience of the self. Individuals with this conflict have an underlying view of themselves as small, powerless, unworthy of others' attention, and unimportant. This self-image is generally a repetition from childhood of how the individual experienced others' views of him or her. As adults, these individuals go to great pains to avoid experiencing or exposing this view of themselves to others. To avoid this, they continually make rejecting comments about others. At other times they may be aware of the negative view of themselves, which leaves them with a sense of vulnerability. Thus, this conflict is common to individuals with both the grandiose and vulnerable manifestations of NPD (Perry, 2009).

  One result of these individuals' underlying negative view of themselves is that they are unable to regulate or to have lasting good feelings about themselves (Kernberg, 1970). The following dynamic operates out of each 'individual's awareness. The individuals continually look to others to foster the belief that they should be seen in a positive light because of alleged positive, praiseworthy qualities. If others see them in this way (or if they believe that they do), then they temporarily feel adequate, deserving, and good. Because these good feelings are only reactive, however, they wear off quickly, leaving the individuals to feel uneasy again. As negative feelings about themselves return closer to consciousness, the individuals reengage in defensive maneuvers. They commonly use defenses to promote a sense of power (i.e., omnipotence), overvalue aspects of themselves (e.g., idealizing exaggerating positive qualities), or idealize certain others as if their positive attributes apply to themselves by association. Conversely, these individuals may devalue themselves or others whenever this negative self-view reaches awareness. The devaluation is global in nature, and the individuals take one fault or shortcoming as evidence that they or someone else is entirely failing or worthless.

- *Resentment of being thwarted by others* is a conflict in which individuals believe that others have no right to impose limits, controls, or sanctions to keep them from doing whatever they want. Rather, they believe that they should be able to do whatever they want, whenever they want. They resent others' imposition of rules or expectations as unwarranted interference, regardless of any rules, laws, or duties that they might otherwise agree should generally be followed. Because this is ego-syntonic, these individuals may not be aware of this resentment. Moreover, they may overtly ascribe to the very expectations, duties, and rules that they covertly resent and resist. The exception is rationalized.

Resentment may show in active–direct or passive–indirect ways. When direct, individuals may complain about and openly transgress any sanctions encountered. Although such transgressions might be impulsive or deliberate, they would be imbued with an angry quality, as in seeking revenge. When indirect, individuals rationalize their complaints to cover up a hypocritical position regarding any sense of duty. Resistance then appears defensible, as a response to injustice, rather than self-centered and based on resentment. They then find innumerable ways to resist demands and evade agreed-upon duties or moral obligations.

- *Counter-dependent conflict* characterizes individuals with a fierce need to maintain independence from others. They continually strive to declare their independence through disavowal of their own dependency needs or those of others. They may reject others' attempts to provide material or emotional support to them in order to maintain a facade of self-sufficiency and strength. Their vulnerabilities lie chiefly in fears of loss of control and autonomy at times when feelings of dependency or affection arise toward another. They eschew nurturing or largesse that others may offer because of the fear of experiencing dependent longings. Such individuals may instead gravitate toward taking care of others' needs, thereby appearing strong. An example of this is the patient with a narcissistic and paranoid personality disorder who entered each therapy session only after handing payment to the therapist, accompanied by a supercilious smile.

- *Dominant goal* is found in individuals who derive their self-esteem largely from seeking to achieve certain goals that override all else in life. They often shun other forms of satisfaction in the single-minded belief that obtaining their chosen goals will result in being valued and treated by others as highly special, in ways reminiscent of childhood praise (Kohut, 1966; Kohut & Wolf, 1978). Fantasies and wishes surrounding the particular dominant goal are used to eschew other sources of satisfaction and meaning in life. The dominant goal conflict leaves these individuals very vulnerable to failure, setback, or other threats to meeting the dominant goal. They are also somewhat insensitive to the emotional support that might otherwise cushion them whenever such disappointments occur. This conflict was described by Arieti and Bemporad (1980) as one of three that predispose individuals to depression. In the Nobel Prize complex, Tartakoff (1966) described a narcissistic variant of dominant goal in which the individual has omnipotent fantasies of power and being special. Goal frustrations and failures can lead to psychological devastation and even suicide because self-esteem and self-image are almost entirely dependent on perceived success (Sperber, 1972).

- *Ambition–achievement*, like dominant goal, characterizes individuals who view themselves as having special personal attributes, such as special talents, abilities, destiny, or goals, and have an intense desire to live up to the expectations of others for their success. Individuals with this type of conflict want the positive feelings that ensue whenever others praise, admire, or otherwise distinguish them for these special attributes or accomplishments. On the other hand, not living up to expectations results in an intense sense of shame and a vulnerability to criticism for disappointing others and oneself. In conflict with this wish to achieve specialness through achievement is that these individuals lack the requisite ambition or real talent or ability to achieve these goals. In childhood, praise may have been directed toward superficial qualities or accompanied partial accomplishments (Kohut & Wolf, 1978), regardless of actual results. This results in some ambivalence about the work necessary to achieve. As a result, these individuals often prefer to plan or fantasize about what they might accomplish to retain special status, rather than actually commit to doing it. Being seen to have the potential for achievement (i.e. making great plans) may paradoxically be preferred to actually striving for achievement. Alternatively, once committed to action, they may self-sabotage, ensuring failure in a way that they can rationalize as accidental. Individuals may derive feeling special for appearing promising regarding future accomplishments, rather than for actual accomplishments in the present.

- *Object hunger* is found in individuals who have an intense need for people to fill an emotional void affecting their sense of continuity of the self. This emotional void leaves them with the feeling that their emotional stability is endangered unless they have an attachment to some person on a day-to-day, hour-to-hour basis; without such an attachment, they have a hunger for attention. This need for attachment is not specific to any one individual or relationship. The individuals may be indiscriminate in their choice of persons to whom they attach. Simply having someone there gratifies the need for another person. The individuals seem grateful for the other's presence and seem to get a sense of stability, meaning, and even identity by the connection, even when that connection is very transient. These individuals may interact in self-centered or promiscuous ways, like Mozart's Don Giovanni. This conflict mirrors the philosopher Berkeley's precept *Esse est percipi* (To be is to be perceived). These individuals seek out others a fair amount of the time in day-to-day as well as social activities. Although they may have some lasting attachments, they also traverse easily from one to another without distress that some attachments are short-lived. The capacity to be alone is very diminished.

Most individuals with NPD have one or more of the conflicts described in degrees varying with their upbringing. Whereas gross childhood traumas, such as physical and emotional abuse, were often absent, there was an accumulation of frequent, even daily, experiences of feeling overvalued, undervalued, or devalued. This resulted in durable disturbances of the self and self-esteem regulation. Kohut and Wolf (1978) described both excessive gratifying and depriving experiences as predominant, whereas Kernberg (1970, 1984) has emphasized the role of severe frustration in the development of pathological internal representations of self and others. As yet, we do not have a systematic empirical understanding of the relationships between factors in the genesis of NPD and associated specific conflicts and defenses. As this becomes available, it should improve our understanding of the pathology and inform our treatment approaches.

DEFENSE MECHANISMS

Whereas the common view is that defenses are usually pathological, their aim is in fact to facilitate adaptation to internal and external stressors and conflict. Research has recurrently found that defenses can be arranged hierarchically as to their general level of adaptiveness. One aspect of character or personality disorder is that individuals tend to rely on specific defenses that often share functions and cluster in certain parts of the hierarchy. Personality disorders rely excessively on so-called immature defenses in the lower half of the hierarchy, but different types of personality disorders have differential preferences for individual defenses (Perry & Bond, 2005).

In his seminal paper, Kernberg (1967) described most patients with NPD as falling within a broad borderline personality organization (BPO), inclusive of other Cluster B personality disorders. He posited that any disorder within BPO is associated with splitting, idealization, projection, devaluation, denial, and grandiosity-omnipotence (Kernberg, 1967). However, this has led to confusion in the personality disorder literature regarding how personality disorders, particularly those within Cluster B, can be differentiated based on defense mechanisms (Presniak et al., 2010). In this section of the chapter, we delineate those defenses characteristic of NPD, indicating how defenses help differentiate NPD from other borderline conditions.

Splitting

Kernberg (1967, 1974, 1984) posited that splitting is the predominant defense mechanism of any disorder falling within BPO. Patients with such conditions show an incapacity to synthesize both positive and negative images of the self and others. Clinically, this is most commonly manifested through alternating between the expression of sides of a conflict, such as the "all good" and "all bad" description of self or others, while denying the complementary side. Although NPD falls within BPO, Kernberg (1974) explained that splitting in NPD manifests itself slightly differently than in other disorders. In NPD, splitting is reflected through the split-off self-states of grandiosity, shyness, and feelings of inferiority that may coexist. However, the latter state is defended through repression and the inflated grandiose state. Therefore, unlike patients with a diagnosis of borderline personality disorder who tend to demonstrate splitting through the vacillation of good and bad images of others and self, patients with NPD tend not to show this vacillation because their split images are defended effectively. It is only through a "narcissistic injury" or during psychotherapy that the devalued self rises into awareness (Gacono, Meloy, & Berg, 1992; Kernberg, 1970). Therefore, splitting is much more difficult to see in patients with NPD, which may explain why the empirical support for splitting in NPD has been weak.

Four studies have examined the association of splitting to NPD, with only one showing a significant positive relationship (Blais et al., 1999; Clemence et al., 2009; Lingiardi et al., 1999; Perry & Perry, 2004). To complicate matters further, one study found a negative correlation between splitting and NPD (Blais et al., 1999). Three studies have compared the use of splitting in NPD compared with other personality disorders, and none found splitting used more in the NPD group (Berg, 1990; Gacono et al., 1992; Hilsenroth, Hibbard, Nash, & Handler, 1993). Paradoxically, these studies may be consistent with Kernberg's assertion that splitting functions slightly differently in NPD compared with how clinicians typically view the defense (i.e., alternating between "all good" and "all bad" images of others). In fact, the report (Clemence et al., 2009) that associated splitting (of others' images only) with NPD studied residential group patients with treatment-refractory disorders who likely experienced narcissistic injuries.

Omnipotence/Grandiosity

The most characteristic defense of NPD patients is their use of omnipotence or grandiosity. Although these two terms have been used synonymously at times, their definitions vary slightly. *Grandiosity* refers to a self-representation (the grandiose self) with attribution of exaggerated positive qualities to the self, wherein the self is seen as superior in comparison with others (MacGregor, Olson, Presniak, & Davidson, 2008). *Omnipotence* refers more specifically to the defense mechanism in which one "acts superior," as though one possesses special powers or abilities (Perry, 1990). Both of these are considered prominent features of NPD. One interesting differentiation between the two patient groups is this: Unlike patients with borderline personality disorder, who have no integrated self-concept, patients with NPD have a highly integrated self-concept. Although pathological in nature, they have a grandiose self-view, which is composed of an amalgamation of aspects of their "real self" (e.g., their specialness as a child that was reinforced), "ideal self" (e.g., self-image as powerful and beautiful), and "ideal object" (e.g., fantasized ever-loving and accepting other; Kernberg, 1970). Thus, individuals with NPD identify with their own ideal self-image and merge this altered view of themselves with how they perceive that others see them. In NPD, the integrated grandiose self-view functions to maintain their relative good functioning, despite the use of lower level defenses or poor object representations or interpersonal relationships.

Two studies have shown that the defense omnipotence is positively associated with NPD (Clemence et al., 2009; Perry & Perry, 2004). However, when NPD is compared to other personality disorders, the results have been mixed. One study found grandiosity to be more prominent in an NPD group (Berg, 1990), but two studies did not replicate this finding (Gacono et al., 1992; Hilsenroth et al., 1993). Overall, it is necessary to clarify measurement issues relating to grandiosity and omnipotence to improve further research on their association to NPD.

Devaluation and Idealization

The use of additional minor image-distorting defenses allows NPD individuals to enhance their self-esteem even further, whenever they are confronted with potential failures or they experience an attack on their self-image (Clemence et al., 2009). The use of devaluation and idealization helps to maintain their grandiose self-view. Devaluation involves attributing exaggerated negative qualities to another object, which allows the NPD individual to dismiss the other as inferior or to dismiss a disappointment as of little import. For individuals with borderline personality disorder, the negative view of others tends to exacerbate feelings of dysphoria and view of the self as damaged (Gacono et al., 1992; Presniak et al., 2010); by contrast, for individuals with NPD, devaluation tends to enhance a grandiose self-view. Others are seen as inferior, which also maintains NPD individuals' interpersonal detachment. Images of others tend to be destructed to such a degree that the internal representations are insubstantial, and although there are some characteristics of real people, they tend to be "lifeless, shadowy people" (Kernberg, 1970, p. 57). In NPD, people are generally divided into those that are special and powerful versus those who are mediocre or diminished. NPD individuals tend to use devaluation of those in the latter category when stress engages their own fear of being ordinary or mediocre.

Narcissistic individuals idealize those who are special, rich, and powerful, which, as Kernberg posited, typically stems from feelings of envy (Kernberg, 1967; Perry & Perry, 2004). However, these objects tend only to be idealized when they are seen as representatives of the self and as objects from which they can gain some value. These relationships tend to be exploitative because NPD individuals feel they have the right to control and possess others and use them to make their own personal gains (Kernberg, 1967). Although the relationships can sometimes appear dependent on others, with closer inspection, it is evident that the NPD individuals are not dependent but instead use the relationships to receive a large amount of adoration. Underneath their exterior, they both distrust and devalue most others. In particular, once a person's value has been acquired, NPD individuals tend to see them as valueless and toss them aside (i.e., they become devalued objects). This is often evident in the therapeutic relationship in which the therapist is initially very strongly idealized, yet, underlying this idealized view, the NPD patient experiences a strong distrust of the therapist. By contrast, Kohut and Wolf (1978) posited that idealization is a reparative process shoring up a weak sense of self, borrowing on the strength of others.

The empirical evidence for idealization and devaluation has been mixed. Three studies have examined the association of these defenses to NPD; two found an association between devaluation and NPD (Clemence et al., 2009; Perry & Perry, 2004), one found an association between idealization and NPD (Clemence et al., 2009), and one found no associations (Blais et al., 1999). Two studies have compared these defenses between personality groups (Gacono et al., 1992; Hilsenroth et al., 1993). Neither found that the NPD group had higher scores on devaluation, whereas both showed higher scores on idealization.

Additional Defenses

The most characteristic defense of NPD is use of omnipotence in support of the grandiose self-view. However, this grandiose self is maintained only through the use of other defenses that disavow their inner experiences and allow them to distort the images of both self and others. Of primary importance is that in NPD their negative self-images (the contradictory splitting state of the self) are repressed and tend to be projected onto other objects (Kernberg, 1970). This sometimes results in a generalized paranoid orientation characterized by distrust and devaluation of others. The association of NPD with projection is generally accepted in the literature (Kernberg, 1970) and is supported by findings from two studies (Clemence et al., 2009; Perry & Perry, 2004). The use of repression has been debated. Some have argued that NPD individuals do not use repression because they have fewer (or even no) unconscious conflicts compared with other patients (Kohut & Wolf, 1978). By contrast, Kernberg (1970) suggested that NPD individuals are often quite successful at repressing material, particularly their negative self-images (Kernberg, 1970). Another possibility is that their ability to keep these aspects of their personality or self-image out of awareness is through their ability to split their self-images and consequently deny the negative self-views. Gacono et al. (1992) described this mechanism as quite characteristic of antisocial personality disorder, but it easily could also be characteristic of NPD. In its most primitive form, any negative images or potential attacks on their grandiose self-image are denied and therefore kept out of consciousness, and in its more advanced level, rationalization is used whereby evidence of any negative self-image or exploitative acts are explained away (Gacono et al., 1992). Regardless of whether repression, denial, or both defenses are used, there is agreement in the literature that for NPD patients to maintain their grandiose self-view, the negative aspects of their self-image are kept out of awareness. Together, the defenses of denial, rationalization, and projection protect self-esteem by disavowing any internal experiences of problems through either denying the problem, covering it up or justifying their responses, or misattributing their experiences to others (Clemence et al., 2009; Millon, 1986; Perry & Perry, 2004).

Very few studies have examined these defenses in NPD, particularly because most studies have used the Rorschach-based Lerner Defense Scales (Lerner, Albert, & Walsh, 1987), which do not assess these four defenses except for denial. Three studies have examined repression, two of which reported a negative association to NPD (Clemence et al., 2009; Perry & Perry, 2004). Four studies have examined denial, of which one found a positive association to NPD (Cramer, 1999). Four studies have examined projection, three of which found a positive association (Clemence et al., 2009; Cramer, 1999; Perry & Perry, 2004). Three studies have examined rationalization, one of which found a positive association (Clemence et al., 2009). Only one study has compared mean differences on any of these defenses between NPD and other personality disorders (Hilsenroth et al., 1993). The authors found that the NPD group did not score higher on denial compared with groups with borderline personality disorder or Cluster C personality disorders. No other defense was assessed.

Discussion

Although there are a larger number of defenses that are used by individuals with NPD, we have described the most characteristic defenses. Individuals with NPD have split off their negative self-images from those that are positive, allowing the grandiose self-image into awareness. Although the defense splitting may not be evident until a narcissistic injury occurs, they tend to idealize those that they envy (those that are rich and powerful) and devalue all others. However, when presented with severe failure they may also devalue themselves. These two defenses typically stem from their own fears of inferiority, which they then project onto others. Additionally, they tend to deny or rationalize any experiences that may be perceived as tarnishing or attacking their grandiose self-image. Although these defenses protect self-esteem, they also contribute to poor interpersonal relationships. Presently, the research support for these defenses is modest, partly because of the sparse number of studies focusing on NPD as well as to measurement differences. Only one study specifically focused on defenses in NPD (Perry & Perry, 2004). Although additional studies have included NPD in their samples, sample sizes of patients who met diagnostic criteria for NPD were very small, often less than 15 (Blais et al., 1999; Clemence et al., 2009). Based on our own experience, this is partly because individuals with NPD typically eschew participation in research. Nonetheless, additional and more comprehensive research on defenses is strongly needed with larger NPD samples.

CASE EXAMPLE

The following case demonstrates the interplay of defenses and conflicts at the moment-to- moment level. (The patient's identity has been disguised to maintain confidentiality.) Mr. F. was a man in his mid-20s who was referred to therapy after the end of his relationship with a girlfriend. He felt he was "a basket case." Following a history of abuse, then dependence on cannabis beginning at age 13, he had been abstinent for over a year. He had no other Axis I disorders, except a history of childhood conduct disorder. On Axis II, he had histrionic and narcissistic personality disorders, with significant antisocial, self-defeating, and borderline traits.

The patient felt loved by his parents in his early years, although his mother was strict, not showing her emotions readily, but unconditionally loving and understanding. He lost an eye at age 5 because of illness and remembered the event as suffused with caring. Grammar school went well; there were no academic problems, and he had friends. The parents argued a lot, and the father was physically abusive to an older brother, who in turn from mid-childhood onward became verbally and physically abusive to the patient. The children could tell that their parents were heading for divorce. While Mr. F. was at summer camp at age 12, his mother was hospitalized, allegedly for anorexia; in fact, she had made a suicide attempt. After discharge, she went to live with relatives. After the divorce, the children lived with their father. He was preoccupied with a new girlfriend and exercised no oversight.

From age 14 onward, the patient felt very alone and became hungry for attention. He started lying to build up his self-image, and he did anything he could to be popular. He began smoking, having lots of sexual encounters, and stealing, first from his father, and later elsewhere, such as at a part-time job. There was no direction, caring, or understanding at home. In his later teenage years, he began using cannabis regularly and worked out an arrangement in which he bought the drug for his father, who gave him a share in return. He repeated a grade of high school and went through college in a desultory fashion, while taking a series of jobs that he quit or left before being fired. He got into financial trouble with credit cards. He had intense relationships with girlfriends, desperate to connect with them. Because he was purposefully exhibitionistic, women found him entertaining, even captivating, but ultimately needy. He had concerns about trust and fidelity and became excessively angry when disappointed by them. At intake he was working as a waiter but hoped to develop a new career in drama or finance, make a lot of money, and be seen as important.

He saw a male therapist weekly for 125 sessions; he terminated therapy after about 2.5 years when he moved across the country for economic reasons. The selection below was taken from Session 26, in which raters identified 70 defenses. In descending order, his most prominent defenses were minor image-distorting (30%), obsessional (24%), disavowal (20%), other neurotic (11%), and high adaptive (7%) levels. The high proportion of minor image-distorting defenses reflected that his narcissistic, and to a lesser extent hysterical, character issues were salient in the session. He also tended to compartmentalize his own affective reactions by use of obsessional defenses.

The following selection concerned an episode at work in which he gave away free coffee at the end of a meal to a group of wealthy customers. He saw this as an issue of how good a salesman he was by pleasing people. This raised a conflict of interest between duty to his employer and self-serving actions (i.e., the effect on the bill vs. his tip), as well as issues of how he experienced himself and others.

Note: The conflict types are listed in the monologues below; abbreviations in the monologue excerpts refer to one of the following defense types: minor-image distorting level defense, MIDLD; disavowal level defense, DLD; and neurotic defense levels, NLD.

Dominant goal: But, uh, again, it's also I look at it, you know, well, [Intellectualization (NLD) begins] selling's an art form and it always will be and it always has been and it's 'cause it's recognizing people's needs and servicing those needs. But how do you get that out of a person? You know, how do you get a person that let you know what they want? You have to make some assumptions at first, then you have to grease and you have to, you know. [Intellectualization ends]

Rejection of others: And it's funny, I saw these four ladies the other day, and I'll tell you, [Idealization-other (MIDLD) begins] I looked at them right away and I knew these women are that they liked the service. You could see they were rich. I didn't have to see—I didn't have to see—they could have paid me with two-dollar bills, I would have known they had money coming out of their "tuckus." I mean, the clothing, the look, the attitude, the way they carried themselves, you know, it's funny. [Idealization-other ends] They sat down at the table and I asked them that same line and I let them know that they're going to be served. And you know it's funny and I see the . . . the faces like this. [Omnipotence (MIDLD) begins] So, I go, "You know, ladies, before I leave this table, you all have to do me a favor, right? Smile." You had to see them, all four of them, like they couldn't believe it. It was nuts. Like I mean, I'm just like in their face telling them, "Relax, kick back. You've waited, folks. The waiting's over. Now it's time to get served," you know.

And it's funny, I said to them, I said, "You know what," I brought the food to the table and they ordered something that didn't include coffee. I looked at all four of them and I said, "You know what? Your waiter's going to buy the coffees for you today. God bless. Enjoy them," right. [Omnipotence ends]

Resentment of being thwarted by others: So then my boss comes to me later and he goes— he knew—like he knew. Like he goes—he goes, "You served those four women," and he goes—and I didn't say anything to them not to say anything to the manager about the free coffees. When they left the restaurant, they had thanked Neil for the free coffees, right. And Neil comes up to me, he goes, "[subject's name], did you give them free coffees?" I said, "Oh, I made a mistake," [Devaluation-other (MIDLD) begins] because I didn't want to get caught in this shit, you know, because they think I'm too generous sometimes. [Devaluation-other ends] [Rationalization (DLD) begins] So I do—like I recognize things that you just call. I mean, if it's coffee, it's a bagel, you just do it and it's good business. Again, you can't teach that to anybody. You got to see it and think for yourself, you know. [Rationalization ends]

And, uh, I go to him, [Rationalization-lying (DLD) begins] "Oh, no, no, Neil, you know what I made a mistake on the computer. I forgot to punch in and I filled them out." [Rationalization-lying ends]. He goes, "Well, you know what? Don't worry about it. I was going to give them the coffees anyway, because those are important people and I want them to be happy," you know.

Rejection of others: [Idealization-self (MIDLD) begins] And in my mind I'm just laughing at myself. I'm saying, "[subject's name], man, you know." I mean, if you could even— I mean, if you would have told him yes, you had given them the free coffees, he would have given you shit from here to tomorrow, but he would have loved you, right. And here you are giving them, because— I mean, and no one had to tell me that, right? I recognized it right away and these ladies, for a cup of coffee are thankful and God knows how many cups of coffee they can buy, right? You know? But how can— you can't tell that to anybody. Either you know it or you don't. And I just saw. I smelt it. I said they want service and they're going to get it. And I gave it to them and they were happy, you know. [Idealization-self ends]

Later in the session they returned to this issue with a segue comparing work to school.

Rejection of others: [Devaluation-other (MIDLD) begins] It's totally—no, I mean, and then the grade's important too, right? I'm going to be upset if I get like a shit grade, if I put a hard effort in, you know. But I'm not going to worry about, like if I'm writing one test and I'm worrying about that A after, you know, when I got to write 10 tests in the semester and I get like a C or a B minus and I'm like, "Oh, my God, I got to get that A," that's a crock of shit. You know, all I got to do is do my best and it'll take care of itself. [Devaluation-other ends] [Rationalization (DLD) begins] And that's why I don't worry about it, because I look at the percentage. I calculate my tip at the end of the night, I do my division there, my tips over my total sales. I get my points. And if I'm in the range, my range from 14.5% to 18%, hey, man, I'm making scratch and I'm getting paid for it, you know, and that's an average. And that's all I will get, you know. I don't care if I make 15 cents on a dollar, I make 15%. That's all I think about. I'm not worried about anything else. [Rationalization ends] And those are good points, man. Waiters make good points. You know, salespeople—most sales jobs you're making 6, 7, 8% and even that much, you know. [Devaluation-other (MIDLD) begins] Telemarketing, scumbag business that is, [Devaluation-other ends] they pay you 20%, you know. So we're pretty high in percentage points, you know.

Therapist: That's why when you got sort of the possible conflict of interest with the coffee, because the likelihood is what you've done is you've knocked five dollars off the bill . . .

Patient: Hoping to get the five dollars in my pocket.

Therapist: Well, the chances are they will appreciate the service and [unclear] . . .

Patient: So, what would it be, it would be about 75 more cents for me, an extra dollar. That's what it would work out to. Actually, yeah, 75 cents. You're right. [Rationalization (DLD) begins] But you know what, when I was doing it, I mean, I know that. I wasn't even thinking about—I won't say—I was thinking about let's serve them, you know, and if that meant, yeah, a better tip, it also meant a better name for the house. Okay, it wasn't just for me. I wasn't selfish in the act. It was really a selfless act. You know, 'cause for me a dollar here, a dollar there is not going to change my life. [Rationalization ends]

Therapist: Yeah, sure. No, it's not that it doesn't sound like it made good business sense, but it sounds as if you were acting more on the basis of being a principal of the outfit, of the restaurant, where you would have that option and that flexibility, where you wouldn't have to answer to somebody else.

Patient: But I am constrained.

Therapist: Sure.

Patient: [Displacement (NLD) begins] Yeah. [laughs] Again, it's so funny, man. The little things that we argue about in the restaurant, like you know, it's funny, you know. I mean, it's like I was telling you about spoons, right? [laughs] It could be about anything. You could take shit for [raises voice] "Why did you leave the mayonnaise in that little . . . " like it would be one little mayonnaise and, "You can't leave it like that." [laughs] And I'm like, "Oh, my God." [Displacement ends]

[Undoing (NLD) begins] But everybody works so hard. I have to say it's a tremendous, tremendous staff and we're being recognized for it, you know. We are being appreciated for it. Yeah, they work us very hard because some of the people didn't stick up front and the ones that stuck are going to carry the load right now. And everybody's putting in, on average, you know, anywhere between 10 and 15 hours a day. [Undoing ends]

Therapist: What were you thinking of when you said you argued with the boss?

Comment

The action of giving away the coffee to the customers encompassed issues of his self-image and self-esteem (a salesman who knows the right things to do) versus his duty to his employer. Thus, three conflicts are intertwined.

Relevant to the story is the importance he has placed on succeeding as a salesman and earning good money in his role as waiter. This is at the lead-in to the vignette. At times this dominant goal focus on success overshadows his other responsibilities. For instance, the therapist interprets that he sees himself as if he were an owner rather than an employee. In the first part, neurotic level defenses predominate.

The conflict rejection of others encompasses the self-esteem boosting function of his role in the vignette. He feels powerful for perceiving the ladies' lucrative potential and powerful in how he appealed to them. ("You know, ladies, before I leave this table, you all have to do me a favor, right? Smile.") In perceiving their qualities, his idealization of them also includes a deeper level devaluation ("I would have known they had money coming out of their tuckus"), which enhances his feeling of power. His self-esteem is enhanced by his sense of having the power to please and to extract good tips. The therapist offers interpretations relating his actions to a wish to be appreciated and later to a wish to be powerful ("being a principal of the outfit"). His defenses reflect minor image-distorting and disavowal levels, including devaluation of others, idealization of self and others, omnipotence, and rationalization–denial. There are also some neurotic level defenses, which are more prominent when other conflicts are operating, such as dominant goal.

Resentment over being thwarted by others is reflected in rationalizing how he knows that he is right and his decision to give the coffee away shouldn't be questioned. Instead of seeing his actions as counter to his employer, he rationalizes them as being in his employer's best interests. His defenses include devaluing the reason for the confrontation by the supervisor and rationalizing his action (by a lie) to his employer. These largely deflect the conflict in favor of boosting his self-regard. They also rationalize the effort to get a larger tip.

Case Conclusion

Mr. F. idealized his early childhood, but frequent parental arguments, his loss of an eye, his brother's verbal abusiveness, and his mother's suicide attempt and subsequent absence contributed to an insecure self-image and self-esteem. Later he rebelled against authority (mother's strictness), substituting a false sense of freedom for a sense of direction, and the omnipotence of antisocial behavior for esteem-building recognition through achievement. In the work vignette, these conflicts play out when he breaks the rules, idealizes his own image, and deceives the boss, while still earning some of the attention he longs for as well as a big tip. The therapist recognizes the wish for self-esteem and is quite gentle in pointing out the self-serving aspect of his behavior, allowing the bravado to pass as an effort to increase his sense of power, recognition, and self-esteem. In general, the therapist's approach was supportive and respectful of the patient's need for self-esteem (see Perry, Petraglia, Olson, Presniak, & Metzger, 2012). The therapist also continually interpreted the patient's immature defenses along with conflicting elements of his wishes and fears, especially in their interpersonal contexts. As a result, after 2.5 years of therapy, his defensive functioning improved considerably (effect size of 0.97), bringing him into the neurotic range. He contacted the study on a return visit to town 5 years later to convey his gratitude, stating that he had found the treatment very helpful and continued to improve in his new city.

REFERENCES

Arieti, S., & Bemporad, J. (1980). The psychological organization of depression. *The American Journal of Psychiatry, 137*, 1360–1365.

Berg, J. L. (1990). Differentiating ego functions of borderline and narcissistic personalities. *Journal of Personality Assessment, 55*, 537–548.

Blais, M. A., Hilsenroth, M. J., Fowler, J. C., & Conboy, C. A. (1999). A Rorschach exploration of the DSM–IV borderline personality disorder. *Journal of Clinical Psychology*, 55, 563–572. doi:10.1002/(SICI)1097-4679(199905)55:5<563::AID-JCLP4>3.0.CO;2-7

Bond, M., & Perry, J. C. (2004). Long-term changes in defense styles with psychodynamic psychotherapy for depressive, anxiety and personality disorders. *American Journal of Psychiatry*, 161, 1665–1671.

Clemence, A. J., Perry, J. C., & Plakun, E. M. (2009). Narcissistic and borderline personality disorders in a sample of treatment refractory patients. *Psychiatric Annals*, 39, 175–184. doi:10.3928/00485713-20090401-05

Cramer, P. (1999). Personality, personality disorders, and defense mechanisms. *Journal of Personality*, 67, 535–554.

Freud, S. (1959). Inhibitions, symptoms and anxiety. In J. Strachey (Ed. & Trans.), *The standard edition of the complete psychological works of Sigmund Freud* (Vol. 20, pp. 75–175). London, England: Hogarth Press. (Original work published 1926)

Freud, S. (1962). The neuro-psychoses of defence. In J. Strachey (Ed. & Trans.), *The standard edition of the complete psychological works of Sigmund Freud* (Vol. 3, pp. 41–61). London, England: Hogarth Press. (Original work published 1894)

Gacono, C. B., Meloy, J. R., & Berg, J. L. (1992). Object relations, defensive operations, and affective states in narcissistic, borderline, and antisocial personality disorder. *Journal of Personality Assessment*, 59, 32–49. doi:10.1207/s15327752jpa5901_4

Hilsenroth, M. J., Hibbard, S. R., Nash, M., & Handler, L. (1993). A Rorschach study of narcissism, defense, and aggression in borderline, narcissistic, and cluster C personality disorders. *Journal of Personality Assessment*, 60, 346–361. doi:10.1207/s15327752jpa6002_11

Kernberg, O. (1967). Borderline personality organization. *Journal of the American Psychoanalytic Association*, 15, 641–685. doi:10.1177/000306516701500309

Kernberg, O. (1970). Factors in the psychoanalytic treatment of narcissistic personalities. *Journal of the American Psychoanalytic Association*, 18, 51–85. doi:10.1177/000306517001800103

Kernberg, O. (1974). Contrasting viewpoints regarding the nature and psychoanalytic treatment of narcissistic personalities: A preliminary communication. *Journal of the American Psychoanalytic Association*, 22, 255–267. doi:10.1177/000306517402200202

Kernberg, O. (1984). *Severe personality disorders*. New Haven, CT: Yale University Press.

Kohut, H. (1966). Forms and transformations of narcissism. *Journal of the American Psychoanalytic Association*, 14, 243–272. doi:10.1177/000306516601400201

Kohut, H., & Wolf, E. S. (1978). The disorders of the self and their treatment: An outline. *The International Journal of Psychoanalysis*, 59, 413–425.

Lerner, H., Albert, C., & Walsh, M. (1987). The Rorschach assessment of borderline defense: A concurrent validity study. *Journal of Personality Assessment*, 51, 334–348.

Lingiardi, V., Lonati, C., DeLucchi, F., Fossati, A., Vanzulli, L., & Maffei, C. (1999). Defense mechanisms and personality disorders. *Journal of Nervous and Mental Disease, 187,* 224–228. doi:10.1097/00005053-199904000-00005

MacGregor, M. W., Olson, T. R., Presniak, M. D., & Davidson, K. (2008). *The Defense-Q: An idiographic Q-Sort measure of defense mechanisms. A manual for clinicians and researchers* (2nd ed.). Unpublished manual.

Millon, T. (1986). Personality prototypes and their diagnostic criteria. In T. Millon & G. L. Klerman (Eds.), *Contemporary direction in psychopathology: Toward the DSM–IV.* New York, NY: Guilford Press.

Perry, J. C. (1990). *The Defense Mechanism Rating Scales* (5th ed.). Cambridge, MA: Cambridge Hospital.

Perry, J. C. (1997). The idiographic conflict formulation method. In T. Eells (Ed.), *Handbook of psychotherapy case formulation* (pp. 137–165). New York, NY: Guilford Press.

Perry, J. C. (2006). *The Psychodynamic Conflict Rating Scales (PCRS).* Available from the author, Montreal, Canada.

Perry, J. C. (2009, August). *Narcissistic personality disorder in two samples entering treatment.* Paper presented at the biannual meeting of the International Society for Personality Disorders, New York, NY.

Perry, J. C., & Bond, M. (2005). Defensive functioning. In J. Oldham, A. E. Skodol, & D. Bender (Eds.), *The American Psychiatric Publishing textbook of personality disorders* (pp. 523–540). Washington, DC: American Psychiatric Press.

Perry, J. C., & Cooper, S. H. (1986). A preliminary report on defenses and conflicts associated with borderline personality disorder. *Journal of the American Psychoanalytic Association, 34,* 863–893. doi:10.1177/000306518603400405

Perry, J. C., Petraglia, J., Olson, T. R., Presniak, M. D., & Metzger, J. (2012). Accuracy of defense interpretation in three character types. In R. Levy S. Ablon, & H. Kächele (Eds.), *Psychodynamic psychotherapy research: Evidenced-based practice and practice-based evidence* (pp. 417–447). New York, NY: Humana Press.

Perry, J. D., & Perry, J. C. (1996). Reliability and convergence of three concepts of narcissistic personality. *Psychiatry: Interpersonal and Biological Processes, 59,* 4–19.

Perry, J. D., & Perry, J. C. (2004). Conflicts, defenses and the stability of narcissistic personality features. *Psychiatry: Interpersonal and Biological Processes, 67,* 310–330. doi:10.1521/psyc.67.4.310.56570

Presniak, M. D., Olson, T. R., & MacGregor, M. W. (2010). The role of defense mechanisms in borderline and antisocial personalities. *Journal of Personality Assessment, 92,* 137–145. doi:10.1080/00223890903510373

Sperber, M. A. (1972). Freud, Tausk, and the Nobel Prize complex. *Psychoanalytic Review, 59,* 283–293.

Tartakoff, H. (1966). The normal personality in our culture and the "Nobel Prize Complex." In R. Lowenstein (Ed.), *Psychoanalysis—A general psychology: Essays in honor of Heinz Hartmann* (pp. 222–252). New York, NY: International Universities Press.

10

PATHOLOGICAL NARCISSISM AND THE RISK OF SUICIDE

PAUL S. LINKS

The risk of suicide is often what brings patients with narcissistic pathology to clinical attention, or a death by suicide might be the first indication of the depth of the individual's pathological narcissism. This phenomenon is illustrated in the song "Richard Cory" by Simon and Garfunkel.[1] The song speaks about a prominent individual who commits suicide and no one had been aware of this risk or possible outcome. Managing the risk of suicide in patients with pathological narcissism can be one of the most important yet perplexing aspects of the care for these patients. In this chapter, I discuss the evidence for the association between pathological narcissism and the risk of suicide, the clinical presentation of suicide risk in narcissistic patients, a theoretical understanding of the risk of suicide in such patients, and an approach to managing narcissistic patients at risk for suicide. I begin by defining the terms used in this chapter.

[1]Lyrics are available at http://www.simonandgarfunkel.com/us/music/sounds-silence/richard-cory

DOI: 10.1037/14041-010

Understanding and Treating Pathological Narcissism, J. S. Ogrodniczuk (Editor)

DEFINITION OF TERMS

Both narcissism and suicide would appear to be topics that are clear and easily defined, but in fact there is ongoing debate about how best to define these concepts. For the purposes of this chapter, Silverman and colleagues' (Silverman, Berman, Sandal, O'Carroll, & Joiner, 2007a, 2007b) nomenclature is used, focusing particularly on *suicide-related behavior*, defined as

> a self-inflicted, potentially injurious behavior for which there is evidence (either explicit or implicit) either that: (a) the person wished to use the appearance of intending to kill himself/herself in order to attain some other end; or (b) the person intended at some undetermined or some known degree to kill himself/herself. Suicide-related behaviors can result in no injuries, injuries or death. (Silverman et al., 2007b, p. 272)

Suicide-related behavior has to be differentiated from self-harm or self-injurious behavior. These behaviors involve purposeful infliction of direct physical harm to the person's body without intent to die (Simeon & Favazza, 2001).

Pincus and Lukowitsky (2010) defined narcissism as

> one's capacity to maintain a relatively positive self-image through a variety of self-, affect-, and field-regulatory processes, and it underlies individual needs of validation and affirmation as the motivation to overtly and covertly seek out self-enhancement experiences from the social environment. (p. 423)

Two clinical phenotypes of pathological narcissism may present themselves: narcissistic grandiosity and narcissistic vulnerability (Gabbard, 2009). Narcissistic grandiosity is characterized by the identifying features of narcissistic personality disorder (*Diagnostic and Statistical Manual of Mental Disorders*, 4th ed., text rev.; American Psychiatric Association, 2000) and this person is "arrogant, grandiose, assertive and aggressive" (Ronningstam, 2009, p. 113; Pincus & Lukowitsky, 2010), whereas the patient with narcissistic vulnerability is "shy, vulnerable, insecure and shame-ridden" (Ronningstam, 2009, p. 113; Pincus & Lukowitsky, 2010). The clinical presentations of narcissistic patients were felt to arise from self-esteem dysregulation, affect dysregulation, and difficulties in interpersonal relationships that characterize pathological narcissism (Ronningstam, 2009).

EVIDENCE FOR THE RISK OF SUICIDE

Narcissistic personality disorder is an uncommon diagnosis in community samples compared with antisocial personality disorder and borderline personality disorder; the respective pooled prevalence estimates are 0.61,

1.77, and 1.16 according to Torgersen (2005). As a result, little data exist regarding the risk of suicide in individuals with this disorder. The most extensive community survey undertaken on narcissistic personality disorder, the National Epidemiologic Survey on Alcohol and Related Conditions, did not provide prevalence rates of suicide-related behavior in survey participants meeting criteria for the disorder (Stinson et al., 2008). Stinson et al. (2008) found that community participants who were separated, divorced, widowed, or never married were more likely to meet criteria for narcissistic personality disorder and that narcissistic personality disorder was highly comorbid with bipolar I disorder, substance use disorders, and anxiety disorders. Given these associations, we should anticipate that individuals meeting criteria for narcissistic personality disorder would be at an increased risk for suicide-related behavior and suicide. In samples of suicide victims studied with the psychological autopsy method, narcissistic personality is infrequently identified. However, Apter et al. (1993) studied 43 consecutive suicides by Israeli males ages 18 to 21 that occurred during their compulsory military service. Psychological autopsies were carried out using preinduction assessment information, service records, and extensive postmortem interviews. Based on this methodology, the most common Axis II personality disorders were schizoid personality in 16 of 43 (37.2%) and narcissistic personality in 10 of 43 (23.3%).

These findings may illustrate the fact that the military attracts individuals with narcissistic pathology, and this disorder may be overrepresented among service personnel who commit suicide and service individuals under psychiatric care. Bourgeois and Hall (1993) found a high prevalence of narcissistic traits and personality disorders in active duty military outpatients: 20% of the outpatients met criteria for narcissistic features. This rate is much greater than that found in civilian samples, where narcissistic features or personality disorder is relatively uncommon. The individuals with narcissistic traits or personality disorder were commonly involved in specialized mission groups within the military. These specialized mission groups were defined as requiring advanced education and/or training, having high visibility roles in combat operational environments, receiving extra compensation and entitlements, and having distinct uniform insignia. The authors noted that "the military services, with their structure that provides tangible rewards, attention to appearance, and public displays of reinforcement, may appeal to the individual with narcissistic personality style" (Bourgeois & Hall, 1993, p. 173). Problems seem to arise for these individuals once the organizational reinforcement decreased, in this case from their military service. In summary, evidence from several studies of military personnel (Bourgeois, Nelson, Slack, & Ingram, 1999; King, 1994) suggested that narcissistic traits may make persons select and be successful within a military role. Yet, outside of their military role and without reinforcements for their military role and/or narcissistic behavior, such individuals appear to be susceptible to a host of impairments, as well as suicide.

Another setting where the association between narcissistic pathology and suicidality has been observed is within older adults under psychiatric care. In a study of geriatric patients attending a depression day-hospital, the presence of narcissistic personality disorder and narcissistic personality compared with those without increased the likelihood of being rated a suicide ideator even after controlling for demographic factors, self-reported depression severity, and cognitive function (Heisel, Links, Conn, van Reekum, & Flett, 2007). Heisel et al. (2007) indicated that older adults with narcissistic pathology may see suicide as a means to escape from "the self," as proposed by Baumeister (1990). Older individuals may follow this pathway to suicide because they experience disappointment and psychological pain when they are unable to meet their extreme self-expectations, when they blame themselves for this shortfall, and when they compare themselves against a standard or against previously achieved goals, responsibilities, or physical accomplishments.

In studies of general psychiatric patients, Stone's (1990) extensive follow-up study of 550 patients admitted to the general clinical service of the New York State Psychiatric Institute provided some information on suicide for individuals hospitalized with the diagnosis of narcissistic personality disorder. According to the 15-year follow-up, patients with the disorder or narcissistic traits were significantly more likely to have died by suicide compared with patients without the disorder or traits (14% vs. 5%; $p < .02$). Blasco-Fontecilla et al. (2009) compared suicide attempts among patients with various Cluster B personality disorders. In contrast to suicide attempters with other Cluster B disorders, those with narcissistic personality disorder were less impulsive in their attempts, suggesting that they were more intentional in their suicidal behavior. Attempters with narcissistic personality disorder also reported significantly higher expected lethality from their attempt compared to suicide attempters without narcissistic personality disorder. The authors concluded that suicide attempters with narcissistic personality disorder may be different from other Cluster B personality disorder attempters in that their suicidal behavior is more intentional and less impulsive.

Some recent evidence suggested that narcissistic pathology may be negatively associated with the risk for suicide. Svindseth, Nottestad, Wallin, Roaldset, and Dahl (2008) examined the relationship between scores on the Narcissistic Personality Inventory-21 Item version and violence, suicidality, and other psychopathology among patients admitted to acute psychiatric wards. In their sample, male gender, involuntary admission, severe violence, and high self-esteem were significantly associated with a high level of narcissism. However, the level of suicidality as measured by the Brief Psychiatric Rating Scale was significantly associated with low levels of narcissism. Anxiety, depression, and withdrawal–retardation were also associated with low levels of narcissism. These results may be a function of the particular qualities of the Narcissistic Personality Inventory-21, which is considered to capture aspects of "adaptive expressions" of the narcissistic concept; therefore, these concepts are likely to be inversely related to psychological distress and risk of suicide (Pincus & Lukowitsky, 2010).

In summary, both empirical and clinical observations suggest that there is an association between the risk of suicide and narcissistic personality. However, the relationships may be complex and changeable; certain adaptive aspects of narcissism may lessen the risk for suicide, whereas other, more pathological narcissistic traits may dramatically increase the risk for serious intended suicide or suicide-related behavior.

CLINICAL PRESENTATION OF SUICIDE RISK IN NARCISSISTIC PATIENTS

Assessing the risk of suicide in patients with narcissistic pathology can be uniquely challenging for the clinician, as the following clinical examples illustrate. The theoretical and clinical significance of each challenge is highlighted. In each example, the patient's identity has been disguised to maintain confidentiality.

Absence of Depression and the Denial of Suicide Intent

Ms. A. was a 29-year-old single woman who was hospitalized when she was seen for assessment of suicide risk. The patient had been an accomplished member of a symphony orchestra and, for most her life, had been focused on her music and performing. Six months prior to hospitalization, she had been unsuccessful in capturing a position with a more prestigious orchestra. For the last 2 months prior to her hospitalization, Ms. A. had stopped performing because of her belief that she was dying of "natural causes." She believed that her body and mind were "breaking down"; as proof of this, she explained, "I can't feel anything. I am in a constant state of numbness," which she took as a forewarning that she was going to "pass away." As a result, she cut herself off from friends, withdrew from her musical career, and stopped attending her individual therapy. Although she denied having suicidal ideation or intent, she often discussed her suicide as a theoretical option given that she felt she was going to die. During the assessment, she denied depressed mood, explaining that she was without emotion. However, she endorsed a history of depression some 5 years earlier during which she did feel suicidal. She had started individual therapy during this prior episode of depression. The other main feature of her history was the loss of her brother to suicide a decade earlier.

Ronningstam and Maltsberger (1998) observed that narcissistic patients are unique because the risk of suicide in these patients can be unrelated to the state of depression. For most other psychiatric disorders, suicide risk is most likely heightened during a time when the patient has evidence of comorbid depression. The importance of comorbid depression leading to the risk of suicide has been demonstrated for most psychiatric disorders such as schizophrenia (Haw, Hawton, Sutton, Sinclair, & Deeks, 2005; Hawton, Sutton, Haw, Sinclair, & Deeks, 2005), alcoholism (Sher, 2006), posttraumatic stress disorder (Krysinska & Lester, 2010), and borderline personality disorder (Kolla, Eisenberg, & Links, 2008). Although the risk of suicide is likely to increase when a patient with pathological narcissism is depressed, the expression of a depressed state is not necessary for such a patient to be acutely suicidal. Suicide risk in narcissistic patients can arise from their need to protect their pathological self-image and to regulate their self-esteem. Ronningstam and Maltsberger (1998) discussed that suicide may serve to "attack or destroy an imperfect, failing, intolerable self"; the belief that "I destroy my failing body so that my perfect soul can survive" (p. 262). In addition, patients with narcissistic pathology may deny or disavow any intent to end their life; thus, interpreting their risk of suicide from their clinical presentations can be difficult. They indicated that such patients may have "no conscious intention to die, or at least their awareness of the deadly nature of their act" may be decreased (p. 263).

Ms. A. appeared to demonstrate these two features. First, she denied any symptoms of depression; even though clinical signs of depression were evident from her presentation. Although risk of suicide in narcissistic patients does not require the coexistence of a depressive episode, Ms. A's case could be understood as using isolation and denial to protect herself from experiencing the deep sense of depression that was demonstrated by her demeanor and loss of functioning. Second, Ms. A. denied suicidal ideation when directly questioned. However, in Ms. A's case it was necessary to hear her fear of dying as an expression of her suicidal intent—as the expression of her desire to rid herself of her defective and failing body that had betrayed her and deserved to die.

As these patients avoid acknowledging their emotional vulnerability or brittleness, their mood disorders may be missed or misdiagnosed. Raja and Azzoni (2007) noted that a similar problem exists with patients with obsessive–compulsive personality disorders. As Ronningstam and Maltsberger (1998) indicated, narcissistic patients' histories often reveal very clear interpersonal events that act as precipitants for their suicidal behavior, although typically these patient may be unable "to identify, feel, admit or understand" the importance of the event to their suicidal crises (p. 266). Ms. A. was unable to verbalize the significance of not being chosen for the more prestigious orchestra as the crucial event in her distress and suicidal thoughts. Because these patients do not directly express their risk of suicide and their experience of depression, it is crucial that the clinician be able to interpret the meaning and significance of the risk of suicide in patients with narcissistic pathology.

Severity of Suicide and the Importance of Shame-Based Risk of Suicide (Death Before Dishonor)

Mr. B. was a 45-year-old corporate executive who had a history of five previous suicide attempts. His first attempt had occurred 15 years earlier during the breakup of his first marriage and during a time when he was off work because of back problems. For the first attempt, he ingested an overdose of fluoxetine but did not experience any ill effects. The second attempt, a month or so later, involved taking pills and alcohol, but he woke up from the attempt, called his psychiatrist, and revealed his overdose. Mr. B.'s third attempt was made while he was hospitalized for depression; he attempted to suffocate himself by placing a plastic bag over his head. In recalling the story, Mr. B. indicated that the attempt quickly came to the attention of the nursing staff because he used a black plastic bag that was very noticeable. Some years later, he made his fourth attempt by (in his words) "combining my two approaches": overdosing on medication and placing a plastic bag over his head. On this occasion, he recalled taking a "whole lot of pills," but before he could place the plastic bag over his head he passed out from the overdose. He was found by his partner and taken to a hospital.

Mr. B.'s latest episode of depression began quickly over a 4- to 6-week period. His corporation had closed his branch office in Eastern Europe and had transferred him back to the home office in Canada. The branch office closure was due to the global economic slowdown; however, Mr. B. felt "put out to pasture" and that his work at the home office was demeaning. He did not feel like a member of his executive group in the home office and quickly began to suspect that he would be terminated. Mr. B. considered that the others in the office were envious of his success and the lavish lifestyle he enjoyed in Eastern Europe. His problems with back pain returned, and he rapidly gained 30 pounds.

Feeling increasingly concerned that he would be terminated in front of his colleagues, he decided to end his life while his girlfriend was out of the country for 4 days. He acquired a hotel room and planned to overdose on a large quantity of pills and to suffocate himself with a plastic bag. Mr. B. researched his plan and made sure he had enough pills to take a fatal overdose. He planned to take alcohol to disinhibit himself and to use Gravol to settle his stomach after the ingestion. He locked himself in the hotel room, left a note on the bedside requesting that the cause of his death remain private, ingested all the pills, and covered his head with the plastic bag. By happenstance, Mr. B. was found by a maintenance person before he expired. During the hospitalization, it was revealed that his great uncle had ingested poison and died by suicide. The uncle had taken his life to save the family embarrassment before his reckless lifestyle became public knowledge.

The case of Mr. B. illustrates the relationship between narcissistic pathology and serious risk of suicide. His final suicide attempt was highly intended, carefully planned, and failed only because of a chance rescue. As indicated previously, narcissistic patients may be characterized by attempts that are intended to be highly lethal (Blasco-Fontecilla et al., 2009). Mr. B. related the story of his increasingly serious attempts in a very matter-of-fact manner. The narcissistic patient typically can approach suicide and death by denying, minimizing, dissociating, or rationalizing loss of life (Ronning-stam & Maltsberger, 1998). This picture is similar to that of patients with obsessive–compulsive personality disorder in that their suicide attempts may be planned to perfection yet their lack of emotional distress may lead others to underestimate the risk and need of psychiatric or medical care (Raja & Azzoni, 2007).

In terms of psychological components that contribute to one's risk for suicide, it is enlightening to consider Mr. B.'s risk in terms of Joiner's (2005) interpersonal–psychological theory of suicide. His theory proposed three components that must be present in a person's life to lead to suicide. Each of these components appears applicable to Mr. B., may be relevant to many patients with pathological narcissism, and may be useful in considering steps to undertake to lessen one's risk for suicide.

1. *Acquired capability.* Joiner proposed that individuals develop fearlessness regarding suicide by engaging in painful experiences or repeated acts of suicidal behavior. Mr. B's history is very consistent with this theory; he has a pattern of escalating behaviors that serve to facilitate the next step to more lethal acts. Therefore, ideation about more lethal means should be taken seriously in narcissistic patients and the family should be informed about preventing access to more lethal means (e.g., guns). I would also speculate that the patient's months of exposure to chronic back pain added to his risk for suicide. Patients with pathological narcissism are often highly focused on their internal reactions and experience, in part to master their dys-regulated emotions (Ronningstam, 2009). Patients often focus on their somatic concerns with their care providers. Joiner suggested that exposure to pain may harden one against suffering

and be an indirect pathway to acquiring the capacity to commit suicide. Therefore, Mr. B's risk of suicide may be lessened by taking steps to ensure that he has help to adequately control his chronic back pain.

2. *Burdensomeness*. This component of risk arises because the person feels ineffective or a burden on others. Mr. B. identified that his life lost much of its purpose when he returned to Canada. He felt that he was not able to contribute in the way he had before and that his work was not as challenging. In conjunction with his loss of purpose and his weight gain, his self-esteem, which is vulnerable to narcissistic injury, was shattered. In the months leading up to his last attempt, he felt very vulnerable to dismissal from and humiliation at work. Joiner recommended long-term psychotherapy to challenge the patient's negative thought patterns that contribute to the patient feeling ineffective or that life is purposeless and to work on factors that will bolster the patient's sense of resilience and self-esteem

3. *Not belonging with a valued group or other relationships*. Thwarted belongingness can be either a true or a distorted belief about the presence of a supportive group. Mr. B. perceived that he did not belong with his colleagues at work. He became preoccupied with suspicions and distrust. His perceived loss of stature made him feel isolated from coworkers and he attributed the cause of the distance between himself and others as their feelings of envy. Helping narcissistic patients maintain their network of supports can be an important buffer against an increased risk of suicide.

Shame as a motive for suicide has been recognized in various circumstances (Lester, 1997). In Mr. B.'s case, he felt demeaned by his loss of stature following his transfer from the branch office to his home office. He experienced this significant career change as a very shameful event and stands as an example of the important role of shame in inducing suicide. From a cross-cultural perspective, shame-motivated suicide appears to be more common in some Asian societies (Lester, 1997). A prototypical story is that of a young married woman in rural China who loses face after being routinely criticized by her husband or mother-in-law. The young woman who lives in a highly conflicted family environment may openly voice that she feels her life is worthless. Following another argument, feeling powerless and humiliated, the young woman impulsively ingests pesticides and succumbs to the poisoning before reaching adequate emergency medical services. Such family disharmony, plus the second-class status of women in China, may contribute to the high rate of suicide in young rural women in China and to the unique overall gender pattern of suicides in that nation, which shows that the rate among females is 25% higher than the rate among men (Law & Liu, 2008).

Shame also has been specifically related to suicide in individuals with borderline personality disorder. According to Linehan (1993), shame is an emotion that patients with borderline personality disorder are unable to process; this difficulty can lead to suicide-related behavior. The patient will experience an intense emotion such as anger or sadness, which the environment will invalidate; in response, the patient then experiences strong feelings of shame. This series of interactions is repeated over time, and the individual learns to always respond to their intense emotions with shame.

Shame is also important in explaining the dramatic and sudden suicidal crises that can occur for patients with pathological narcissism. Theoretically, shame may make such individuals more vulnerable because they are already struggling with unregulated self-identity (Ronningstam, 2009). Shame may result from transgressions or failed behaviors that are directed inward, altering self-consciousness and leading to reappraisals of self-worth. Shame leads to humiliation, or the "sense of having been exposed and rendered childlike in stature, diminished in power, status, worth, and importance" (Wilson, Drozdek, & Turkovic, 2006, p. 127). Intense shame is accompanied by a disintegration of the dimensions of the self structure: "the essential vitality of the self feels drained" and the person's ability to take productive action can become immobilized (Wilson et al., 2006, p. 134). Wilson and colleagues (2006) elaborated that "the intensity and severity of shame is directly correlated with high suicide potential and fantasies of killing oneself to obliterate the inner experience of shame" (p. 133). Although clinical theorists have always considered individuals with narcissistic pathology as prone to experiencing shame (H. B. Lewis, 1987), Tangney, Stuewig and Mashek (2007) found that shame proneness was negatively correlated with narcissism but positively associated with the risk of increased psychological distress, suicide ideation, egocentricity, social withdrawal, and drug and alcohol use. Again, the definition of narcissism, which can encompass both negative and positive characteristics, may explain the contradictory findings. Shame also impairs the individual's ability to maintain the dimensions of self and the self becomes "diminished, lost, dissolved, broken apart" (Wilson et al., 2006, p. 134). In this state of mind, rational safe action will often not be available to the patient with narcissistic pathology. Taken together, shame-induced suicide in individuals with narcissistic pathology explains many of the clinical phenomena that are characteristic of this crisis:

1. Suicidal crises can be sudden and unrelated to periods of clinical depression.
2. The patient becomes withdrawn and does not communicate a risk for suicide.

3. The patient feels powerless, worthless, exhausted, and unable to take constructive action.
4. Suicidal behaviors may be very lethal and accompanied with the intent for "self-obliteration."
5. The crisis may pass quickly if circumstances restore the patient's self-esteem. Often with recovery, the patient denies or suppresses the severity of the crisis.

MANAGING SUICIDAL PATIENTS WITH PATHOLOGICAL NARCISSISM

The clinician can take five approaches to manage the risk of suicide and suicide-related behavior in outpatients with pathological narcissism.

- Patients should be routinely monitored for evidence of co-existing major depression or for an acute episode of lowered self-esteem resulting from a felt narcissistic injury. When narcissistic people feel ashamed, they hide their emotions and withdraw from the therapist. To avoid being exposed, narcissistic patients may be deceitful by acts of omission rather than outright lying. Therefore, the therapist has to be sensitive to signs of withdrawal, missed sessions, sudden guardedness, or defensive anger. The therapist probably will have to directly inquire about suicidal thoughts, planning, and intent. To address these issues, patients who have experienced a serious narcissistic injury have to experience a sense of safety within the therapeutic relationship.
- When working with suicidal patients with narcissistic pathology, the therapist should anticipate that during crises, patients will become isolated from family and be less communicative. From the outset of therapy, the therapist should contract to have permission to speak with the patient's significant supports. With this initial consent, the patient's family and other significant supports should be aware of the risk for suicide and for the potential for an acute onset of suicidal feelings. The family must understand how to access help if a crisis arises.
- Because suicide-related behavior in narcissistic individuals tends to arise abruptly, the risk can be lessened by preventing the patient from having access to a means of suicide. Specific inquiries should be made about access to guns or large quantities of pills or proximity to high venues. If guns or large quantities of

pills are accessible in the home, the therapist should enlist a responsible family member or support to remove the items in question. Simon (2007) outlined the principles of gun safety management in patients at risk for suicide and cautioned that the therapist must receive firsthand evidence from the enlisted family member that the means of suicide has been removed and safely secured away from the patient.

- The creation of a stable therapeutic relationship seems to be an important factor that can lessen the risk of suicide in patients with pathological narcissism and should be recommended in the ongoing management of suicidal patients with narcissistic pathology. In the early phases of therapy, narcissistic individuals may require that the therapist attend to their need for acknowledgement and accept their feelings of entitlement. For example, acknowledging the patient's importance and need for recognition often deescalates the narcissistic patient's distress and defensiveness. When some of the narcissistic need is acknowledged and met, further engagement and cooperative dialogue is possible. Kohut (1972) suggested that narcissistic patients may be at less risk of acting out suicidal behavior after they have established a stable transference within a therapeutic relationship and the therapist has established some empathic closeness to the patient's fragmented self. Contrary to other theorists, Kohut (1971) developed the concept that narcissistic patients could form stable transference relationships if they had their narcissistic and exhibitionistic needs met. According to Kohut (1971), a "mirroring relationship" with the therapist, which corresponds to the parental reflection of a growing child's development of healthy narcissism, can provide a therapeutic environment in which a narcissistic individual can achieve some early stability and later growth.

- In some instances, patients with narcissistic pathology are thrown into a suicidal crisis when their intimate relationship is threatened. Ronningstam and colleagues (1995) noted that a meaningful and durable relationship can be corrective for patients with pathological narcissism. J. M. Lewis (1998, 2000) has written about the healing aspects of intimate relationships even with individuals suffering from disorders that are notoriously difficult to treat. When a suicidal crisis is driven by a rupture or perceived rupture in the narcissistic patient's intimate relationship, couple therapy should be considered both to lessen the immediate crisis and to address the underlying relationship issues (Links & Stockwell, 2002).

SUMMARY

Patients with pathological narcissism are unique because of their propensity to become highly suicidal even though they may not be suffering with clinical depression. Often these suicidal crises are driven by shame-based emotions. The assessment of suicide risk is challenging and requires that the clinician not underestimate the risk in such patients. However, strategies are available to manage risk. Often the establishment of a trusting therapeutic alliance is the key to the ongoing management of the suicidal patient with pathological narcissism.

REFERENCES

American Psychiatric Association. (2000). *Diagnostic and statistical manual of mental disorders* (4th ed., text rev.). Washington, DC: Author.

Apter, A., Bleich, A., King, R. A., Kron, S., Fluch, A., Kotler, M., & Cohen, D. J. (1993). Death without warning! A clinical postmortem study of suicide in 43 Israeli adolescent males. *Archives of General Psychiatry, 50,* 138–142. doi:10.1001/archpsyc.1993.01820140064007

Baumeister, R. F. (1990). Suicide as escape from self. *Psychological Review, 97,* 90–113. doi:10.1037/0033-295X.97.1.90

Blasco-Fontecilla, H., Baca-Garcia, E., Dervic, K., Perez-Rodriguez, M., Lopez-Castroman, J., Saiz-Ruiz, J., & Oquendo, M. A. (2009). Specific features of suicidal behavior in patients with narcissistic personality disorder. *Journal of Clinical Psychiatry, 70,* 1583–1587. doi:10.4088/JCP.08m04899

Bourgeois, J. A., & Hall, M. J. (1993). An examination of narcissistic personality traits as seen in a military population. *Military Medicine, 158,* 170–174.

Bourgeois, J. A., Nelson, J. L., Slack, M. B., & Ingram, M. (1999). Comorbid affective disorders and personality traits in alcohol abuse inpatients at an Air Force Medical Center. *Military Medicine, 164,* 103–106.

Gabbard, G. O. (2009). Transference and countertransference: Developments in the treatment of narcissistic personality disorder. *Psychiatric Annals, 39,* 129–136. doi:10.3928/00485713-20090301-03

Haw, C., Hawton, K., Sutton, L., Sinclair, J., & Deeks, J. (2005). Schizophrenia and deliberate self-harm: A systematic review of risk factors. *Suicide and Life-Threatening Behavior, 35,* 50–62. doi:10.1521/suli.35.1.50.59260

Hawton, K., Sutton, L., Haw, C., Sinclair, J., & Deeks, J. J. (2005). Schizophrenia and suicide: Systematic review of risk factors. *British Journal of Psychiatry, 187,* 9–20. doi:10.1192/bjp.187.1.9

Heisel, M. J., Links, P. S., Conn, D., van Reekum, R., & Flett, G. L. (2007). Narcissistic personality and vulnerability to late-life suicidality. *The American Journal of Geriatric Psychiatry, 15,* 734–741.

Joiner, T. E. (2005). *Why people die by suicide*. Cambridge, MA: Harvard University Press.

King, R. E. (1994). Assessing aviators for personality pathology with the Millon Clinical Multiaxial Inventory (MCMI). *Aviation, Space, and Environmental Medicine, 65,* 227–231.

Kohut, H. (1971). *Anaylsis of the self.* New York, NY: International Universities Press.

Kohut, H. (1972). Thoughts on narcissism and narcissistic rage. *The Psychoanalytic Study of the Child, 27,* 360–400.

Kolla, N. J., Eisenberg, H., & Links, P. S. (2008). Epidemiology, risk factors and psychopharmacological management of suicidal behavior in borderline personality disorder. *Archives of Suicide Research, 12,* 1–19. doi:10.1080/13811110701542010

Krysinska, K., & Lester, D. (2010). Post-traumatic stress disorder and suicide risk: A systematic review. *Archives of Suicide Research, 14,* 1–23. doi:10.1080/13811110903478997

Law, S., & Liu, P. (2008). Suicide in China: Unique demographic patterns and relationship to depressive disorder. *Current Psychiatry Reports, 10,* 80–86. doi:10.1007/s11920-008-0014-5

Lester, D. (1997). The role of shame in suicide. *Suicide and Life-Threatening Behavior, 27,* 352–361.

Lewis, H. B. (1987). Shame and narcissistic personality. In D. Nathanson (Ed.), *The many faces of shame* (pp. 93–133). New York, NY: Guilford Press.

Lewis, J. M. (1998). For better or worse: Interpersonal relationships and individual outcome. *The American Journal of Psychiatry, 155,* 582–589.

Lewis, J. M. (2000). Repairing the bond in important relationships: A dynamic for personality maturation. *The American Journal of Psychiatry, 157,* 1375–1378. doi:10.1176/appi.ajp.157.9.1375

Linehan, M. (1993). *Cognitive behavioral treatment of borderline personality disorder.* New York, NY: Guilford Press.

Links, P. S., & Stockwell, M. (2002). The role of couple therapy in the treatment of narcissistic personality disorder. *American Journal of Psychotherapy, 56,* 522–538.

Pincus, A. L., & Lukowitsky, M. R. (2010). Pathological narcissism and narcissistic personality disorder. *Annual Review of Clinical Psychology, 6,* 421–446. doi:10.1146/annurev.clinpsy.121208.131215

Raja, M., & Azzoni, A. (2007). The impact of obsessive-compulsive personality disorder on the suicide risk of patients with mood disorders. *Psychopathology, 40,* 184–190. doi:10.1159/000100366

Ronningstam, E. (2009). Narcissistic personality disorder: Facing DSM–V. *Psychiatric Annals, 39,* 111–121. doi:10.3928/00485713-20090301-09

Ronningstam, E., Gunderson, J. G., & Lyons, M. (1995). Changes in pathological narcissism. *The American Journal of Psychiatry, 152,* 253–257.

Ronningstam, E. F., & Maltsberger, J. T. (1998). Pathological narcissism and sudden suicide-related collapse. *Suicide and Life-Threatening Behavior, 28,* 261–271.

Sher, L. (2006). Risk and protective factors for suicide in patients with alcoholism. *The Scientific World Journal*, 6, 1405–1411. doi:10.1100/tsw.2006.254

Silverman, M. M., Berman, A. L., Sandal, N. D., O'Carroll, P., & Joiner, T. E. (2007a). Rebuilding the Tower of Babel: A revised nomenclature for the study of suicide and suicidal behaviours. Part 1: Background, rationale, and methodology. *Suicide and Life-Threatening Behavior*, 37, 248–263. doi:10.1521/suli.2007.37.3.248

Silverman, M. M., Berman, A. L., Sandal, N. D., O'Carroll, P., & Joiner, T. E. (2007b). Rebuilding the Tower of Babel: A revised nomenclature for the study of suicide and suicidal behaviours. Part 2: Suicide-related ideations, communications and behaviors. *Suicide and Life-Threatening Behavior*, 37, 264–277. doi:10.1521/suli.2007.37.3.264

Simeon, D., & Favazza, A. R. (2001). Self-injurious behaviors: Phenomenology and assessment. In D. Simeon & E. Hollander (Eds.), *Self-injurious behaviors. Assessment and treatment* (pp. 1–2). Washington, DC: American Psychiatric Publishing.

Simon, R. I. (2007). Gun safety management with patients at risk for suicide. *Suicide and Life-Threatening Behavior*, 37, 518–526. doi:10.1521/suli.2007.37.5.518

Stinson, F. S., Dawson, D. A., Goldstein, R. B., Chou, S. P., Huang, B., Smith, S. M., . . . Grant, B. F. (2008). Prevalence, correlates, disability, and comorbidity of DSM–IV narcissistic personality disorder: Results from the Wave 2 National Epidemiologic Survey on Alcohol and Related Conditions. *Journal of Clinical Psychiatry*, 69, 1033–1045. doi:10.4088/JCP.v69n0701

Stone, M. H. (1990). *The fate of borderline patients*. New York, NY: Guilford Press.

Svindseth, M. F., Nottestad, J. A., Wallin, J., Roaldset, J. O., & Dahl, A. A. (2008). Narcissism in patients admitted to psychiatric acute wards: Its relation to violence, suicidality and other psychopathology. *BMC Psychiatry*, 8, 13. doi:10.1186/1471-244X-8-13

Tangney, J. P., Stuewig, J., & Mashek, D. J. (2007). Moral emotions and moral behavior. *Annual Review of Psychology*, 58, 345–372. doi:10.1146/annurev.psych.56.091103.070145

Torgersen, S. (2005). Epidemiology. In J. M. Oldham, A. E. Skodol, & D. S. Bender (Eds.), *The American Psychiatric Publishing textbook of personality disorders* (pp. 129–141). Washington, DC: American Psychiatric Publishing.

Wilson, J. P., Drozdek, B., & Turkovic, S. (2006). Posttraumatic shame and guilt. *Trauma, Violence, and Abuse*, 7, 122–141. doi:10.1177/1524838005285914

11

SEX AND RACE–ETHNIC DIFFERENCES IN PSYCHIATRIC COMORBIDITY OF NARCISSISTIC PERSONALITY DISORDER

ATTILA J. PULAY AND BRIDGET F. GRANT

Narcissistic personality disorder (NPD) is characterized by a pervasive pattern of grandiosity, need for admiration, interpersonal exploitativeness, and lack of empathy, beginning in early adulthood and manifested in a variety of contexts. Among the 10 personality disorders defined in the *Diagnostic and Statistical Manual of Mental Disorders* (4th ed.; *DSM–IV*; American Psychiatric Association, 1994), NPD has received the least empirical attention (Cramer, Torgersen, & Kringlen, 2006; Miller, Campbell, & Pilkonis, 2007). Despite the highly disabling nature of the disorder with its major adverse impact on the relationships of affected individuals with those around them, including family, friends, and coworkers (Miller et al., 2007), the lack of information on its prevalence and comorbidity in major subgroups of the

The views and opinions expressed in this report are those of the authors and should not be construed to represent the views of sponsoring organizations, agencies, or the U.S. government. The National Epidemiologic Survey on Alcohol and Related Conditions is funded by the National Institute on Alcohol Abuse and Alcoholism, with supplemental support from the National Institute on Drug Abuse. This research was supported in part by the Intramural Program of the National Institutes of Health, National Institute on Alcohol Abuse and Alcoholism.

DOI: 10.1037/14041-011
Understanding and Treating Pathological Narcissism, J. S. Ogrodniczuk (Editor)

population creates gaps in our knowledge concerning etiology, economic costs, planning of mental health services, and treatment.

Most of the research on NPD comorbidity has been conducted in clinical samples (George, Miklowitz, Richards, Simoneau, & Taylor, 2003; Mantere et al., 2006; Oldham et al., 1995; Ronningstam, 1996; Skodol et al., 1995; Skodol, Oldham & Gallaher, 1999; Skodol, Stout, et al., 1999; Zimmerman, Rothschild, & Chelminski, 2005). In most of the clinical studies, no significant associations were found between NPD and most mood and anxiety disorders, with the possible exception of bipolar disorder. Evidence linking NPD with substance use disorders, though strong in earlier clinical work (Ronningstam, 1996), remains mixed when more recent clinical studies are considered (Fossati et al., 2000; Skodol, Oldham, et al., 1999). By contrast, NPD has consistently been shown to be associated with histrionic, antisocial, obsessive–compulsive, and schizotypal personality disorders (Fossati et al., 2000; Marinangeli et al., 2000; Stuart et al., 1998), with mixed evidence for a relationship with border-line personality disorder (Grilo, Sanislow, & McGlashan, 2002; Marinangeli et al., 2000; Stuart et al., 1998; Zanarini et al., 1998).

Relative to clinical work on NPD, very little is known about disability and comorbidity of NPD in general population samples. Although prevalence estimates of NPD are available from several early community surveys (Black, Noyes, Pfohl, Goldstein, & Blum, 1993; Ekselius, Tillfors, Furmark, & Fredrikson, 2001; Klein et al., 1995; Lenzenweger, Loranger, Korfine, & Neff, 1997; Maier, Lichtermann, Minges, & Heun, 1992; Moldin, Rice, Erlenmeyer-Kimling, & Squires-Wheeler, 1994; Reich, Yates, & Nduaguba, 1989; Zimmerman & Coryell, 1989), these surveys were geographically restricted, in addition to being limited by small sample sizes ($Ns = 229–797$). Others (Coid, Yang, Tyrer, Roberts, & Ullrich, 2006; Lenzenweger, Lane, Loranger, & Kessler, 2007; Samuels, Nestadt, Romanoski, Folstein, & McHugh, 1994) used statistical techniques to impute prevalence rates of NPD from small subsamples of individuals to larger general population samples, further limiting the precision of prevalence estimates.

Only one large epidemiologic survey (Torgersen, Kringlen, & Cramer, 2001) conducted in Oslo, Norway, yielded prevalence estimates of basic sociodemographic factors of NPD, reporting 0.8% prevalence of NPD in their sample. Two more recent studies (Pulay, Goldstein, & Grant, 2011; Stinson et al., 2008) using the Wave 2 National Epidemiologic Survey on Alcohol and Related Conditions (NESARC; Grant, Kaplan, & Stinson, 2005) reported data on the prevalence, correlates, and comorbidity of NPD across sociodemographic characteristics and found a substantially larger rate of NPD (6.2%) in the U.S. general population. Stinson et al. (2008) reported high co-occurrence rates of NPD with substance use, mood, anxiety, and other personality disorders and found independent associations between NPD and bipolar I disorder, posttraumatic stress disorder, generalized anxiety disorder (GAD), borderline and schizotypal personality disorders. Their findings also suggested that a sex-specific comorbidity pattern exists in NPD, with men having greater odds to develop substance use disorders and histrionic and obsessive–compulsive personality disorders and women being more prone to anxiety and mood disorders. Although this study provided valuable information on the psychiatric comorbidity of NPD, its scope was restricted to sex and did not analyze the comorbidity pattern from other important aspects, such as racial–ethnic differences.

Race–ethnicity is an important determinant in psychiatric epidemiology; it influences both Axis I (Smith et al., 2006) and Axis II psychopathology (Alarcón, 2005). Despite its significance, no prior epidemiologic or clinical work has examined race–ethnicity differences in NPD comorbidity. To address this gap in our knowledge, we present comprehensive information on the comorbidity of *DSM–IV* NPD with Axis I and II disorders both by sex and race–ethnicity using a large, nationally representative survey of the United States, the Wave 2 NESARC. The large sample size and high response rate of the Wave 2 NESARC allow for reliable, precise estimation of lifetime NPD comorbidity, even for less frequent psychiatric conditions, especially among these important subgroups of the general population. By assessing an extensive set of *DSM–IV* Axis I and II disorders, sociodemographic characteristics and standardized, dimensional measures of mental functioning, the Wave 2 NESARC provides an excellent source of information on the comorbidity pattern of NPD and its impact on mental functioning.

BACKGROUND OF THE WAVE 2 NESARC STUDY

The 2004–2005 Wave 2 NESARC is the second wave follow-up of the Wave 1 NESARC, conducted in 2001–2002 and described in detail elsewhere (Grant, Kaplan, et al., 2005; Grant, Moore, Shepard, & Kaplan, 2003). The Wave 1 NESARC provided a representative sample of the civilian population of the United States ages 18 years and older that resides in households and group quarters. Face-to-face interviews were conducted with 43,093 respondents, oversampling Blacks, Hispanics, and young adults 18 to 24 years old, with an overall response rate of 81.0%.

Attempts were made in Wave 2 to conduct a second round of face-to-face interviews with all Wave 1 respondents. Respondents were excluded from the Wave 2 if they were mentally or physically impaired, deported, or on active military duty over the entire follow-up period. The Wave 2 had a response rate of 86.7%, reflecting 34,653 completed interviews with a cumulative response rate at Wave 2 of 70.2%. As in Wave 1, the Wave 2 NESARC data were weighted to reflect design characteristics of the survey and account for oversampling.

Diagnoses of NPD were made at Wave 2 using the Alcohol Use Disorder and Associated Disabilities Interview Schedule—*DSM–IV* Version (AUDADIS–IV; Grant, Dawson, & Hasin, 2001, 2004), a fully structured diagnostic instrument designed for use by experienced nonclinician interviewers. Because the diagnosis of NPD requires evaluation of long-term patterns of functioning (American Psychiatric Association, 1994), all NESARC respondents were asked a series of NPD symptom questions about how they felt or acted most of the time throughout their lives, regardless of the situation or whom they were with. Respondents were also instructed to exclude symptoms that occurred only when they were depressed, manic, anxious, drinking heavily, using medicines or drugs, experiencing withdrawal symptoms, or physically ill. NPD symptom items ($n = 18$), representing NPD criteria, were similar to those in the Structured Clinical Interview for *DSM–IV* Personality Disorders (First, Gibbon, Spitzer, Williams, & Benjamin, 1997), the International Personality Disorder Examination (Loranger, 1999), and the Diagnostic Interview for *DSM–IV* Personality Disorders (Zanarini, Frankenburg, Sickel, & Yong, 1996). Reliability of the NPD diagnosis and symptom scales were good ($\kappa = 0.70, 0.72$; Ruan et al., 2008).

Wave 2 AUDADIS-IV measures of substance use (alcohol and drug-specific abuse and dependence and nicotine dependence), mood (major depressive disorder [MDD], dysthymia, bipolar I, and bipolar II), and anxiety (panic disorder with and without agoraphobia, social phobia, specific phobia, and GAD) disorders were identical to those measured in Wave 1, whereas posttraumatic stress disorder was assessed only in Wave 2. For this study, all disorders were assessed on a lifetime basis, occurring over the life course as assessed in both Wave 1 and Wave 2.

A comprehensive set of questions covered *DSM–IV* criteria for alcohol and drug-specific abuse and dependence, including sedatives, tranquilizers, opioids other than heroin, cannabis, cocaine or crack, stimulants, hallucinogens, inhalants and solvents, heroin, and other illicit drugs. Consistent with Wave 1 diagnoses, Wave 2 12-month abuse required one of more of four abuse criteria and dependence required three or more of seven dependence criteria to be met in any 1-year period covered by Waves 1 and 2 surveys. Drug-specific abuse and dependence were aggregated in this study to yield diagnoses of any drug abuse and any drug dependence.

The reliability and validity of AUDADIS-IV alcohol and drug diagnoses are documented in clinical and general population samples (Grant, Dawson, et al., 2003; Grant, Harford, Dawson, Chou, & Pickering, 1995; Hasin, Carpenter, McCloud, Smith, & Grant, 1997; Hasin & Paykin, 1999; Hasin et al., 2003; Ruan et al., 2008), including in the World Health Organization/

National Institutes of Health International Study on Reliability and Validity (Chatterji et al., 1997; Hasin, Grant, et al., 1997; Vrasti et al., 1998), in which clinical reappraisals documented good validity (Canino et al., 1999; Cottler et al., 1997).

Mood, anxiety, and personality disorders only included DSM–IV primary disorders excluding substance-induced disorders and those caused by general medical conditions. Diagnoses of MDD also ruled out bereavement, whereas diagnoses of personality disorders also excluded symptoms that only occurred when respondents were depressed, manic, or anxious. Test–retest reliability and validity for AUDADIS-IV mood, anxiety, and personality disorder diagnoses in the general population and clinical samples were fair to excellent (Grant et al., 2006; Grant, Hasin, Blanco, et al., 2005; Grant, Hasin, Stinson, et al., 2005; Grant, Hasin, et al., 2004; Grant, Stinson, et al., 2005; Hasin, Goodwin, Stinson, & Grant, 2005; Ruan et al., 2008; Stinson et al., 2007).

Disability was derived from the Short Form-12 Health Survey, version 2 (SF-12v2; Gandek et al., 1998). The SF-12v2 scores measures impairment in three dimensions of mental functioning: social functioning, role emotional functioning, and mental health. Standard norm-based scoring techniques were used to transform each score ranging from 0 to 100 to achieve a mean of 50 and a standard deviation of 10 in the U.S. general population. Lower scores indicate greater disability.

NOVEL FINDINGS FROM THE WAVE 2 NESARC STUDY

As noted previously, data on race–ethnic differences in the comorbidity of NPD have not been reported. The nationally representative Wave 2 NESARC study provided an excellent opportunity to examine psychiatric comorbidity of NPD in the general adult population. In this section, we describe the statistical procedures used in these analyses and present our findings on the sex- and race-specific co-occurrence and association of NPD with DSM–IV Axis I and II disorders and mental disability.

Statistical Procedure

Weighted frequencies and cross-tabulations were computed to calculate (a) lifetime prevalences of NPD among respondents with other psychiatric disorders and (b) prevalences of other psychiatric disorders among respondents with NPD. Weighted mean SF-12v2 scores were computed to assess mental disability. Pairwise t statistics were used to test sex and race–ethnic differences in rates of co-occurrence of NPD with other psychiatric disorders. Because of sample size limitations, detailed analyses among race–ethnic groups were carried out only for Whites, Blacks, and Hispanics (excluding Asians and Native Americans).

Odds ratios of NPD and other *DSM–IV* disorders were calculated by using series of multivariable logistic regression models. Relationships between NPD and the dimensions of mental disability measures were assessed with multiple linear regression analyses. All logistic and linear regression models controlled for sociodemographic characteristics and comorbid psychiatric disorders by using Software for Survey Data Analysis (Research Triangle Institute, 2006).

Co-Occurrence of Lifetime *DSM–IV* NPD and Lifetime Axis I and II Psychiatric Disorders

Co-occurrences of NPD with other psychiatric disorders by sex and by race–ethnicity are shown in Tables 11.1 and 11.2, respectively. Prevalences of substance use, mood, anxiety, and other personality disorders among respondents with NPD were 64.5%, 49.1%, 54.6%, and 62.7%, respectively. Rates of substance use disorders were higher among men than women with NPD, whereas rates of MDD and anxiety disorders except social phobia were higher among women with NPD than men with NPD. Men with NPD were also more likely than women to have antisocial personality disorder, whereas women with NPD were more likely than men to have paranoid, avoidant, and borderline personality disorders. With regard to race–ethnicity, White respondents with NPD had higher rates of substance use disorders than Blacks and Hispanics, except for drug dependence, whereas rates of alcohol dependence were higher among Whites than Blacks. Furthermore, Whites with NPD had higher rates of MDD and GAD than Blacks. Among Axis II disorders, schizotypal personality disorder was more prevalent among Blacks than Whites and Hispanics with NPD, rates of avoidant personality disorder was significantly higher among Whites than Blacks, whereas rates of obsessive–compulsive personality disorder were higher among Whites than Blacks and Hispanics.

In the total sample, prevalence rates of NPD among respondents with lifetime substance use, mood, and anxiety disorders were 8.7%, 11.8%, and 11.4%. Rates of NPD were significantly higher among men than women with all Axis I disorders except dysthymia, bipolar II disorder, and panic disorder with agoraphobia. Rates of NPD were also higher among men with histrionic, borderline, and obsessive–compulsive personality disorders relative to women with these disorders.

With regard to race–ethnicity, the prevalences of NPD among respondents with all substance use and mood, anxiety, and personality disorders, except for histrionic, avoidant, and dependent personality disorders, were higher among Blacks than Whites. Rates of NPD were higher among Blacks with alcohol dependence, nicotine dependence, MDD, specific phobia, and schizotypal, schizoid, and obsessive–compulsive personality disorders compared with Hispanics. Prevalences of NPD were also higher among Hispanics with

TABLE 11.1
Co-Occurrence Rates of Lifetime *DSM–IV* Narcissistic Personality Disorder (NPD) and Axis I and II Lifetime Psychiatric Disorders by Sex

Psychiatric disorder	Prevalence of other psychiatric disorders among respondents with NPD			Prevalence of NPD among respondents with other psychiatric disorders		
	Total % (SE)	Men % (SE)	Women % (SE)	Total % (SE)	Men % (SE)	Women % (SE)
Any substance use disorder	64.5 (1.35)	73.4 (1.72)	51.1 (1.94)[a]	8.7 (0.34)	9.9 (0.45)	6.9 (0.41)[a]
Any substance abuse	35.5 (1.43)	43.6 (1.88)	23.4 (1.66)[a]	8.2 (0.39)	9.2 (0.52)	6.4 (0.52)[a]
Any substance dependence	50.5 (1.45)	56.4 (1.97)	41.7 (2.12)[a]	10.0 (0.45)	11.7 (0.60)	7.8 (0.52)[a]
Any alcohol use disorder	51.4 (1.43)	62.7 (1.76)	34.4 (1.76)[a]	9.0 (0.36)	10.0 (0.45)	7.2 (0.46)[a]
Alcohol abuse	20.4 (1.08)	25.4 (1.55)	12.9 (1.04)[a]	6.4 (0.36)	7.2 (0.49)	4.8 (0.44)[a]
Alcohol dependence	30.9 (1.25)	37.3 (1.75)	21.5 (1.68)[a]	12.4 (0.61)	13.6 (0.77)	10.2 (0.87)[a]
Any drug use disorder	26.2 (1.27)	31.7 (1.63)	17.9 (1.71)[a]	13.4 (0.68)	15.3 (0.87)	10.2 (1.04)[a]
Any drug abuse	19.7 (1.11)	24.3 (1.45)	12.8 (1.52)[a]	11.9 (0.69)	13.4 (0.93)	8.9 (1.08)[a]
Any drug dependence	11.8 (0.94)	14.4 (1.30)	7.9 (1.06)[a]	21.9 (1.63)	26.0 (2.14)	15.4 (2.06)[a]
Nicotine dependence	35.8 (1.39)	39.5 (1.83)	30.2 (1.86)[a]	9.5 (0.45)	11.6 (0.67)	7.1 (0.49)[a]
Any mood disorder	49.1 (1.36)	44.2 (1.80)	56.5 (1.81)[a]	11.8 (0.47)	17.0 (0.84)	8.7 (0.45)[a]
Major depressive disorder	20.3 (1.03)	17.4 (1.33)	24.6 (1.39)[a]	7.6 (0.42)	12.0 (0.88)	5.5 (0.40)[a]
Dysthymia	3.9 (0.42)	3.2 (0.57)	5.0 (0.69)	7.1 (0.75)	10.6 (1.82)	5.4 (0.74)
Bipolar I	20.0 (1.05)	18.5 (1.46)	22.2 (1.48)	23.8 (1.31)	29.5 (2.17)	19.1 (1.41)[a]
Bipolar II	4.4 (0.53)	3.4 (0.69)	6.0 (0.79)	16.1 (1.73)	18.3 (3.25)	14.6 (1.86)
Any anxiety disorder	54.6 (1.33)	46.6 (1.99)	66.4 (1.89)[a]	11.4 (0.44)	16.5 (0.81)	8.6 (0.44)[a]
Panic with agoraphobia	5.8 (0.67)	3.3 (0.85)	9.7 (1.18)[a]	19.2 (2.11)	22.0 (4.90)	18.1 (2.22)
Panic without agoraphobia	11.4 (0.80)	9.1 (1.00)	14.8 (1.37)[a]	12.0 (0.91)	17.5 (1.92)	9.3 (0.90)[a]
Social phobia	15.1 (1.02)	13.0 (1.29)	18.4 (1.70)	13.4 (0.87)	16.9 (1.62)	11.0 (1.03)[a]

(continues)

TABLE 11.1

Co-Occurrence Rates of Lifetime *DSM–IV* Narcissistic Personality Disorder (NPD) and Axis I and II Lifetime Psychiatric Disorders by Sex   *(Continued)*

Psychiatric disorder	Prevalence of other psychiatric disorders among respondents with NPD			Prevalence of NPD among respondents with other psychiatric disorders		
	Total % (SE)	Men % (SE)	Women % (SE)	Total % (SE)	Men % (SE)	Women % (SE)
Specific phobia	27.5 (1.29)	20.5 (1.67)	38.0 (1.96)[a]	11.1 (0.56)	15.3 (1.18)	9.2 (0.56)[a]
Generalized anxiety	19.7 (1.12)	14.5 (1.28)	27.6 (1.88)[a]	15.9 (0.92)	22.6 (1.89)	12.9 (0.95)[a]
Posttraumatic stress	18.0 (0.99)	13.5 (1.30)	24.7 (1.68)[a]	17.1 (1.06)	24.9 (2.42)	13.7 (1.05)[a]
Any other personality disorder	62.7 (1.36)	60.3 (1.80)	66.3 (1.90)	20.2 (0.66)	23.1 (0.92)	17.3 (0.81)[a]
Any Cluster A	38.0 (1.36)	35.6 (1.69)	41.5 (2.03)	26.2 (1.05)	30.8 (1.58)	22.1 (1.25)[a]
Paranoid	14.9 (0.97)	12.9 (1.21)	17.9 (1.44)[a]	21.8 (1.25)	27.7 (2.42)	17.7 (1.35)[a]
Schizoid	8.7 (0.73)	8.1 (1.01)	9.7 (1.11)	17.6 (1.42)	20.4 (2.43)	15.0 (1.67)
Schizotypal	27.3 (1.16)	25.6 (1.52)	29.8 (1.77)	42.8 (1.69)	46.0 (2.48)	39.2 (2.31)
Any other Cluster B	45.0 (1.38)	43.6 (1.69)	47.1 (2.08)	28.4 (0.99)	30.1 (1.35)	26.4 (1.30)
Antisocial	11.6 (0.92)	14.0 (1.26)	8.1 (1.10)[a]	19.0 (1.35)	18.5 (1.53)	20.3 (2.50)
Borderline	36.8 (1.31)	33.8 (1.67)	41.3 (1.98)[a]	38.9 (1.47)	47.8 (2.28)	31.7 (1.67)[a]
Histrionic	9.6 (0.84)	10.0 (1.12)	9.0 (1.05)	33.1 (2.25)	41.7 (3.39)	24.7 (2.58)[a]
Any Cluster C	24.6 (1.29)	23.4 (1.65)	26.3 (1.70)	16.0 (0.80)	19.7 (1.34)	12.8 (0.91)[a]
Avoidant	6.8 (0.70)	5.2 (0.87)	9.2 (1.22)[a]	18.2 (1.73)	21.6 (3.23)	16.1 (1.91)
Dependent	1.7 (0.42)	1.5 (0.61)	2.0 (0.51)	25.4 (4.94)	37.8 (9.59)	18.5 (4.52)
Obsessive–compulsive	21.7 (1.24)	21.9 (1.61)	21.4 (1.57)	16.5 (0.89)	20.7 (1.47)	12.6 (1.01)[a]

Note. DSM–IV = *Diagnostic and Statistical Manual of Mental Disorders* (4th ed.).
[a]Prevalence rates for women are significantly different ($p < .01$) than prevalence rates for men.

TABLE 11.2
Co-Occurrence of Lifetime *DSM–IV* Narcissistic Personality Disorder (NPD) and Axis I and II Lifetime Psychiatric Disorders by Race–Ethnicity

Psychiatric disorder	Prevalence of other psychiatric disorders among respondents with NPD			Prevalence of NPD among respondents with other psychiatric disorders		
	White % (SE)	Black % (SE)	Hispanic % (SE)	White % (SE)	Black % (SE)	Hispanic % (SE)
Any substance use disorder	70.8 (1.65)	54.8 (2.17)[a]	54.0 (2.76)[b]	7.2 (0.32)	18.6 (1.14)[a]	12.1 (1.14)[b,c]
Any substance abuse	41.6 (1.82)	24.8 (2.11)[a]	27.9 (2.73)[b]	7.1 (0.39)	16.4 (1.48)[a]	11.3 (1.45)[b]
Any substance dependence	55.2 (1.89)	44.6 (2.33)[a]	41.0 (2.71)[b]	8.3 (0.43)	21.1 (1.43)[a]	13.8 (1.44)[b,c]
Any alcohol use disorder	57.5 (1.76)	39.8 (2.24)[a]	44.4 (3.05)[b]	7.6 (0.36)	19.0 (1.39)[a]	12.6 (1.31)[b,c]
Alcohol abuse	23.9 (1.51)	14.6 (1.82)[a]	15.4 (1.88)[b]	5.5 (0.38)	13.5 (1.63)[a]	9.2 (1.26)[b]
Alcohol dependence	33.6 (1.67)	25.2 (2.14)[a]	29.1 (2.71)	10.4 (0.62)	25.0 (2.31)[a]	15.7 (1.90)[c]
Any drug use disorder	28.8 (1.63)	21.5 (1.85)[a]	22.8 (2.39)	11.3 (0.68)	26.1 (2.09)[a]	18.5 (2.57)[b]
Any drug abuse	22.8 (1.47)	14.2 (1.67)[a]	15.8 (2.12)[b]	10.3 (0.70)	22.1 (2.42)[a]	15.4 (2.53)
Any drug dependence	12.4 (1.38)	10.9 (1.34)	10.3 (1.45)	18.3 (1.88)	41.6 (4.35)[a]	26.8 (4.05)
Nicotine dependence	40.6 (1.84)	31.5 (2.39)[a]	22.8 (2.33)[b]	7.9 (0.46)	20.7 (1.56)[a]	13.0 (1.69)[b,c]
Any mood disorder	50.3 (1.97)	47.3 (2.02)	47.2 (3.06)	9.5 (0.46)	25.7 (1.66)[a]	15.3 (1.23)[b,c]
Major depressive disorder	22.1 (1.43)	15.8 (1.74)[a]	20.1 (2.21)	6.2 (0.42)	17.7 (1.96)[a]	11.0 (1.40)[b,c]
Dysthymia	4.1 (0.62)	2.8 (0.64)	5.1 (1.02)	5.6 (0.81)	14.0 (2.97)[a]	12.4 (2.43)
Bipolar I	20.3 (1.45)	20.5 (1.75)	18.1 (2.42)	20.2 (1.41)	38.5 (3.22)[a]	26.9 (3.10)
Bipolar II	4.0 (0.76)	5.2 (0.94)	5.0 (1.10)	12.2 (2.05)	29.2 (4.24)[a]	23.4 (4.78)
Any anxiety disorder	55.8 (1.94)	53.9 (2.07)	50.5 (3.01)	9.1 (0.43)	23.6 (1.51)[a]	15.1 (1.16)[b,c]
Panic with agoraphobia	6.7 (1.04)	4.8 (0.77)	4.1 (1.05)	16.7 (2.48)	38.7 (5.70)[a]	21.2 (5.00)
Panic without agoraphobia	12.7 (1.21)	9.2 (1.33)	9.7 (1.41)	10.1 (0.95)	25.8 (3.89)[a]	16.0 (2.68)
Social phobia	16.0 (1.44)	14.0 (1.81)	13.6 (1.85)	10.5 (0.91)	32.3 (3.77)[a]	20.4 (2.81)[b,c]

(continues)

TABLE 11.2
Co-Occurrence of Lifetime *DSM–IV* Narcissistic Personality Disorder (NPD) and Axis I and II Lifetime Psychiatric Disorders by Race–Ethnicity *(Continued)*

Psychiatric disorder	Prevalence of other psychiatric disorders among respondents with NPD			Prevalence of NPD among respondents with other psychiatric disorders		
	White % (SE)	Black % (SE)	Hispanic % (SE)	White % (SE)	Black % (SE)	Hispanic % (SE)
Specific phobia	27.9 (1.75)	29.9 (2.31)	22.1 (2.27)	9.0 (0.61)	23.8 (1.79)[a]	12.5 (1.39)[c]
Generalized anxiety	21.8 (1.55)	16.7 (1.34)[a]	16.0 (2.31)	13.2 (0.96)	32.4 (3.00)[a]	22.1 (2.52)[b]
Posttraumatic stress	15.9 (1.31)	21.4 (1.86)	21.0 (2.26)	12.6 (1.08)	33.7 (2.42)[a]	25.0 (2.86)[b]
Any other personality disorder	63.7 (1.89)	64.0 (2.15)	56.7 (2.72)	17.1 (0.70)	33.9 (1.57)[a]	22.3 (1.65)[b,c]
Any Cluster A	35.8 (1.85)	45.1 (2.32)[a]	35.8 (2.85)	22.6 (1.25)	38.7 (1.99)[a]	26.9 (2.47)[c]
Paranoid	14.0 (1.27)	17.1 (1.91)	15.2 (1.82)	19.3 (1.67)	29.4 (2.73)[a]	21.9 (2.60)
Schizoid	9.0 (1.06)	9.4 (1.12)	6.6 (1.23)	16.3 (1.78)	25.2 (3.19)	14.2 (2.52)[c]
Schizotypal	25.0 (1.55)	34.8 (2.04)[a]	24.8 (2.50)[c]	35.5 (1.99)	63.6 (2.83)[a]	47.9 (4.59)[c]
Any other Cluster B	46.3 (1.88)	43.7 (2.12)	42.0 (2.99)	24.4 (1.11)	45.3 (2.05)[a]	33.0 (2.65)[b,c]
Antisocial	12.9 (1.34)	9.4 (1.20)	9.9 (1.57)	17.1 (1.60)	31.7 (3.64)[a]	18.7 (2.98)
Borderline	37.1 (1.75)	37.5 (2.11)	34.8 (2.86)	33.2 (1.63)	57.0 (2.77)[a]	49.6 (3.26)[b]
Histrionic	11.2 (1.23)	7.9 (1.04)	6.3 (1.38)	31.9 (2.88)	40.1 (4.50)	30.7 (5.89)
Any Cluster C	28.5 (1.84)	19.7 (1.45)[a]	16.4 (2.33)[b]	14.4 (0.91)	27.3 (2.27)[a]	15.9 (2.13)[c]
Avoidant	8.3 (1.06)	4.1 (0.85)[a]	4.9 (1.08)	17.3 (2.04)	28.7 (5.46)	16.4 (3.54)
Dependent	2.3 (0.66)	0.7 (0.20)	1.0 (0.40)	25.7 (5.76)	27.9 (9.65)	20.8 (8.49)
Obsessive–compulsive	25.2 (1.76)	17.9 (1.35)[a]	13.5 (2.40)[b]	14.8 (1.00)	27.9 (2.34)[a]	16.6 (2.57)[c]

Note. *DSM–IV* = *Diagnostic and Statistical Manual of Mental Disorders* (4th ed.).
[a]Prevalence rates for Blacks are significantly different (*p* < .01) from prevalence rates for Whites.
[b]Prevalence rates for Hispanics are significantly different (*p* < .01) from prevalence rates for Whites.
[c]Prevalence rates for Hispanics are significantly different (*p* < .01) from prevalence rates for Blacks.

alcohol abuse, nicotine dependence, MDD, social phobia, GAD, posttraumatic stress disorder, and borderline personality disorder relative to Whites.

Associations Between Lifetime DSM–IV NPD and Lifetime Axis I and II Psychiatric Disorders

Associations of lifetime NPD with Axis I and II disorders in the total sample and by sex are shown in Table 11.3 and by race–ethnicity in Table 11.4, controlling for sociodemographic characteristics and other psychiatric disorders. Among men and women, NPD was significantly associated with bipolar I disorder, posttraumatic stress disorder, and borderline and histrionic personality disorders. Among men, NPD was also positively associated with drug dependence and obsessive–compulsive personality disorders, whereas NPD was positively associated with specific phobia and GAD but negatively associated with dysthymia among women.

The odds of NPD were higher among respondents with bipolar I disorder, posttraumatic stress disorder, and schizotypal and borderline personality disorders across all race–ethnic groups. Among Whites, the odds of NPD were higher among respondents with GAD and histrionic and obsessive–compulsive personality disorders, but the odds of NPD were significantly lower among respondents with dysthymia. NPD was also positively associated with any substance use disorder and specific phobia among Blacks and positively associated with bipolar II disorder among Hispanics.

Disability

Table 11.5 shows the associations between NPD and mental disability by sex and race–ethnicity, controlling for sociodemographic characteristics and other psychiatric disorders. NPD was associated with all three SF-12v2 mental disability scores among men and women. Men and women with NPD had greater disability relative to their counterparts without NPD. NPD was also associated with all three mental disability scores among Whites, with social functioning and role emotional functioning scores among Blacks and with the mental health score among Hispanics. In each of these cases, respondents with NPD had greater disability relative to those without NPD.

CONTEMPORARY UNDERSTANDINGS OF NPD COMORBIDITIES

The lifetime prevalence of NPD in this general population sample was 6.2%, with higher rates among men compared with women and higher among Blacks relative to Whites and Hispanics. Rates of NPD were also higher among Hispanics than Whites (Pulay et al., 2011; Stinson et al., 2008).

TABLE 11.3

Adjusted Odds Ratios (OR) of Lifetime *DSM–IV* Narcissistic Personality Disorder and Lifetime Axis I and II Psychiatric Disorders by Sex

Psychiatric disorder	Total OR (99% CI)	Men OR (99% CI)	Women OR (99% CI)
Any substance use disorder	**1.3** (1.08-1.54)	**1.4** (1.06–1.82)	1.2 (0.95–1.49)
Any substance abuse	1.1 (0.89–1.25)	1.1 (0.86–1.34)	1.0 (0.79–1.33)
Any substance dependence	**1.2** (1.05–1.49)	**1.3** (1.04–1.69)	1.2 (0.90–1.55)
Any alcohol use disorder	1.1 (0.92–1.35)	1.1 (0.88–1.47)	1.1 (0.83–1.45)
Alcohol abuse	1.1 (0.87–1.33)	1.1 (0.84–1.47)	1.0 (0.75–1.34)
Alcohol dependence	1.2 (0.92–1.46)	1.2 (0.86–1.59)	1.2 (0.81–1.74)
Any drug use disorder	1.1 (0.91–1.37)	1.2 (0.89–1.51)	1.1 (0.73–1.60)
Any drug abuse	1.0 (0.80–1.21)	1.0 (0.73–1.28)	1.1 (0.69–1.61)
Any drug dependence	1.3 (0.97–1.86)	**1.6** (1.07–2.32)	1.0 (0.63–1.70)
Nicotine dependence	1.1 (0.90–1.30)	1.2 (0.90–1.47)	1.0 (0.75–1.27)
Any mood disorder	**1.3** (1.06–1.50)	**1.3** (1.03–1.73)	1.2 (0.93–1.50)
Major depressive disorder	0.9 (0.72–1.06)	1.0 (0.73–1.31)	0.8 (0.61–1.01)
Dysthymia	**0.5** (0.39–0.74)	0.6 (0.32–1.02)	**0.5** (0.34–0.83)
Bipolar I	**1.8** (1.44–2.37)	**1.9** (1.30–2.78)	**1.8** (1.30–2.50)
Bipolar II	1.3 (0.86–1.84)	1.1 (0.57–2.03)	1.4 (0.89–2.24)
Any anxiety disorder	**1.7** (1.43–2.05)	**1.7** (1.31–2.17)	**1.7** (1.35–2.21)
Panic with agoraphobia	1.2 (0.82–1.84)	0.8 (0.36–1.93)	1.5 (0.97–2.43)
Panic without agoraphobia	1.1 (0.87–1.47)	1.2 (0.77–1.73)	1.1 (0.79–1.58)
Social phobia	0.9 (0.70–1.11)	0.8 (0.59–1.20)	0.9 (0.69–1.27)
Specific phobia	1.2 (0.96–1.46)	1.1 (0.77–1.55)	**1.3** (1.02–1.62)
Generalized anxiety	**1.4** (1.09–1.72)	1.3 (0.91–1.78)	**1.5** (1.08–2.06)
Posttraumatic stress	**1.9** (1.45–2.38)	**2.0** (1.34–3.05)	**1.8** (1.32–2.35)
Any other personality disorder	**5.5** (4.59–6.53)	**4.8** (3.79–5.96)	**6.6** (5.09–8.67)
Any Cluster A	**2.6** (2.10–3.29)	**2.6** (1.93–3.49)	**2.6** (1.87–3.69)
Paranoid	1.2 (0.92–1.52)	1.3 (0.90–1.99)	1.0 (0.71–1.46)
Schizoid	0.9 (0.67–1.21)	0.9 (0.57–1.44)	0.9 (0.57–1.34)
Schizotypal	**5.3** (4.22–6.69)	**4.9** (3.52–6.87)	**5.9** (4.32–8.18)
Any other Cluster B	**4.3** (3.54–5.32)	**3.6** (2.81–4.74)	**5.7** (4.20–7.70)
Antisocial	1.2 (0.90–1.62)	1.1 (0.79–1.55)	1.5 (0.94–2.49)
Borderline	**6.9** (5.57–8.58)	**7.2** (5.15–10.09)	**7.0** (5.20–9.37)
Histrionic	**2.2** (1.55–3.00)	**2.6** (1.70–3.94)	**1.7** (1.04–2.82)
Any Cluster C	1.2 (0.95–1.58)	1.3 (0.90–1.80)	1.2 (0.83–1.74)
Avoidant	0.9 (0.65–1.31)	0.8 (0.47–1.44)	1.0 (0.67–1.64)
Dependent	1.2 (0.60–2.50)	1.4 (0.46–4.58)	1.0 (0.44–2.49)
Obsessive–compulsive	**1.4** (1.10–1.82)	**1.6** (1.13–2.22)	1.2 (0.87–1.73)

Note. Ratios are adjusted for sociodemographic characteristics and comorbid substance use, mood, anxiety, and attention-deficit/hyperactivity disorders and other personality disorders. *DSM–IV = Diagnostic and Statistical Manual of Mental Disorders* (4th ed.). CI = confidence interval. Estimates in boldface are statistically significant ($p < .01$).

TABLE 11.4
Adjusted Odds Ratios (OR) of Lifetime *DSM–IV* Narcissistic Personality Disorder and Lifetime Axis I and II Psychiatric Disorders by Race–Ethnicity

Psychiatric disorder	White OR (99% CI)	Black OR (99% CI)	Hispanic OR (99% CI)
Any substance use disorder	**1.3** (1.01–1.63)	**1.3** (1.01–1.70)	1.3 (0.93–1.93)
Any substance abuse	1.1 (0.89–1.38)	0.9 (0.60–1.26)	1.0 (0.66–1.56)
Any substance dependence	1.2 (0.95–1.54)	**1.5** (1.10–1.93)	1.3 (0.89–1.76)
Any alcohol use disorder	1.1 (0.87–1.44)	1.0 (0.69–1.35)	1.4 (0.88–2.08)
Alcohol abuse	1.1 (0.83–1.44)	0.8 (0.55–1.25)	1.3 (0.80–2.10)
Alcohol dependence	1.1 (0.84–1.56)	1.1 (0.70–1.75)	1.4 (0.82–2.40)
Any drug use disorder	1.1 (0.85–1.43)	1.3 (0.86–1.81)	1.1 (0.68–1.92)
Any drug abuse	1.0 (0.79–1.32)	1.1 (0.65–1.74)	0.8 (0.45–1.45)
Any drug dependence	1.3 (0.83–1.93)	1.8 (0.98–3.31)	1.4 (0.69–2.77)
Nicotine dependence	1.0 (0.81–1.34)	1.4 (0.94–2.06)	0.9 (0.59–1.38)
Any mood disorder	1.1 (0.89–1.46)	**1.5** (1.12–2.11)	1.4 (0.09–2.33)
Major depressive disorder	0.8 (0.64–1.05)	1.0 (0.66–1.65)	1.0 (0.61–1.58)
Dysthymia	**0.5** (0.34–0.83)	0.5 (0.23–1.12)	0.6 (0.33–1.28)
Bipolar I	**1.7** (1.24–2.37)	**2.1** (1.40–3.19)	**2.2** (1.08–4.30)
Bipolar II	1.0 (0.58–1.84)	1.4 (0.73–2.83)	**2.2** (1.01–4.58)
Any anxiety disorder	**1.7** (1.29–2.12)	**1.8** (1.33–2.44)	**1.8** (1.16–2.88)
Panic with agoraphobia	1.3 (0.80–2.21)	1.2 (0.58–2.60)	0.8 (0.34–1.99)
Panic without agoraphobia	1.2 (0.83–1.63)	1.1 (0.61–1.84)	1.1 (0.63–1.91)
Social phobia	0.8 (0.57–1.06)	1.3 (0.73–2.19)	1.1 (0.65–1.92)
Specific phobia	1.2 (0.87–1.53)	**1.5** (1.04–2.13)	0.9 (0.58–1.51)
Generalized anxiety	**1.5** (1.13–1.96)	1.1 (0.75–1.73)	1.2 (0.73–2.04)
Posttraumatic stress	**1.7** (1.23–2.45)	**1.9** (1.33–2.72)	**2.4** (1.48–3.98)
Any other personality disorder	**5.9** (4.58–7.63)	**5.3** (4.00–7.04)	**4.1** (2.95–5.79)
Any Cluster A	**2.5** (1.86–3.41)	**3.1** (2.09–4.64)	**2.6** (1.55–4.36)
Paranoid	1.4 (0.98–1.96)	0.8 (0.52–1.30)	1.2 (0.73–1.96)
Schizoid	1.1 (0.75–1.59)	0.7 (0.42–1.08)	0.6 (0.31–1.01)
Schizotypal	**4.5** (3.26–6.17)	**8.8** (5.66–13.80)	**5.3** (3.10–9.07)
Any other Cluster B	**4.5** (3.38–5.88)	**4.0** (2.88–5.66)	**4.2** (2.69–6.59)
Antisocial	1.2 (0.86–1.75)	1.0 (0.59–1.69)	1.2 (0.62–2.47)
Borderline	**6.9** (5.06–9.41)	**6.8** (4.72–9.80)	**8.3** (5.22–13.29)
Histrionic	**2.6** (1.76–3.93)	1.3 (0.71–2.32)	1.6 (0.70–3.61)
Any Cluster C	**1.4** (1.05–1.99)	0.9 (0.58–1.48)	0.8 (0.39–1.75)
Avoidant	1.1 (0.71–1.68)	0.7 (0.33–1.50)	0.6 (0.27–1.22)
Dependent	1.5 (0.65–3.31)	0.7 (0.20–2.50)	0.7 (0.16–3.09)
Obsessive–compulsive	**1.6** (1.18–2.22)	1.1 (0.74–1.64)	1.0 (0.48–2.15)

Note. Ratios are adjusted for sociodemographic characteristics and comorbid substance use, mood, anxiety, and attention-deficit/hyperactivity disorders and other personality disorders. *DSM–IV = Diagnostic and Statistical Manual of Mental Disorders* (4th ed.). CI = confidence interval. Estimates in boldface are statistically significant ($p < .01$).

TABLE 11.5
Associations Between Lifetime Narcissistic Personality Disorder and Mental Disability by Sex and Race–Ethnicity

Sex and race–ethnicity	Social functioning		Role emotional functioning		Mental health	
	x̄ (SE)	β (SE)	x̄ (SE)	β (SE)	x̄ (SE)	β (SE)
Total	47.7 (0.29)	−1.6 (0.29)[a]	45.5 (0.29)	−1.8 (0.28)[a]	47.1 (0.31)	−1.8 (0.28)[a]
Sex						
Men	48.8 (0.39)	−1.5 (0.40)[a]	46.7 (0.40)	−1.8 (0.42)[a]	48.5 (0.40)	−1.8 (0.40)[a]
Women	46.0 (0.46)	−1.7 (0.46)[a]	43.7 (0.46)	−1.9 (0.41)[a]	45.1 (0.45)	−1.8 (0.42)[a]
Race–ethnicity						
White	48.1 (0.39)	−1.5 (0.40)[a]	45.7 (0.42)	−2.0 (0.41)[a]	47.2 (0.42)	−1.9 (0.42)[a]
Black	46.3 (0.48)	−1.3 (0.49)[a]	44.6 (0.48)	−1.3 (0.45)[a]	46.7 (0.55)	−1.3 (0.58)
Hispanic	48.1 (0.75)	−1.5 (0.63)	46.2 (0.54)	−1.5 (0.62)	47.9 (0.67)	−1.9 (0.61)[a]

Note. Associations refer to multiple linear regression analyses controlled for all sociodemographic characteristics and other Axis I and II psychiatric disorders. Mental disability is assessed through the Short Form-12 Health Survey, version 2 (Gandek et al., 1998) score; a lower score indicates higher disability. *DSM–IV = Diagnostic and Statistical Manual of Mental Disorders* (4th ed.).
[a]Regression coefficients are statistically significant (*p* < .01).

In general, co-occurrence rates of other psychiatric disorders among individuals with NPD were much higher than co-occurrence rates of NPD among individuals with other psychiatric disorders, a result that generalized to men, women, and each race–ethnic subgroup. Similar to the distribution of psychiatric disorders in the general population, co-occurrence rates of substance use disorders and antisocial personality disorder were higher among men than women with NPD, whereas rates of MDD, most anxiety disorders, and paranoid, borderline, and avoidant personality disorders were higher among women compared with men with NPD. New data from the NESARC also indicated that co-occurrence rates of most substance use disorders and obsessive–compulsive personality disorder were higher among Whites than Blacks and Hispanics with NPD.

In contrast, co-occurrence rates of NPD among men with substance use disorders, most mood and anxiety disorders, and paranoid, histrionic, and obsessive–compulsive personality disorders were greater than those among women. In general, the prevalence of NPD among individuals with substance use; mood and anxiety disorders; and borderline, schizotypal, histrionic, obsessive–compulsive, and antisocial personality disorders was greater among Blacks than Whites. Prevalence of NPD among individuals with alcohol abuse, nicotine dependence, MDD, social phobia, GAD, posttraumatic stress disorder, and borderline personality disorder was greater among Hispanics than Whites.

Taken together, the co-occurrence rates observed in the NESARC data suggest increased vigilance in assessing substance use disorders and antisocial personality disorder among men with NPD and assessing mood, anxiety, paranoid, borderline, and avoidant personality disorders among women with NPD. Similarly, Whites with NPD should be screened for substance use disorders and avoidant and obsessive–compulsive personality disorders. Equally important is the assessment of NPD among males, Blacks, and Hispanics with all substance use, mood and anxiety disorders, and personality disorders.

These newest findings from the NESARC study highlight the importance of controlling for other psychiatric disorders (in addition to sociodemographic characteristics) that are highly comorbid with each other, when examining associations between NPD and other specific disorders by sex and race–ethnicity. The positive and invariant relationship between bipolar I disorder, posttraumatic stress disorder, and schizotypal and borderline personality disorders across sex and race–ethnic subgroups is consistent with earlier clinical research (Fossati et al., 2000; Marinangeli et al., 2000; Ronningstam, 1996; Stuart et al., 1998) and one epidemiologic study (Stinson et al., 2008) that demonstrated that for the samples as a whole, NPD was most strongly related to these disorders. However, sex- and race–ethnic–specific differences observed for NPD and anxiety disorder comorbidity in the NESARC data are at variance with most previous clinical research (Oldham et al.,

1995; Ronningstam, 1996; Skodol, Oldham, et al., 1995; Zimmerman et al., 2005) that found no associations between NPD and specific anxiety disorders. Furthermore, the strong relationships between NPD and histrionic personality disorder found in earlier studies (Fossati et al., 2000; Marinangeli et al., 2000; Stuart et al., 1998) were also observed in the NESARC data among men, women, and Whites, whereas the association with obsessive–compulsive personality disorder observed in some prior clinical studies (Marinangeli et al., 2000; Stuart et al., 1998) was found only among males and Whites.

There was a significant but negative association between NPD and dysthymia among women and Whites. That women and Whites with NPD were significantly less likely to have dysthymia than their counterparts without NPD could be viewed in the context of the increased co-occurrence rates of substance use disorders among Whites relative to Blacks and Hispanics with NPD and the higher rates of anxiety disorders among women relative to men with NPD. There may be a propensity among women and Whites with NPD to self-medicate to maintain a sense of grandiosity and self-esteem and to ameliorate feelings of depression and worthlessness associated with dysthymia (Oldham et al., 1995; Ronningstam, 1996; Skodol, Oldham, et al., 1995; Zimmerman et al., 2005). The lack of a negative association between NPD and dysthymia among men may reflect the generally lower base rate of dysthymia and greater presence of heavy drinking among men; that is, self-medication of depressive symptoms among men may be more widespread and successful at least in the short term, making the NPD-specific changes less detectable.

NPD was associated with social dysfunction, consistent with findings from one clinical study (Miller et al., 2007). These results generalized to men and women, but disability was more strongly associated with NPD among Whites relative to Blacks and Hispanics. These findings suggest that NPD may have a more severe expression among Whites compared with other race–ethnic groups. Further longitudinal research is needed to understand sex and race–ethnic differences in disability of NPD and its impact on development, course, outcome, and comorbidity.

THEORETICAL AND CLINICAL IMPLICATIONS

Examination of sex and race–ethnic differences in patterns of NPD comorbidity can provide a starting point for future etiological research on this highly disabling personality disorder. The NESARC findings can generate new hypotheses about those factors underlying sex differences in the vulnerability to NPD, for instance, the possible shared risk factors between NPD and obsessive–compulsive personality disorder among men. Moreover, the race–ethnic differences in NPD comorbidity revealed in the NESARC data underscore the importance of culture on personality psychopathology that may arise from variations in NPD symptom expression, response styles, and social desirability responding, all of which may also be stable personality characteristics. Cultural experiences and expressions of NPD symptomatology among various subgroups of Blacks, Hispanics, and Whites may differ markedly, highlighting the need for larger epidemiologic surveys of NPD to understand the unique cultural factors influencing NPD and their interaction with the powerful effect of sex.

Furthermore, these results should also inform the clinical, diagnostic, and treatment guidelines of NPD. Taken together, the earlier findings and the current results of the NESARC study clearly indicate that NPD already is a severe and disabling disorder in its own right, but it is also highly comorbid with other disabling psychiatric conditions, most importantly substance use disorders, bipolar disorders, and borderline and schizotypal personality disorders. However, given the aforementioned race–ethnic and sex specific variations in the comorbidity, practicing clinicians should be aware that different complications in NPD may arise as a result of these characteristics. Knowledge of these differences will contribute to the development of appropriate and efficient preventive or therapeutic interventions.

That NPD is a highly prevalent and disabling disorder in the general population serves as a powerful stimulus for efforts to understand the contributions of sex and race–ethnicity to the development and course of NPD within a cultural formulation and to develop models of prevention and effective treatment.

REFERENCES

Alarcón, R. D. (2005). Cross-cultural issues. In J. M. Oldham, A. E. Skodol, & D. S. Bender (Eds.), *Textbook of personality disorders* (pp. 561–578). Washington, DC: American Psychiatric Publishing.

American Psychiatric Association. (1994). *Diagnostic and statistical manual of mental disorders* (4th ed.). Washington, DC: Author.

Black, D. W., Noyes, R., Jr., Pfohl, B., Goldstein, R. B., & Blum, N. (1993). Personality disorder in obsessive–compulsive volunteers, well comparison subjects, and their first-degree relatives. *American Journal of Psychiatry, 150,* 1226–1232.

Canino, G., Bravo, M., Ramírez, R., Febo, V. E., Rubio-Stipec, M., Fernández, R. L., & Hasin, D. (1999). The Spanish Alcohol Use Disorder and Associated Disabilities Interview Schedule (AUDADIS): Reliability and concordance with clinical diagnoses in a Hispanic population. *Journal of Studies on Alcohol, 60,* 790–799.

Chatterji, S., Saunders, J. B., Vrasti, R., Grant, B. F., Hasin, D., & Mager, D. (1997). Reliability of the alcohol and drug modules of the Alcohol Use Disorder and Associated Disabilities Interview Schedule—Alcohol/Drug–Revised (AUDADIS-ADR): An international comparison. *Drug and Alcohol Dependence, 47,* 171–185. doi:10.1016/S0376-8716(97)00088-4

Coid, J., Yang, M., Tyrer, P., Roberts, A., & Ullrich, S. (2006). Prevalence and correlates of personality disorder in Great Britain. *The British Journal of Psychiatry, 188*, 423–431. doi:10.1192/bjp.188.5.423

Cottler, L. B., Grant, B. F., Blaine, J., Mavreas, V., Pull, C., Hasin, D., . . . Mager, D. (1997). Concordance of DSM–IV alcohol and drug use disorder and diagnoses as measured by AUDADIS-ADR, CIDI and SCAN. *Drug and Alcohol Dependence, 47*, 195–205. doi:10.1016/S0376-8716(97)00090-2

Cramer, V., Torgersen, S., & Kringlen, E. (2006). Personality disorders and quality of life. A population survey. *Comprehensive Psychiatry, 47*, 178–184. doi:10.1016/j.comppsych.2005.06.002

Ekselius, L., Tillfors, M., Furmark, T., & Fredrikson, M. (2001). Personality disorders in the general population: DSM–IV and ICD-10 defined prevalence as related to sociodemographic profile. *Personality and Individual Differences, 30*, 311–320. doi:10.1016/S0191-8869(00)00048-9

First, M. B., Gibbon, M., Spitzer, R. L., Williams, J. B. W., & Benjamin, L. S. (1997). *User's guide for the Structured Clinical Interview for DSM–IV Personality Disorders.* Washington, DC: American Psychiatric Press.

Fossati, A., Maffei, C., Bagnato, M., Battaglia, M., Donati, D., Donini, M., . . . Prolo, F. (2000). Patterns of covariation of DSM–IV personality disorders in a mixed psychiatric sample. *Comprehensive Psychiatry, 41*, 206–215. doi:10.1016/S0010-440X(00)90049-X

Gandek, B., Ware, J. E., Aaronson, N. K., Alonso, J., Apolone, G., Bjorner, J., . . . Sullivan, M. (1998). Tests of data quality, scaling assumptions, and reliability of the SF-36 in eleven countries: Results from the IQOLA Project. International Quality of Life Assessment. *Journal of Clinical Epidemiology, 51*, 1149–1158. doi:10.1016/S0895-4356(98)00106-1

George, E. L., Miklowitz, D. J., Richards, J. A., Simoneau, T. L., & Taylor, D. O. (2003). The comorbidity of bipolar disorder and axis II personality disorders: Prevalence and clinical correlates. *Bipolar Disorders, 5*, 115–122. doi:10.1034/j.1399-5618.2003.00028.x

Grant, B. F., Dawson, D. A., & Hasin, D. S. (2001). *The Alcohol Use Disorder and Associated Disabilities Interview Schedule—DSM–IV version.* Bethesda, MD: National Institute on Alcohol Abuse and Alcoholism.

Grant, B. F., Dawson, D. A., & Hasin, D. S. (2004). *The Wave 2 National Epidemiologic Survey on Alcohol and Related Conditions Alcohol Use Disorder and Associated Disabilities Interview Schedule—DSM–IV version.* Bethesda, MD: National Institute on Alcohol Abuse and Alcoholism.

Grant, B. F., Dawson, D. A., Stinson, F. S., Chou, P. S., Kay, W., & Pickering, R. (2003). The Alcohol Use Disorder and Associated Disabilities Interview Schedule–IV (AUDADIS-IV): Reliability of alcohol consumption, tobacco use, family history of depression and psychiatric diagnostic modules in a general population sample. *Drug and Alcohol Dependence, 71*, 7–16. doi:10.1016/S0376-8716(03)00070-X

Grant, B. F., Harford, T. C., Dawson, D. A., Chou, P. S., & Pickering, R. P. (1995). The Alcohol Use Disorder and Associated Disabilities Interview Schedule (AUDADIS): Reliability of alcohol and drug modules in a general population sample. *Drug and Alcohol Dependence, 39,* 37–44. doi:10.1016/0376-8716(95)01134-K

Grant, B. F., Hasin, D. S., Blanco, C., Stinson, F. S., Chou, S. P., Goldstein, R. B., . . . Huang, B. (2005). The epidemiology of social anxiety disorder in the United States: Results from the National Epidemiologic Survey on Alcohol and Related Conditions. *Journal of Clinical Psychiatry, 66,* 1351–1361. doi:10.4088/JCP.v66n1102

Grant, B. F., Hasin, D. S., Stinson, F. S., Dawson, D. A., Chou, S. P., Ruan, W. J., . . . Pickering, R. P. (2004). Prevalence, correlates, and disability of personality disorders in the United States: Results from the National Epidemiologic Survey on Alcohol and Related Conditions. *Journal of Clinical Psychiatry, 65,* 948–958. doi:10.4088/JCP.v65n0711

Grant, B. F., Hasin, D. S., Stinson, F. S., Dawson, D. A., Goldstein, R. B., Smith, S., . . . Saha, T. D. (2006). The epidemiology of DSM–IV panic disorder and agoraphobia in the United States: Results from the National Epidemiologic Survey on Alcohol and Related Conditions. *Journal of Clinical Psychiatry, 67,* 363–374. doi:10.4088/JCP.v67n0305

Grant, B. F., Hasin, D. S., Stinson, F. S., Dawson, D. A., Ruan, W. J., Goldstein, R. B., . . . Huang, B. (2005). Prevalence, correlates, co-morbidity, and comparative disability of DSM–IV generalized anxiety disorder in the United States: Results from the National Epidemiologic Survey on Alcohol and Related Conditions. *Psychological Medicine, 35,* 1747–1759. doi:10.1017/S0033291705006069

Grant, B. F., Kaplan, K. K., & Stinson, F. S. (2005). *Source and accuracy statement for the Wave 2 National Epidemiologic Survey on Alcohol and Related Conditions.* Bethesda, MD: National Institute on Alcohol Abuse and Alcoholism.

Grant, B. F., Moore, T. C., Shepard, J., & Kaplan, K. (2003). *Source and accuracy statement: Wave 1 National Epidemiologic Survey on Alcohol and Related Conditions (NESARC).* Bethesda, MD: National Institute on Alcohol Abuse and Alcoholism.

Grant, B. F., Stinson, F. S., Hasin, D. S., Dawson, D. A., Chou, S. P., Ruan, W. J., . . . Huang, B. (2005). Prevalence, correlates, and comorbidity of bipolar I disorder and Axis I and II disorders: Results from the National Epidemiologic Survey on Alcohol and Related Conditions. *Journal of Clinical Psychiatry, 66,* 1205–1215. doi:10.4088/JCP.v66n1001

Grilo, C. M., Sanislow, C. A., & McGlashan, T. H. (2002). Co-occurrence of DSM–IV personality disorders with borderline personality disorder. *Journal of Nervous and Mental Disease, 190,* 552–554. doi:10.1097/00005053-200208000-00010

Hasin, D., Carpenter, K. M., McCloud, S., Smith, M., & Grant, B. F. (1997). The Alcohol Use Disorder and Associated Disabilities Interview Schedule (AUDADIS): Reliability of alcohol and drug modules in a clinical sample. *Drug and Alcohol Dependence, 44,* 133–141. doi:10.1016/S0376-8716(97)01332-X

Hasin, D., Goodwin, R. D., Stinson, F. S., & Grant, B. F. (2005). Epidemiology of major depressive disorder: Results from the National Epidemiologic Survey on Alcohol and Related Conditions. *Archives of General Psychiatry, 62,* 1097–1106. doi:10.1001/archpsyc.62.10.1097

Hasin, D., & Paykin, A. (1999). Alcohol dependence and abuse diagnoses: Concurrent validity in a nationally representative sample. *Alcoholism: Clinical and Experimental Research, 23,* 144–150. doi:10.1111/j.1530-0277.1999.tb04036.x

Hasin, D. S., Grant, B. F., Cottler, L., Blaine, J., Towle, L., Üstün, B., & Sartorius, N. (1997). Nosological comparisons of alcohol and drug diagnoses: A multisite, multi-instrument international study. *Drug and Alcohol Dependence, 47,* 217–226. doi:10.1016/S0376-8716(97)00092-6

Hasin, D. S., Schuckit, M. A., Martin, C. S., Grant, B. F., Bucholz, K. K., & Helzer, J. E. (2003). The validity of DSM–IV alcohol dependence: What do we know and what do we need to know? *Alcoholism: Clinical and Experimental Research, 27,* 244–252. doi:10.1097/01.ALC.0000060878.61384.ED

Klein, D. N., Riso, L. P., Donaldson, S. K., Schwartz, J. E., Anderson, R. L., Ouimette, P. C., . . . Aronson, T. A. (1995). Family study of early-onset dysthymia: Mood and personality disorders in relatives of outpatients of dysthymia and episodic major depression and normal controls. *Archives of General Psychiatry, 52,* 487–496. doi:10.1001/archpsyc.1995.03950180073010

Lenzenweger, M. F., Lane, M. C., Loranger, A. W., & Kessler, R. C. (2007). DSM–IV personality disorders in the National Comorbidity Survey Replication. *Biological Psychiatry, 62,* 553–564. doi:10.1016/j.biopsych.2006.09.019

Lenzenweger, M. F., Loranger, A. W., Korfine, L., & Neff, C. (1997). Detecting personality disorders in a nonclinical population: Application of a 2-stage procedure for case identification. *Archives of General Psychiatry, 54,* 345–351. doi:10.1001/archpsyc.1997.01830160073010

Loranger, A. W. (1999). *International Personality Disorder Examination: DSM–IV and ICD-10 Interviews.* Odessa, FL: Psychological Assessment Resources.

Maier, W., Lichtermann, D., Klingler, T., Heun, R., & Hallmayer, J. (1992). Prevalences of personality disorders (DSM–III–R) in the community. *Journal of Personality Disorders, 6,* 187–196. doi:10.1521/pedi.1992.6.3.187

Mantere, O., Melartin, T. K., Suominen, K., Rytsälä, H. J., Valtonen, H. M., Arvilommi, P., . . . Isometsä, E. T. (2006). Differences in Axis I and Axis II comorbidity between bipolar I and II disorders and major depressive disorder. *Journal of Clinical Psychiatry, 67,* 584–593. doi:10.4088/JCP.v67n0409

Marinangeli, M. G., Butti, G., Scinto, A., Di Cicco, L., Petruzzi, C., Daneluzzo, E., & Rossi, A. (2000). Patterns of comorbidity among DSM–III–R personality disorders. *Psychopathology, 33,* 69–74. doi:10.1159/000029123

Miller, J. D., Campbell, W. K., & Pilkonis, P. A. (2007). Narcissistic personality disorder: Relation with distress and functional impairment. *Comprehensive Psychiatry, 48,* 170–177. doi:10.1016/j.comppsych.2006.10.003

Moldin, S. O., Rice, J. P., Erlenmeyer-Kimling, L., & Squires-Wheeler, E. (1994). Latent structure of DSM–III–R Axis II psychopathology in a normal sample. *Journal of Abnormal Psychology, 103,* 259–266. doi:10.1037/0021-843X.103.2.259

Oldham, J. M., Skodol, A. E., Kellman, H. D., Hyler, S. E., Doidge, N., Rosnick, L., & Gallaher, P. E. (1995). Comorbidity of Axis I and Axis II disorders. *The American Journal of Psychiatry, 152,* 571–578.

Pulay, A. J., Goldstein, R. B., & Grant, B. F. (2011). Sociodemographic correlates of DSM–IV Narcissistic Personality Disorder: Results from the Wave 2 National Epidemiologic Survey on Alcohol and Related Conditions (NESARC). In J. D. Miller & W. K. Campbell (Eds.), *The handbook of narcissism and narcissistic personality disorder: Theoretical approaches, empirical findings, and treatment* (pp. 167–180). New York, NY: Wiley-Interscience.

Reich, J., Yates, W., & Nduaguba, M. (1989). Prevalences of DSM–III personality disorders in the community. *Social Psychiatry and Psychiatric Epidemiology, 24,* 12–16. doi:10.1007/BF01788194

Research Triangle Institute. (2006). *Software for Survey Data Analysis (SUDAAN), Version 10.0.1.* Research Triangle Park, NC: Author.

Ronningstam, E. (1996). Pathological narcissism and narcissistic personality disorder in Axis I disorders. *Harvard Review of Psychiatry, 3,* 326–340. doi:10.3109/10673229609017201

Ruan, W. J., Goldstein, R. B., Chou, S. P., Smith, S. M., Saha, T. D., Pickering, R. P., . . . Grant, B. F. (2008). The Alcohol Use Disorder and Associated Disabilities Interview Schedule–IV (AUDADIS-IV): Reliability of new psychiatric diagnostic modules and risk factors in a general population sample. *Drug and Alcohol Dependence, 92,* 27–36. doi:10.1016/j.drugalcdep.2007.06.001

Samuels, J. F., Nestadt, G., Romanoski, A. J., Folstein, M. F., & McHugh, P. R. (1994). DSM–III personality disorders in the community. *The American Journal of Psychiatry, 151,* 1055–1062.

Skodol, A. E., Oldham, J. M., & Gallaher, P. E. (1999). Axis II comorbidity of substance use disorders among patients referred for treatment of personality disorders. *The American Journal of Psychiatry, 156,* 733–738.

Skodol, A. E., Oldham, J. M., Hyler, S. E., Stein, D. J., Hollander, E., Gallaher, P. E., & Lopez, A. E. (1995). Patterns of anxiety and personality disorder comorbidity. *Journal of Psychiatric Research, 29,* 361–374. doi:10.1016/0022-3956(95)00015-W

Skodol, A. E., Stout, R. L., McGlashan, T. H., Grilo, C. M., Gunderson, J. G., Shea, M. T., & Oldham, J. M. (1999). Co-occurrence of mood and personality disorders: A report from the Collaborative Longitudinal Personality Disorders Study (CLPS). *Depression and Anxiety, 10,* 175–182. doi:10.1002/(SICI)1520-6394(1999)10:4<175::AID-DA6>3.0.CO;2-2

Smith, S. M., Stinson, F. S., Dawson, D. A., Goldstein, R., Huang, B., & Grant, B. F. (2006). Race/ethnic differences in the prevalence and co-occurrence of substance use disorders and independent mood and anxiety disorders: Results from the National Epidemiologic Survey on Alcohol and Related Conditions. *Psychological Medicine*, 36, 987–998. doi:10.1017/S0033291706007690

Stinson, F. S., Dawson, D. A., Chou, S. P., Smith, S., Goldstein, R. B., Ruan, W. J., & Grant, B. F. (2007). The epidemiology of DSM–IV specific phobia in the USA: Results from the National Epidemiologic Survey on Alcohol and Related Conditions. *Psychological Medicine*, 37, 1047–1059. doi:10.1017/S0033291707000086

Stinson, F. S., Dawson, D. A., Goldstein, R. B., Chou, S. P., Huang, B., Smith, S. M., . . . Grant, B. F. (2008). Prevalence, correlates, disability, and comorbidity of DSM–IV narcissistic personality disorder: Results from the Wave 2 National Epidemiologic Survey on Alcohol and Related Conditions. *Journal of Clinical Psychiatry*, 69, 1033–1045. doi:10.4088/JCP.v69n0701

Stuart, S., Pfohl, B., Battaglia, M., Bellodi, L., Grove, W., & Cadoret, R. (1998). The co-occurrence of DSM–III–R personality disorders. *Journal of Personality Disorders*, 12, 302–315. doi:10.1521/pedi.1998.12.4.302

Torgersen, S., Kringlen, E., & Cramer, V. (2001). The prevalence of personality disorders in a community sample. *Archives of General Psychiatry*, 58, 590–596. doi:10.1001/archpsyc.58.6.590

Vrasti, R., Grant, B. F., Chatterji, S., Ustün, B. T., Mager, D., Olteanu, I., & Badoi, M. (1998). Reliability of the Romanian version of the alcohol module of the WHO Alcohol Use Disorder and Associated Disabilities Interview Schedule—Alcohol/Drug–Revised. *European Addiction Research*, 4, 144–149. doi:10.1159/000018947

Zanarini, M. C., Frankenburg, F. R., Dubo, E. D., Sickel, A. E., Trikha, A., Levin, A., & Reynolds, V. (1998). Axis II comorbidity of borderline personality disorder. *Comprehensive Psychiatry*, 39, 296–302. doi:10.1016/S0010-440X(98)90038-4

Zanarini, M. C., Frankenburg, F. R., Sickel, A. E., & Yong, L. (1996). *The Diagnostic Interview for DSM–IV Personality Disorders*. Belmont, MA: McLean Hospital, Laboratory for the Study of Adult Development.

Zimmerman, M., & Coryell, W. (1989). DSM–III personality disorder diagnoses in a nonpatient sample: Demographic correlates and comorbidity. *Archives of General Psychiatry*, 46, 682–689. doi:10.1001/archpsyc.1989.01810080012002

Zimmerman, M., Rothschild, L., & Chelminski, I. (2005). The prevalence of personality disorders in psychiatric outpatients. *The American Journal of Psychiatry*, 162, 1911–1918. doi:10.1176/appi.ajp.162.10.1911

IV

TREATMENT CONSIDERATIONS AND APPROACHES

12

COUNTERTRANSFERENCE ISSUES IN THE TREATMENT OF PATHOLOGICAL NARCISSISM

GLEN O. GABBARD

In contemporary discourse among psychotherapists and psychoanalysts, the term *narcissistic* is often used as an insult. One may use the term to refer to colleagues who are self-confident or who seem to think more about themselves than others. The implication of the label is that the colleague who is self-absorbed and insensitive to the needs of others presents a challenge to others. Specifically, this individual may seem so "toxic" that others may prefer to spend their time in the company of someone else. Patients with pathological narcissism may be experienced similarly by clinicians because they often produce characteristic feelings in those around them that are recreated in the therapeutic setting. Indeed, the success of the treatment may rest on the therapist's capacity to tolerate the countertransference reactions that are evoked by narcissistic patients and to forge a therapeutic alliance (the most potent predictor of outcome in psychotherapy) despite those feelings. One might even say that the therapist is facing the core difficulty of narcissistic

DOI: 10.1037/14041-012
Understanding and Treating Pathological Narcissism, J. S. Ogrodniczuk (Editor)
Copyright © 2013 by the American Psychological Association. All rights reserved.

patients: How can they improve their capacity to develop gratifying relation-ships with others when so many people are alienated by their interpersonal style? Hence, a discussion of what is transpiring in the consulting room between therapist and patient often leads to the heart of their problems outside the therapeutic setting.

Countertransference today is regarded as intimately and inextricably related to transference (Gabbard, 1995). Although the construct was classically regarded as the analyst's transference to the patient (i.e., feelings that stemmed from the analyst's past relationships displaced onto the patient), today most psychoanalytically oriented clinicians would agree that countertransference is jointly created by the patient and the therapist. In other words, the patient's transference to the therapist induces a set of feelings in the therapist that are in turn influenced by the preexisting internal object relations of the therapist. Some induced feelings are a better "fit" than others.

Transference and countertransference are best conceptualized as the unconscious recreation of the patient's internal object world in the relation-ship with the psychotherapist. Indeed, the character dimension of personality is usefully conceptualized as involving an ongoing attempt to actualize certain patterns of relatedness that are ubiquitous in the patient's life (Gabbard, 2005a). Through interpersonal pressure in the here-and-now of the clinical setting, narcissistic patients try to impose on the therapist a particular way of respond-ing and experiencing. What are called character traits, then, can be viewed as the attempt to actualize a wish-fulfilling internal object relationship that is firmly entrenched in the patient's unconscious (Sandler 1981). A patient may wish to be admired by the therapist and therefore boast about his many accomplishments to elicit an admiring response. The method, however, may backfire; the therapist may become increasingly irritated and alienated by the patient's boasting. Hence, the tragedy of patients with pathological narcissism is that they are unable to elicit the responses from others that will stabilize their self-esteem that they so desperately long for.

The mode of actualization within the analytic relationship is often referred to as *projective identification* (Gabbard, 1995; Ogden, 1979). Stemming from the thinking of Klein (1946/1975) and Bion (1962), this model involves the notion that patients tend to behave in a characterologically driven way that leads them to "imagine" the therapist into assuming a role that origi-nates within the patient. In other words, by behaving in a particular way, the patient influences the therapist to take on characteristics of an internal object representation or representation of the self. A narcissistic patient who makes contemptuous comments about the therapist may eventually trigger in the therapist feelings of anger or hatred.

The repetitive relationships established in the transference and counter-transference of the clinical setting may approximate real relationships in the patient's past. However, relationships based in fantasy may also be part of a patient's internal world. Transference longings often reflect intensely wished-for relationships that never really materialized in the patient's childhood. Children who grow up with neglect and abuse may long for an idealized rescuer who will save them from abuse, and they may approach others with that wish activated in a variety of different settings.

EMPIRICAL DATA

Most of our knowledge about narcissistic personality disorder has emerged from psychoanalysis and intensive psychoanalytic psychotherapy. We have little research to provide a systematic understanding of transference and countertransference phenomena in large series of patients with the diagnosis. Recently, a growing body of empirical data has helped illuminate those characterological features that are hallmarks of narcissistic personality disorder.

Betan et al. (2005) studied countertransference processes in clinical practice and related it to personality pathology. A randomly selected national sample for this study consisted of 181 clinical psychologists and psychiatrists in North America, and each of these clinicians completed a battery of instruments on a patient in their care. Included among these instruments was the Countertransference Questionnaire (Zittel & Westen, 2003). When the responses to the Countertransference Questionnaire underwent factor analysis, an aggregated portrait of countertransference responses to patients with narcissistic personality disorder provided an empirically based description that strongly resembled clinical and theoretical accounts. Clinicians reported feeling resentment, anger, and dread when treating such patients. They also found themselves behaving in avoidant or distracted ways and harboring wishes to terminate the treatment. In addition, they described feeling criticized and devalued by the patient. These feelings were independent of the therapist's theoretical preferences.

These typical countertransferences are obviously responsive to a set of characterological features that typify narcissistic personality disorder. These traits are the source of characteristic interpersonal problems. Ogrodniczuk et al. (2009) studied 240 consecutively admitted patients to a day treatment program. These patients completed measures of narcissism, interpersonal problems, and general psychiatric distress. Those individuals that were characterized as "highly narcissistic" had several features in common: They were domineering, vindictive, and prone to intrusive behavior. The domineering behavior was composed of controlling and aggressive features that reflected an inability to empathize with others. The vindictive behavior was characterized by vengeful and suspicious features, suggesting an incapacity to enjoy another person's happiness or to be supportive of another's goals in life. The intrusive behavior was composed of exhibitionistic features and reflected an inability to keep things private and to respect the personal boundaries of others. The investigators also found that a failure to complete treatment in the program was associated with high scores in narcissism.

The defining features of the narcissistic patients in the study can be viewed as accounting for the typical countertransference problems that were described in the study conducted by Betan et al. (2005). If we understand transference as involving the continuation in the treatment setting of habitual modes of object relatedness by the patient, then characteristic patterns of response occur in the clinician's countertransference. As discussed in Chapter 2 of this volume, narcissistic personality disorder is not a monolithic entity but a spectrum of subtypes (Gabbard, 2005b; Russ et al., 2008).

The research suggests that the principal subtypes share several key features: conceit, self-indulgence, and disregard for others. However, the vulnerability–sensitivity group is characterized as introverted, anxious, defensive, and vulnerable to life's traumas. By contrast, the grandiosity–exhibitionism group was extroverted, self-assured, aggressive, and exhibitionistic. Hence, one might say that a critically important distinction revolves around narcissistic vulnerability. The hypervigilant narcissist is exquisitely vulnerable to narcissistic wounding, whereas the oblivious narcissist is more intensely defended against that vulnerability.

COMMON PATTERNS OF COUNTERTRANSFERENCE

The empirical literature identifies prototypes—personality subtypes in ideal or pure form. In clinical work, one commonly finds patients who have characteristics of more than one subtype and who reside along the continuum between the oblivious or overt subtype and the hypervigilant or narcissistically vulnerable subtype. Hence, the transferences that develop are related to the constellation of features stemming from the various subtypes identified in the aforementioned research, as well as by idiosyncratic patterns of object relatedness that have been internalized in childhood. It is clinically useful to identify themes that occur in the psychotherapy or psychoanalysis of these patients that are relevant to specific countertransference challenges.

Therapist as Sounding Board

The oblivious narcissistic patient uses the therapist as a sounding board, a listening ear that exists primarily to enhance the patient's self-esteem. Such patients do not really "connect" with the therapist in the way that neurotically organized patients do. They talk on and on about themselves in a self-aggrandizing way without studying the therapist's face to see what is happening in the therapist's internal world. This absence of mentalizing is connected with a lack of curiosity about the therapist. Indeed, the oblivious narcissist may induce a feeling in the therapist that "this patient has no transference." The astute clinician, however, knows that this apparent absence is in fact the transference (Brenner, 1982).

This apparent mode of nonrelatedness is the way that some narcissistic individuals relate to everyone. Kohut (1971) viewed this style of relating to the analyst as a version of the mirror transference, where the patient is hoping to receive confirming and validating responses from others as a way of shoring up a fragmented self and increasing his or her sense of self-esteem. Kohut referred to these as *selfobject transferences* because the other person is used as a missing part of the self. Hence in this form of narcissistic transference, the patient is not aware of the therapist's separate subjectivity and internal world; the therapist is only there to affirm the patient's self-worth.

Clinicians who practice psychotherapy tend to have a need to be needed (Gabbard, 2005b). Narcissistic patients deprive the therapist of fulfilling that need to a large extent. The oblivious subtype often is experienced as speaking "at" the therapist instead of "to" the therapist (Gabbard, 1998). Being used as a sounding board makes one feel isolated, what Kernberg (1970) referred to as a "satellite existence." Therapists feel that their independent center of autonomy, their unique subjectivity, their very "personhood" is not being acknowledged. The therapist may feel ineffectual, colorless, invisible, and deskilled. The common defensive response to this feeling of uselessness is to become bored and disengaged. The therapists may feel a sense of dread when the patient's session is due to begin, and they may count the minutes until the end of the session.

Steiner (2008) wrote about the transference to the analyst as an excluded observer. Indeed, in the presence of an oblivious and grandiose narcissistic patient, therapists may feel chronically excluded, as though they are consigned to the role of silent or approving observer whose insights are not welcome. Steiner stressed that this particular transference is conducive to counter-transference enactments. Therapists may wish to force themselves back into the primary role with the patient or to take sides in an argument involving moral dilemmas. Hence, therapists may find themselves behaving in an overly assertive or judgmental manner that, on reflection, they recognize as being counterproductive. One of the paradoxes is that this sort of patient comes to therapy ostensibly to receive help, feedback, and observations from the therapist but then does not allow the therapist to do the job that he or she is being paid for.

Many of those who choose careers in psychotherapy harbor a wish to be loved and idealized (Finell, 1985); thus, there is potential for therapists to experience narcissistic wounding that parallels what the patient experiences.

Because the narcissistic patient tends to treat the therapist as a self-extension, the patient is likely to evoke certain states in the therapist that reflect the patient's own internal conflicts. It is also true, however, that patients may use projective identification to externalize an aspect of their self-experience into the therapist. Therefore, a therapist who is feeling excluded and bored may be experiencing what the patient went through as a child who was distanced or excluded by a parent. In other words, some narcissistic patients may attempt to master their childhood trauma by unconsciously recreating it in the therapeutic situation (Gabbard, 1998).

Contempt

Therapist feelings of being the object of contempt are unavoidable with narcissistic patients. Therapists must keep in mind that narcissistically organized individuals characteristically stabilize their self-esteem by devaluing others. We expect narcissistic patients to carry their usual defensive styles of object-relatedness into the treatment, so therapists must prepare themselves for being a devalued object much of the time. Betan et al. (2005) found that the hallmarks of countertransference to narcissistic patients were feelings of being devalued and criticized by the patient, accompanied by anger, resentment, and dread in working with such patients.

A variety of responses can result from feelings of being treated with contempt day in and day out. Some therapists may use reaction formation against their growing feelings of anger and hurt. They may become overly empathic and overly kind to the patient as a way of denying their true feelings. This stance may simply activate the patient's envy and rage to a greater extent, leading to a vicious cycle of greater contempt followed by greater reaction formation in the therapist. Patients may also feel that they are being ineffectual in trying to produce the desired response in the therapist.

Other therapists may react by becoming more aggressive and competitive with the patient. They may become so exasperated with being denigrated that they become defensive and demonstrate that they are more intelligent, well-read, worldly, and knowledgeable than the patient. Of course, this reaction only provides the patient with further ammunition to devalue the therapist as a hypersensitive and narcissistically vulnerable individual who has to "show off" his knowledge. Hence, these kinds of countertransference enactments allow patients to projectively disavow their own narcissistic vulnerability and see it only in the therapist.

As one attempts to tolerate the patient's contempt, it is useful to remember that the fundamental disturbances in narcissistically organized patients are feelings of inadequacy associated with difficulties in regulating their self-esteem. One common defensive strategy is to devalue others as a way of making oneself feel superior and less inadequate. Patients who come for help may immediately feel in a one-down position with respect to the therapist and need to treat the therapist with contempt as a way of trying to level the playing field. The grandiose–malignant patient may engage in this contempt, but the fragile or hypervigilant narcissistic individual may also devalue the therapist, especially when feeling narcissistically wounded, ignored, or rejected by the therapist. A small change in the therapist's appearance may lead the patient to erupt in narcissistic rage. This rage may be accompanied by contemptuous and devaluing comments about the therapist's capacities.

Another useful strategy that helps therapists to tolerate the patient's contempt is to remember that it often is related to envy. Narcissistic patients are frequently envious of those who seem to have things that they do not. The therapeutic situation presents narcissistic patients with a dilemma: To receive help, they must acknowledge that the therapist knows something that they do not. This situation results in their feeling diminished in comparison with the therapist, who appears to have wisdom and knowledge. A common response to envy is to try to spoil and devalue what one cannot have, much like the "sour grapes" story in Aesop's Fables (Kernberg 1970, 1984). By insisting that the therapist is incompetent and does not really know anything useful, patients can convince themselves that there is nothing to envy and hence they do not need to feel inferior about themselves. A variation on this envy was noted in the findings of the day hospital study reported by Ogrodniczuk et al. (2009) when they characterized vindictive behavior as reflecting an inability to feel good about another person's happiness or to be supportive of another's goals in life. To do so would be to recognize envy of something good that someone else has.

Idealization

In addition to the mirror transference, Kohut (1971, 1977, 1984) also recognized other types of selfobject transferences in narcissistically organized individuals. To shore up shaky self-esteem and to achieve more cohesion of the self, some patients may idealize the therapist. They may perceive the therapist as an all-powerful parent whose presence soothes and heals. By basking in the reflected glory of an idealized therapist, they vicariously have a sense of self-esteem conferred upon them. Such patients may come to therapy just to be in the presence of a therapist and not really show any initiative to analyze or understand the problems that brought them to therapy. They may feel that being with a therapist is an end in itself—they have found the ideal person and do not need to look any further.

Being idealized may not enter the therapist's radar screen as a form of transference. Therapists who need to be idealized may experience the transference simply as an example of a patient who recognizes the therapist's talents and empathy or the reflection of a good therapeutic alliance. Thus, one reaction to being the object of idealization is to have a blind spot regarding the idealizing transference.

Other therapists may find being idealized to be acutely uncomfortable, as Kohut (1984) himself described. The experience of idealization may make therapists feel conflicted about the activation of their own grandiosity. Their secret or not-so-secret wish to be idealized is being gratified in a way that may make them feel grandiose or extraordinarily narcissistic. A common enactment is to prematurely interpret the idealization rather than recognize the patient's need for idealization as a way of regulating self-esteem.

Omnipotent Control

One of the most common transferences, regardless of the narcissistic subtype, is an effort to control the therapist. Rosenfeld (1964) stressed that for a narcissistically organized person, the greatest concern is an experience of separateness between subject and object. Much of what transpires is an effort to prevent that separateness. This fantasy of controlling what the therapist does manifests in a variety of ways in the transference. Patients may use the therapist as an extension of the self and not allow the therapist any space to make comments from an outside perspective that might challenge the patient's experience of fusion. Hypervigilant or fragile narcissistic individuals may never take their eyes off the therapist, as though through intense scrutiny of the therapist's every move, they maintain the fantasy that the therapist is completely under their control. Erupting in narcissistic rage when the therapist does not conform to the patient's expectations also may be related to a fantasy that bullying and intimidating the therapist with anger will enable them to subjugate him or her.

Symington (1990) once noted that projective identification can be construed as an attempt by the patient to control the therapist's freedom of thought. With narcissistic patients, therapists may feel subjugated by their omnipotent control and therefore feel that they are allowed only a narrow range of thoughts and words. Even one's movements may feel under the control of the patient. If they fidget too much, glance at the clock, clear their throat, or take their eyes off the patient, they may induce a narcissistic injury in a hypervigilant narcissistic patient.

Although the countertransference as an excluded observer and the countertransference of feeling subjugated both grow out of the patient's need to deny separateness from the therapist, these two states may feel quite different. In contrast to the excluded observer countertransference, therapists of hypervigilant patients may feel that they are anything but excluded; they may feel under intense scrutiny, as though a police interrogation light is shining on their faces. They may not feel able to reflect on their own thoughts and allow themselves the freedom of their own associations because they feel they must comply with patients' needs for omnipotent control.

Mutual Admiration

Russ et al. (2008) identified a high-functioning narcissistic individual who may actually produce feelings of envy and admiration in the therapist, especially if the patient is charming and entertaining. Therapists may find themselves "enjoying the show" rather than working therapeutically to help the patient (Gabbard 1998). They may have difficulty recognizing that they are being treated as an extension of the self who is designed to meet the needs of the patient for validation and affirmation rather than interpreting the patient's interpersonal strategies. These kinds of therapies may end up in a stalemate of a mutual admiration society, where both therapist and patient admire and complement one another.

CONCLUSION

Although many of the countertransference developments that occur with narcissistic patients are challenging to tolerate, there is often an advantage in allowing oneself to be steeped in the transference–countertransference experience because it reflects the characteristic patterns of difficulty in relationships outside the treatment setting. The challenges inherent in treating patients with narcissistic personality disorder make brief treatment an inadequate option. These patients generally require long-term psychoanalytic psychotherapy or psychoanalysis to adequately address the entrenched problems that have haunted them throughout their lives. Hence, the capacity to contain and process uncomfortable affect states for extended periods becomes an essential component of the treatment. Therapists who prematurely attempt to "unload" these feelings may find that their patient is not prepared to accept the return of those unpleasant affects. On the other hand, those who can allow themselves to be used in the service of the patient's needs can hope to make significant long-term progress.

REFERENCES

Betan, E., Hein, A. K., Conklin, C. Z., & Westen, D. (2005). Countertransference phenomena and personality pathology. *The American Journal of Psychiatry, 162,* 890–898. doi:10.1176/appi.ajp.162.5.890

Bion, W. R. (1962). *Learning from experience*. New York, NY: Basic Books.

Brenner, C. (1982). *The mind in conflict*. New York, NY: International Universities Press.

Finell, J. S. (1985). Narcissistic problems in analysts. *The International Journal of Psychoanalysis, 66*, 433–445.

Gabbard, G. O. (1995). Countertransference: The emerging common ground. *The International Journal of Psychoanalysis, 76*, 475–485.

Gabbard, G. O. (1998). Transference and countertransference in the treatment of narcissistic patients. In E. F. Ronningstam (Ed.), *Disorders of narcissism: Diagnostic, clinical, and empirical implications* (pp. 125–145). Washington, DC: American Psychiatric Publishing.

Gabbard, G. O. (2005a). Psychoanalysis. In J. M. Oldham, A. E. Skodol, & D. S. Bender (Eds.), *The American psychiatric publishing textbook of personality disorders* (pp. 257–273). Arlington, VA: American Psychiatric Publishing.

Gabbard, G. O. (2005b). *Psychodynamic psychiatry in clinical practice* (4th ed.). Arlington, VA: American Psychiatric Publishing.

Kernberg, O. F. (1970). Factors in the psychoanalytic treatment of narcissistic personalities. *Journal of the American Psychoanalytic Association, 18*, 51–85. doi:10.1177/000306517001800103

Kernberg, O. F. (1984). *Severe personality disorders: Psychotherapeutic strategies*. New Haven, CT: Yale University Press.

Klein, M. (1975). Notes on some schizoid mechanisms. In *Envy and gratitude and other works, 1946–1963* (pp. 1–24). New York, NY: Free Press. (Original work published 1946)

Kohut, H. (1971). *The analysis of the self: A systematic approach to the psychoanalytic treatment of narcissistic personality disorders*. New York, NY: International Universities Press.

Kohut, H. (1977). *The restoration of the self*. New York, NY: International Universities Press.

Kohut, H. (1984). *How does analysis cure?* (A. Goldberg, Ed.). Chicago, IL: University of Chicago Press.

Ogden, T. H. (1979). On projective identification. *The International Journal of Psychoanalysis, 60*, 357–373.

Ogrodniczuk, J. S., Piper, W. E., Joyce, A. S., Slanberg, P. I., & Duggal, S. (2009). Interpersonal problems associated with narcissism among psychiatric outpatients. *Journal of Psychiatric Research, 43*, 837–842. doi:10.1016/j.jpsychires.2008.12.005

Rosenfeld, H. (1964). On the psychopathology of narcissism: A clinical approach. *The International Journal of Psychoanalysis, 45*, 332–3377.

Russ, E., Shedler, J., Bradley, R., & Westen, D. (2008). Refining the construct of narcissistic personality disorder: Diagnostic criteria on subtypes. *The American Journal of Psychiatry, 165*, 1473–1481. doi:10.1176/appi.ajp.2008.07030376

Sandler, J. (1981). Character traits and object relationships. *The Psychoanalytic Quarterly, 50*, 694–708.

Steiner, J. (2008). Transference to the analyst as an excluded observer. *The International Journal of Psychoanalysis, 89*, 39–54. doi:10.1111/j.1745-8315.2007.00005.x

Symington, N. (1990). The possibility of human freedom and its transmission (with particular reference to the thought of Bion). *The International Journal of Psychoanalysis, 71*, 95–106.

Zittel, C., & Westen, D. (2003). *The countertransference questionnaire*. Departments of Psychology & Psychiatry and Behavioral Sciences (Emory University). Retrieved from http://www.psychsystems.net/lab

13

MAINTAINING BOUNDARIES IN THE TREATMENT OF PATHOLOGICAL NARCISSISM

ANDREW F. LUCHNER

It is clear that narcissism is not a unitary construct that is defined solely by grandiosity, entitlement, and selfishness, but that it also manifests as deficits in self-esteem (a depleted or devalued self), lack of confidence, conformity, and hypersensitivity to slights and negativity (Dickinson & Pincus, 2003; Gabbard, 1994; Masterson, 1993; Miller, 1997; PDM Task Force, 2006; Wink, 1991). The two subtypes of narcissism have been termed *grandiose* and *vulnerable*, respectively. (See Chapter 2 in this volume for further explanation and discussion of vulnerable and grandiose narcissistic subtypes.) Patients with pathological narcissistic characteristics are among the more difficult to treat in psychotherapy because they use others (e.g., therapists) to define themselves, are fragile and easily affected by perceived slights and mistakes, and are per-fectionistic in their attempts to elicit admiration from others to neutralize internal experiences of devaluation (Ivey, 1995; McWilliams, 1994). The source of self-satisfaction for narcissistic patients does not exist within them-selves; thus, in psychotherapy, therapists are depended on to fulfill absent

DOI: 10.1037/14041-013
Understanding and Treating Pathological Narcissism, J. S. Ogrodniczuk (Editor)

self-definition and self-worth. The pressure that therapists feel is a function of the demands that narcissistic patients place on them to exist as separate people and to exist as an extension of their devalued and critical self. Because patients with grandiose and vulnerable narcissism lack clearly defined boundaries between themselves and others, therapists can have difficulty managing and maintaining boundaries.

Pathological narcissistic patients may be additionally challenging to treat because of therapists' strivings for admiration, acceptance, and recognition for selflessness—core aspects of vulnerable narcissism. Many therapists tend to be giving, caring, and willing to accommodate to the needs of others, including their patients. It is hyper-responsibility, aversion to wrongdoing, and the wish to provide and take care of others that increases the probability that difficulties maintaining boundaries in psychotherapy will occur. For example, grandiose narcissistic patient characteristics may force therapists to confront their inability to help, whereas vulnerable narcissistic patient characteristics may leave therapists blinded by identification and the fantasy that providing psychotherapy can resolve past and current needs for helpfulness and selflessness. Although vulnerable narcissistic characteristics are not emblematic of all therapists, it is common to hear therapists talk about their special role in personal relationships as the one who has always been the "good listener" or the one whose friends "go to when they need to talk." At the expense of one's own needs and authentic responses in the moment, therapists may have learned early to deny their own self (e.g., denial of their own need to be gratified and attended to) as a way to feel some sense of self-worth, identity, and helpfulness to others. To care more about others than oneself has been linked to the choice of psychotherapy as a profession (Miller, 1997), and therapists are drawn to want to be the most helpful, the most effective, and the most sought out for their ability to engender change.

The interaction between characterological qualities of many therapists and the vicissitudes of therapeutic practice make working with patients with pathological narcissism challenging and taxing. As a result, psychotherapy with narcissistic patients affects therapists' ability to attend to therapeutic boundaries that are a necessary component not only for patient care (e.g., managing the therapeutic relationship) but for therapist self-care as well (Kottler, 2010; McWilliams, 2004).

This chapter begins with a discussion of boundaries and their definitions and further delineates the susceptibility of therapists to patients with vulnerable narcissism. The link between patient pathological narcissism and boundaries is then addressed, emphasizing how different patient characteristics may lead to separate struggles with maintaining boundaries within the context of the therapeutic relationship.

BOUNDARIES AND BOUNDARY MAINTENANCE

Although there are no specific American Psychological Association (APA) ethical standards that pertain to the maintenance of boundaries, psychotherapists widely agree that boundaries play a crucial role in the therapeutic process (Gelso & Hayes, 1998). The establishment of boundaries is directly related to the professional standards of conduct, notably the importance of upholding the principle of Beneficence and Nonmaleficence (APA, 2002). However, clear definitions and clear agreement of what differentiates healthy boundaries from boundary violations are lacking (Gabbard & Lester, 1995; Glass, 2003; McWilliams, 2004). For the purpose of this discussion, *boundaries* are defined as therapeutic limits that allow for the protection of the patient's best interests, thereby allowing for safety, reliability, and dependability (Gabbard & Lester, 1995; Gelso & Hayes, 1998; Glass, 2003; Gutheil & Gabbard, 1998; Smith & Fitzpatrick, 1995). The psychotherapist attempts to protect boundaries by maintaining focus on the patient's difficulties as they relate to therapeutic goals, reducing or attending to the role of therapist opinion, and enhancing opportunities to increase patient independence and autonomy (Epstein, 1994; Smith & Fitzpatrick, 1995). The purpose of establishing and maintaining boundaries is to ensure that therapy is geared toward helping the patient and not motivated by therapist needs, wishes, or agendas (Smith & Fitzpatrick, 1995). When boundaries are compromised, boundary transgressions occur, which exist on a continuum ranging from *adaptive* (i.e., ethical and therapeutically useful boundary crossings) to *maladaptive* (i.e., antitherapeutic and unethical; Frank, 2002; Zur, 2007). *Boundary violations*, which stand at the maladaptive end of the boundary continuum, are "serious" and "harmful" (Gabbard & Lester, 1995, p. 123), do not involve careful consideration by anyone involved in the therapy, and occur when the therapist crosses the line of appropriate, decent, and ethical behavior (Zur, 2007). Furthermore, boundary violations are characterized by an absence of attenuation, involving the therapist's inability or refusal to address the enactments, being pervasive in nature, and causing harm. Many theorists consider boundary violations as inherently unethical and exploitative, departing from normal practice, involving the misuse of power and influence, and causing harm to the patient (Gabbard & Lester, 1995; Smith & Fitzpatrick, 1995; Zur, 2007). Some examples of boundary violations include establishing romantic and sexual relationships with patients and manipulating patients for financial gain.

It is important to emphasize that boundary crossings in isolation are not inherently pathological, negative, or to be avoided (Wolf, 1988). Some interventions that cross boundaries are potentially therapeutic (Luchner, Mirsalimi, Moser, & Jones, 2008; Smith & Fitzpatrick, 1995; Williams,

1997). For example, therapists may disclose their awareness of and reactions to patients' enactment of past patterns in an attempt to provide patients with a new understanding and experience of themselves and others in relationships. Much of the discourse on enactments and more recent definitions of countertransference support the usefulness of therapist reactions to inform and benefit the patient in psychotherapy. Additionally, it has been argued that crossing therapeutic boundaries intentionally may be clinically useful for certain patients and populations (e.g., patients from diverse cultural backgrounds that emphasize more flexible boundaries) and when performed by certain therapists with varying theoretical orientations (Luchner et al., 2008).

However, boundary crossings and ineffective maintenance of boundaries may negatively affect the patient and the therapeutic relationship when they are (a) not attended to, (b) for the therapist's benefit, (c) outside of awareness (e.g., unconscious), (d) automatic, or (e) not part of an understanding of the patient's patterns and dynamics. Although boundary crossings are not inherently unethical, they have a powerful impact on the therapeutic relationship and process. Furthermore, the proper maintenance and examination of boundaries may be one of the most important experiences for patients as they learn that they are capable of being treated as independent adults and having mature relationships in which clear distinction is made between themselves and others (Binder, 2004; Epstein, 1994; McWilliams, 1994). Determining when boundary transgressions are helpful or harmful remains difficult because boundaries are flexible, idiosyncratic to particular work with a particular patient (i.e., a therapeutic boundary crossing with one patient may be a violation with another), and tailored to specific therapeutic situations (Glass, 2003; Harper & Steadman, 2003). Because there is a fine line between appropriate and inappropriate boundary transgressions, it is crucial to be aware of the many problems that may arise as a result of one's own narcissistic susceptibility that may have led to the choice of psychotherapy as a profession.

PSYCHOTHERAPISTS AND VULNERABLE NARCISSISM

Two important aspects of providing psychotherapy appear to connect to descriptions of vulnerable narcissism: the importance of attunement and the one-sided nature of therapeutic work. Attunement with and interest in the needs of the patient are skills that psychotherapists depend on to form a collaborative therapeutic relationship with patients (Binder, 2004; Gelso & Hayes, 1998). These abilities have been described as "emotional antennae" that allow the therapist to provide important qualities such as "sensibility, empathy" and "responsiveness" (Miller, 1997, p. 19). The qualities that allow therapists to center their attention and suspend focus on themselves also create pressure to feel that they must provide more when patients express or communicate displeasure or dissatisfaction (McWilliams, 2004). Second, psychotherapy is focused on helping one person, which leaves the therapist relatively protected from being known by the patient (Coen, 2007; Epstein, 1994; Smith & Fitzpatrick, 1995; Wolf, 1988). Therapy has the potential to create ongoing and repetitive interpersonal experiences of not getting needs met. For example, psychotherapy depends greatly on a working alliance, which is established by focusing on the needs and goals of the patient in order to establish trust and safety (Gabbard & Lester, 1995; Gelso & Hayes, 1998). Therefore, the necessary conditions for the establishment of a therapeutic alliance (e.g., attunement, establishment of trust and safety) create ample opportunities for the therapist to rescue (Masterson, 1993) and fulfill the need to be selfless, caretaking, giving, and self-sacrificing—aspects of vulnerable narcissism.

Although one's own narcissistic needs may be met as part of being a therapist, it is important to recognize that striving for admiration and affirmation may be healthy and appropriate. For example, therapists may feel good or capable when a timely and accurate intervention is made in the service of furthering patient exploration and growth, and there is nothing inherently problematic about reacting positively. Experiences of narcissism are important in the development of the self and are part of healthy development for every individual (Gabbard, 1994; Kohut, 1971; Kohut & Wolf, 1986; Wink, 1991; Wolf, 1988). Indeed, it is quite appropriate for psychotherapy to feel rewarding and satisfying for both patient and therapist in a mutual way.

Therapist vulnerabilities are likely to be ignited when working with pathologically narcissistic patients, irrespective of their own struggles with narcissism. Therapist effectiveness is tied to patient responsiveness, and when patient responsiveness is compromised it affects the therapist's ability to feel worthy, energized, competent, and effective (Ivey, 1995). The extent to which therapists are motivated to attend selflessly to patients in an attempt to receive admiration may depend on the interaction between the severity of the patient's narcissistic disturbance and therapists' narcissistic vulnerability (Ivey, 1995), although either in isolation may be sufficient to affect boundary maintenance. Difficulty maintaining boundaries may occur when there is too much of a focus on therapist needs for admiration and acceptance (Wolf, 1988), especially when therapists identify or counteridentify with patient struggles for admiration and self-definition.

PATHOLOGICAL NARCISSISM:
IDENTIFICATION AND COUNTERIDENTIFICATION

It has been noted that patients who are vastly different from their therapists may provide the greatest challenge to treat; they tend to defy therapist attempts to help, to be empathic, and to model balance within therapy (McWilliams, 2004). It is equally important to consider the power of identification and how strongly therapists are drawn to patients that remind them of themselves. Similarities between therapists and patients may compromise the ability of the therapist to be a participant observer, as the wish to assist patients becomes the wish to heal oneself and to provide what the therapist never received from others. At times, therapists overidentify and become overinvolved in their patients' concerns and progress, because patients remind therapists of themselves and their own internal struggles. At other times, therapists struggle to identify with patients that they perceive as different, especially if they flaunt their grandiosity, arrogance, or self-assuredness.

Feeling satisfaction for attending selflessly to the needs of patients is most likely to be frustrated when working with patients with grandiose pathological narcissism or gratified when working with those possessing more vulnerable traits (Ivey, 1995). As might be expected, it is the grandiose patient who most obviously creates discordance in treatment and leads therapists to feel used, engulfed, and exploited (Shulman, 1986); experience fantasies of avoidance; struggle with conflict and anger; and harbor guilt and fears of ineptitude, failure, and responsibility. Because therapists "identify with victims rather than with oppressors" (McWilliams, 2004, p. 105), working with patients who exhibit grandiosity, entitlement, and selfishness is particularly taxing. However, therapists working with patients suffering from pathological vulnerable narcissism are susceptible to imposing their own needs onto patients and identifying too strongly with the deficits of patients (e.g., selflessness, subversion of needs to serve others, empathy, attunement to others' needs). It seems reasonable to expect that patients who are likeable, approachable, agreeable, and giving remind therapists of themselves and their struggles to be liked, respected, and appreciated, thereby potentially creating blind spots and boundary maintenance difficulties. Conversely, patients whom therapists dislike pose specific problems with maintaining therapeutic boundaries and managing boundary crossings because therapists want to be admired for their empathic attunement and selflessness. There are no rules for determining whether one type of patient may compromise therapeutic boundaries more or less. Yet, awareness of how patients with narcissistic pathology affect the therapeutic relationship and compromise therapists' ability to maintain intentional delivery of interventions and interpretations remains a crucial aspect of understanding narcissistic pathology in patients and recognizing when narcissistic difficulties are affecting therapeutic work for patients and therapists alike.

BOUNDARIES AND PATHOLOGICAL NARCISSISM

Although it is difficult to anticipate how a particular therapist will react to a particular patient, some common themes regarding boundary crossings and maintenance have emerged in the clinical literature and pertain specifically to work with patients with narcissistic pathology. Because the potential for difficulty in maintaining boundaries with narcissistic patients exists specifically because of identification and counteridentification, it is important to highlight areas or indicators of boundary crossings that might exist or appear in therapy (Ivey, 1995). Each of the following sections addresses the connection between areas of potential risk for boundary transgressions based on specific traits of vulnerable and grandiose narcissism. I hope that this discussion encourages self-reflection, self-awareness, consultation, and supervision as these themes emerge within the unique context of the therapeutic relationship.

Overinvesting in Caretaking or Overinvesting in Rejection: The Misuse of Empathy

Patients with vulnerable narcissism are challenging because they tend to pull from therapists approval, advice, soothing, caretaking, and over-involvement that ultimately affects the therapeutic process and the boundary between patient and therapist (Wolf, 1988). Therefore, the pull to bolster the self-esteem of the patient with vulnerable narcissism may involve a misuse of empathy; the therapist may erroneously believe that empathy entails "doing something good for the patient" (Wolf, 1988, p. 132) and performing acts of kindness (Gabbard, 2009). For example, the therapist, in an effort to reduce negative reactions in the patient, may attempt to emphasize positive aspects of the relationship (e.g., progress, closeness) and deemphasize any negative aspects (e.g., failure, ruptures) that may be affecting the therapeutic relationship (Miller, 1997). Controlling the discourse in therapy so that only positive experiences occur may be conceptualized as empathy, but it can be problematic because it leads to overinvestment in taking care of the patient. By extending sessions past normal time limits and by making special concessions, the therapist may be trying to protect the patient from negative experience, sacrificing boundary maintenance in an effort to avoid creating an atmosphere where negativity exists. Additionally, a psychotherapist may pay an inordinate amount of attention to the patient's strengths, avoid confrontation, and constantly reframe patient difficulties in an attempt to reduce their own and the patient's discomfort with negativity. Difficulties accepting patients' negative reactions may create an environment in which patients cannot see the therapist as anything but positive and may serve to convey the message that negative emotions should be avoided because they may injure others. This may serve to reinforce patients' expectations that they must take care of the therapist and support the belief that they too must negate their feelings of anger and frustration in an attempt to remain close to others. The freedom for the patient to express the full range of human emotion and see the therapist as human with flaws and inabilities is thwarted, thereby possibly halting movement toward change (Wolf, 1988).

Reactions to grandiose narcissistic characteristics of grandiosity and entitlement may leave therapists unable to invest emotionally, leaving them unempathic, critical, and rejecting (Glickauf-Hughes & Wells, 1997; McWilliams, 1994). Particular emphasis on the negative aspects of grandiose narcissistic patients may be tempting because the constant devaluation and scorn that such a patient expresses may lead therapists to withhold empathy (Ivey, 1995; Shulman, 1986) or to make "vengeful comments or ill-advised management decisions as a way to get back at the patient" (Gabbard, 1994, p. 483). Therefore, therapist rejection may reduce opportunities for grandiose narcissistic patients (once a therapeutic relationship has been firmly established) to admit to or express any need of or dependence on the therapist. As empathy provides the necessary conditions for full disclosure of an integrated self, one made up of independent and dependent strivings, an absence of empathy is tantamount to rejecting the patient's need and wish to feel understood and supported. Empathy provides the necessary boundary that allows for a full range of experience by the patient. Therefore, erosion of empathy that creates rejection of the patient's inherent worth reaffirms the patient's need to protect oneself from showing weakness, vulnerability, and fallibility—core fears of grandiose narcissistic patients. Insufficient empathy may ultimately lead to treatment failure (Ivey, 1995; Wolf, 1988).

Attempting to Engender Closeness or Attempting to Engender Distance

Closeness to and "tranquil union" (Shulman, 1986, p. 146) with patients is a common experience when working with vulnerable narcissistic patients (Shulman, 1986). Therapists are drawn to patients who appear selfless, weak, and helpless, and vulnerable narcissistic patients often implicitly communicate fantasies of rescue and merger (Wolf, 1988). Although attraction to and interest in patients are expected and understandable phenomena, overinvestment in how close therapists feel toward patients may limit authenticity in treatment. The closeness that therapists feel toward their patients may limit therapeutic flexibility and an awareness of negative countertransferential reactions.

Additionally, awareness and understanding of patients' experiences may be limited as therapists are drawn to join with patients who yearn to be close to and known by others. For example, therapists working with patients who exhibit vulnerable narcissistic traits may struggle to separate their own experience from that of patients, potentially leading to misguided reflections, validations, and interpretations. Therapists may believe that they can understand their clients because they are the same (thinking to themselves, "I know how you must feel") and therefore share similar reactions, perceptions, and experiences. Patients may ultimately feel like they must acquiesce to attempts to engender closeness to avoid separation. Additionally, patients may accept attempts by the therapist to provide understanding while simultaneously believing that they must agree in order to receive approval and remain close to the therapist, leading to further entrenched inauthenticity and selflessness.

Boredom is a common countertransferential reaction when working with patients with grandiose narcissistic characteristics; it takes many forms, including daydreaming, tiredness, detachment, forgetfulness, and an inability to focus attention (Gabbard, 2009; Ivey, 1995; Kernberg, 2004). Boredom ultimately creates psychological and emotional withdrawal (Glickauf-Hughes & Wells, 1997), limiting therapists' ability to attend to patients, track therapeutic dialogue, or attend to the therapeutic relationship (McWilliams, 2004). The distance that is created as a result of the grandiose narcissistic patient's attempts to separate from and not be dependent on the therapist causes difficulty for the therapist in attempting to attend to the patient, possibly recapitulating the patient's past experience of being ignored, invalidated, and devalued. For example, psychological and emotional distance from the patient (e.g., the sense that "I am too different to understand or relate") with grandiose pathological narcissism may compromise the ability of the therapist to be a participant observer; the therapist might withdraw from participation in the relationship and become unable to observe, recognize, or inquire about cognitive-affective phenomena that arise.

Devaluing and Criticizing or Idealizing and Praising: The Role of Therapist Self-focus

Vulnerable narcissistic patients "respond to their falling short by feeling inherently flawed rather than forgivably human" (McWilliams, 1994, p. 174). Therapists might misinterpret the patient's internal experience of devaluation as a therapeutic failure; their constant criticism of themselves is likely to set the stage for a multitude of difficulties that can compromise the therapeutic relationship and the treatment itself. These difficulties may include being less responsive, more hesitant, less attentive, and more doubtful about accomplishments, therapeutic gain, and therapeutic ability. As a result, therapists who struggle with doubt about their effectiveness focus too much on their own performance, potentially replicating patients' past experience of feeling unimportant and devalued themselves.

A significant trap that therapists can easily fall into when working with patients who display grandiose narcissistic tendencies is identification with the patient's grandiose and inflated sense of self (Coen, 2007; McWilliams, 1994). Such patients can be charming, extroverted, and attractive, qualities that therapists may aspire to but have difficulty owning and believing apply to themselves. By using these qualities, patients with grandiose narcissism can be very convincing in their attempts to exude greatness and infallibility. Therapists can easily be drawn to patients' grandiose presentations and collude with them in believing in their greatness and also begin to identify with this illusion (Gabbard, 2009). For example, therapists may become increasingly confident about their abilities, such as their greatness to heal, attend, and help. Idealization may result in both parties reinforcing grandiose and entitled strivings, never allowing for growth or challenge of grandiose behavior and defense.

Taking Responsibility or Avoiding Responsibility

Vulnerable narcissistic patients tend to attribute too much error to their own behavior; they feel that they must perfectly attend to others or be rejected and left without purpose. In turn, they may create in therapists the wish to protect, increasing the therapist's susceptibility to taking too much responsibility for lack of progress and difficulty in the therapeutic relationship. Because patients with vulnerable narcissism come across as selfless, eager to assist, giving, agreeable, and caretaking, therapists may feel guilty when they become aware of a lack of improvement or change. For example, therapists may take responsibility for blame too easily or too often when patients express self-blame or fault in terms of lack of progress. Therapists who excessively admit fault and vulnerability may inadvertently reinforce self-devaluation and self-blame to vulnerable narcissistic patients. Boundaries are compromised when patients shift attention to managing therapist distress, placing patients with vulnerable narcissism in the familiar role of caretaker and protector of others.

Patients who exhibit grandiose narcissistic characteristics challenge therapists to admit vulnerabilities, fallibilities, and mistakes, the same fears that exist for the patient. Grandiose narcissistic patients pull therapists to disown their own sense of responsibility and blame the patient for the lack of progress, for difficulty establishing a therapeutic relationship, and for negative countertransference feelings (e.g., anger). In turn, the therapist's inability to accept responsibility may limit the ability of patients to accept their own fallibility, denying them self-expression and subjective experience. For example, a therapist may communicate that patients are "responsible for their own change" while thinking that patients' lack of change is "not my responsibility."

Unconditionally Accepting or Competing and Arguing

The patient with vulnerable narcissistic tendencies often attempts to demonstrate to the therapist his or her capacity to provide constant affection and admiration. As a result, the therapist may feel obligated to unconditionally accept the patient and return the experience of admiration and affection (especially if the therapist struggles with similar difficulties). Boundary transgressions of a more implicit nature can occur as a result of the wish to provide unconditional acceptance (and at its most extreme, love) of the patient. For example, the psychotherapist may frequently and persistently attempt to actively soothe the patient, potentially compromising boundaries because of the motivation and wish to be the perfect parent who is capable of providing unconditional love to the child (Gabbard & Lester, 1995). Improvement in therapy for patients, however, may become increasingly difficult to achieve because therapists' attempts to provide unwavering acceptance may stunt patients' ability to acknowledge their own unrealistic wish to be unconditionally loved. Furthermore, it can shift the focus of psychotherapy to the therapist's needs to provide and soothe, leaving patients in the familiar role of providing constant support and comfort to others. For example, providing unconditional acceptance may leave patients unexposed to the inevitable and necessary frustration inherent in therapeutic work that ultimately contributes to motivation for and awareness of change, depriving them of the opportunity to develop their own internal means (e.g., confidence) for self-soothing.

The seeming self-assuredness and sense of entitlement of patients with grandiose narcissism invites therapists to argue, confront, and be competitive with them (Gabbard, 2009) in an attempt to show or prove to them that their sense of grandiosity is false and not based in reality. Additionally, therapists may feel annoyed, frustrated, and angry at patients who constantly attempt to prove their infallibility and perfection; they may become overly invested in arguing and competing with their patients as a result of their own struggle to manage negative reactions (e.g., criticism, condemnation) toward them (Kohut & Wolf, 1986; Masterson, 1993). Therapists may engage in competitive strivings to win arguments, prove their worthiness to their patients, or prove the unworthiness of the patient's grandiosity. As a result, argumentativeness may ultimately lead to further devaluation, leading to entitlement in the therapist. For example, a therapist may become competitive and argumentative with patients, which in turn conveys to patients that the therapist is correct while simultaneously communicating the belief that patients are incorrect and invalid (most likely resonating with the patient's past experiences and supporting the need for the grandiosity and arrogance).

Making Connections or Withholding Intervention

The selfless and helpless qualities of patients with vulnerable narcissistic characteristics tend to make them seem needy. Therapists may attempt to gratify the needs of vulnerable narcissistic patients by providing early and frequent interpretations and connections (Gabbard, 2009). Misguided attempts to interpret or intervene may compromise the boundary between therapist and patient (Ogrodniczuk, Piper, Joyce, & McCallum, 1999), as the therapist's attempts to provide for patients may in fact support their pathological belief in their own weakness and helplessness (Miller, 1997). Therapist attempts to further the conscious awareness of patients' past and/or present struggles by constantly attempting to provide greater cognitive and emotional under-standing for vulnerable narcissistic patients may recreate past experiences of patients who have never been allowed to engage in self-direction or self-discovery (Gabbard, 2009; Kohut, 1971), thereby supporting feelings of shame and worthlessness. For example, a therapist may be more active than usual in order to feel more helpful and useful (Wolf, 1988), but in doing so may not take into account the vulnerable narcissistic patient's chronic self-doubt and vulnerability. Autonomy, collaboration, and participation might be discour-aged (Epstein, 1994), and dependency may be created as the therapist takes on greater responsibility in the relationship by not allowing the patient to confront feelings of weakness and helplessness or confront defenses against guilt and exhibitionistic desires.

The withholding of intervention by the therapist may occur in response to the grandiose narcissistic patient's devaluation of the therapist's attempts to understand, interpret, and connect (Kernberg, 1986). Therapists may feel unnecessary in sessions because patients are not interested in the therapists' independent existence (McWilliams, 1994). Additionally, a patient's rejection of interpretation and intervention may tap into a thera-pist's fears of being an imposter, of not being worthy enough to help others. Withholding of interpretation may foster greater independence and fear of dependency in the patients, who are not offered the opportunity for a different experience or increased insight into their own pathology. For example, a therapist may withhold attempts to intervene (e.g., "There is no use to provide anything because nothing I do matters"), which may enhance and support the patient's devaluation of and emotional disconnection from the therapist.

Avoiding Termination or Prematurely Terminating

Because patients with vulnerable narcissism tend to be agreeable, giving, accommodating, and pleasing, termination can be a difficult process as therapists are pulled to not relinquish the patient. Avoidance of termination diverts attention away from issues relating to separation, independence, and one's ability to exist separately from others, thereby creating difficulty for the therapist to manage boundaries that aim to support patient growth and development. When vulnerable narcissistic patients (who are adept at recognizing the needs of others) detect therapists' need to remain connected, they are discouraged from ending psychotherapy when termination may be in their best interest. For example, psychotherapists may dissuade patient independence by communicating to patients the importance of remaining in therapy as the only way to maintain change and positive results. Additionally, hindering patients from terminating therapy directly (e.g., "I think you have more work to do" or "You are not ready to terminate") or indirectly (e.g., "Are you sure you have met your goals?" or errors of commission that avoid recognition of change) when there is evidence that they have progressed may serve to remind them that they are unable to achieve support, help, or improvement without others, most notably the therapist.

As patients with pathological grandiose narcissism consistently and repeatedly devalue, criticize, reject, and use therapists to fulfill unmet needs for mirroring, therapists may begin to act out wishes and fantasies for premature termination (Betan, Heim, Conklin, & Westen, 2005; Kernberg, 2004). The wish to vanquish the patient who exhibits grandiose narcissistic characteristics is a product of the patient's unyielding debasement of others. Therapists may encourage premature termination and may justify such acts as ethical or moral (e.g. "The patient has made progress," "I will only do more harm," or "I am not qualified to treat this patient"). Because patients with grandiose narcissistic characteristics challenge therapists to withstand their onslaught of devaluation and entitlement, therapists may push patients toward termination through inappropriate use of intervention (e.g., premature confrontation, expression of anger) as a means of reducing their own discomfort and fear of failure (Glickauf-Hughes & Wells, 1997). It may begin with gradual disinterest in upcoming sessions and relief when cancellations or no-shows occur. These same feelings of dread or relief may then transform into therapist encouragement of independence, deemphasizing the importance of connection and an integrated sense of self (e.g., one that relies on a relative balance of independence and dependence). These messages implicitly support the grandiose belief of overtly narcissistic patients that connections to others are undesirable or that the only way to exist is through independence. Premature encouragement to seek support and empathy from others may accomplish the therapist's desire to separate and end treatment but further reinforces patients' fears of dependence and engulfment.

CONCLUSION

Working with patients with pathological narcissism is undeniably challenging. Inherent in the treatment of such patients are difficulties in maintaining therapeutic boundaries. Patients' narcissistic tendencies can incite a variety of reactions in therapists, which have the potential to lead to boundary violations. Therapists who themselves possess vulnerable narcissistic traits may be particularly susceptible to experiencing difficulties in maintaining therapeutic boundaries (Luchner et al., 2008). Moreover, therapists who are dealing with environmental struggles (e.g., relational, financial, familial) of their own might be especially challenged by a narcissistic patient's behaviors and find that therapeutic boundaries are threatened (Wolf, 1988). However, all therapists can be expected to face challenges in maintaining therapeutic boundaries with narcissistic patients. Appropriate management of therapeutic boundaries requires a persistent focus on how a patient's narcissistic tendencies are manifesting in treatment and one's own reactions to these manifestations (Coen, 2007). Therefore, awareness of common reactions to narcissistic patients and recognition of deviation from known patterns of relating may be especially important for determining whether boundary crossings have moved away from having a useful place in treatment to impeding treatment by limiting therapist flexibility and autonomy. Training, supervision, and consultation are important to help therapists develop the skills for maintaining appropriate boundaries with narcissistic patients, especially for beginning therapists who may be especially susceptible to the pressure to please others and embarrassment about mistakes (Huprich, 2008). Persistent awareness of one's reactions to patients remains necessary to prevent undue boundary crossings and more serious boundary violations from occurring when working with all patients, but particularly with patients struggling with pathological narcissism.

REFERENCES

American Psychological Association. (2002). Ethical principles of psychologists and code of conduct. *American Psychologist, 57,* 1060–1073. doi:10.1037/0003-066X. 57.12.1060

Betan, E., Heim, A. K., Conklin, C. Z., & Westen, D. (2005). Countertransference phenomena and personality pathology in clinical practice: An empirical investigation. *The American Journal of Psychiatry, 162,* 890–898. doi:10.1176/appi. ajp.162.5.890

Binder, J. L. (2004). *Key competencies in brief dynamic psychotherapy: Clinical practice beyond the manual*. New York, NY: Guilford Press.

Coen, S. J. (2007). Narcissistic temptations to cross boundaries and how to manage them. *Journal of the American Psychoanalytic Association, 55,* 1169–1190. doi:10.1177/000306510705500404

Dickinson, K. A., & Pincus, A. L. (2003). Interpersonal analysis of grandiose and vulnerable narcissism. *Journal of Personality Disorders, 17,* 188–207. doi:10.1521/pedi.17.3.188.22146

Epstein, R. S. (1994). *Keeping boundaries: Maintaining safety and integrity in the psychotherapeutic process*. Washington, DC: American Psychiatric Press.

Frank, K. A. (2002). The "ins and outs" of enactment: A relational bridge for psychotherapy integration. *Journal of Psychotherapy Integration, 12,* 267–286. doi:10.1037/1053-0479.12.3.267

Gabbard, G. O. (1994). *Psychodynamic psychiatry in clinical practice: The DSM–IV edition*. Washington, DC: American Psychiatric Press.

Gabbard, G. O. (2009). Transference and countertransference: Developments in the treatment of narcissistic personality disorder. *Psychiatric Annals, 39,* 129–136. doi:10.3928/00485713-20090301-03

Gabbard, G. O., & Lester, E. P. (1995). *Boundaries and boundary violations in psychoanalysis*. Washington, DC: American Psychiatric Publishing.

Gelso, C. J., & Hayes, J. A. (1998). *The psychotherapy relationship: Theory, research, and practice*. New York, NY: Wiley.

Glass, L. L. (2003). The gray areas of boundary crossings and violations. *American Journal of Psychotherapy, 57,* 429–444.

Glickauf-Hughes, C., & Wells, M. (1997). *Object relations psychotherapy: An individualized and interactive approach to diagnosis and treatment*. Northvale, NJ: Jason Aronson.

Gutheil, T. G., & Gabbard, G. O. (1998). Misuses and misunderstandings of boundary theory in clinical and regulatory settings. *The American Journal of Psychiatry, 155,* 409–414.

Harper, K., & Steadman, J. (2003). Therapeutic boundary issues in working with childhood sexual-abuse survivors. *American Journal of Psychotherapy, 57*(1), 64–79.

Huprich, S. K. (Ed.). (2008). *Narcissistic patients and new therapists: Conceptualization, treatment, and managing countertransference*. London, England: Jason Aronson.

Ivey, G. (1995). Interactional obstacles to empathic relating in the psychotherapy of narcissistic disorders. *American Journal of Psychotherapy, 49,* 350–370.

Kernberg, O. F. (1986). Factors in the psychoanalytic treatment of narcissistic personalities. In A. P. Morrison (Ed.), *Essential papers on narcissism* (pp. 213–244). New York, NY: New York University Press.

Kernberg, O. F. (2004). *Aggressivity, narcissism, and self-destructiveness in the psychotherapeutic relationship: New developments in the psychopathology and psychotherapy of severe personality disorders*. New Haven, CT: Yale University Press.

Kohut, H. (1971). *The analysis of the self*. Madison, CT: International Universities Press.

Kohut, H., & Wolf, E. S. (1986). The disorders of the self and their treatment: An outline. In A. P. Morrison (Ed.), *Essential papers on narcissism* (pp. 175–196). New York: New York University Press.

Kottler, J. A. (2010). *On being a therapist*. San Francisco, CA: Jossey-Bass.

Luchner, A. F., Mirsalimi, H., Moser, C. J., & Jones, R. A. (2008). Maintaining boundaries in psychotherapy: Covert narcissistic personality characteristics and psychotherapists. *Psychotherapy: Theory, Research, Practice, Training, 45*(1), 1–14. doi:10.1037/0033-3204.45.1.1

Masterson, J. F. (1993). *The emerging self: A developmental, self, and object relations approach to the treatment of the closet narcissistic disorder of the self*. New York, NY: Brunner/Mazel.

McWilliams, N. (1994). *Psychoanalytic diagnosis: Understanding personality structure in the clinical process*. New York, NY: Guilford Press.

McWilliams, N. (2004). *Psychoanalytic psychotherapy: A practitioner's guide*. New York, NY: Guilford Press.

Miller, A. (1997). *The drama of the gifted child: The search for the true self* (Rev. ed.). New York, NY: Basic Books.

Ogrodniczuk, J. S., Piper, W. E., Joyce, A. S., & McCallum, M. (1999). Transference interpretations in short-term dynamic psychotherapy. *Journal of Nervous and Mental Disease, 187*, 571–578. doi:10.1097/00005053-199909000-00007

PDM Task Force. (2006). *Psychodynamic diagnostic manual*. Silver Spring, MD: Alliance of Psychoanalytic Organizations.

Shulman, D. G. (1986). Narcissism in two forms: Implications for the practicing psychoanalyst. *Psychoanalytic Psychology, 3*, 133–147. doi:10.1037/0736-9735.3.2.133

Smith, D., & Fitzpatrick, M. (1995). Patient–therapist boundary issues: An integrative review of theory and research. *Professional Psychology: Research and Practice, 26*, 499–506. doi:10.1037/0735-7028.26.5.499

Williams, M. H. (1997). Boundary violations: Do some contended standards of care fail to encompass commonplace procedures of humanistic, behavioral and eclectic psychotherapies? *Psychotherapy, 34*, 239–249.

Wink, P. (1991). Two faces of narcissism. *Journal of Personality and Social Psychology, 61*, 590–597. doi:10.1037/0022-3514.61.4.590

Wolf, E. S. (1988). *Treating the self: Elements of clinical self psychology*. New York, NY: Guilford Press.

Zur, O. (2007). *Boundaries in psychotherapy: Ethical and clinical explorations*. Washington, DC: American Psychological Association. doi:10.1037/11563-000

14

TRANSFERENCE-FOCUSED PSYCHOTHERAPY FOR NARCISSISTIC PERSONALITY

BARRY L. STERN, FRANK YEOMANS, DIANA DIAMOND,
AND OTTO F. KERNBERG

S. was a 23-year-old man who was referred to the lead author (BLS) for treatment pursuant to his withdrawing from his first year at a prestigious law school.[1] Overwhelmed by academic challenges that demanded great persistence, focus, and collaboration with peers, S. became severely depressed and withdrawn; disgusted with himself, he had feelings of inferiority and hopelessness and suicidal thoughts, all resulting in a late-semester withdrawal from school and an inpatient admission. S.'s inpatient treatment team noted his condescending attitude toward them and his fellow patients, his minimal engagement in the program, and his sarcastic, nonchalant attitude. Although he was aware that he was roundly disliked by the staff and fellow patients (a fact confirmed by the staff), he also stated that he felt chronically misunderstood, unappreciated, and neglected.

S. was pleased with his initial sessions; he experienced his therapist as earnest, knowledgeable, and forthright. Soon after the evaluation, however,

DOI: 10.1037/14041-014

Understanding and Treating Pathological Narcissism, J. S. Ogrodniczuk (Editor)

[1]The patient's identity has been disguised to maintain confidentiality.

S.'s complaints grew—about the therapist's techniques, the inefficiencies in billing and office security practices, and the therapist's attitude, which S. experienced as condescending. When asked about his increasingly cynical and critical attitude and his sense that most people had little to offer him, S. responded unguardedly. He discussed his awareness of the air of superiority he exudes, admitted that he had little patience for those whom he saw as being beneath him, and conveyed a sense of justification in his typically oppositional stance toward those superior to him, specifically when their requests of him were, in his view, short-sighted or otherwise not to his liking. Surprisingly, S. recognized the contradiction between his superior attitude and his current, seriously compromised life situation. S. could discuss with convincing depth his sense of fragility and proneness to humiliation, and he demonstrated some awareness of the defensive function of his arrogance and its self-defeating effects. Nevertheless, and despite genuinely viewing his demeanor and attitude as a character flaw, his conscious, predominant presentation and experience of self was one of brittle superiority.

In the initial sessions, the therapist suggested that S. seemed to hold two competing views of himself, each linked to a corresponding view of others: one in which he was superior, desirable, and competent, in relation to teachers, peers, and therapists who were naïve and weak, unjustifiably arrogant, with little to offer him; and a second view, in which he himself was the devalued, incompetent naïf, lacking in confidence or direction while posturing a snide rebellion against an authority unworthy of his respect. The therapist suggested that S.'s split sense of himself and experience of others is characteristic of individuals with a personality disorder, in his case, one marked by a particular difficulty associated with maladaptive self-esteem regulation (i.e., narcissistic personality disorder). His treatment recommendation was an exploratory psychodynamic psychotherapy called transference-focused psychotherapy (TFP).

INTRODUCTION

What follows are some preliminary considerations on the application of TFP (Caligor, Clarkin, & Kernberg, 2007; Clarkin, Yeomans, & Kernberg, 2006) for patients with narcissistic pathology. TFP is a twice-weekly psychodynamic treatment approach grounded in contemporary object relations theory; it posits that borderline pathology, including Axis II borderline personality disorder and other severe personality disorders, results from a fragmented sense of identity, one in which positive and negative representations of self and others are segmented in the mind for defensive purposes. The treatment approach combines elements of standard psychodynamic technique (e.g., attention to unconscious processes, a focus on transference, interpretation of conflict and defense), with a higher level of therapist activity, within a set of mutually agreed-upon behavioral parameters designed to set up a viable therapeutic framework that limits acting out and promotes the unfolding of the patient's full emotional experience and psychic life in the treatment setting. The ultimate goal of TFP is to promote the mental integration of the patient's extreme, unintegrated representations of self and others, and in doing so help the patient to more adaptively tolerate negative affects (e.g., aggression, anxiety, envy, guilt) and sustain meaningful engagements in interpersonal relationships and work.

Two well-controlled randomized clinical trials (Clarkin, Levy, Lenzenweger, & Kernberg, 2007; Doering et al., 2010) provided evidence that TFP is an effective treatment for patients with borderline personality disorder. Our collective clinical experience suggests that borderline and narcissistic personalities share core structural features (i.e., identity pathology, supported by the operation of "primitive" defensive strategies for managing intolerable self states and affects) and has led us to think that TFP would be effective in the treatment of narcissistic pathology. We discuss borderline personality organization (BPO), the syndrome characterized by identity pathology in combination with the predominance of primitive defensive strategies, and which, in our view, encompasses many of the personality disorders described on Axis II of the *Diagnostic and Statistical Manual of Mental Disorders* (American Psychiatric Association, 2000); then we explore narcissistic personality disorder as a specific case of BPO. We then address the question of how TFP could be extended to work with narcissistic patients.

THE SYNDROME: BORDERLINE PERSONALITY ORGANIZATION

As experiences of the self in relation to others unfold in early childhood, they are structured by the mind into representations, conceived as cognitive/ affective structures that serve as lenses through which the self, interpersonal exchanges, and life are subsequently perceived and experienced. Rewarding/ gratifying and frustrating/negative experiences with caretakers are internalized, grouped together in the mind, and form the bedrock for the internal world of self and object representations. The first stage of organization of these dyads, before the integration that comes with healthy psychological development, is into two sets of dyads, one characterized by totally negative affects and representations (the *persecutory* dyad) and the other by a set of ideal affects and representations (the *idealized* dyad). Some of the persecutory self–object dyads frequently encountered in our work with borderline patients include a *deprived child* in relation to an *absent, neglectful, or withholding parent;*

or a *threatened, weak, vigilant victim* in relation to a *sadistic, persecutory, or mercurial parent*. A generalized example of such a dyad in a narcissistic patient might involve a *grandiose, fully independent self*, in relation to an *ineffectual, depreciated, dependent other*. An example of an idealized dyad might be that of a *dependent, yet perfectly nurtured self* linked with longing to an *admiring, caring, and loving parent*.

The internal array of these self–object dyads (dyads that are more prominent, regularly experienced, affectively charged, and those that are defended against) defines the quality of the individual's developing identity and shapes both the structure (integrated, flexible vs. split, rigid) and outward expression of the individual's personality. Healthy identity is characterized by a sense of self that is stable, differentiated, integrated, and flexible. In contrast, identity pathology corresponds to a subjective sense of self and others that is (a) unstable (i.e., rapidly and unpredictably shifting); (b) poorly differentiated (i.e., the descriptions of self and other are impoverished or caricatured, idealized, or devalued); (c) unintegrated, meaning that positively and negatively imbued qualities of self and other are defensively segregated; and (d) inflexible, meaning that the individual cannot shift from the dominant, more ego-syntonic self- and object representations (even if these are negatively valenced), to dyads or representations that are defended against, because these are too painful or uncomfortable to experience.

Identity pathology is maintained by the operation of *primitive defenses*, also referred to as *splitting-based defenses*, including projection and projective identification, omnipotent control, externalization, and idealization/devaluation. All of these defenses function, at various levels of awareness, at times to ward off the persecutory dyad and at other times to ward off the threatening aspects of the idealized dyad (because of the anxieties associated with holding onto a very stimulating and positively valenced but also tenuous and brittle relationship). Essentially, the function of these defenses is to keep the camps of negative and positive affect separate insofar as their integration would pose a threat to the patient's psychic equilibrium (i.e., a fear that the aggression associated with the negative affect would destroy the brittle segments of positive affect; Kernberg, 1984; Kernberg & Caligor, 2005; Klein, 1946).

The treatment process in TFP involves using the affect in a session to track the emergence of self and object dyads in the treatment relationship; specifically, which are most prominent, and how the roles in the dyad are alternatingly enacted or projected onto the therapist in the moment-to-moment process. As one example of a negatively valenced, surface dyad, the narcissistic patient often protests against therapeutic interventions that he or she experiences as reflecting an arrogant, depreciatory, or authoritarian attitude, suggesting that in the moment the patient is the helpless victim of a critical attack or that the therapist is exploiting the patient's weak position to

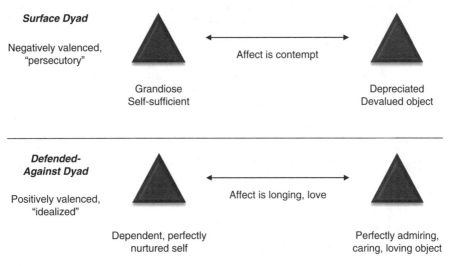

Surface Dyad

Negatively valenced, "persecutory"

Affect is contempt

Grandiose
Self-sufficient

Depreciated
Devalued object

Defended-Against Dyad

Positively valenced, "idealized"

Affect is longing, love

Dependent, perfectly
nurtured self

Perfectly admiring,
caring, loving object

Figure 14.1. A pictorial representation of object-relations dyad interactions. The figure depicts one object-relation dyad defending against a deeper dyad.

demonstrate his or her own superiority. Invariably, however, the roles in this dyad alternate, so that the therapist experiences the patient as dismissing or ridiculing the therapist and his efforts (see Figure 14.1 for a graphic illustration of this dynamic). It is crucial to emphasize that one of the distinguishing features of BPO is that upon internalizing these dyads (in this example, a specific instance of a persecutory dyad), the patient becomes identified with both roles, with both the aggressor and the victim, although each identification is experienced at different times and the identification with the aggressor is often enacted without awareness or justified as "self defense."

In tracking these linked self- and object-representational dyads as they emerge in the treatment process, the therapist must also be mindful of the *layering* of dyads, that is, which dyad on the surface defends against another at greater depth. An example of such layering would be the manner in which the dyad of the negatively valenced, fully independent, grandiose self in relation to a depreciated, dependent object defends against a deeper, positively valenced, idealized dyad, that of a dependent and perfectly nurtured self, linked with longing to an admiring, caring, and loving parent.[2] (See Figure 14.1 for a graphic illustration of the layering of dyads.) Said differently, it is our experience that whereas the fears, negative expectancies, and aggression

---

[2]Note that we do not presume that these dyads are historically accurate; rather, they reflect internal representations of earlier experiences, now reworked in terms of the individual's present motivations, wishes, and defenses.

often dominate the transference, these negatively valenced affects and experiences often protect patients from painful longings for a positively tinged, gratifying relationship that holds the promise, unrealistically, of nurturance, support, and love devoid of any conflict and frustration. Similar to the negatively valenced, persecutory dyads often encountered on the surface, the defended-against idealized dyads are equally extreme in their characteristics and equally influential in the patient's distorted experience of reality.[3] At the same time, however, the idealized dyad is generally less consciously accessible to the narcissistic patient, even transiently, because of the intolerable feelings of envy that would be provoked by an object that the patient might need or depend on.

PATHOLOGICAL NARCISSISM AND BORDERLINE PERSONALITY ORGANIZATION

Our understanding of narcissistic personality disorder is as a specific subtype of BPO, a specific configuration of self- and object representations characterized by the pathological grandiose self (Kernberg, 1984), in which the self becomes the repository for all that is good, combining realistic representations of the self, idealized representations of the self (what one wishes one would be, or that which significant others wish one to be, *becomes* the self representation), and idealized representations of the others (as though they were one's own). Starting early in childhood, this defensive maneuver is thought to protect the nascent self, developing under conditions characterized by an excess of frustration, painful neglect, abuse, and/or trauma, often in combination with temperamental factors that compromise the child's emergent coping and affect regulation skills. The pathological grandiose self is thus compensatory in that it can be thought of as a structure superimposed upon the divided sense of self described in the general case of BPO, providing a semblance of integration by warding off any experience of the self that is negatively valenced, including feelings of inferiority, incompetence, vulnerability, aggression, and envy, all of which are ascribed to others, individuals, groups, institutions, and the therapist.

Like the more general case of BPO, the fragmented identity of the narcissistic patient is supported by primitive defenses. Kernberg, drawing on Rosenfeld (1964, 1971) and Klein (1946), suggested that the patient's fantasy

---

[3]In contrast to persecutory dyads, which are generally quite visible in borderline and narcissistic patients, idealized dyads are often hidden from view, with patients tending to deny the need for a longed-for relationship experience because that experience regularly fails to live up to its idealized form, thus corrupting the idealized vision with even deeper feelings of pain and disappointment.

of omnipotence serves to eliminate the experience of frustration and pain, that of a humiliating sense of need or dependency, and related feelings of envy. (Of whom would an omnipotent, grandiose self be envious?) When enacted interpersonally, the narcissistic patient unconsciously seeks to omnipotently control others, as if to guarantee the admiration, validation, or accommodation from others that he requires. The patient's sense of omnipotence is threatened, and the prospect of actualizing some limitation or failure becomes more real, when he comes into increased contact with the demands posed in his work situation or relationships. It is for this reason that many narcissistic patients functioning in the BPO range have difficulties in work and relationships, often responding to the reasonable demands of the same with an indignant withdrawal from real-life commitments.

In contrast to typical cases of borderline personality disorder, which are characterized by extreme and unpredictable shifts in the self- and object representations activated in a given moment, the narcissistic dyad is often particularly stable and, for periods of time, inflexible. The artificially stable pathological grandiose self is kept firmly in place through the use of primitive defenses, such as omnipotent control, which involves the use of aggression, the threat of aggression, and the induction of a "walking on eggshells" feeling in the therapist and others. Such control facilitates an avoidance of any sense of inferiority, injuries to self-esteem, or anything that would suggest to the patient something lacking in the self and residing in others, something the patient might need to depend on or might envy. Unconscious as well as conscious feelings of envy may lead to the impulse to destroy the good aspects and experience of others, particularly those qualities admired in the other but that one does not possess (Kernberg, 1984; Rosenfeld, 1964). Pathological envy is a dominant experience and ever-present threat for narcissistic patients, one that is frequently warded off in the clinical process through the patient's grandiosity and devaluation of others, including the therapist. Idealization allows the patient to feel admired by those surrounding him, individuals and institutions worthy of his company and communion. Paradoxically, however, the patient needs to devalue those same individuals in order to stave off the awareness of any humiliating deficiency in the grandiose self, as well as feelings of envy. The episodes of rage characteristic of many narcissistic personalities (Kernberg, 2003; Kohut, 1972) reflect threats to or breakdowns in the pathological grandiose self, incited by situations in which the patient is forced to confront some aspect of reality that challenges the splitting off of negative self representations or that does not suit the patient's narcissistic needs at the moment (to have their brilliance reflected and admired by a brilliant object/therapist, or to be perfectly understood). When operating effectively (from the patient's perspective), this defensive style complicates the treatment process by contributing to a strong subjective sense of superiority and self-sufficiency, eliminating the feelings of humiliation that accompany the narcissistic patient's need to depend on anyone other than the self, including the therapist.

TREATMENT

The work of TFP with narcissistic patients is complicated by the tenacity of their defensive processes, the degree of underlying aggression, the enactment and enabling of patients' entitlement and grandiosity in their lives outside the treatment, and by their heightened sensitivity to envy, with its associated affects of humiliation, shame, and inferiority.[4] Nevertheless, if the therapist works with the patient to construct a mutually acceptable treatment frame, the containing and interpretive process can be used to slow down the interactions (and the projective processes) enough to access breaches in the patient's fantasy of omnipotence and to begin to examine the shifts in self and object representations as they play out with the therapist. The consistent exploration of these patterns can help patients become increasingly familiar with the parts of themselves that they have to recognize and integrate in order to move toward a sense of self in which positive and negative, aggressive and libidinal, hateful and loving affects are increasingly integrated (i.e., a "whole-object" position).

Evaluation and Anamnesis

The treatment always begins with a careful evaluation designed to determine whether the patient is operating in the borderline or higher levels of personality organization, and to derive his or her phenomenological diagnosis (for a more in-depth view of our assessment procedure, please consult our writings on the "structural interview" [Kernberg, 1984] and the Structured Interview of Personality Organization [Stern et al., 2010]). In addition to assessing the patient's representations of self and other, the quality of the patient's internalized values system (e.g., the presence thereof, capacity for guilt and remorse, presence of antisocial tendencies) and aggression (self- and other-directed, including self-injury/suicidality) are carefully assessed insofar as they are essential for determining the severity of the patient's pathology within the borderline personality organization spectrum and have prognostic implications.

The narcissistic structure and the operation of primitive defenses often make it very difficult to obtain a clear picture of the patient's self and object

---

[4]The underlying aggression may be more defensive in higher level and more primary in patients with low-level narcissistic personality disorder.

representations and of the quality of his or her engagement with external reality (work, recreation, romantic and sexual relations). One can often begin to formulate a diagnosis as one notices descriptions of self and others that are overly idealized or depreciatory, lacking depth and differentiation, or largely self-referential. It is also during the evaluation period that for the first time the therapist may sense being under the hostile, omnipotent control of someone who is threatened by close contact with an independent other (such as the therapist); in the patient's view, an uncontrolled therapist might enact the aggressive affects that the patient is denying and projecting. Conversely, the therapist may experience feelings of self-doubt and even humiliation when the patient systematically dismisses or evaluates his or her attempts to elicit history; these early countertransference responses can signal the operation of projective identification (Feldman, 2009; Kernberg, 1984), a primitive defensive procedure by which the patient reduces anxiety by unconsciously using the therapist as a repository of negative self representations and feelings that cannot be tolerated internally. In such circumstances, the countertransference can provide important clues about the dreaded and devalued aspects of self against which the pathological grandiose self defends.

The Treatment Contract and Setting the Frame

Subsequent to the evaluation, the therapist and the patient must determine the conditions under which TFP with this particular patient can succeed. The discussion of the "treatment contract" includes elements characteristic of all TFP treatments, such as session length and frequency, management of fees and absences from the treatment, and guidelines for free association (i.e., discussing what comes to mind without editing or censoring). Discussion of the treatment contract also includes individual elements designed (a) to address and limit patient-specific behaviors that have the potential to disrupt the treatment frame (e.g., recommendations of adjunctive treatment for eating disorders or alcoholism); and (b) to create safe conditions for both patient and therapist by establishing parameters for the management of acting out and suicidality. TFP is also premised on the notion that the patient's life activities are integral to the treatment process. Effective treatment requires that patients be productively engaged in some structured activity while they are in treatment (a job or an educational or training program) and that the treatment itself does not support secondary gain of the illness. Having patients engaged in life outside of treatment forces them to confront their capabilities and limitations and to bring into the treatment the conflicts associated with submission, collaboration, and empathy; the struggles over ambition and striving; and the related impulse, under stress, to retreat. As might be expected, patients with significant narcissistic pathology often experience this process as a coerced submission to authority, a relinquishment of cherished autonomy and control. It is nevertheless essential that patients, buffered by the containing and explanatory function of the treatment, confront the world from which they have psychically, and in the case of patient S., actually withdrawn. S.'s ready agreement to find a full-time job prior to returning to school, and to continue sessions upon his subsequent return to school, was prognostically positive. It demonstrated a willingness to compromise some of his autonomy in the service of growth and a developing ego strength that allowed him to confront his limitations and frailties while persisting in his work.

Treatment Process

After mutually acceptable treatment conditions have been established, the treatment proceeds, with the first phase generally focusing on the containment of suicidal and self-destructive behaviors through the patient's testing of the treatment contract. Issues related to fees and attendance and breaches in agreed-upon treatment parameters (e.g., those related to substance abuse or parasuicidality) are discussed. These behaviors, which tend to diminish over the first few months of treatment, are understood in the transference because they reflect the patient's self and object world as enacted in the treatment process with the therapist. Our efforts in this early stage involve clarifying the emergence of the actors, roles, or part-self and part-objects involved in the patient–therapist interaction (e.g., roles of dominance–submission, superior–inferior).

Transferences

There are several typical transferences that tend to develop in the treatment of narcissistic personalities, each derivative of the self-structure described earlier, and each with origins in the patient's earliest object relations. It is not unusual for psychodynamic clinicians to experience narcissistic patients as failing to develop any transference at all. Therapists may get the sense that they do not exist, or, to the extent that they do, it is only as impersonal "ATM therapists," valued to the extent that they dispense support, guidance, and interpretations on demand, and dismissed or devalued to the extent that they (properly) focus on the patient's internal world (self and object representations) rather than on solving the problems of the day.

Therapists frequently experience a transference in which a grandiose, omnipotent self stands in relation to an object (therapist) as passive audience. Patients relentlessly strive to be in charge of their narratives, whether or not these narratives correspond to objective reality, while at the same time complaining that the therapist, who struggles against the powerful influence of patients' omnipotent control, is passive or otherwise unhelpful. The therapist's efforts to exert influence are dismissed or ignored, experienced as a threat, promising either intolerable envy of whatever good the therapist might possess or disappointment or rage at the therapist's reasonable limitations.

When the therapist steps out of the role of being the passive audience, what is often revealed, through affects related to contempt and rage, is the dyad of a grandiose, omnipotent self in relation to the depreciated, devalued object (therapist). The emergence of this underlying dyad, which is typical of patients with narcissistic personality disorder and borderline organization, may be staved off for a time by techniques that reflect, validate, or empathize with the patient's productions. Yet, in our experience, this underlying dyad will emerge and must be addressed within the transference in order for the pathological grandiose self to be analyzed. The manifestation of this dyad in the transference can take several forms. At times we observe the devaluation of the therapist through passive acceptance or a thinly veiled pseudo-idealization of the therapist's communications ("Oh, that is such a brilliant idea"; "I'm so lucky to have you"). The limitations of this superficial gratitude are revealed as the therapist's communications are in turn forgotten ("What did we talk about last time?"), ignored, or as patients repeatedly fail to use them to deepen their understanding or to link them meaningfully to their difficulties ("hmmm, how interesting . . . anyway."). In other expressions of this same transference, our efforts are met with an overtly contemptuous response, with an outright hostile, knee-jerk rejection of whatever is offered, without any apparent reflection. We understand such immediate, dismissing reactions to our interventions in several ways. The rapid consumption and concurrent surface dismissal allow patients (a) to eliminate any awareness of something good existing outside of themselves that they did not possess, thus preventing them from experiencing envy; (b) to eliminate any sense of unfulfilled need within herself, which would provoke feelings of helplessness and dependency (Rosenfeld, 1964); and (c) to stave off potential feelings of humiliation associated with having been made aware of a deficiency in the self or the feeling of having submitted to an authority (Steiner, 2006). Other explanations for the rejection of the therapist's interpretive efforts involve the patient's experience of another's viewpoint and mind as overwhelming and annihilating, replicating earlier experiences of the self being used for the parents' narcissistic aims (Britton, 2004).

In patients with more intense aggression and a less well-developed and internalized system of moral values, one may see the transference of a grandiose, omnipotent self in relation to a projected exploitive, envious object (therapist), or at lower levels on the same spectrum, a persecutory, dangerous object (therapist). In such cases, the therapist is experienced as exploitive, interested in the patient for money or wisdom, or as enhancing himself or herself through the glow of the patient's special talent and ability. We understand this as a defense against the patient's insecurities and sense of emptiness, resulting in a need to greedily take in whatever resources on the outside might supplement or complete the sense of perfection strived for in the self. Episodic reversions to a paranoid stance in turn stave off the patient's sense of emptiness and inadequacy while at the same time protecting his or her fragile self-esteem from painful feelings of envy. Finally, in the syndrome of malignant narcissism, characterized by more pervasive and significant paranoid, aggressive, and antisocial tendencies, the therapist is experienced as dangerous, an object that needs to be neutralized and defeated (Kernberg, 1984). In such cases, the only gratification derived by the patient may be in the defeat of the therapist and of all goodness in the external world, represented to the patient as a grandiose triumph over external persecutory, exploitive forces. The danger of negative therapeutic reactions resulting from this transference, including the potential triumph through self-destructiveness and destructiveness over the therapist (who at times inevitably comes to represent all external sources of neglect and mistreatment), or over the perceived strength of persecutory objects, is severe, and such cases must be treated with the utmost caution.

Countertransference Management

The countertransferences that develop in treatments with narcissistic patients tend to be intense and unstable, to develop rapidly, and to be confusing to the therapist. Countertransference pressures are intimately related to the topic of technical neutrality in that they often involve intolerable feelings of anger, self-doubt, and even humiliation in the therapist—the very feelings that the patient is warding off through projection—that may lead to enactments. As such, these intense countertransferences can disrupt our ability to reflect upon and understand a patient's inner world and to effectively communicate with the patient. The capacity to recognize, tolerate, and process such countertransference feelings is an essential aspect of the treatment process. Bion's notion of containment (Bion, 1967; Ogden, 2004), in which the inexpressible, inchoate, projected elements of the patient's experience are "contained" in the mental and emotional experience of the therapist in the service of ultimately being returned in more organized, elaborated, and tolerable form to the patient, is central to the intersection of countertransference management and the interpretation process in TFP (Caligor, Diamond, Yeomans, & Kernberg, 2009).

At times, therapists experience feelings of boredom with narcissistic patients. This countertransference may signal the operation of the patient's omnipotent control, with the threat of the combination of the patient's rage and narcissistic vulnerability working to render the therapist powerless to introduce anything other than weak, validating responses. This is particularly problematic under conditions in which the patient accepts no outside influence yet is engaging in parasuicidal or otherwise self-destructive behaviors. The therapist's feelings of irritation with the patient are often associated with a patient's brittle idealizing stance, with its strong undercurrent of devaluation. A therapist's feelings of hopelessness are not only a logical outcome of the relentless depreciation experienced in some treatment processes, but can also be thought of as the result of a complementary countertransference (Racker, 1957), in which the hopeless and defeated representations of the patient's self are projected, induced in, and experienced by the therapist, whereas the patient, ensconced in the pathological grandiose self, acts as though he or she has no problems whatsoever. For the therapist, fear of patients and for his or her own physical and legal safety can at times represent a realistic attunement to a patient's rageful expressions of envy and wishes for revenge. Fear of one's own rage toward the patient, in response to accusations of greed, ignorance, neglect, or aggression; the patient's effort to enact boundary violations; or the rejection by the patient of therapeutic efforts, are prominent countertransference reactions that the therapist must recognize and address. The failure to tolerate and contain one's fear, resentment, or even rage toward a patient can have damaging or even disastrous consequences, resulting in the therapist's ignoring the extent of the patient's self- or other-directed aggression or contributing to boundary violations and other forms of acting out on the part of the therapist. The supportive and organizing function of peer consultation groups in addressing these powerful countertransference reactions cannot be overemphasized.

Interpretation

The core process of TFP takes place largely through one broad technical strategy, long viewed as central to the psychoanalytic process, but modified somewhat in the case of TFP, namely, interpretation. Interpretation in TFP (Caligor, Diamond, Yeomans, & Kernberg, 2009) involves repeatedly identifying the actors in the therapeutic dyad as they are experienced and shift across a session, tracking their emergence, projection, and oscillation in the moment-to-moment process, and eventually developing hypotheses about their defensive function. The goal of these efforts is to help the patient gain awareness of and tolerate the confusion in their inner world by examining how it unfolds in the transference.

Interpretation is conceived as a series of interventions that build on one another. In the language of traditional psychoanalysis, the cycle of interpretation consists of three elements: (a) requesting *clarification*, seeking information from patients regarding their subjective experience so as to clarify which dyads are being enacted on the surface in a given exchange; (b) *confrontation*, which is an attempt to invite the patient's collaborative reflection upon an apparent contradiction in the patient's communication (either a contradiction between how the patient presents at different moments, or a discrepancy between the patient's words, or between the verbal report and the patient's affect and/or behavior); and (c) what is thought of as *interpretation* proper, a linking of the content of the clarification and/or confrontation to a hypothesis about the unconscious determinants of the patient's surface experience. (For a detailed depiction of the interpretive process in TFP, see Caligor et al., 2009.)

The guiding principle that helps to focus the therapist's attention when selecting the subject of an interpretation is that of affective dominance. What is affectively dominant at a given point in the session can be expressed through the content of the patient's communications, his or her behavior in the session, and, as is often the case with narcissistic patients, through the counter-transference, the affect avoided by the patient and now displaced, resonating in the therapist. Interpretation ultimately helps patients integrate the present, conscious experience with that which has been split off, either projected onto others, dissociated from a different self experience, or repressed. Throughout the treatment process, the therapist works to intervene and interpret from a standpoint of "technical neutrality," that is, a concerned but objective observer of the patient and his difficulties, rather than one clearly identified with one side or the other of the patient's conflict. Rather than implying indifference to the patient's concerns, technical neutrality simply dictates that the therapist does not actively take sides in the patient's conflicts (i.e., those between opposing internal wishes, between internal wishes and external prohibitions, and between wishes and the constraints of external reality). The technically neutral stance thus allows for the therapist's empathy with each side of the patient's conflict, in service of understanding the patient's unconscious motivations and determinants and helping the patient become better able to understand and resolve internal conflicts.

The full cycle of interpretation can be illustrated in the case of S. Early clarifications focused on S.'s shifting experiences of the therapist in the developing transference. S.'s defensive response to inquiries about his failure to follow up on inquiries he made in search of summer employment prior to his academic withdrawal led to the suggestion that he was experiencing the therapist as a critical, demanding parent. In response to this clarification, S. noted how his experience of the therapist matched his typical experience of his father, whose demands for academic perfection were exceeded only by his exasperation at his son's torpor (in the father's view, S.'s actively wasting his intellectual gifts and talent). In summary, the earliest object-relation dyad to emerge in the treatment, a persecutory dyad, was of the therapist as a critical parent, linked by affects of fear and shame, to a depreciatory self-representation of S. as incompetent and ineffectual.

As S. complained about the various critical authorities dictating his life to him, the therapist became increasingly aware of becoming alternately annoyed with and disengaged from him. S. had several instances in which he was "confused" about logistical matters, citing a "miscommunication," resulting in missed sessions and his failure to follow through in a timely manner with some of what he had agreed to in the treatment contract (his working to obtain a temporary job and to reinstate his academic status). S. became angry when the therapist suggested that these misunderstandings were all emotionally beneficial to him, allowing him to avoid situations that would provoke his anxiety or threaten his self-esteem. S. shared his sense that he should not have to follow up on policies with which he did not agree, that it was important to him to move at his own pace as opposed to the therapist's, and that he was the expert on his emotional needs. At this point S.'s attention could be drawn to the oscillation in the dominant, surface dyad; it was now S. who was in the role of the critical parent, silently but actively undermining the authority of the therapist, which he viewed as wrongheaded and ineffectual. Through repeated observation of this pattern to S., in and beyond the particular treatment setting (recall that the hospital staff experienced him as imperious and depreciatory), both he and his therapist came to understand how the two sides of this dyad alternated in defending against one another: first, how his arrogant, critical attitude toward others (including the therapist) staved off feelings of his own inadequacy and smallness; and second, how his self-representation as weak and ineffective allowed him both an excuse to withdraw from challenges that could elevate him (albeit at the risk of humiliation and failure) and the diminished but secure position from which to enviously mock anyone actively working to succeed, including those attempting to help him.

On a more positive note, even at the earliest stages of S.'s therapy, the therapist had a palpable, although intermittent sense of a positive, warm working relationship. S. would speak freely, associating in rich images to his daily goings on, hopes, and pleasures, and providing a window into his internal world. The freedom of S.'s speech, and the disinhibition and suspension of vigilance which it implied, is typical of higher level narcissistic personalities and suggested that S. was not always threatened by the possibility of his mind happening upon unwanted or threatening self-representations, and likewise, that he did not always feel threatened by the therapist's independent mind, the function of which he implicitly recognized as being to help him access and tolerate aspects of his experience that would otherwise be felt as overwhelmingly negative. This more benign, positive transference was associated with a dyad, warded off in much of S.'s life by the vicissitudes and behavioral consequences associated with his experiences of persecutory dyads, in which a dependent, satisfied, and curious child was linked by affects associated with respect and affection, to a loving, admiring, and nurturing parent. In this dyad, we see the counterweight to the narcissistic patient's sense of omnipotence and self-sufficiency, the nascent ability to tolerate some measure of healthy dependency. S. was indeed able to think of his tendency to become arrogant and contemptuous of others, while at other times demeaning himself, feeling inferior and weak, as a defensive position, protecting him against longings for reliable and consistent closeness, affection, and support that had historically proved fleeting.

Interpretation, the effort to observe with the patient the object-relations dyads operating on the surface and the way they defend against dissociated or projected experiences of the self and other, thus poses a major threat to the pathological grandiose self. Therapist efforts to breach the patient's protective armor can touch off a range of affects, including rage and shame, and is experienced frequently by patients as an intentional enactment by the therapist of a humiliation (Steiner, 2005), one that often results in projections of increased force and rigor. S. was unusual in his ability to tolerate the therapist's interpretation of his arrogance as a defense against a weak and devalued sense of self and to deepen through his associations the mutual understanding of this frequently projected part of himself. S. and the therapist were able to form, relatively quickly, a working alliance that could survive the onslaught of his pathological grandiose self, and in which S. could tolerate the therapist as a partner in what is usually a long and painful process of analyzing the pathological grandiose self. Analysis of the pathological grandiose self in the transference is essential to TFP and is considered to be the factor that allows for lasting, durable changes in the patient's personality, going above and beyond the more limited goal of shorter term relief of the narcissistic patient's symptoms of anxiety or depression. Patients at lower levels of BPO, whose use of aggression-fueled primitive defenses to keep the depreciated, devalued self more firmly projected onto the object world, require more protracted attention to periods of clarification. Steiner's (1994) notion of "therapist-centered" interpretations, in which the patient's experience of the therapist is clarified and simply accepted for the moment, without linking this experience to more sensitive self representations or interpreting the oscillation in the dyad or the operation of the patient's projective defenses, can be helpful. Such interventions may help the patient to feel understood and supports a containment in the treatment dyad of intolerable self states usually managed through projective processes. (For a more complete discussion of the interpretive process, see Caligor et al., 2009; Diamond, Yeomans, & Levy, 2011.)

SUMMARY

TFP begins with the establishment of a treatment framework that optimally facilitates an exploratory process, one in which the representations of self and other that so powerfully shape the patient's life experiences come alive in the treatment relationship, wherein their firsthand examination becomes a powerful therapeutic tool. Through the recognition of these part–self and part–object representations as they unfold in the treatment, and the repeated interpretation of their meaning and defensive functions in the transference and in the patient's life outside of treatment, patients become more aware of motivations that were previously hidden, yet highly determinative of their subjective experience. Increasingly, patients can tolerate the negative self experiences they had projected onto the outside world, while also tolerating more realistic, imperfect, and ambivalent representations of self and others. This process ideally allows patients an enhanced control over their emotions and a greater sense of freedom, choice, and pleasure in the totality of their lives.

REFERENCES

American Psychiatric Association. (2000). *Diagnostic and statistical manual of mental disorders* (4th ed., text rev.). Washington, DC: Author.

Bion, W. R. (1967). *Second thoughts: Selected papers on psycho-analysis.* New York, NY: Jason Aronson.

Britton, R. (2004). Subjectivity, objectivity, and triangular space. *The Psychoanalytic Quarterly, 73,* 47–61.

Caligor, E., Clarkin, J. F., & Kernberg, O. F. (2007). *Handbook of dynamic psychotherapy for higher level personality pathology.* Washington, DC: American Psychiatric Publishing.

Caligor, E., Diamond, D., Yeomans, F., & Kernberg, O. F. (2009). The interpretive process in psychoanalytic psychotherapy of borderline pathology. *Journal of the American Psychoanalytic Association, 57,* 271–301. doi:10.1177/0003065109336183

Clarkin, J. F., Levy, K. N., Lenzenweger, M. F., & Kernberg, O. F. (2007). Evaluating three treatments for borderline personality disorder: A multiwave study. *The American Journal of Psychiatry, 164,* 922–928. doi:10.1176/appi.ajp.164.6.922

Clarkin, J. F., Yeomans, F., & Kernberg, O. F. (2006). *Psychotherapy of borderline personality: Focusing on object relations.* Washington, DC: American Psychiatric Publishing.

Diamond, D., Yeomans, F., & Levy, K. N. (2011). Psychodynamic psychotherapy for narcissistic personality disorder. In K. Campbell & J. Miller (Eds.), *The handbook of narcissism and narcissistic personality disorder: Theoretical approaches, empirical findings, and treatment* (pp. 423–433). New York, NY: Wiley.

Doering, S., Hörz, S., Rentrop, M., Fischer-Kern, M., Schuster, P., Benecke, C., . . . Buchheim, P. (2010). Transference-focused psychotherapy v. treatment by community psychotherapists for borderline personality disorder: Randomized controlled trial. *British Journal of Psychiatry, 196,* 389–395. doi:10.1192/bjp.bp.109.070177

Feldman, M. (2009). *Doubt and conviction in the analytic process: Selected papers of Michael Feldman*. London, England: Routledge.

Kernberg, O. F. (1984). *Severe personality disorders*. New Haven, CT: Yale University Press.

Kernberg, O. F. (2003). The management of affect storms in the psychoanalytic psychotherapy of borderline patients. *Journal of the American Psychoanalytic Association, 52*, 517–545.

Kernberg, O. F., & Caligor, E. (2005). A psychoanalytic theory of personality disorders. In J. F. Clarkin & M. F. Lenzenweger (Eds.), *Major theories of personality disorder* (2nd ed., pp. 114–156). New York, NY: Guilford Press.

Klein, M. (1946). Notes on some schizoid mechanisms. *The International Journal of Psychoanalysis, 27*, 99–110.

Kohut, H. (1972). Thoughts on narcissism and narcissistic rage. *Psychoanalytic Study of the Child, 27*, 360–400.

Ogden, T. H. (2004). On holding and containing, being and dreaming. *The International Journal of Psychoanalysis, 85*, 1349–1364. doi:10.1516/T41H-DGUX-9JY4-GQC7

Racker, H. (1957). The meanings and uses of countertransference. *The Psychoanalytic Quarterly, 26*, 303–357.

Rosenfeld, H. (1964). On the psychopathology of narcissism: A clinical approach. *The International Journal of Psychoanalysis, 45*, 332–337.

Rosenfeld, H. (1971). A clinical approach to the psychoanalytic theory of the life and death instincts: An investigation into the aggressive aspects of narcissism. *The International Journal of Psychoanalysis, 52*, 169–178.

Steiner, J. (1994). Patient-centered and analyst-centered interpretations: Some implications of containment and countertransference. *Psychoanalytic Inquiry, 14*, 406–422. doi:10.1080/07351699409533994

Steiner, J. (2005). The conflict between mourning and melancholia. *The Psychoanalytic Quarterly, 74*, 83–104.

Steiner, J. (2006). Seeing and being seen: Narcissistic pride and narcissistic humiliation. *The International Journal of Psychoanalysis, 87*, 939–951. doi:10.1516/AL5W-9RVJ-WKG2-B0CK

Stern, B. L., Caligor, E., Clarkin, J., Critchfield, K., Horz, S., McCornack, V., . . . Kernberg, O. F. (2010). Structured Interview of Personality Organization (STIPO). Preliminary psychometrics in a clinical sample. *Journal of Personality Assessment, 92*, 35–44. doi:10.1080/00223890903379308

15

KOHUT'S SELF PSYCHOLOGY APPROACH TO TREATING PATHOLOGICAL NARCISSISM

M. DAVID LIBERMAN

Heinz Kohut was born in Vienna in May 1913. He graduated from the University of Vienna medical program in 1938 and emigrated shortly afterward. "Kohut, like Freud, initially started out in Neurology and did so, reportedly, quite successfully" (Strozier, 2002, p. 44). Kohut published a number of papers as well as two books that were both groundbreaking and controversial. These publications began his career-long reconsideration of the basic tenets of psychoanalysis. His ideas continued to evolve until his death in 1981. Kohut's last book was published posthumously.

SELF PSYCHOLOGY: AN OVERVIEW

Self psychology is the school of psychoanalysis that grew out of Heinz Kohut's work. Kohut, a classically trained psychoanalyst, was thoroughly steeped in the ego psychology of the time. However, his experiences with

DOI: 10.1037/14041-015
Understanding and Treating Pathological Narcissism, J. S. Ogrodniczuk (Editor)

narcissistic patients ultimately led him to develop a radical reformulation of psychoanalytic theory and practice. Classical analysis held that there was one developmental line that reached from narcissism (i.e., self-investment) to object love (i.e., the ability to invest in others) and that the narcissistic individual was someone who had failed to progress along this continuum. Kohut proposed a very different conceptualization. He believed that there were two normal developmental lines. One of these was the development of object relations as described by Freud. The other, equally important, line was the developmental line of narcissism. Kohut began to understand narcissism as an immature or yet-to-be-developed form of self-esteem. The narcissistic individual is "stuck" and needs to resume the development toward mature self-esteem and a resilient sense of self (Kohut, 1966). In so doing, Kohut removed from narcissism the stigma of being implicitly pathological. In classical psychoanalysis, it was believed that narcissistic patients were incapable of developing transferences. Freud (1912/1958) saw the development of the transference as absolutely crucial for successful treatment. In the psychoanalytic thinking of the time, the inability to develop a transference meant that the patient was unanalyzable (i.e., untreatable). In a second major departure from the classical analytic position, Kohut clearly stated that individuals suffering from narcissistic disorders did, in fact, develop transferences, albeit of a different variety, and were therefore treatable (Kohut, 1968).

EVOLUTION OF SELF PSYCHOLOGY THEORY

Initially, Kohut attempted to fit his ideas into prevailing psychoanalytic thought and phrased his understanding in the metapsychological language of the time (Kohut, 1971). Eventually, however, he began to offer a different vision of psychoanalysis. Stolorow (1978) referred to Kohut's new framework as a

> psychology of the self . . . The phrase "developmental phenomenology of the self" would be more accurate since it is concerned with the ontogenesis of the self-experience, its conscious and unconscious constituents, and their normal and pathological developmental vicissitudes. . . . In short, Kohut enjoined analysts to shift their conceptual framework from one that assumes the motivational primacy of instinctual drives to one that postulates the motivational primacy of self-experience. (p. 329)

By the end of his life, Kohut had clearly separated his ideas from classical psychoanalysis. Rather than seeing psychopathology as resulting from a clash among psychic structures caused by difficulties in drive processing, Kohut envisioned a psychoanalysis that focused on the individual's self experience and how it might reflect successful and failed experiences with past relationships.

THE SELF

Although he was known to be very precise in his definitions of all matters psychoanalytic, Kohut remained purposely imprecise in his definition of the self. He later explained that he was deliberately vague in his discussion of how the essence of self should be defined because it was not possible to know the essence of the self. "Only its introspectively or empathically perceived psychological manifestations are open to us" (Kohut, 1977, pp. 310–311). Kohut considered the self to be a "comparatively low-level, i.e. comparatively experience-near psychoanalytic abstraction" as compared with the ego, id and superego, which are "high level, i.e., experience-distant, abstraction in psychoanalysis" (Kohut, 1977, pp. 310–311). Furthermore, he described the self as "a content of the mental apparatus" and that "it has continuity in time, i.e., it is enduring" (Kohut, 1971, pp. xiv–xv). Self psychology thus became the psychoanalytic study of our ongoing self experience as we perceive its continuities and discontinuities.

HEALTHY DEVELOPMENT

Kohut (1959) was convinced that empathy was absolutely crucial to psychological development, referring to it as the "oxygen" of self development, without which the self would not develop (Kohut, 1977). Serious empathic failures by the child's caretakers would cripple the developing self and leave it open to fragmentation and collapse. According to Kohut, there were two requirements for healthy self development. First, there was a basic "intuneness" or empathic connection between the caretakers and the child. Second, psychic structure was developed because of nontraumatic failures in empathy by the child's caretakers. Kohut referred to these nontraumatic failures as *optimal frustrations* (Kohut & Seitz, 1960). This meant that the child was disappointed just enough to be able to absorb the frustration of an unmet need without being overwhelmed by the feelings of frustration. Kohut's view was that human beings needed to feel understood throughout the life span and that these developments prepared the developing self to get this need for understanding filled by engaging in more mature relationships (Kohut, 1984).

The healthy child was envisioned as initially born into a blissful state of tensionless existence. Empathically attuned parents provide for the child's comforts, and the child is unaware of an inner or outer world. In time, the child becomes uncomfortably aware that all is not perfect, as the environment fails to seamlessly provide for his or her needs. In an attempt to hold onto that original blissful state, the child develops a belief in his or her own perfection and omnipotence and that all "good" resides within. Kohut initially termed this state of the child's perception of being perfect as the *narcissistic self* (Kohut, 1966) and later changed the term to the *grandiose self* (Kohut, 1968). The child's feelings of "greatness" and perfection are mirrored back to the child by the parents through their constant attention to his or her needs. "This attention reassures the child of its greatness, vigor and perfection" (Kohut & Wolf, 1978, p. 413).

Selfobjects

As a result of continuing optimal frustrations, the child begins to develop some awareness that there is something else "out there." At this point, the child would not see these others (the psychoanalytic term for *other* is *object*) in his or her environment as separate people but as actually part of himself or herself. Kohut described these "others" as narcissistic objects and later renamed them *self-objects* to convey the sense of the child that these others were really part of himself or herself much in the same way as an adult would see an arm or a leg (Kohut, 1971). Later still, he eliminated the hyphen between the words *self* and *object* to convey even more dramatically the image of merger.

Eventually, the child becomes more aware that the selfobjects respond to its level of tension. The child feels empathically merged with his or her parents, and this allows him or her to feel that the parents' tension-regulating capacities are actually part of the child. This merger leads to the child's development of the grandiose self (Kohut, 1968). Kohut saw the development of the grandiose self as ultimately supplying the child with the ability to regulate tension, self-soothe, and feel vigorous and joyful.

Simultaneously, the child becomes increasingly aware that these others also provide a feeling of calm, security, safety, and power that can protect the child and dispel fears when he or she feels threatened or helpless. The child idealizes these others and sees them as all knowing and all powerful. Kohut termed these others the *idealized parent imagoes* (Kohut, 1971, p. 25). They become the external representations of the child's former feeling of omnipotence. The developing child empathically merges with the idealized parent and feels that the parents' calmness, power, and wisdom are also part of himself or herself (Kohut, 1966).

The Role of Frustration

Because of continuing optimal frustrations, the mirroring and idealizing functions of the parents are ultimately converted into a psychic structure by the child through the process of transmuting internalization—*transmuting* inasmuch as the raw idealization is changed into a more realistic appraisal and freed of its painful origins and *internalization* as it steadily becomes part of the individual's own psychic structure. The child then takes some small portion of these processes and makes it part of his or her own mind. Successful internalization takes place in a way that is both fractionated and removes the "personal" elements from what is internalized (Kohut, 1971). The child is able to take over the soothing and admiring functions of the mirroring selfobject as well as the calming and inspiring functions of the idealized parent imago. For Freud (1917), the mourning process was necessary to the development of psychic structure through the process of internalization. Kohut saw a similar process taking place in the developing individual (Kohut & Seitz, 1960). Clinicians often see the same thing taking place in the clinical situation. When our patients find that we have let them down in some small way, they withdraw their idealizing or mirroring needs back from us and begin to perform these functions for themselves.

Motivation

Motivation stemmed from the synthesis of the grandiose self and the idealized parent imago into what Kohut called the *bipolar self*. The bipolar self was the inheritor of these two earlier imagoes. The mirroring of the early maternal object that accepts and confirms the child's exhibitionism and perfection becomes the grandiose self, which ultimately gives rise to the child's ambitions. The child's idealization of and subsequent merger with the idealized selfobject develops into the idealized parent imago, which ultimately gives rise to the child's ideals (Kohut, 1977). Kohut saw these two poles as being connected by a *tension arc*, which is the area of skills and talents that the individual possesses. These native skills and talents give the developing self the ability to pursue its ambitions and goals. Kohut described the self as being "pushed" by the ambitions that were developed from the grandiose self and "pulled" by the ideals that were incorporated from the idealized parent imago (Kohut, 1977).

PATHOLOGICAL DEVELOPMENT

Kohut saw the narcissistic disorders as resulting from early damage to the self-structure resulting in a defective self. It was not the content of a particular experience that was traumatic to the self but rather the intensity of it (Kohut & Seitz, 1963). A damaged self was one that was prone to weakness, fragmentation, and disharmony. This was the result of disturbances in the self-selfobject processes in early life (Kohut, 1984). Damage could result if tension relief was unpredictable or the waiting time for relief exceeded the child's tolerance (Kohut & Seitz, 1963). Kohut identified two symptom patterns that characterized the narcissistic disorders: He found that the self-esteem of narcissistically injured individuals was very labile and also that they were extremely sensitive to failures, disappointments, and slights (Kohut & Wolf, 1978).

Disorders

Four primary categories of psychopathology were conceptualized: (a) the psychoses, in which the individual either had no sense of self or one that was seriously fragmented, such as in schizophrenia; (b) the borderline condition, in which there was a defensive covering of a psychotic or fragmented self; (c) the narcissistic disorders; and (d) the neurotic or oedipal disorders, the latter two having an intact but compromised self. Of the four, it was only the last two that were analyzable (Kohut & Wolf, 1978). Initially, Kohut believed that oedipal and narcissistic disorders could coexist in the same person (Kohut, 1977). However, by the time of his death, Kohut had begun to question whether the neurotic disorders were, in reality, just another form of narcissistic disorder (Kohut, 1984).

Kohut (1977) delineated two general types of narcissistic disorders: the narcissistic personality disorder and the narcissistic behavior disorder. In the former, the symptoms were autoplastic; patients might seek therapy because they just did not feel right but could not say how or why. They might also experience feelings of emptiness or detachment. In the narcissistic behavior disorder, the symptoms were alloplastic; individuals have resorted to some form of acting out, such as shoplifting, compulsive sexual activity, or substance abuse in order to calm or soothe themselves.

Narcissistic problems could be expressed in many ways. The narcissistic individual's fear of the breakdown of the self leads to a fear of fragmentation or disintegration anxiety. One patient in analysis experienced the breakdown of his vulnerable self-structure in his sleep. After he had suffered a narcissistic injury, he would report vivid dreams of being disemboweled, dissected, or eaten alive. It was not the symbolism that was important to him but the helplessness and agony that he felt in the dream.

Splitting of the self could also result. The *horizontal split* was something that was long established in classical analysis. This was the separation of conscious from unconscious processes. Kohut described the *vertical split* in which two ideas that are totally contradictory could simultaneously exist in consciousness without the individual seeing the contradiction (Kohut, 1971). A former patient used to complain bitterly about his wife's weight. She was terribly heavy and did not seem to be doing anything about it. Yet he would go shopping and bring home large amounts of sweets and other tempting foods. He was incredulous when I questioned this. He knew that she overate and that her weight upset him, but he could not understand what his shopping choices had to do with that. Another consequence of the weakened self can be episodes of narcissistic rage. Kohut viewed these narcissistic rages as the response of a weakened self structure to some threat to its already fragile integrity and described the considerable intensity of the anger that his patients would display toward him when they felt either misunderstood or wronged in some way (Kohut, 1977). Kohut noted that unlike healthy aggression, the motive for these rages is a feeling of revenge or of an unfairness that had to be righted (Kohut, 1972). I have worked with a number of men and women who, on discovering their spouse's infidelity, experienced intractable rage, which they struggled with for years as a narcissistic injury that could not be absorbed.

Causes

Self psychologists believed that narcissistic disorders resulted from failures in necessary self experiences with either the mirroring that is needed for development of the grandiose self or in some disruption of the idealization process between the child and the idealized parent imago. If there have been failures in mirroring, then the grandiose self will continue to strive for fulfillment of its archaic aims. One patient had been told by his mother that he could do anything, including being president of the United States. He was convinced that she was right, and he continued to struggle to achieve this end. Lesser achievements meant nothing to him. If there had been failures in idealization, then the individual may feel helpless and will continue searching for someone to idealize and with whom to merge. One somewhat well-known local mental health professional had become a bit of a professional "embarrassment" as he was known for going from sitting at the feet of one famous psychiatrist to sitting at the feet of another, seemingly in a continuing search to find an all-knowing other.

TREATMENT

The process of self psychological treatment is like other forms of psychoanalytic therapy: The patient attempts to speak freely while the therapist listens and makes interpretations, paying particular attention to the transferences that arise. Kohut (1984) wrote that for a successful treatment "the analysand must be able to engage the analyst as a selfobject by mobilizing the sets of inner experiences that we call selfobject transferences" (p. 70). Kohut believed that it was absolutely necessary that the therapist be truly able to accept the phase-appropriate demands for mirroring or idealization and not be critical of them. If the therapist was able to interpret to the patient that his or her demands were at one time appropriate, then the patient will be able to gradually modify and integrate them as the self moves toward cohesion (Kohut, 1968).

Kohut articulated a very specific perspective on the selfobject transferences. Rather than seeing the transference as a breakthrough of repressed drives or the displacement of past experiences onto the current situation, he began to see them as different kinds of necessary experiences (Kohut & Wolf, 1978). The child needed a selfobject, a "parent," who enjoyed the child's joyousness and vigor. Kohut went on to say that that the developing child needed a figure "to whom the child can look up and with whom he can merge as an image of calmness, infallibility and omnipotence" (Kohut & Wolf, 1978, p. 414). In so doing, Kohut moved the transference from being a distortion of the past to being a necessity of the present.

Process

Treatment was conceptualized as a three-step process. First, there was analysis of the patient's general defensiveness. Second, there was the unfolding of the transferences. And finally, there was as opening of an empathic "path" between the self and selfobject on a mature adult level (Kohut, 1984). The mobilization of the selfobject transferences was critical. The establishment of the selfobject transferences permits the patient to develop the necessary relationship with the therapist to allow the thwarted selfobject needs to unfold. This unfolding allows the patient to experience, understand, and, in time, work through the feelings that initially caused the thwarting of those needs. The empathy provided by the self psychological therapist is a critical component of self development. In addition to the empathic responses provided by the therapist, his or her provision of mirroring responses and willingness to be viewed as the needed idealized objects provide these necessary experiences for the narcissistically injured individual.

Kohut (1979) described the establishment, interpretation, and working through of various selfobject transferences in detail in his paper "The Two Analyses of Mr. Z." The patient had originally undergone a successful classical analysis with Kohut. Kohut had noted, however, that the patient's attempts to give up his narcissistic organization made him feel inadequate and humiliated. Some years later, the patient found that his love relationships were shallow and that his life felt joyless and empty of excitement. In the patient's second analysis, Kohut allowed himself to observe some things about the patient: He seemed to crave an interested and involved other to whom he could reveal himself without fear of embarrassment. He also appeared to desperately need another who would appear to be knowledgeable and strong. In the first analysis, Kohut had interpreted these transferences as defenses. In the second analysis, Kohut allowed these transferences to develop and unfold. As he did so, Kohut found that Mr. Z was developing a very different picture of his childhood. Kohut began to see the patient's issues as problems in development rather than as conflicts.

The self psychological approach to treatment focuses on establishing the narcissistic transference: keeping the transference alive while it is repetitively worked through and providing optimal frustration for the patient so that growth will continue (Kohut, 1971). The therapist's empathy and emotional participation keep the patient's narcissistic tensions from getting too high. The patient feels free to explore his exhibitionistic demands and grandiose fantasies because the therapist does not disapprove of them; rather, they are echoed and reflected (Kohut, 1971). Resistance to the transferences is motivated by fears of revealing fantasies and urges of the grandiose self rather than the fear of revealing conflicts.

Transference

Kohut described two major categories of transference: the mirroring transferences in the broad sense and the idealizing transferences. Kohut initially saw three kinds of mirroring transferences. He termed these the *merger transference*, the *alter ego* or *twinship transference*, and the *mirroring transference* in the narrow sense. As suggested previously, Kohut used the term *mirroring transference* in two ways: in the broad sense as a general category of transference and in the narrow sense as a particular kind of mirroring transference (Kohut, 1971).

Merger transferences result from early failures in mirroring, whereby early parental failures to vigilantly attend to the child's needs left the merger-hungry individual constantly searching for another with whom to develop an intense relationship that would allow him or her to regulate chronic feelings of tension and emptiness. This was seen in the treatment of a young woman who would go into a rage whenever I failed to repeat exactly what she had said.

Developmentally, the next transference configuration was the alter ego or twinship transference. In this form of mirroring transference, the narcissistic individual needed another who could be viewed as a contemporary who shared the patient's values and ideas. I have had a number of patients of different ages and political persuasions who were convinced that I shared their tastes in music, politics, literature, or religion. Some were much younger than I, yet saw me as being their age. Kohut later reconsidered this transference and decided that it was not a form of mirroring transference but rather a third major category of transference. It reflected the individual's need for someone who shared his or her attributes in the tension arc of the bipolar self (Kohut, 1984). The function of the therapist in the twinship or merger transference "is to allow himself to be included in the patient's grandiosity and exhibitionism as an anonymous part" (Kohut, 1971, p. 175). Not an easy thing to do. One patient who had required intense mirroring began insisting that since he had read a book on narcissism, he was now much more competent than I was to conduct his therapy.

The mirroring transference in the narrow sense arose from developmentally later problems in the mirroring process. In this form of transference, individuals are subject to sudden bouts of feelings of worthlessness, discouragement, or disconnection. In the case of one patient, failures on the part of his parents to appreciate his achievements or efforts left him feeling totally discouraged and ready to give up. When this happened, he would suddenly lose all hope, become completely discouraged, and begin to entertain, and on occasion act out, suicidal feelings. The function of the therapist in the mirror transference is to reflect and be a friendly echo of the patient's grandiosity and exhibitionism. The goal of treatment in the mirroring transference is to transform the grandiose self, firm the ego's potential for action through increasing the realism of the ambitions, and strengthen realistic self-esteem (Kohut, 1971).

The *idealizing* transferences were the second general category of transferences described by Kohut. Unmanageable disappointments in the idealized parent imago can leave the child fearful and suspicious. The child is left constantly searching for someone who fulfills the need to feel safe, protected, and inspired and for someone who can be viewed as a hero. This is a frequently occurring transference in therapy. Patients begin to attribute wisdom, attractiveness, success, and fame to the therapist to the point where the therapist becomes uncomfortable and needs to make them more aware of his or her limitations. Although Kohut did not name specific transference constellations in the idealization process, as he had done with mirror transferences, he did note the different consequences of early and later disruptions in the idealization process. If disruptions occurred early in the pre-oedipal period, then the individual was not able to regulate tension. Their feelings of self-worth could fluctuate widely, and the child or the patient may feel empty and powerless when separated from the idealized selfobject (Kohut, 1968). In therapy, these individuals often experienced terrible feelings of emptiness, helplessness, and worthlessness during weekend separations or when the intervals between sessions became too great. Kohut wrote that if disruptions occurred later in the pre-oedipal period, patients' superegos were not sufficiently idealized for them to feel guided by the principles that they had learned or to be able to raise their self-esteem in times of stress. Unmanageable disappointments in the idealized parent imago leaves the individual unable to develop goals and ideals or doubtful of the possibility of successfully working toward them. In the idealizing transference, the goals of treatment are to strengthen the basic neutralizing structure of the psyche and to help in both the acquisition and strengthening of the patient's ideals (Kohut, 1968). One patient, who had suffered severe injuries in this area of development, told me of an incident in which he found himself in a multistory shopping mall going up the escalator after having stolen, and then putting on his head, a large Mexican sombrero from a mall store. He said that as he watched the security men chasing him up the escalators, he first felt powerful and invulnerable and then became aware of how terribly empty and worthless he felt inside. When I repeated this back to him immediately after he had spoken, he denied that he had ever said it. He couldn't remember having said these words even though they were spoken literally seconds before.

Self-State Dreams

In classical psychoanalytic theory, a dream is a symbolic representation of a conflict between psychic structures. Kohut observed that the dreams of his patients during separations appeared to portray the fragmenting state of the self rather than a structural conflict (Kohut, 1971). The dreams of many of his patients were not amenable to interpretation. Kohut found that associations to these kinds of dreams did not lead to deeper meanings. It was productive, however, if the analyst could tell the patient, based on his knowledge of the patient's vulnerabilities of self, how a specific situation was affecting the patient to stir up the kind of anxiety portrayed in the dream (Kohut, 1977). Kohut called these kinds of dreams *self-state dreams* (Kohut, 1971).

In my practice, a man who was deeply into his analysis brought in a dream in which he was standing in the engine room of a large zeppelin. He looked at a wall of dials, gauges, and handles and had not the faintest idea of what to do with them. He was hugely impressed at the size and complexity of what it took to run the airship. Standing off to the side was the captain. He appeared silent, quiet, and unapproachable. The patient was increasingly irritated by my attempts to get him to associate to the dream. I realized later that this was a self-state dream. The man was overawed at the momentousness of our analytic endeavor. It was both frightening and intriguing to him. Furthermore, it had been up to me to have understood and offered that observation to him.

Sometime later, he brought in a second dream. He was flying high in a helicopter above a hilly green landscape. Looking down on all the foliage and trees, he was quite pleased with what he was seeing. He was in the back section, looking out the window. He could see the pilot and co-pilot sitting up ahead of him. He was comfortable and confident in their skill at flying. This was someone who had come from an emotionally deprived family. His early dreams had been filled with images of arid deserts and lifeless mountains.

He was feeling growth and comfort. This time I was able to convey to him that I understood how far he had come, how much richer his experiences had become, and how much safer he felt in our journey.

Resistance

Resistance is also viewed differently in a self psychological therapy. Patients attempt to minimize their growing transference to the therapist by saying things such as the relationship with the therapist is not a real relationship or that the only thing the therapist cares about is the fee. The self psychological therapist recognizes and interprets these resistive statements as being due to patients' apprehension that they will reexperience earlier empathic failures and disappointments. Through the understanding and interpretation of these fears, the therapist can help patients to overcome these resistances and deepen both the transference and their experience of themselves. A second avenue of resistance comes from the possibility that the therapist is simply out of tune with patients (Kohut, 1977). Patients can become legitimately distressed when the therapist fails to empathize with something that they were experiencing or when there is a failure to recognize their progress. These failures are referred to as *empathic breaks* (Kohut, 1971).

Regression

Kohut noted that the regressive swings that occur during the treatment of narcissistic patients can be dramatic and disturbing. At times, a patient may sound delusional. For example, a young man who was very much in the throes of a deep regression in a mirroring transference insisted to me that he and his friends had invented a "Q" bomb that could destroy the earth. These deep regressions sometimes preceded the patient's acknowledgement of the painful incidents or circumstances that caused his narcissistic difficulties. Empathic breaks by the therapist may also cause these dramatic regressive responses. If the therapist realizes that a mistake has been made, then a careful and noncritical explanation to the patient of what happened and why it affected the patient so profoundly may not only repair the breach but also lead to further strengthening of the patient's developing self (Kohut, 1971).

Countertransference

The management of countertransference plays a particularly important role in the treatment of narcissistic disorders. Kohut discussed two general countertransference reactions that can interfere with the progress of the treatment. In dealing with the mirroring transferences, the therapist may feel marginalized or continuously diminished by the patient depending on mirroring transference (Kohut, 1971). In a *mirroring transference*, one may feel irrelevant, useless, or deadened. Narcissistic patients have left me feeling as if there was nothing that I could possibly offer them that would be of any value. The intensity of the need to feel both special to and understood by the therapist is indicative of the developmental level of the patient. I have had patients who felt deeply injured or enraged when they felt that my attention had wandered. They needed to feel that they were the constant and intense focus of my attention through each moment of the session.

The idealizing transference can make therapists feel so uncomfortable that they point out their own limitations so that the patients can develop a more realistic perception of them (Kohut, 1971). The therapist may initially feel special to the patient or feel that both of them are unique and extraordinary. This is a common reaction to individuals who are in search of the idealized parent imago. Several years ago, a supervisee of mine came to his supervisory session feeling quite distressed. He had arrived home hours later than he had told his wife he would because he had completely lost track of time while seeing a very narcissistic patient who was deeply into an idealizing transference. He told me that he had felt like he was gliding home on a cloud until he walked into his house and was confronted by his very angry wife. He was stunned to realize that time had just slipped away from him without his having any awareness of its passage.

The self psychologically oriented therapist must constantly be aware of his or her feelings in dealing with the patient and be prepared to work through the feelings that the narcissistically troubled patient will inevitably evoke. In addition to the two general countertransference reactions described above, there is a third countertransference difficulty: A therapy can get stalled when the therapist does not recognize that an issue for the patient has also been a problem in the therapist's life. This situation results in a continuing empathic break. A seemingly stalemated treatment can again begin to move forward when therapists are finally able to accept and work through their own resistances to this kind of recognition (Liberman, 2006). A male patient, who had been in weekly therapy, repeatedly expressed the need and wish for analysis. I was finally able to offer him an analysis at a greatly reduced rate. Shortly after starting the analysis, however, he began to complain of the terrific sacrifice he was making by coming more frequently, as well as the added expense. I was shocked and dismayed. All I could think was that he was now getting the intense treatment that he had asked for and that he was paying a fraction per session of what he had been paying for weekly sessions. The analysis was stalemated. Finally, I was able to work through my feelings and understand his. From his perspective, the analysis was a big investment in time and a bigger investment of his income. Once I was able to understand his perspective and convey this understanding to him, the analysis began to again move forward.

TREATMENT GOALS

The traditional analytic view of cure was that the patient had come to recognize and resolve the oedipal neurosis and was, therefore, now cured of the conflict between ego, id, and superego. Kohut began to see the idea of cure quite differently. From his perspective, cure was not the resolution of conflict as much as the development of resilience. He distinguished between the "guilty man" of classical analysis who was the victim of internal conflict and strife and the "tragic man" who was unable to feel alive and pursue the nuclear program of his inborn talents (Kohut, 1984). As part of this, Kohut differentiated between what he called *compensatory structures* and *defensive structures*. A structure was termed *defensive* when it merely covered over a defect in the self. A defensive structure might be compulsive masturbation or endless daydreaming. A structure that actually compensated for this defect was termed *compensatory* (Kohut, 1977). Kohut saw the development of compensatory structures as an important step in development of a resilient (i.e., healthy) self. Several years ago, a married man who was very disappointed in his life consulted me. He appeared to have no goals or ambitions. He had been engaging in a series of emotionally meaningless one-night stands that seemed to happen when he was disappointed at work or upset with his wife. It turned out that he was regulating both his tension and his despair by engaging in these infidelities. His sexual acting out was clearly a defensive structure. Later in his therapy, he recalled that he had once hoped to be a writer. His desire to write had clearly been a compensatory structure to achieve the appreciation and valuing that he had missed. However, he had never been able to sit down and write. As we worked through his feelings, his ambitions became mobilized. He eventually changed careers and got into a writer's workshop where his work was well received. His sexual acting out faded away as he was increasingly able to recognize and enjoy his successes.

Kohut saw the goal of a successful treatment as the achievement of vitality and purpose. The narcissistically injured individual suffers from an enfeeblement of the self-structure. This weakness could be manifested not only as an inability to self-soothe, manage tension, and regulate self-esteem but also in a lack of ambition or inability to pursue goals. Kohut envisioned the narcissistically sound individual as one who felt alive and vital and who was able to manage tension and feeling upset without falling apart or relying on substance abuse. A narcissistically healthy person has ideals that guide and ambitions that motivate him or her to pursue goals and dreams. Such people are realistic about their talents and abilities and use them successfully to pursue their ambitions. Finally, they will have moved from a position of self-centeredness and self-preoccupation to one of awareness of and concern for the feelings of others: in other words, the ability to be empathic. Kohut (1984) saw the achievement of these ends as realistic goals for a successful self psychological treatment of pathological narcissism.

REFERENCES

Freud, S. (1912). The dynamics of transference. In J. Strachey (Ed.), *The standard edition of the complete psychological works of Sigmund Freud* (Vol. 12, pp. 99–108). London, England: Hogarth Press. (Original work published 1958)

Freud, S. (1917). Mourning and melancholia. In J. Strachey (Ed.), *The standard edition of the complete psychological works of Sigmund Freud* (Vol. 14, pp. 229–258). London, England: Hogarth Press. (Original work published 1957)

Kohut, H. (1959) Introspection, empathy and psychoanalysis. *Journal of the American Psychoanalytic Association, 7,* 459–483.

Kohut, H. (1966). Forms and transformations of narcissism. *Journal of the American Psychoanalytic Association, 14,* 243–272. doi:10.1177/000306516601400201

Kohut, H. (1968). The psychoanalytic treatment of narcissistic personality disorders. In R. S. Eissler, A. Freud, E. Glover, P. Greenacre, W. Hoffer, H. Hartmann, . . . Spitz, R. A. (Eds.), *The psychoanalytic study of the child* (Vol. 23, pp. 86–113). New York, NY: International Universities Press.

Kohut, H. (1971). The analysis of the self: A systematic approach to the psychoanalytic treatment of narcissistic personality disorders [*The psychoanalytic study of the child, Monograph No. 4*]. New York, NY: International Universities Press.

Kohut, H. (1972). Thoughts on narcissism and narcissistic rage. In R. S. Eissler, A. Freud, M. Kris, & A. J. Solnit (Eds.), *The psychoanalytic study of the child* (Vol. 27, pp. 360–400). New York, NY: Quadrangle Books.

Kohut, H. (1977). *The restoration of the self.* New York, NY: International Universities Press.

Kohut, H. (1979). The two analyses of Mr. Z. *The International Journal of Psychoanalysis, 60,* 3–27.

Kohut, H. (1984). *How does analysis cure?* (A. Goldberg & P. E. Stepansky, Eds.). Chicago, IL: The University of Chicago Press.

Kohut, H., & Seitz, P. (1960). Beyond the bounds of the basic rule—Some recent contributions to applied psychoanalysis. *Journal of the American Psychoanalytic Association, 8,* 567–586. doi:10.1177/000306516000800312

Kohut, H., & Seitz, P. (1963). Concepts and theories of psychoanalysis. In P. H. Ornstein (Ed.), *The search for the self: Selected writings of Heinz Kohut* (Vol. 1, pp. 113–141). New York, NY: International Universities Press.

Kohut, H., & Wolf, E. (1978). The disorders of the self and their treatment: An outline. *The International Journal of Psychoanalysis, 59,* 413–425.

Liberman, M. D. (2006). The psychoanalytic approach to the treatment of conduct disorder. In W. M. Nelson, A. J. Finch, & K. J. Hart (Eds.), *Conduct disorders: A practitioner's guide to comparative treatments* (pp. 27–47). New York, NY: Springer.

Stolorow, R. (1978). The restoration of psychoanalysis. *PsycCRITIQUES, 23,* 229–230.

Strozier, C. B. (2002). *Heinz Kohut: The making of a psychoanalyst.* New York, NY: Farrar, Strauss and Giroux.

16

TREATING PATHOLOGICAL NARCISSISM WITH SHORT-TERM DYNAMIC PSYCHOTHERAPY

MANUEL TRUJILLO

The normal development of the sense of self leads most people to develop a sturdy individual identity and to achieve the ability to successfully pursue cherished personal goals, values, and ideals. In addition, such "good enough" development liberates the capacity to value and love other people and to connect with significant aspects of the real world (e.g., nature, history, culture). The developmental pathway to such achievements includes the repeated experiencing of an inner core of physical, emotional, and intellectual characteristics that form one's unique identity. This identity becomes increasingly solid as the person perceives and trusts the acceptance and enjoyment of such core identity by parents and by other key people in the person's life. At the core of such developments lay the experiencing and blissful enjoyment of the essence and functionality of the child's body: the pleasure of being dry, warm, fed, in motion when appropriate, and the delight of being absorbed in the warm, welcoming, and celebratory parental embrace. The next layer incorporates deep feelings of joy and exuberance that, when appropriately shared and

DOI: 10.1037/14041-016
Understanding and Treating Pathological Narcissism, J. S. Ogrodniczuk (Editor)
Copyright © 2013 by the American Psychological Association. All rights reserved.

mirrored, yield deep feelings of wholeness and an emotional conviction of being worthy of love and of being desired. Thus, as the normal developmental phases unfold and the unique individuality of the growing child is recognized and celebrated, the sense of self and identity acquires sufficient robustness and consistency. One can then talk about certain confidence in the self and a somewhat expansive ambition, later to be enhanced by its integration with actual capacities (i.e. ego functions). If it is said that the journey of classical psychoanalysis can be described by the dictum "where the *id* is, the *ego* shall be," the travel through the developmental pathway of the normal self can be denoted as "where *grandiose omnipotence* is, *mature competence* shall be."

At the end of this process of self development, the person is equipped with a healthy, enduring, and robust sense of self and with effective and rewarding relationship with others and the world of culture and ideas that provide significant avenues for sublimation. The subjective awareness of such accomplishments is mediated by particular (positive) types of self-experiences and self-representations. The sense of physical joy and vigor (vs. depletion), the experience of wholeness (vs. emptiness), the mobilization of curiosity, and many other emotional parameters can be described as normal and fulfilling self-experiences. Experiencing oneself as desirable (vs. rejected) and as possessing value and capacities can be denoted as a normal range of positive self-representations.

This developmental pathway can be impinged on, and impaired, by a host of factors that are important to consider when evaluating and treating patients who present with narcissistic pathologies, regarded as disorders of the self. In terms of the developmental process, the life histories of many of these patients are filled with potentially pathogenic experiences, such as excessive and repeated praise unrelated to behavior or performance, or conversely, excessive and relentless criticism. Therapists often find evidence of exploitation of the child's talents and capacities for parental purposes, such as intense demands for exceptional performance, often unrelated to the emotional needs or wishes of the growing child. Cumulatively, such experiences may interfere with the optimum integration between the early, unformed ("archaic") and grandiose self-images and the child's emerging talents and capacities. As such, alignment between ambitions and talents is key to the development of self-esteem and healthy functioning; when the necessary integration fails it may generate an exaggerated sense of entitlement (or its negative twin, a sense of worthlessness). Severe emotional neglect or abuse can also affect the normal developmental process of the evolving self. A common cause of derailment of self-development is the disdain or frank and aggressive contempt of parents for the core identity (sexual, temperamental, artistic, or vocational) of their child. The excess shame that accrues in this process is toxic to the sense of self.

DYNAMICS OF PATHOLOGICAL NARCISSISM

Heinz Kohut (1971) described the core dynamics of pathological narcissism as flowing from the developmental failures that impede both the growth and maturation of the basic structures of the self and of the progressive relatedness of the evolving self to the world of objects. Such relatedness grows from childhood through an appropriately primitive (i.e., selfish) use of objects at the service of the self (self-objects) and goes on to achieve mature relatedness and adult mutuality. Such developmental failures may affect the attainment of a personal identity and of mature love.

If this healthy process is not accomplished, the person's identity is impaired by repressed childlike, immature, grandiose self-images. The repression of such entities requires significant and tiresome efforts on the part of the ego, and the control is, in any case, so tenuous that the person often lives in dread of a breakthrough of such primitive experiences—experiences such as a grandiose sense of self-importance; a preoccupation with fantasies of unlimited success, power, brilliance, beauty, or ideal love; and the belief that he or she is "special" and unique and can only be understood by, or should associate with, other special or high-status people.

A second set of consequences of the developmental failures that give rise to pathological narcissism affect the person's relationships to others. To the degree that such relationships are suffused with omnipotence and magical thinking, they are also plagued by endless conflict: conflict generated by the patient's overt or covert demands for excessive admiration and by their feeling entitled to especially favorable treatment. These patients are often interpersonally exploitative, lack empathy, are envious of others, and demonstrate arrogant, haughty behaviors or attitudes.

In addition, persons suffering from pathological narcissism experience shame as a characteristic main affect. Shame is mobilized when the narcissistic person fails to live up to his grand self-image or when suffering the perceived interpersonal slights to which narcissistic individuals are ever so sensitive. The shame is intertwined with a tyrannical perfectionism that imposes impossible demands on the person and on others. This perfectionism may serve to compensate for the conscious or unconscious sense of inferiority that often plagues these patients and may also fuel the relentless drive to live up to their grandiose fantasies. This perfectionism may extend to large domains of the person's functions such as the appearance and function of the body, sexual fantasies or activities, and emotional or intellectual dispositions. The implacable demands (on self and others) of such perfectionism erode any sense of self-esteem and may give rise to considerable self-hatred.

The overt psychopathology displayed by people with pathological narcissism relates to two sets of forces. The first is the lack of maturation, integration, and realization of large segments of grandiose self that leads to problems of identity formation, maintenance of self-esteem, and development of appropriate and satisfying values, ideals, and accomplishments for the patient. The second pathological process involves the derailment of drive–developmental processes. In this regard, the presence of significant, unresolved self-developmental pathology affects the patient's ability to cope with object losses and to resolve triangular oedipal pathology. Kohut (1971), in fact, is said to have stated that clinically significant Oedipus complexes occur because the developing child's normal drives and conflicts were previously disturbed by unresolved narcissistic wounds related to unempathic parental responses.

SHORT-TERM DYNAMIC PSYCHOTHERAPY FOR PATHOLOGICAL NARCISSISM

I have developed a short-term treatment option for patients suffering from pathological narcissism that builds on some of the technical contributions of David Malan (1976) and Peter Sifneos (1992); Habib Davanloo (2000) in his intensive short-term dynamic psychotherapy (ISTDP); and on the contributions of Heinz Kohut to self psychology.

ISTDP was developed to deal with the problems of patients whose pathology is generated by complicated foci of oedipal psychopathology and by pathological grief resulting from object loss but who manifest intense and rigid defenses that render their unconscious conflict practically inaccessible to dynamic techniques based on free association. Meta-analytic reviews (Abbass, Hancock, Henderson, & Kiesly, 2006; Leichsenring, 2001) have found that ISTDP is effective for a variety of patient problems, including anxiety and depressive disorders or Axis II Cluster C disorders such as avoidant, dependent, obsessive–compulsive, and passive–aggressive personality disorders, precisely because it has developed techniques that can reach these affects by effectively confronting and reducing such defenses. My extensive clinical experiences suggest that modified forms of ISTDP are potentially powerful treatments for some of the problems of these patients, but they are not sufficient to mobilize and resolve the specific narcissistic unconscious pathology, constituted by rigid dissociative defenses and by primitive self and object representations.

Davanloo (2000) elegantly systematized the techniques required to obtain an early breakthrough into the unconscious of highly resistant patients. The core of Davanloo's techniques flows from his research on the twin dynamics of transference and resistance. The central aim of Davanloo's system of ISTDP is the rapid reduction or removal of resistance through a system of planned interventions that, when successful, result in direct access to the unconscious as a result of the breakdown of the major resistance system with mobilization of unconscious therapeutic alliance and with the emergence of long repressed impulses and feelings such as intense anger and deep sadness. However, Davanloo's techniques alone are not sufficient to break through such patients' strong dissociative defenses or to mobilize the primitive self-experiences and self-representations necessary for a successful therapeutic process.

THERAPY PROCESS

The techniques that I developed, referred to as *empathy based short term dynamic psychotherapy* (EB-STDP; Trujillo, 2002, 2009), use some of the techniques proposed by Davanloo to treat the oedipal and loss problems that also plague patients with narcissistic psychopathology but add specialized techniques to reach the narcissistic core of these patients through the barrier of defensive dissociation. My techniques are based on empathy and on the early uncovering, and therapeutic use, of the unique complex transferences that these patients typically develop.

Clinical Assessment and Trial Therapy

Initiation of the process of therapy with narcissistic patients requires a careful diagnostic evaluation to determine whether they meet selection criteria for a trial of EB-STDP. Trial therapy, when successful, permits rapid and profound access to the patient's unconscious conflicts, repressed feelings, painful self-experiences, and primitive self-representations. The diagnostic evaluation, which can last a few sessions, must, like in any other psychiatric examination, obtain a five-Axis diagnosis according to the *Diagnostic and Statistical Manual of Mental Disorders* (4th ed., text rev.; DSM–IV–TR; American Psychiatric Association, 2000). Beyond such clinical evaluation, the clinician must develop a complete psychodynamic assessment that includes a comprehensive description of the patient's living and adaptive problems, the dynamic forces that fuel such problems, and the genetic and developmental experiences that give rise to such forces. The paradigmatic characteristics of patients suffering from narcissistic disorders, traits, or vulnerabilities are represented by the existence, at the deepest genetic developmental levels, of deeply repressed and dissociated pathological self-experiences and self-representations. As these experiences and views of themselves are uncovered and experienced in the therapy sessions, patients appear full of pain, shame and grief, dread and anxiety, helplessness, and narcissistic rage; they may never have experienced these feelings with such intensity or immediacy before.

These emotions represent the narcissistic core of these patients. This core, and the long repressed feelings contained in it, must be accessed through the barrier of complex defenses (resistance) that these patients have erected if they are to be treated with EB-STDP. To reach that core, the therapist needs to blend some technical interventions derived from Davanloo's ISTDP with interventions specially designed for narcissistic psychopathology. This dynamic evaluation, when successful, often provides great relief to patients and mobilizes positive transference feelings including any of the classical narcissistic transferences: idealized, mirroring, or twinship. When such results are obtained, patients are considered good candidates.

STDP-Derived Techniques

The planned sequence of steps to deal with resistance during the trial therapy starts with what Davanloo (2000) referred to as the *central dynamic sequence*. The sequence includes the following technical steps: (a) a relatively brief phase of inquiry into the patient's clinical and interpersonal difficulties (e.g., "Could you describe the problems that you have with your husband?"); (b) the exertion of pressure to confront the avoided or repressed feelings (e.g., "You say that you are angry with him but how do you experience that anger toward him?"); (c) the initiation of challenges to the defensive system, through an intense and rapid sequence of interaction where the patient holds on to his resistances and the therapist highlights it and challenges it repeatedly (e.g., "You are still not describing your feelings"); (d) the analysis of the transference resistance that when successful, provides direct access to the unconscious, facilitating the visceral experience of intense primitive rage and murderous impulses followed by the eruption of profound sadness and guilt, feelings that are often experienced with a vivid sense of immediacy (e.g., "What are your feelings towards me now?"); (e) systematic analysis of the transference and dynamic exploration of the unconscious configuration of the patient's psychodynamic conflicts; and (f) consolidation and preparation for the working through phase and development of the therapeutic contract.

Goals of Therapy

The ultimate goal of EB-STDP for patients with pathological narcissism is the resolution of emotional and interpersonal problems through the reactivation of primitive, dissociated, anxiety-provoking self and object perceptions and structures, to a degree that permits the resumption and completion of normal development. As such dissociated perceptions, emotions, and ambitions emerge, patients may share, with considerable shame and trepidation, how they fantasize about achieving much more in life than the therapist (e.g., a better office address, better furniture, car, clothes). The supportive response of the therapist ("What would be wrong with that?") can lead to the sudden experience of a joyful giddiness and later give way to a feeling of entitlement to achieve (through his efforts and capacities) and enjoyment of such successes. Steps like this often lead to a gradual but significant resolution of symptoms, gains in self-esteem, and more fulfilling relationships with others and with work. The assertion, attributed to Freud, that freedom from neurosis enhances the capacity to love and work applies here as well. The time frame for such process hovers around 50 one-hour sessions held once or twice a week.

The paradigmatic interventions for core self-problems are the empathic understanding and interpretation and the active and pervasive use of the transference, which develops rapidly as a function of breaking through the defense barrier and reaching deep emotions and core narcissistic phenomena. In this realm, empathy involves an accurate grasp, both cognitive and affective, of what others experience. Its presence creates a supportive milieu in which the patient can either bask in the use of the therapist as an optimum self-object, or bitterly but safely complain about the therapist's failure to satisfy the patient's unconscious demand for a perfect object. The working through of that failure is critical for the acceptance of adversity, now without the catastrophic tint that those experiences typically acquire in persons with narcissistic vulnerabilities.

Techniques Used During EB-STDP

To the degree that the narcissistic vulnerabilities of many patients are hidden behind a well-defended wall of character defenses, they can be reached only after achieving significant breakthroughs into patients' unconscious rage and/or grief. For this part of the process, Davanloo's techniques, as described earlier, are crucial. These techniques, however, must be complemented by the use of interventions specifically tailored to reach the narcissistic core of these patients. (Note that in all clinical examples in this chapter, the patient's identity has been disguised to maintain confidentiality.)

- Active and empathic attention to the development of various types of self-object transferences. A patient of mine made an off-hand remark at the beginning of the initial evaluation alluding to the rudeness of the doorman who attended to her as she entered the building. The patient repeatedly avoided my invitation to focus on that comment, and after challenging some of her defenses ("Why are you afraid to share this experience with me?"), she broke down in tears—the doorman's rudeness had evoked the fear that I would be equally dismissive of her, with catastrophic consequences for her self-esteem and for the therapeutic process. Feeling safe, after this exchange, she could open and explore her intense need for my admiration and applause.

- Early detection and reactivation (largely through active inquiry) of primitive, dissociated, grand, or grandiose self-images while containing the defensive and inhibiting affects, such as dissociative anxiety, fragmentation anxiety, and embarrassment and shame. A patient of mine, a historian who suffered an incapacitating writer's block while attempting to write his first book, declared—after considerable challenges to his resistances were made—that his ambition was to write the "definitive" book on his chosen subject. The declaration made him blush intensely while he experienced considerable fear and shame. These feelings were related to his conviction that I would dismiss him with contempt for declaring his ambition. Following this interaction, which occurred in the first assessment session, the patient suddenly remembered a dream from the night before. In it, a man was helping him to load a backpack with tools in preparation for a very important trip. This dream expressed his yearning for a relationship that would allow him to identify his true talents and capacities and allow him to develop his own life project without exploitation or excessive protectiveness.

- Facilitating the experience of the special form of corrective emotional experience, which I call *imaginary reconstruction*. In the example just described, I asked the patient–writer the following question: "What would it feel like to you to write a book like that and to have such an impact?" He experienced my remark as an expression of confidence in him and of my support and comfort with his engaging in grand fantasies and ambitions. As result, he felt entitled to hold such ambitions and to consider himself as potentially worthy of admiration.

The middle phase of therapy is characterized by the repeated reactivation and working-through of the pathogenic foci uncovered during the assessment phase and aims toward the systematic resolution of those multiple foci. The following principles apply to the working-through process:

- To undo the effects of the defense of dissociation, the therapist should highlight and promote the patient's actual, visceral experience of feelings, avoiding intellectualization and challenging cognitive distancing. Feelings such as intense grief, sadness, and rage, followed by guilt and remorse, appear again and again in the psychodynamic focus facilitating patients' working-through and resolution and promoting healthy adaptive growth.

- Often, as a result of the breakdown of resistance systems, the patient experiences vivid reactivation of memories and dreams, which enrich the working-through process as long as the therapist holds the focus on the direct affective experience of the recovered memories and dreams.

- The working-through process must include the meaningful, and affect-laden, links between three conceptual layers of the mental apparatus: problems of adaptation; dynamic forces; and genetic problems. The problems of adaptation are expressed in symptoms, performance problems, and interpersonal difficulties. The dynamic forces represent bridges between the genetic roots of the patient's problems and the actual adaptive problems that they cause. For instance, the presence of abuse, neglect, and longing for a genetic figure (mother or father) in the patient's past may give rise to dynamics of unconscious rage and self-sabotage, which are expressed in the daily life of the patient in the form of many failed interpersonal relationships.

- The frequent use of transference is another hallmark of EB-STDP. Transference appears early, it is ubiquitous throughout the treatment, and it changes very frequently even within the same session. For example, a patient may respond at one moment with a statement of admiration or affection for the therapist; a short while later, a perceived slight may precipitate torrents of contempt and ridicule.

The therapy process can be portrayed by the triangle of the self depicted in Figure 16.1, where the myriad of repressed feelings, impulses, self-experiences, and self-representations are repeatedly reactivated and viscerally experienced as the strong defenses are weakened through repeated breakthroughs. The reactivation of feelings, impulses, and self-experiences initially evoke considerable anxiety and shame, which must be contained, progressively tolerated, and ultimately resolved. While dealing with the defense component of the triangle, therapists must pay special attention to defensive activities such as splitting and cognitive affective dissociation.

Distorted negative self-images, as they emerge, are deactivated through exposure; they can be seen more realistically in the "light of day." Positive self-images flow through the barriers of dissociation and are reactivated (experienced by patients as rightfully belonging to them) and appropriately linked to hopes, dreams, skills, and values. In this way, profoundly personal

Defenses   Shame and anxiety

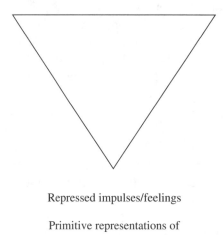

Repressed impulses/feelings

Primitive representations of

self and objects

Figure 16.1. Triangle of the self.

projects of much meaning to the patient can reemerge as valued blueprints for purposeful and meaningful life plans and actions.

Termination of Therapy

Mutually agreed-upon termination of therapy with patients with pathological narcissism requires the fulfillment of several criteria. First, there must be significant reduction of Axis I symptoms and substantive lessening of the interpersonal and work dysfunctions that brought the patient into treatment. Second, there should be evidence of significant reactivation of the grand(iose) self: increasing acceptance and enjoyment of aspects of self and the capacity to experience vitality and well-being independent of the approval of an admiring self-object. Often, patients experience wonder and pleasure on reflecting, or discovering, self-functions such as imaginativeness and playfulness. It is as if they say to themselves, "This is who I am and I like it." As this function grows and expands, patients come to expect that a large part of the pleasure of living will come from the exercise of these self-functions and from their ability to develop life projects, and build human relationships, stemming from this deep source of being, rather than from empty social conventions or from a compulsive need for perfection. As pleasure and pride accrue from the exercise of these self-functions, tyrannical perfectionistic demands on self or others lessen, and empathy may appear in intimate relationships, together with tolerance for the self-object shortcomings of others. Finally, there should be significant resolution of pathological grief reactions for others and for self. I supervised the treatment of a patient who epitomized the process of pathological grief resolution while describing a particular moment of well-being achieved while hiking a few months after he had been able to grieve the deaths of his parents and his wife.

> I came to this point on the road where I could see the whole valley down the road; struck by the beauty of the place, I had what I would call an epiphany: for the first time in a long time I felt totally at peace with myself and, I guess with life: there was no anxiety, no fear, no guilt. I thought about my wife, I thought about my mother and my father, and I could imagine the three of them looking at me from high in the sky and I could see {tears streaming down his face} that they were pleased with my success, that they were proud of me.

This experience summarizes several features present in the resolution of pathological grief reactions: People from whom the patient has felt ambivalently alienated are restored to an optimal, emotionally meaningful, contact; anxiety and guilt disappear from those relationships and are replaced by peace and harmony.

The closer the process comes to the fulfillment of these criteria, the better the outcome and the easier the termination process. Active work on the transference can solidify the process. When the patient above was asked by his therapist, "And where would I be in that picture?" he answered, "You made it possible. You created the peace treaty. You gave them all back to me." The patient thus indicated the termination of the therapist function as a self-object who functions in lieu of the parental self-object; they are now restored to their sublimated self-object function in memory. The transference can now be deactivated and the therapist becomes the real object who mediated and facilitated the changes in the patient's subjective emotional life.

PARADIGMATIC CASE

I.T. is a 46-year-old unmarried, professional man who first consulted because of unbearable anxiety, depression, and loneliness. These feelings appeared a few months after the death of his father following surgery for heart problems. His relationship with his father was a tortuous one, and one of the reasons for his consultation is that he could not let go of his feelings of rage toward his dead father. Not that he felt guilty for having those feelings: "He died without giving me the respect and love that I need and deserve . . .

I had to take care of him far more than he ever took care of me." A large portion of his conscious experience of life and self was filled with bitter complaints and laments about the failures of others. The other large part of his conscious awareness was related to his unshakable conviction that he was special and that others were there to serve him. He required from others an exquisite attention and responsiveness to the endless flow of his physical and emotional needs. In his romantic life, he treated women with a mixture of cruel devaluation and condescension, promptly eroding their self-esteem, and then demanding that they recognize his superiority and submit to his needs for confirmation and affection. As a result, few people lasted long in his life, and when they left him, he suffered months of intense anxiety, complaining bitterly about their abandoning him despite his uniqueness and "generosity." "She is nothing without me," he would typically say after the breakup of one of these relationships. In other contexts, he relished the thought of "getting over" on people by being successfully manipulative and had no concern about the cost to the other person of his exploitiveness. The dynamics of "specialness" and exploitiveness also appeared at work, impairing his performance and his relationships with bosses and colleagues. As a result, he often changed jobs and even careers, performing and earning well below his intellectual potential.

His conscious life was dominated by the need to ensure that others were there to meet his needs and that no one ever cheated him of anything. In therapy, he was always trying to extend the session beyond the agreed upon time, experiencing a sense of triumph when he succeeded at it, while reacting with considerable rage when the therapist was even one or two minutes late, whatever the reason for such delay. The thought of being cheated met with a cascade of subjective affects such as unbearable anxiety and pervasive rage, which often led to prolonged, sadistic devaluing, and attacks on the offender.

The dynamic picture for this patient can be represented as follows:

- Ongoing, conscious experience of entitled grandness or frank grandiosity, with large segments of the patient's adaptive behavior devoted to seeking opportunities for confirmation of his sense of being special.
- Bouts of primitive anxiety, rage, and despair, often accompanying the experience of rejection by any of the persons that he chose as self-objects. These bouts, at times, included painful episodes of fragmentation anxiety, depression, and self-devaluation, and prolonged experiences of emptiness.
- An unconscious life dominated by negative self-images and experiences of rejection and devaluation or anticipation of such

states. These experiences color the patient's conscious fears and frequently appear in his dreams.

At the end of the evaluation phase, I.T.'s dynamic assessment appeared to have the following configuration:

- Problems
  - Inability to channel professional activities to reasonable success despite evident intellectual assets.
  - History of stormy failed relationships with several women despite craving to achieve stability, be married, and have a family.
  - Chaotic life dominated by a craving for emotionally intense professional and emotional relationships (self-object like); the frantic attempts to mold such relationships to his needs; and the aftermath of rage, anxiety, and depression when facing their inevitable failure.
- Dynamics
  - An all-consuming and compulsive need to find the perfect (i.e., all-admiring, all-giving, and mirroring) partner, which dominated his personal and professional life.
  - Primitive rage and vindictiveness triggered by perceived or actual failure of chosen partners.
  - Ongoing professional and personal self-sabotage.
- Core narcissistic conflicts
  - Impulse/feeling. Ambivalence toward paternal object complicated by life-long rage and unresolved pathological grief, with consequent disruption to the formation of dynamically equivalent actual relationships.
  - Self-representations. Split-off primitive un-integrated self-images. The grandiose self-images are acted out in consciousness in the form of demands to be met by partners; the helpless self feeds enormous self-doubts and constant neediness.

The comprehensive dynamic picture described above represents a road map for the unfolding of the therapeutic experience. For I.T., therapy proceeded through repeated runs around the triangle of impulses, person, and self. The two key pathogenic foci for him are the focus of self and the focus of pathological grief reaction for the death of his father. The pathogenic capacity of each focus reinforces the pathogenic capacity of the other. The images of helplessness and utter fragility derived from his repressed disturbed negative self-images are reinforced first by identification with the failed aspects of his father's life as a way to maintain some bond with the father, charged again by his need to expiate guilt for his unconscious murderous impulses toward him. The trigger for such destructive feelings relates to his father's failure to act as an adequate narcissistic self-object (optimum mirror).

The working through of these problems required revisits to the experience of anger and destruction in relationship to the people in his current life, toward the therapist in the transference, and subsequently toward his father. In different sessions and several contexts, he had visceral experiences of rage toward his father yet almost simultaneously remembered normal life events and positive or neutral interactions with him, which facilitated a nuanced reconstruction of his life with his father. A feeling of acceptance and serenity replaced the former stormy anguish and made possible the acceptance of his father's death and the working through of grief. Often, this process brought with it the awareness that the emotional acceptance of his father's death led to relinquishing the long-held unconscious hope that his father would ever be the mirroring object that he had needed all his life and that he would ever experience the "perfect" warmth, love, and admiration that he had so much craved. When successful, this process makes possible a growing and lasting sense of peace and emotional understanding.

A modicum of closure and closeness then ensued for the patient in relationship to memories of his father. Simultaneously, overt and covert demands for closeness, support, feedback, extra time, and extra resources showed up in the therapeutic situation. The slightest disappointment in the therapist evoked feelings of desolation and devastation in the session. The technique described as imaginary reconstruction allowed the patient to evoke emotionally satisfying moments of optimum mirroring. The following vignette describes the use of such techniques.

> *Therapist:* How do you feel toward me as a person?
>
> *Patient:* That is a good question. I really don't know that you truly care . . . How could you possibly care for all your patients?
>
> *Therapist:* What it would be like to be cared for the way you want to?
>
> *Patient:* [surprised] Wow, that would be something . . . I cannot even . . . fathom it . . . a certain warmth . . . trust . . . contentment [eyes moisten]
>
> *Therapist:* And how do you imagine I feel toward you?
>
> *Patient:* Never thought of that—I think you want me to succeed, I don't think you are jealous of me . . . I think you like me [gets emotional] . . . maybe even love me . . .
>
> *Therapist:* And how do you feel about that?

Patient:	Warm, great . . . it makes me think of my father. I think that if he would have been able to, he definitely would have loved me, how sad!
Therapist:	What would he have loved especially about you?
Patient:	My wit, my creativity . . . that I am caring for my mother as I promised him I would. [crying]
Therapist:	How would he feel if he could see you right now?
Patient:	Proud . . . proud . . . prouder than he ever felt . . . or at least expressed to me that he felt.

CONCLUSION

In this chapter, the EB-STDP approach to the treatment of pathological narcissism was described and elucidated. Prior efforts to extend the applications of short-term dynamic techniques to patients with relatively uncomplicated psychoneurotic disorders (Sifneos, 1992) and to complicated multifocal psychopathology (Davanloo, 2000) required the honing and refinement of the psychotherapeutic techniques needed to break through complex characterological barriers. The application of these techniques to self-disordered patients requires their adaptation to the metapsychology of self and self-development (as distinct from the metapsychology of impulse/feeling, derived conflict). The aim is similar: to achieve rapid access to unconscious pathogenic structures and their attendant repressed feelings and to promote rapid healing through early, active, and abundant recourse to the transference. It is my hope that the successful marriage between well-established short-term techniques and the emerging metapsychology of narcissistic pathology will yield increasingly effective treatments for these patients.

REFERENCES

Abbass, A., Hancock, J. T., Henderson, J., & Kiesly, S. (2006). *Short-term psychodynamic psychotherapies for common mental disorders*. The Cochrane Library. Chichester, England: Wiley. doi:10.1002/14651858.CD004687.pub3

American Psychiatric Association. (2000). *Diagnostic and statistical manual of mental disorders,* (4th ed., text rev.). Washington, DC: Author.

Davanloo, H. (2000). *Intensive short-term dynamic psychotherapy*. Chichester, England: Wiley.

Kohut, H. (1971). *The analysis of the self*. New York, NY: International University Press.

Leichsenring, F. (2001). Comparative effects of short-term dynamic psychotherapy and cognitive–behavioral therapy in depression: A meta-analytic approach. *Clinical Psychology Review, 21*, 401–419. doi:10.1016/S0272-7358(99)00057-4

Malan, D. (1976). *Towards the validation of dynamic psychotherapy.* New York, NY: Plenum Press. doi:10.1007/978-1-4615-8753-8

Sifneos, P. (1992). *Short-term anxiety provoking psychotherapy: A treatment manual.* New York, NY: Basic Books.

Trujillo, M. (2002). Short-term dynamic psychotherapy of narcissistic personality disorders. In J. J. Magnavita (Ed.), *Comprehensive handbook of psychotherapy* (Vol. I, pp. 345–364). New York, NY: Wiley.

Trujillo, M. (2009). Intensive short-term dynamic psychotherapy. In B. J. Sadock, V. A. Sadock, & P. Ruiz (Eds.), *Comprehensive textbook of psychiatry* (9th ed., pp. 2893–2910). Baltimore, MD: Lippincott Williams & Wilkins.

17

SCHEMA THERAPY FOR PATHOLOGICAL NARCISSISM: THE ART OF ADAPTIVE REPARENTING

WENDY T. BEHARY AND EVA DIECKMANN

Schema therapy, an integrative model of psychotherapy developed by Young, Klosko, and Weishaar (2003), was developed to treat personality and chronic symptom disorders. Included in this thoughtfully assembled, evidence-based approach to treatment (Giesen-Bloo et al., 2006) are elements from gestalt, object relations, psychodynamic, cognitive–behavioral, and emotion-focused therapies. One of the hallmark features of schema therapy is the concept of (adaptive) limited reparenting. Emphasis is placed on (a) identifying core unmet needs and attachment ruptures in the patient's early development and (b) working to help the patient get those needs met. Although no specific clinical trials of schema therapy for narcissistic personality disorder (NPD) have been conducted, anecdotal observations and reports suggest that it may have potential as an effective treatment.

This chapter discusses the use of schema therapy for NPD. We begin by discussing the primary tenets of schema therapy and then illustrate how this can be applied to the treatment of NPD.

DOI: 10.1037/14041-017
Understanding and Treating Pathological Narcissism, J. S. Ogrodniczuk (Editor)

TABLE 17.1
Eighteen Early Maladaptive Schemas / Developmental
Domains and Unmet Needs

Schema domain	Frustrated basic need	Schemas
I. Disconnection and Rejection	Secure attachment (stability, empathy, nurturance, guidance, acceptance)	1. Abandonment 2. Mistrust/Abuse 3. Emotional Deprivation* 4. Defectiveness/Shame* 5. Social Isolation*
II. Impairment of Competence and Autonomy	Autonomy, competence, and sense of identity	6. Dependence/ Incompetence 7. Vulnerability to Harm 8. Enmeshment/ Undeveloped Self 9. Failure*
III. No Limits	Realistic limits and self control	10. Entitlement/ Grandiosity* 11. Insufficient Self-Control/Self-Discipline*
IV. Other Directedness	Freedom to express valid needs and emotions	12. Subjugation* 13. Self-Sacrifice 14. Approval Seeking*
V. Overvigilance and Inhibition	Spontaneity and play	15. Negativity/Pessimism 16. Emotional Inhibition 17. Unrelenting Standards* 18. Punitiveness

Note. An asterisk denotes a schema that is specific to narcissistic personality disorder. From *Schema Therapy: A Practitioner's Guide* (pp. 14–17), by J. E. Young, J. S. Klosko, and M. E. Weishaar, 2003, New York, NY: Guilford. Copyright 2002 by Jeffrey Young. Also from http://www.schematherapy.com. Copyright 2003 by Jeffrey Young. Adapted with permission.

EARLY MALADAPTIVE SCHEMAS

Young (1999) proposed 18 early maladaptive schemas that are defined as self-defeating cognitive and emotional patterns that underlie maladaptive coping styles and behaviors (see Table 17.1). These schemas begin in early development and get repeated throughout life. They represent the interplay between the temperament of the child and early experiences during which certain core needs were not adequately met, and at an extreme, created ruptures in healthy human development. This proposal is consistent with attachment theory, positing that early unmet needs may result in insecure attachment to others (Bowlby, 1988). Young et al. (2003) postulated that we have five core emotional needs; the goal of schema therapy is to help patients find adaptive ways to meet these needs:

1. connection to others (includes safety, stability, nurturance, and acceptance);
2. autonomy, competency, and identity;
3. freedom to express valid needs, ideas, and emotions;
4. spontaneity and play; and
5. realistic limits, reciprocity, and self-control.

A common schema profile of narcissism is one whereby the child's experience included caregivers who were intolerant of the child's sensitivity, vulnerability, and less than superior performance. The child was overly indulged when it came to rules and material objects and inadequately disciplined when it came to limit setting. The emerging young adult is often unprepared to live in the world where healthy relationships require empathy, responsibility, frustration tolerance, and give-and-take. This profile corresponds to Twenge and Campbell's (2009) conceptualization of NPD. Described as "raising royalty," the pairing of emotional deprivation and special privilege can influence the child's relationship with the world as one where material acquisitions, status, and recognition become substitutes for true connection.

As shown in Table 17.1, patients with NPD tend to present with schemas relating to Entitlement, Insufficient Self-Control, and Unrelenting Standards. Their tendency to cut themselves off from their emotions keeps them unaware of the Emotional Deprivation, Defectiveness and Shame, and Failure schemas that are bundled together in the roots of the lonely little child. Social Isolation, Subjugation, and Approval Seeking schemas develop in response to unmet needs, thus ensuring that these needs do not get properly fulfilled.

THE SCHEMA MODE APPROACH

Schema therapy uses a mode-based approach to treatment with NPD patients. *Schema mode* refers to "those schemas, coping responses, or healthy behaviors that are currently active for an individual" (Young et al., 2003, p. 37). A schema mode is activated when particular schemas or coping responses have erupted into strong emotions or rigid coping styles that take over and control an individual's functioning. "An individual may shift from one schema mode into another; as that shift occurs, different schemas or coping responses, previously dormant, become active" (Young et al., 2003, p. 40). Ten schema modes have been identified, including child modes, maladaptive coping modes, maladaptive parent modes, and the healthy adult mode (for a complete mode listing, see http://www.schematherapy.

com). Patients with NPD tend to have the following schema modes (Young & First, 2004):

- Vulnerable Child Mode: feels mostly lonely, unlovable, and ashamed in response to the conditional love based on extraordinary performance along with the critical and demanding expectations for emotional control and achievement;
- Impulsive Child Mode: acts on noncore desires or impulses in a selfish or uncontrolled manner to get his or her own way and often has difficulty delaying short-term gratification; often feels intensely angry, enraged, infuriated, frustrated, or impatient when these noncore desires or impulses cannot be met; may appear "spoiled";
- Detached Self-Soothing/Self-Stimulating Coping Mode: pursues activities in a compulsive manner (to help cut off access to painful emotions and loneliness), such as excessive work, substance abuse, intellectual dialogues, pornography, and other addictive behaviors;
- Overcompensating Mode: bullies, acts entitled and controlling, demands approval and attention, usually triggered by feelings of inadequacy or disregard;
- Demanding Parent Mode: feels that the "right" way to be is to be perfect or achieve at a very high level, to keep everything in order, and to strive for high status, typically in response to the underlying sense of defectiveness and emotional deprivation; and
- Healthy Adult Mode: nurtures the vulnerable child mode, sets limits for impulsive child mode and the entitled overcompensator, promotes and supports a healthy child mode, eventually replaces the maladaptive detached coping mode; neutralizes or moderates the demanding parent.

The schema mode approach allows the therapist to align with the healthy and strong parts of the patient's personality, in an effort to weaken the maladaptive or self-defeating parts that interfere with and sabotage relationships and the overall health of the patient, as detailed in the following case example. (The patient's identity has been disguised to maintain confidentiality.)

Therapist: Hello, Stephen.

Patient: Hello . . . Uh [looking at his watch as he takes a seat], do you think we can wrap this up a little faster today? I have a telephone conference in about an hour. I really have nothing much to talk about, and I am parked in what I believe may be a no-parking area outside. I was rushed getting here, almost canceled.

Therapist: [smiling—looking inquisitive] Hmm . . . What's going on, Stephen? You "almost canceled, wrap this up, nothing to say" . . . Feels like "Detached Stephen" has entered the room? The side of you that does not want to be here . . . doesn't want to open up . . . sees this as a waste of time? You've been in this mode before. I am wondering why today?

Patient: Oh, geez . . . I don't know . . . You [therapists] make such a big deal out of everything [scowling]. Let's just move on. Forget it . . . it's not important.

Therapist: You seem annoyed with me, Stephen. What's triggered you? Why so anxious to "move on"?

Patient: [cynically] You know, there are more important things in the world than wallowing in my feelings. I am managing a major deal right now at the firm, timing is critical, and I cannot afford to lose my focus. That's all I need right now! More people in my life to be fed up with me.

Therapist: Stephen, if you are saying that you need to dodge the painful feelings today because you are fearful of losing your edge and facing tough consequences, you can just say so, and we can see if that makes sense. I know it's hard for you to ask for what you need, or talk about your fears. I know that you have never expected anyone to understand, given your background, right? It was always important to your parents that you stay at the top of your game, and never show "weakness." I understand your story and the challenges you have had to deal with, but it's hard to care about you when you use that hurried, cynical, and off-putting tone. I can imagine the impact this must have on Carla [wife], who isn't your therapist and isn't trained to connect all the dots.

Patient: [softer] Yeah, yeah, you're right. I know I am a pain in the ass . . . sorry.

Therapist: [smiles, tongue-in-cheek] Yeah, you are. Thanks for owning it. But seriously Stephen, don't brush it off so fast. You are really just a guy who is not comfortable letting down his guard, always has to be performing and meeting those unrelenting standards. Now, let's start over. This time you tell me what you are afraid of, but in an open and respectful way. It's me, remember? I do care about you. I am not the enemy.

Patient: [eye roll] Okay, okay . . . but you are a pain too [sheepishly smiling]. And yes, I could really use a break from all of the constant demands in my life. I am so tired . . . but I am afraid to let Carla and my kids down . . . to disappoint them. I don't know how to turn that switch off.

Therapist: When do you think you developed this one-way switch . . . the one that makes you feel like you have to be "on" all the time for everyone?

Patient: I just can't remember not having it. . . . It's just who I am . . .

Therapist: Yes . . . But actually it's "how" you are, Stephen. "Who" you are is a person who simply longs to be loved without conditions, without feeling that you always have to prove yourself. It's a long-standing and, actually, very lovable part of you that you had to learn 'how' to conceal. Carla and the children just want *you*—not "Mr. Outstanding" senior partner in the firm. They just want to love *you* and laugh with you and play together and share the joys and burdens of daily life.

Patient I know, but I don't know "how" to be that guy.

Therapist: Yes, that's why you are here.

[The use of empathic confrontation and leverage in the therapy relationship.]

The therapist identifies and labels the "Detached Stephen" mode as one whereby he attempts to close down access to his emotions, avoid responsibility, and hyperfocus on his performance and productivity. She (the therapist) points out the impact on others, namely, his wife, in an effort to keep the leverage high enough—we say more about what this means later—and widen his awareness of the consequences he may face if he does not take ownership of his maladaptive behaviors. She also empathically links this mode, and the inherent frustration he exhibits, to the early learned experiences of a boy who had to answer to the unrelenting expectations of his parents. This strategy promotes differentiation of "then" and "now" experiences, along with empathy for long-standing and automatic responses to discomfort. Without blame, the therapist can hold the patient accountable for poor interpersonal responses.

Schemas are self-perpetuating, implicitly informing an individual's maladaptive reactions and self-defeating patterns. For example, narcissistic individuals who implicitly experience shame and loneliness when they are not the center of attention may become interruptive in conversation and ramble on, trying to impress listeners with self-boasting stories. They usually end up feeling lonely (and sometimes ashamed) because their obnoxious behavior results in people distancing themselves, not following up with them as promised, or becoming annoyed and critical of them. The very experience they are attempting to avoid (shame and disconnection) is the very thing they perpetuate with their poor coping habits. Patients are taught about this phenomenon in treatment as a means of normalizing these challenges and painful outcomes. Schema therapists emphasize their belief that this phenomenon is part of a universal truth: We all have core needs, we all have schemas, and we are creatures of habit, not "pathetic" or "crazy" and not mere masochistic beings.

Organized within the memory system, implicit experiences, held outside of our awareness, can prompt schemas and schema modes to become activated, causing intensely disruptive affect and dysfunctional behavioral reactions. Conditions might include interpersonal interactions that are deemed capable of exposing shame or rejection and attributions: "He thinks I am brilliant," "He is not worth my time," "He does not find me acceptable." Such attributions are not uncommon for narcissistic types who are usually summing up their interpersonal exchanges based on approval and recognition achievement to bolster their sense of worth. They seek to mask their core sense of defectiveness and emotional loneliness with an overcompensating style of orating, showing off, controlling or dominating behavior, acting entitled, or entertaining others with their wit, charm, and intelligence. They can also easily detach and become dismissive or preoccupied, shifting to their often compulsive outlets like work, gambling, drugs, shopping, sex, drinking, or intellectual (fact-finding) dialogues, to soothe their inner turmoil. Sensory stimuli can also activate schemas and schema modes (i.e., smells, sounds, tactile elements, and bodily sensations).

GENERAL APPROACH TO SCHEMA THERAPY WITH NARCISSISTIC PATIENTS

The goal of schema therapy is to provide adaptive reparenting within the limits of the therapy relationship, in an effort to strengthen the healthy adult mode so that patients can engage in healthier interpersonal and intimate relationships; function better in work and school environments; develop a more integrated sense of self; and improve their capacity to tolerate, manage, and communicate difficult emotions. Patients learn to identify their schemas, coping styles, and schema modes as they arise in the context of current life issues. The therapist points out the links between these current life challenges and the early maladaptive experiences of the child–adolescent. The therapist validates and empathically confronts modes as they arise and sets limits when appropriate. Experiential strategies such as imagery and gestalt techniques are used to help patients connect with emotions linked to their child modes, to weaken avoidant modes, and to challenge and fight punitive and demanding parent modes, all the while maintaining an attuned awareness of the in-the-moment interactions within the therapy relationship. Schema therapists act as healthy models for patients' healthy adult mode; reorganizing biased beliefs; empathizing with, nurturing, guiding, and protecting child modes; and identifying shifts in the treatment room as a means for generalizing these experiences and response patterns to patients' daily life. For example, schema therapists notice out loud that the long-winded, condescending monologue of narcissistic patients, in response to a question about feelings, can feel burdensome and off-putting (even though they are trained to understand patients' need to avoid emotions and assume a superior role in most relationships). They point out that despite their awareness of the underlying motivation for this recognition-seeking mode, their "humanness" detects what it might be like for significant others who lack the training to understand their makeup and simply want to feel connected. The therapy relationship is relevant to patients' therapeutic goals, such as developing reciprocity, openness, and empathy in relationships. Collaboration between the therapist and the patient's healthy adult mode promotes the healing of these lifelong patterns formed in response to the unmet needs of the lonely and deprived child. As patients become more aware of their modes and activating conditions and work to strengthen the healthy adult modes (with the help of the therapist), they experience a weakening of imbedded schema-driven inclinations and begins responding more openly and adequately to their longings, which arise from core unmet needs. They also achieve quicker recovery from the tightly held grip of turbulent emotions related to their early maladaptive blueprints.

The Issue of Therapist Competence

Finding clinicians who are willing (and specifically trained) to work with patients with NPD is a serious challenge. Yet, many therapists have a strong desire to develop the clinical skills necessary to treat such patients. Therapists often reveal that no matter what method they have used, there is rare "success" with NPD patients. Thus, most therapists choose to not work with them, because they expect enduring change to be a hopeless endeavor. Additionally, it is not uncommon for therapists to state that they experience their own intense schema activation when working with these patients, making their access to empathy untenable. There are probably few patient populations that can provoke the same sense of intimidation, incompetence, anger, and self-doubt as narcissistic patients. During training and supervision in schema therapy, a good deal of time is spent on *parallel process*, meaning that for therapists to become sturdy, credible, and competent experts with this population, they need to heal personal schemas and modes that are likely to be triggered by the narcissistic patient, who can become highly critical of the therapist's credentials, style, and even office décor. It is not uncommon for clinicians to report self-sacrifice, subjugation, defectiveness/shame, emotional deprivation, unrelenting standards, and/or abandonment schemas (see Table 17.1). Left unattended, the therapist's vulnerability becomes fodder for the narcissistic patient's game of wits.

The Concept of Leverage

Patients with NPD are among the most challenging in any clinician's caseload. They avoid exposing their vulnerability and can be cynically unwilling to engage in experiential work in therapy. This is why they rarely enter therapy voluntarily. Even when they do, they often arrive armed with a sense of entitlement and hold everyone else accountable for their dilemma—and it is usually not long before the therapist joins the cast of the blamed. The usual scenario is one in which they reluctantly agree to go to therapy because a significant someone is posing a threat to their general state of comfort, their reputation, or status if they refuse therapy. In the schema therapy model, it is typically this leverage—the avoiding of certain consequences—that sets up the possibility for patient motivation, compliance, and an effective treatment outcome. However, the therapist must keep the leverage high, as was demonstrated in the vignette with Stephen, who came to therapy because Carla threatened to divorce him unless he did. After years of trying to cope with his grandiose, demeaning, controlling, and dismissive behaviors, Carla expressed her readiness to terminate the marriage if things did not change. Stephen's therapist continued to remind him of the likely and unwanted loss he would face should he exit treatment prematurely. She also kept Stephen keenly aware of those moments in the therapy relationship when he acted in ways that Carla (reasonably) refused to tolerate.

Schemas and Modes

The patient with NPD has a schema profile that includes emotional deprivation, defectiveness–shame, mistrust–abuse, failure, approval seeking, unrelenting standards, a sense of entitlement, and insufficient self-control schemas. In some cases, therapists may also see subjugation, abandonment, punitiveness, and negativity schemas. The male pronoun is used for ease of writing and reading in the following discussion; it is reported that males represent a greater number of patients with NPD, and when compared to their female counterparts, the differentiating behaviors in the male profile usually show up with greater emphasis on achievement, competitiveness, and dominance (Behary, 2008a, 2008b; Twenge & Campbell, 2009).

A typical background story is one in which the child received a confusing message based on conditional love. One parent (usually the mother) doted on him because she needed him to bolster her sense of security and worth; she praised him for being the "special child" but didn't stand up to the other parent (usually the father), who was unavailable, critical of his performance, and placed high demands on the child to be extraordinary (i.e. the concept of never feeling good enough, except through third-party boasting to friends, family, and "important" people). The child learns that it is not enough to simply be a spontaneous, curious, playful, and lovable little person. Success and celebrity-like stature in the community have sometimes gained these families a type of special VIP status. The child is expected to meet the obligations of an ascribed child prodigy. As the child grows, he learns that he is entitled to live by a separate set of rules, different from the "ordinary people" in the world.

But NPD is not limited to a "high society" family, nor is such a family background an absolute predictor for narcissism. A schema profile of narcissism can also be anchored to an average family where the mother was passive or depressed and needed her child to be the strong side of her. The father may have been a man who worked long hours, drank too much, and had little time or tolerance for his son's needs for love and attention. His interests and enthusiasm regarding his child may have been mostly based on the child's competitive self-expression and productivity. The child's need for a genuinely secure sense of connection and acceptance is exchanged for the relief he finds in the absence of his dad's disappointment, criticism, and disdain for his innate emotional longings.

As patients learn about their modes, schema therapists help them to choose suitable terminology to identify their Lonely Child, Detached Side, and Self-Aggrandizing Side. Patients find it more emotionally illustrative and less clinical when they use personal expressions to characterize their modes. For example, we know of a patient who referred to his detached side as "Freezer Boy" and the lonely child as "Lost Edward."

(Vulnerable) Lonely Child Mode

Emotional deprivation is a hallmark schema for narcissistic patients because the need for physical and emotional affection, protection, guidance, and understanding was not adequately met. Instead, the only attention or praise the child received was conditioned by his meeting certain expectations. He learned to be loved for "doing," not "being." Yet, approval for a well-done performance did not meet the child's need for a secure attachment. Patients will sometimes state that they still feel deprived, inadequate, and lonely, in spite of immense success. However, unaware of the impact of this void in the parent–child relationship, they often respond to initial interviews by casually stating that their childhood was "normal." This extraordinary form of detachment is akin to forgetting that you are starving. We can also view it as a type of habituated adaptation.

In addition to the deprivation of positive attunement, any sign of emotional neediness—the need to be held, hugged, comforted, reassured—is deemed a weakness and is met with either direct criticalness or further withdrawing of attention and praise, leaving the child feeling ashamed and defective for having these (natural) needs. This creates the onset of the defectiveness–shame schema. Our patients express sentiments like, "I learned to not need anyone, from the age of four. I was dedicated to just working hard to get the goodies." And when asked, "But what happened to 'little so-and-so'?" they usually reply with, "He's gone—and good riddance. He was too weak, too sensitive." What the patient is describing is the detached, self-soothing mode that was constructed early on as a way of not feeling the pain associated with his emotional loneliness and his sense of shame and insecurity. The absence of this important needs constellation, founded in secure attachments, can have implications for treatment, informing clinicians of the deeply imbedded implicit belief that no one could ever really love and understand him just for being him.

Detached Protector (Self-Soother) Mode

Many (enlightened) patients with NPD say that they had to become hyperautonomous and self-reliant so that they would never have to count on someone else to be there for them. Their unrelenting standards schema is often spawned by the high expectations put forth by their parent(s), along with a striving for the kind of perfection that puts them at the top of the heap, where others can only look up to them. They find places to turn their attention to ward off and soothe the empty feelings of the lonely, vulnerable child within their implicit memory. The Detached Protector (Self-Soother) is one of the default modes of patients with NPD. Some examples of this (maladaptive) mode in adult patients include a variety of compulsive behaviors, such as working, gambling, eating, drugs, alcohol, spending, pornography, sex, debates, and intellectual monologues.

Because mom essentially "used" the child for her own sense of purpose and connection, the child develops a mistrust schema, the idea that people are nice only because they want something. In therapy, patients with NPD tend to be moderately suspicious of kind and caring gestures toward them. They may even mock the therapist for being too sensitive or too soft. One of our patients once said, "You're paid to care about me. What kind of real care is that?" The reply was:

> You pay me for my training and expertise in guiding this process and understanding your makeup. You cannot pay me to care for you. I either do or I don't. So, if I do—it's free. It's on me. But when you accuse me of being manipulative and use that critical tone, it's hard to care about you. That's on you.

(Overcompensating) Self-Aggrandizing Mode

The "fight" or overcompensating mode is also used to cope with the triggering of schema clusters. Narcissistic patients are likely to show up as overly charming, entitled, competitive and aggressive, controlling, or critical. They can also show up impatiently in treatment rooms, with little to no tolerance for "things" (including approval and recognition) not coming easily and rapidly to them. This is when they are likely to yell, demand, embarrass, and dominate the people who they perceive to be a threat to their immediate comfort and security. This is another (disowned) method for keeping the lonely and shameful little boy tucked away, never to be felt, never again to be ignored or punished. Narcissistic individuals engage in human interactions as if they are in a game, consistently manipulating their sense of importance and acceptance by maneuvering the "one up–one down" position.

Other Modes

The demanding parent mode—the one responsible for the undying competitiveness, unrelenting standards, and compulsivity—is almost always operating just a scratch below the surface, much like the stage mother who refuses to relinquish her post just beyond the curtain. The healthy adult mode is present when the narcissistic patient is not reacting to a triggering condition and has not flipped into a maladaptive coping mode.

GOALS AND STRATEGIES

The chief goal in schema therapy for patients with NPD is to weaken the maladaptive coping modes, so that the lonely child can be accessed for reparenting, first by the therapist and eventually by the healthy adult side of his personality and ultimately by others who have chosen to remain in his life. As a result, he learns to drop his guard(s) and empathize not only with the resonant feelings coming from his early internal world but for others as well. In so doing, he creates the opportunity for intimacy with others. The therapist may use imagery and chair work to facilitate dialogues for the purpose of schema mode differentiation and to assess the relevant strength of the modes. These strategies are also aimed at freeing and reparenting the lonely child and at helping the healthy adult side confront the detached and entitled sides (Kellogg, 2009; Young et al., 2003).

Experiential or emotion-focused techniques are also used (Behary, 2008a). For example, the therapist uses *self-disclosure* in an effort to generalize micro clashes in the therapy relationship to macro clashes in the patient's world. By pointing out the negative and off-putting effects of the narcissistic patient's tone, facial expression, and word crafting when he is "covering up" his feelings, the patient comes to appreciate the impact he has on others. For example, the therapist would self-disclose by empathically confronting the patient when he is being condescending:

> I understand that getting things right and being in control has always been very important to you, given the standards placed upon you by your parents when you were growing up. Being in therapy means letting down your guard sometimes, and I know this is hard for you. But when you use that disparaging tone and language with me, despite my understanding of your issues, I can feel enough of the negative resonance to imagine how off-putting that must be for your wife and children who are not trained to understand your makeup and can only feel hurt and disconnected from you.

The use of an mp3 audio device can assist therapists in capturing these moments and playing them back to the patient to assess shifts in the treatment room. Perhaps surprisingly, patients tend to be very receptive to this technique. The audio device can also be highly effective for creating audio coaching files that the patient can use as practice homework. Listening to the therapist's voice guiding his focus to such things as schema triggers and mode shifts, to dropping in on his inner world to pay attention to his vulnerable child, to scripting a remorseful statement to a loved one that best reflects his role in a hurtful interaction, keeps him anchored to the treatment process and to the therapist—the one who is safe and helping him to heal.

Limit Setting and the Therapy Relationship

Limit-setting strategies are used to address the unmet need for defined boundaries, reciprocity, and responsibility. Limit setting also creates a platform for the development of frustration tolerance. Many narcissistic patients grow up with few limits and lots of "things" that replace their emotional nurturing with a warped sense of specialness. They are used to having someone clean up their interpersonal untidiness and take them off the hook for their bullying, acting out, impetuousness, demanding, and disrespectful behaviors. One of our patients once reported the following:

> When my mom (who was hosting her monthly ladies luncheon at our house) found out about how mean I had been to my classmate; and how upset I was when he said he would never play with me again—she told me that I was too good for him.

This is a classic precursor for the self-aggrandizing, recognition-seeking mode.

Another example of limit setting in the therapy relationship would include confronting the narcissistic patient's whimsical demands for extra time when he arrives late. The therapist must be careful not to collude with the patient's sense of entitlement in order to install a better sense of how the world really works if people want to be accepted. He or she might describe it like this:

> I know it's hard for you when you cannot have what you want, and you are not treated as if you are special, because this was the way that you learned to feel cared for. It's what you're used to . . . the way the world gives in to you, given your status at work, and your style at home. Ironically, because I do care about you, it is important that I help you to reassemble this biased (and incorrect) expectation. I need to help you to realize that while it is not your fault that there was a traffic jam, it is your responsibility to manage your time as best you can; and to be respectful of mine and the other clients who are awaiting their sessions. It is unfortunate that you will not have a full session today, but it is also important for you to understand the reasonableness of this and not feel that it makes you any less important to me. It is not a measure of how special you are. It is just the way to treat everyone as fairly as possible.

Empathic Confrontation

The schema therapist uses strategies like empathic confrontation to address issues of entitlement, found in the ("I'll show you") overcompensating mode, as well as the ("I don't need anyone") detached mode. In the case of Stephen, the therapist was empathic to the origins of Stephen's struggle when it came to letting down his guard and his difficulty looking inward. She also showed empathy for the little boy who learned that impressing people was the way to fit in and be connected. She kept a photo of Stephen as a child in the chart so that she could remind herself of the vulnerable boy beneath the brassy camouflage. She might hold it up for him to view and ask him whether he could feel this side of himself, the one who had to always "do" something for love. Typically he would change the subject or challenge her motives, and she would immediately point out the shift to his dismissive/aggressive and detached modes and suggest that it must be (although he cannot feel it) hard to bear the pain held by this part of him. As the schema therapist empathically joined the dots between "then and now" experiences, she was also readily engaged in holding him accountable for his self-defeating behaviors, the ones that caused him to produce the very outcome that he was trying to avoid.

The narcissistic patient seeks to avoid appearing foolish, defective, or needy, but his method for preempting this outcome is often, ironically, the very thing that perpetuates it. He starts out as the entertaining, bright, and witty guy in the room. But as soon as you attempt to reach beyond his wall of masterful trivia or profoundly esoteric stories to his emotional side, he excuses himself for an "important call" or glazes over and becomes bored, annoyed, or distracted. He may also attempt to turn the tide, asking why you would ask such a "foolish" question.

There is irony in the fact that the response pattern (when he is uncomfortable) that causes those in his company to often find him unbearable, undesirable, boorish, and obnoxious is the very thing he is trying to avoid. He merely wants to fit in, and the only way he knows how to achieve this is by grandstanding and attention seeking or by shutting down and distracting himself. The major idea behind empathic confrontation is, "It's not your fault, but it is your responsibility to do something now."

Obstacles in Treatment

The change phase of treatment can take a good deal of time, sometimes lasting 1 to 2 years or more, depending on other comorbid issues. The narcissistic patient, with little frustration tolerance, may not withstand the process. There may also be the issue of limited financial resources. Additionally, there is the question of how much leverage the therapist can maintain to strengthen patient compliance. It is our experience that without leverage, treatment is likely to fail. It is like teaching a lesson of "choices and consequences," one that is rarely a part of such patients' early interpersonal building blocks.

CONCLUSION

Against the background of the growing importance of pathological narcissism, it is remarkable that there are no empirical studies concerning the identification of effective treatments for people suffering from this debilitating disorder. Perhaps such a void is understandable. Doing research with people whose hallmark trait consists of not wanting to follow the same rules as everyone else is unquestionably not an effortless undertaking. Furthermore, there must be an adequate supply of therapists who are confident in their competence in treating NPD (Dieckmann & Behary, 2010). Nonetheless, schema therapy offers a thoughtful and exciting contribution to the collection of treatment models for NPD. We look forward, with great enthusiasm, to gathering more verified evidence of what we have come to observe, appreciate, and celebrate in our clinical experience thus far.

REFERENCES

Behary, W. T. (2008a). *Disarming the narcissist*. Retrieved from http://www.disarming thenarcissist.com

Behary, W. T. (2008b). *Disarming the narcissist: Surviving and thriving with the self-absorbed*. Oakland, CA: New Harbinger.

Bowlby, J. (1988). *A secure base: Parent–child attachment and healthy human development*. New York, NY: Basic Books.

Dieckmann, E., & Behary, W. (2010). Schematherapie: Ein ansatz zur behandlung narzisstischer persönlichkeitsstörungen [Schema therapy: A beginning for the treatment of narcissistic personality disorder]. *Psychiatrie und Psychotherapie Up2date, 1*, 53–68.

Giesen-Bloo, J., van Dyck, R., Spinhoven, P., van Tilburn, W., Dirksen, C., van Asselt, T., . . . Arntz, A. (2006). Outpatient psychotherapy for borderline personality disorder: Randomized trial of schema-focused therapy vs. transference-focused psychotherapy. *Archives of General Psychiatry, 63*, 649–658. doi:10.1001/archpsyc.63.6.649

Kellogg, S. H. (2009). Schema therapy: A gestalt-oriented overview. *Gestalt! 10*. Retrieved from http://www.g-gej.org/10-1/schematherapy.html

Twenge, J. M., & Campbell, W. K. (2009). *Living in the age of entitlement: The narcissism epidemic*. New York, NY: Free Press.

Young, J. E. (1999). *Cognitive therapy for personality disorders: A schema-focused approach* (3rd ed.). Sarasota, FL: Professional Resource Exchange.

Young, J. E., & First, M. (2004). *Schema therapy: An integrative therapy for personality change*. Retrieved from http://www.schematherapy.com

Young, J. E., Klosko, J. S., & Weishaar, M. (2003). *Schema therapy: A practitioner's guide*. New York, NY: Guilford Press.

18

COGNITIVE BEHAVIORAL PERSPECTIVES ON THE THEORY AND TREATMENT OF THE NARCISSISTIC CHARACTER

ARTHUR FREEMAN AND SUZY FOX

According to the *Diagnostic and Statistical Manual of Mental Disorders* (4th ed., text rev.; *DSM–IV–TR*; American Psychiatric Association, 2000), the individual with narcissistic personality disorder (NPD) *suffers* from a "pervasive pattern of grandiosity (in fantasy or behavior), lack of empathy, and hypersensitivity to the evaluation of others" (p. 689; italics added). Whether the individual actually "suffers" depends on how the narcissism is perceived and responded to by others and how it is perceived and used by the individual. The pattern of grandiosity occurs whether or not an objectively accurate evaluation of talent, accomplishment, physical prowess, intelligence, competence, physical attractiveness, sense of humor, or creativity is made. If the self-assessment is reinforced by others, the narcissistic individual has reason to maintain and support this self-view. Narcissistic individuals often seem unable or unwilling to see the impacts of their actions on others when those impacts are negative. Their view of the cognitive triad (i.e., how they view the self, the world, and the future) is colored by their self-referent schema.

DOI: 10.1037/14041-018
Understanding and Treating Pathological Narcissism, J. S. Ogrodniczuk (Editor)

Furthermore, they may seem to have a poor understanding of self and of their motives. Their sense of self can be easily threatened, and they may be willing to go through sometimes painful experiences rather than be less than the special person that they believe themselves to be and that they expect or demand others to see in them. Their "suffering" comes when their self-view is not accepted or supported by those around them, when they collect the approbation of others, or when they experience a loss of narcissistic pleasures or tributes. In most cases, the negative response of others is often a mystery; narcissistic individuals have difficulty understanding why others do not subscribe to the view they have of themselves.

Narcissism ranges from mild to severe. A mild form may be interpreted as high self-esteem and may be seen by parents and teachers as a positive aspect of the child's personality. The moderate to severe manifestations are less easily excused or seen as positive. Another available lens through which to view narcissistic behavior is on the altruist–narcissist spectrum. At one end would be the altruist, whose major concern would be for others, even if that entails a loss of personal safety, recognition, or profit. On the other end, the narcissistic individual evidences a greater self-concern with a concomitant lack of caring or empathy for others. Rather than fall into the diagnostic dichotomy of narcissism, the clinician must recognize that the only place one can find a "pure" narcissist is in the pages of *DSM–IV–TR* (American Psychiatric Association, 2000). The clinical presentations generally include Axis I disorders (depression and anxiety) as well as Axis II, Cluster B combinations of narcissistic/histrionic, narcissistic/antisocial, and narcissistic/borderline disorders.

Federn (1952) differentiated between healthy and pathological narcissism. Healthy narcissism contributes to hope and ambition, motivating the individual to grow and to be creative. Pathological narcissism serves as a substitute for hope and ambition. In healthy narcissism, the boundaries of the ego are firm and resilient. In pathological narcissism, ego boundaries are unstable. The fantasies of the normal or healthy narcissistic individual, on both the conscious and unconscious levels, are more in accord with reality and are less infantile. The grandiose and magical elements that are the hallmark of narcissistic fantasies are related to how far the narcissistic style differs from the normal and the acceptance by the individual of certain schema.

Horney (1937) also differentiated between healthy strivings for power and neurotic strivings:

> The feeling of power, for example, may, in a normal person be born of the realization of his own superior strength, whether it be physical strength or ability, mental capacities, or maturity of wisdom. Or his striving for power may be connected with some particular cause; family, political, or

professional group, native land, a religious or scientific idea. The neurotic striving for power, however, is born out of anxiety, hatred and feelings of inferiority. To put it categorically, the normal striving for power is born of strength, the neurotic of weakness. (p. 163)

Horney saw the narcissistic striving and the resultant behavior as being expressions of weakness and deprivation for which the self-glorying and self-righteousness of the narcissistic individual are not functions of self-love, but rather self-hate. The narcissistic style

has nothing to do with any kind of self-love; it does not even contain any element of complacency or conceit, because contrary to appearances, there is never a real conviction of being right, but only a constant desperate need to appear justified. (p. 210)

Narcissistic individuals who are highly intelligent may, in fact, have good impulse control and social functioning with the capacity for active and consistent work, which may allow them to achieve success. They "can be found as leaders in industrial organizations or academic institutions; they may also be outstanding performers in some artistic domain" (Kernberg, 1975, p. 229). Researchers in the areas of industrial–organizational psychology and leadership have found evidence that certain occupational roles requiring or rewarding a confident social presentation, persuasiveness, authoritativeness, nonconventional creativity, and certain styles of leadership favor certain types of narcissistic individuals. With their unusually high expectations of themselves (task-specific self-efficacy), preferences for challenging goals (need for achievement), beliefs in their personal control (internal locus of control), and self-serving assertiveness in organizational politics, many narcissistic individuals rise to positions of leadership in their work organizations (Hill & Yousey, 1998; Lubit, 2002; Rosenthal & Pittinsky, 2006). This form of narcissism can arguably be considered "adaptive" as long as the individuals continue to receive and perceive "evidence" of their importance and success. Their difficulty will surface when they no longer have the accoutrement and trappings of recognition, success, and the perceived appreciation of others.

In discussing the etiology of a narcissistic personality, Millon and Everly (1985) and Millon, Millon, Meagher, and Grossman (2004) described three factors in the development of a narcissistic style: parental indulgence and overevaluation, learned exploitative behavior, and only-child status. These "learnings" are coded as rules or schema that direct the individual's behavior and serve as filters for receptive and expressive data. In terms of parental indulgence, the parents view the child as special and perhaps even better than siblings or relatives. These children draw several conclusions from this parental view: (a) that they deserve to be treated with distinction and do not have to earn such treatment; (b) that they are special, superior people; (c) that they can expect compliance and even subservience from other not-so-special people; (d) that they can expect commendation and praise for virtually everything they do; and (e) that the world revolves around their whims and wishes. They are egotistical in their perspectives and narcissistic in their expressions of love and emotion (Millon & Everly, 1985, pp. 75–76).

As these individuals move outside the favored position within the family, they expect to be treated in ways similar to those to which they had become accustomed. They quickly learn to manipulate others and situations so as to receive the special status that they have learned that they should get, regardless of their performance or ability. They learn the "buttons" and idiosyncrasies of others and use this information to manipulate and exploit others in order to get the recognition that they believe that they deserve. "Exploitation of others seems to be powerfully reinforcing and, therefore, difficult to bring to extinction" (Millon & Everly, 1985, p. 77).

Hamner and Turner (1985) made three assumptions about the development of self-concept: that it is learned, that this learning occurs early in the socialization process, and that the self-concept is a powerful determinant of behavior. This view implies that inappropriate early socialization could result in the individual's learning an unrealistically high appraisal of his or her capabilities and for developing a pathological level of narcissism, but it does not specify the type of socialization that would produce this problem.

Theories regarding the development of the self-concept provide another perspective on narcissism. During normal development, a major part of the parental role is to help a child develop a positive self-image and a strong sense of self-concept or self-esteem (Hamner & Turner, 1985). These schemas would ideally translate into a sense of personal efficacy, a feeling of satisfaction that is derived from successfully dealing with stressors and limitations imposed by one's environment. This may lead to what we might term *healthy narcissism*, that is, a positive sense of self that is developed by having an awareness and acceptance of one's abilities and limitations and a striving to further develop one's abilities without the need to flaunt one's accomplishments.

Narcissistic individuals often go to considerable lengths to maintain their high opinion of themselves. Maintaining physical health may take an exaggerated form (e.g., fad dieting; working out to maintain the illusion of strength, health, or beauty). They may seek and use reconstructive surgery to "correct" physical flaws to the point of body dysmorphia. The need for the individual's academic success may result in a joyless school experience that centers on grades and recognition rather than on learning or enjoying the learning process. This may be strongly reinforced by family, peers, and teachers. Similarly, the narcissistic individual's need for professional success and recognition may result in a career strongly focused on the acquisition of status and power at the expense of the well-being of coworkers, subordinates, and clients and the interests of the organization and the society in which it is embedded.

Finally, there is only-child status. This status may not be the sole province of only children. Children whose next sibling is several years younger may be treated as only children inasmuch as the child is, in effect, an only child for many years. The only-child experience may contribute to the child's self-perception as special. The perception of specialness may then pervade all of the individual's experiences.

A COGNITIVE BEHAVIOR THERAPY PERSPECTIVE

The focus of cognitive behavior therapy (CBT) is on helping individuals identify and respond to their misattributions, impaired or limited problem-solving, cognitive distortions, negative automatic thoughts, maladaptive schemas, and misperceptions (Freeman, Pretzer, Fleming, & Simon, 2004). These interventions may prove to be difficult for individuals who may have limitations in describing their experiences, labeling emotions, and identifying relationships between their thoughts and feelings (Knell & Ruma, 2003). In such a case, the therapist who uses a CBT approach may be faced with the following options: (a) simplify the interventions or assist the individual in developing the skills necessary to benefit from such techniques, and (b) help to develop the motivation to change. As with all forms of therapy, the patient must be invested (or at least interested) in finding value in treatment to even allow change to develop. CBT therapists simultaneously focus on four aspects of cognitive or behavioral functioning: cognition (how individuals perceive and understand their experiences), mood (their affective responses), environment (how others in their system respond), and behavior (observed actions). Because of the inherent interplay of these functions, a change in one might be assumed to effect changes in the others. CBT works to bring about direct change in one's environment, cognition, and behavior and indirect change in one's affect. The emphasis is on helping individuals to detect and more adaptively interpret internal and environmental cues. In essence, events alone are not inherently good or bad, right or wrong, fearful or calming; one's interpretation of the event is what matters. How or why people perceive situations in varying manners, and the result of doing so, is the foundation of cognitive theory and treatment.

In every human action, reaction, and interaction, individuals are guided by templates of personal, cultural, family, religious, gender, and age-related schemata that have developed over the years (Beck, Freeman, Davis, & Associates, 2004; Freeman, Pretzer, Fleming, & Simon, 1990, 2004). Schemata shape behavior and affect in particular directions and help to give meaning to one's world. The schemata are involved in memory (what is selected for recall or what is "suppressed"), cognition (the abstraction and interpretation of information), affect (the generation of feelings), motivation (wishes and desires), and action and control (self-monitoring, inhibition, or direction of action; Beck, Freeman, & Associates, 1990; Beck et al., 2004). By this selectivity, the schemata allow for more efficient information processing (Mandler, 1984; Taylor & Crocker, 1981).

Schemata are not isolated; they are interlocking and appear in various constellations. For example, although most individuals in Western cultures have learned and would subscribe to the basic personal/religious/cultural schema "Thou shalt not steal," they might still take something belonging to another individual. The rationale of the narcissistic individual might be based on other parallel "rules" such as "I deserve it," "It is due to me," or "If anyone has something that I do not have it is intolerable for me."

Through the use of selective abstraction, these individuals overattend to schema-consistent information and underattend to information inconsistent with those assumptions. It is an instance of confirmatory bias in information processing. Narcissistic individuals continually seek information consistent with their positive (or grandiose) views of self, world, and future, and do not seek, perceive, or see as valid, information that contrasts with or contradicts this view.

Overgeneralization involves applying conclusions appropriate to a specific instance to an entire class of experience based on perceived similarities and is an instance of global reasoning. Having been successful at one task (no matter how circumscribed or limited), narcissistic individuals conclude that they will be successful or superior at all similar tasks.

Magnification and minimization occur when the person over-attends to and exaggerates the importance of aspects of experience and discounts or underestimates the relevance of negative or nonconfirmatory experience.

Narcissistic persons are more likely to inaccurately interpret situations when their self-worth is on the line. Thus, when an event is most in need of critical analysis, the person may be less likely to accommodate and more likely to attempt to assimilate the new situation into the existing repertoire of knowledge and responses. In the best of circumstances, this has adaptive purposes: A quick assessment of a strange situation, using old knowledge, may save one's life. Unfortunately, it becomes problematic when the assessment discounts essential information that would call for a different response

THE NARCISSISTIC FAMILY

Based on Freeman and Rigby (2003), we can identify several family and systemic conditions that contribute to the development of a narcissistic schema:

1. Parents fail to teach the child frustration tolerance.
2. The child is not taught the meaning and importance of boundaries and limits.
3. Overly permissive parents do not impose consequences for inappropriate behavior.
4. A skewed parental value system awards the child as special.
5. The parental style of manifesting self-esteem is often reflected by the child. If a parent is narcissistic, he or she models certain behaviors and a general style for the child.
6. Parental neglect and/or rejection leads to narcissistic over-compensation.
7. An only child or only grandchild is rewarded for little achievement.
8. Parents act out their frustrations at never having been able to achieve the goals that they (or their parents) had for them and that they get vicariously through the child.
9. Parents are unskilled in child rearing and agree to every request or demand made by the child.
10. Systems reward every behavior as special, whether or not the award is earned (e.g., all children get a trophy to avoid injuring the child's fragile "ego").

TREATMENT ISSUES

The clinician must think in terms of the individual's temperament, which represents the genetic contribution (genotype) to development and behavioral style. Is narcissism a genetic predisposition designed for survival? The alpha animal gets more food, the choice food and bed, choice of mates, control over others, and death or banishment of adversaries; does this position imply narcissism? The observable behavior and physical appearance are together labeled as the phenotype. It is this level that is observed and used as grist for the diagnostic mill. The cultural, family, and environmental context within which the child develops can be thought of as the sociotype. There are several cultures that view their own culture or ethnic group as superior and therefore have rights and dominion over other "lesser" groups of people; the results of such beliefs include the Holocaust, slavery, and prejudice. The interplay of these elements makes for the colors and shading of the disorder.

Several questions are raised regarding the treatment of the narcissistic individual. First, what brings the individual into therapy? A second and probably more important question is, what keeps the individual in treatment? Third, what are the goals of therapy? Fourth, who is involved in the therapy?

Inasmuch as narcissistic individuals may not be aware of the upset that they create in others or in systems, they may have little motivation to change their behavior, their view of the world, or their opinion of themselves or of others with whom they interact. Often the individual's significant other makes the referral for treatment, while the referred individual does not understand why family members are so upset or annoyed. Similarly, a narcissistic employee might be referred for coaching or therapy by a supervisor or through a human resources disciplinary process.

ASSESSMENT

To ensure a useful referral, it is essential to request concrete examples of the problematic behavior rather than vague, amorphous goals such as "become easier to live with." (Appendix 18.1 provides a specific approach to assessment of narcissism.) Rather than viewing the narcissism in a uni-dimensional manner, clinicians must view narcissistic behavior in terms of several differing though overlapping styles, each of which requires a different therapeutic approach.

- Narcissistic individuals with *positive self-esteem* can accept and state that they feel good about themselves. They rely on the consensually accepted and validated perspective of others to support the idea that they have special skills and abilities. For example, few would argue with the self-view of Itzhak Perlman that he is a great violinist or with Michael Jordan's view that he was a great basketball player.
- *Healthy* narcissistic individuals have attributes that they recognize as special or superior to their age-mates, family members, or colleagues. They do not, however, flaunt their "gifts." For example, Bill Gates has proven his perspicacity but remains a rather humble individual (at least from what the public can discern).
- *Group* narcissistic individuals' special status is conferred and maintained by membership in a group. The group might be a gang, a religious group, a family or school group, or a work organization. Without the group, the status is lost and is not transferable. For example, the members of a particular country club or association may see themselves as special and members of "lesser" clubs as "lesser" people.
- *Helpful* narcissistic individuals may be unaware that their "helpfulness" at guiding and correcting others is negatively perceived. They offer to help even when their help is not sought

or appreciated. They may correct peers, colleagues, or strangers. For example, parents who continue to comment on and correct an adult child's marriage, housekeeping skills, child-rearing behavior, or job in the interest of being "helpful" may be doing so because "father (or mother) knows best." They continue their "helpful" behavior even after being asked to cease.

- *Real* narcissistic individuals believe that they are superior to others. This view may be justified and consensually validated. They are not, however, hesitant to point out their "gifts" to others, often frequently and loudly.

- *Compensated* narcissistic individuals feel so badly about themselves that they create a superperson to make up for their perceived lacks and failures. For example, individuals who feel so badly about themselves or their abilities inflate themselves in unrealistic ways to appear more competent or inflate their image by denigrating others. This is the type of person referred to earlier by Horney (1937).

- *Oblivious* narcissistic individuals are unaware of their effect on others. They may be excluded from groups or social settings and have no idea why they are excluded. For example, these individuals are constantly making social gaffes and seem to stride through life with little ill-intent but a blind eye to where they have just overstepped.

- *Hypervigilant* narcissistic individuals are constantly scanning for any tiny insult, denigration, or for any sign of being discovered to not be as powerful or able as they see themselves. To not be powerful is to be vulnerable. For example, these individuals may be seen or diagnosed as having a paranoid personality inasmuch as they are on constant guard for any slight or affront from all quarters.

- *Ruthless* narcissistic individuals gain satisfaction and enjoyment from the discomfort of others. They may often be the cause of the discomfort by teasing, insulting, or pointing out the flaws and foibles of others, and they may gain sadistic gratification from "putting others down" or embarrassing others publicly. They may even see this behavior as humorous.

- *Helpless* narcissistic individuals are often diagnosed with refractive anxiety or depression. No treatment or therapist seems to be able to treat their persistent problems. For these individuals, the goal is winning. By beating therapists at their therapeutic game, they gain power, but at the cost of other, more adaptive life experiences.

DEVELOPING A THERAPEUTIC RELATIONSHIP

A key ingredient in CBT is the development of a collaborative set. This generally involves the development of a therapeutic alliance or treatment bond. Often thought of as synonymous, they are, in fact, quite different, with different goals and foci. The *treatment bond* involves the relationship between the therapist and the patient. The *therapeutic alliance* involves the treatment plan, treatment goals, and agreement to work on those goals. A treatment bond may be far more difficult to establish and maintain with narcissistic individuals, who may, in fact, be resistant to the emotional connection that is part of the treatment bond. In light of their difficulty in establishing and maintaining relationships and their tendency to push the bounds of acceptable behavior, the therapeutic alliance is, for them, a far safer treatment focus than a treatment bond. To help avoid the challenges and "contests" that are part of the treatment bond, the alliance can be structured so that the focus and goals are aligned with their informed and enlightened self-interest.

A continual theme in treatment is the patient's informed and enlightened self-interest. Simply put, the therapist repeats the questions, "How do you profit from this?" "How does this help *you?*" "Why continue behavior that seems to keep getting you less of what you want rather than more?" In effect, the therapist uses the narcissism rather than fights against it; the therapist uses the patient's pathology in the service of the therapy rather than fighting the pathology, which for the patient is not pathology but simply a lack of perceived acceptance of their special status. The building of a strong collaborative relationship that focuses on the alliance is essential because participation in psychotherapy requires that narcissistic individuals be asked to do things which they have had great difficulty doing, have never had to do, or have never learned to do: tolerating frustration, bearing great amounts of anxiety without the usually employed avoidant behavior or usual coping strategies (e.g., abusing drugs, taking flight, abusing others, acting out in some form, disciplining themselves and talking about their ideas and feelings). Collaboration can be difficult both because of the characteristics of the patient and the reactions the patient elicits from the therapist. Unless the therapist has a clear, strong, reasonable, and realistic idea and image of what the desired outcome will be, treatment cannot be successful or will succeed only by accident. The therapist must be able to collaborate with the patient to outline what the "finished product" will look like, act like, and sound like. The patient must agree as part of the therapeutic alliance.

The patient's narcissism, most naturally, becomes a focus of therapy as it often impedes progress toward accomplishing more concrete goals. In practice, it may be far more realistic to work on changing specific behaviors and on helping individuals be more moderate in their narcissism than to plan to change a life-long narcissistic pattern. As noted earlier, insofar as possible, the therapist must work with, rather than against, the narcissistic pattern in order to minimize unproductive conflict and to engage patients in therapy. The therapist who is not willing or able to tolerate the narcissistic patient's behavior and accommodate to it will have difficulty inducing the patient to remain in therapy. Conversely, the therapist who is unwilling to confront the narcissistic patient because he or she is so easily offended or is concerned about being the target of the patient's tantrum is likely to be unable to have any therapeutic impact. It is essential for the therapist to establish and maintain firm guidelines and limits for patients early in therapy. This may be as straightforward as asking patients to not put muddy shoes on a couch in the office or to not steal magazines from the waiting room. The rules and limits should cover as many potentialities as possible (e.g., frequency of phone calls, length of phone calls, and attendance at support groups). Offering unconditional positive regard may feed into the narcissism (i.e., all behaviors cannot be accepted). Clearly, the bond alone is not sufficient for change. The therapeutic alliance requires that there be an agreement or contract on the goals, tasks, and focus of therapy.

THE NARCISSISTIC INJURY

The therapist must also be educated to the nature of the narcissistic injury or insult. Narcissistic individuals may become very upset by challenges to their narcissistic striving or to previously uninterrupted behavior. They may respond to the perceived loss or threat of loss of the narcissistic "prizes" with anger, frustration, or aggression. They may try to "heal" the injury, or recoup the perceived loss, or even perceive the need to injure the perpetrator. They may escalate their demands, increase the frequency and volume of their protests, or threaten injury to themselves or others unless they are allowed to proceed as they wish. What is interesting, and unexpected, is that even small covert actions may be satisfying enough to heal the loss and "injury"; an apology from another may soothe the roiled waters and calm what appeared to be an emotional tsunami.

CBT TREATMENT PLANNING

The treatment goals must meet a number of criteria.

1. The goals of the treatment must be realistic. A realistic goal is to reduce the narcissism to manageable and more acceptable proportions.

2. Treatment must be reasonable in terms of timing and frequency of sessions, attendance at sessions, or pacing of the sessions and the therapy more generally.
3. The therapy goals must be hierarchical and sequential. The treatment plan must be set out so that it can be mapped with goals; in this way, the therapy can build on present skills and later acquired skills.
4. Treatment goals must be proximal so that the therapist can improve the chance of the goals being reached.
5. The therapeutic goals must be well-delineated to enhance the chances for therapeutic success. Vague goals lead to vague therapy, which leads to vague results.
6. The therapist must make a careful assessment of the emotional, behavioral, contextual, and cognitive repertoire of the patient. When the baseline repertoire is established, the treatment map dictates what additional skills need to be developed.
7. The treatment goals must be agreed to by the individual before treatment can proceed.
8. The goals of treatment must be seen by the individual as valuable. Among all the requirements of treatment, this is perhaps the most important. To have the individual give up what has been so very rewarding for so long must require a value that can potentially equal or even exceed that of the more dysfunctional behavior.
9. The therapist must be informed and willing to set and maintain limits and to offer the patient appropriate feedback on his or her behavior and rewards that are reasonable and that would defuse or no longer fuel the narcissism.

CASE EXAMPLE

In this case example, the patient's identity has been disguised to maintain confidentiality. Veronica Acres, recently hired as an executive vice-president of sales and marketing of a large corporation, is facing her first major crisis. In her first month in her executive position, she has been deluged by complaints from her division directors (as well as their department managers, vendors, and even customers). The complaints focused on Bill Bronson, whose promotion last year to director of marketing topped a meteoric rise in the company. Veronica has been stunned by the revelations about Bill's management and communication styles and behavior. She finds it hard to reconcile his apparently brilliant success with the disastrous performance being brought to her attention now. In the past 2 weeks alone, three managers in the marketing department have asked for transfers to other departments or tendered their resignations, the union is threatening to file several grievances, and morale is at an all-time low. Most strikingly, two long-term clients have withdrawn from discussions of major new projects.

Veronica promised the CEO to get to the bottom of this. As a first step, she contacted her predecessor, Bill's former boss, who expressed amazement when informed of Bill's problems. According to him, Bill was one of the most promising junior marketing managers he had ever encountered. Bill demonstrated the drive, enthusiasm, creativity, and assertive ambition that are considered so vital in the highly competitive marketing environment. He had been impressed with Bill's total focus on success, his skills in bringing attention to his accomplishments, and his charismatic way of pulling others together to accomplish challenging goals. It seemed there was no challenge too difficult for Bill to take on—he plunged right in, cut to the chase, made the tough calls, and enjoyed the well-deserved attention and prestige when he scored. Bill was seen as a magnetic, engaged champion of his projects who did what it took to succeed.

Bill himself was taken aback when Veronica spoke with him about his performance. He struggled noticeably to control his reactions when she relayed some of the feedback she had received from subordinates, peers, and clients. As the conversation proceeded, Bill grew frustrated and angry—he stated that he was offended that "his superior efforts" were not recognized by many of the same people who so benefitted from his accomplishments. He further suggested that envy might be playing a role and that people simply did not want to admit that they were overshadowed by his energy, work ethic, and abilities. He lamented the time he had spent covering for errors of judgment or lackadaisical performance by his subordinates or teammates: "They should be thanking their lucky stars that I took charge, went the extra mile, and ultimately made them all look good. Sure, I had to break a few eggs now and then, but what an omelet they had to feast upon! Hurt feelings and whining have no place in such a demanding, competitive industry particularly in today's market!" Bill believed he was doing a stellar job and was entitled to the status and respect his position commanded.

When Veronica questioned Bill's colleagues and subordinates, she heard a different story. His communication style consisted of asserting his point of view—ignoring or cutting off comments by other team members, making snide remarks or rolling his eyes at suggestions, and consistently interrupting presentations with his own point of view. When disagreements arose, he seemed energized and aggressive, almost coercive in his efforts to prevail. He often tried to pit other team members against one another, taking one or the other into his "confidence" and derogating the work, ideas, or personal characteristics of targeted team members. In this atmosphere of intimidation, subordinates were reluctant to criticize or question Bill's plans and directives for fear of becoming the next target of his snide comments, glares, finger pointing, slamming objects, cursing, and obscene gestures.

Veronica thus learned that Bill had been highly successful in navigating the politics of this competitive organizational culture. He had some real accomplishments under his belt and had made sure his status and achievements were recognized. However, his grandiose self-importance; exaggerated concern with success, power, status, and admiration; sense of entitlement; and, above all, the exploitativeness, envy, arrogance, and bullying that characterized his relationships with peers and subordinates were threatening the future of the organization. Bill demonstrated several of the narcissistic styles described above in the Assessment section.

- *Positive self-esteem.* Clearly Bill believed he had contributed energy, creativity, hard work, managerial talent, and charismatic leadership to the organization. He saw his rapid rise in the management hierarchy as validation of his marketing and managerial excellence.
- *Healthy narcissism.* Bill was frankly surprised that the very people who had so benefitted from his hard work and talent did not recognize how indebted they and the organization really were to him. He was especially critical of those whose own careers had been saved by Bill's extraordinary job of covering for their alleged errors of judgment and lackadaisical performance.
- *Group narcissism.* Although Bill recognized that he may have "broken a few eggs" along the way, he believed it had been necessary for the survival of the team and the organization in such a competitive economic environment.
- *Helpful narcissism.* Bill remained amazed that all the subordinates and colleagues he had helped did not seem to appreciate his concern and efforts. He seemed unaware that his extraordinary career success had been, in part, due to his skills at impression management—that is, taking on visible tasks with potential to highlight his own superiority—and effectively taking credit for successes while scapegoating others for failures. This of course had not gone unnoticed by his subordinates and peers, whom he claimed to have "helped" along the way.
- *Real narcissism.* Again, Bill's skill at impression management had enabled him to play up to his bosses, making sure that all were aware of his talents and achievements. He pursued a strategy of taking on only those tasks that overtly demonstrated his

"superiority," and he avoided tasks that appeared mundane or had a low probability of success (Wallace & Baumeister, 2002).

- *Hypervigilant narcissism.* Bill responded to Veronica's implied criticism with frustration and anger; he considered the complaints against his management style and indeed the lack of adulation for his "superior efforts" to be offensive. He attributed complaints to envy and ignorance by incompetent, jealous inferiors.

- *Ruthless narcissism.* Bill admitted he had not always handled his subordinates and peers with kid gloves, but he maintained that "whiners" and "babies" have no place in such a competitive industry.

What would be the most effective and appropriate direction for Veronica's intervention? If Veronica believed that Bill's personality could be channeled to the benefit of the organization and its members, she might strongly encourage (or require) him to enter an executive coaching process in order to learn to use his strengths rather than experiencing his worst nightmare (failure). Alternatively, she might do nothing and allow the group process to unfold. It is possible that the group would come together and force or compel Bill to alter what he was doing. A third possibility would be for Veronica to "sacrifice" Bill's strengths and terminate his employment because of its costs in terms of staff productivity, morale, creativity, satisfaction, and allegiance to the organization, and its potential external direct and indirect costs such as litigation, workers' compensation, and corporate reputation.

Veronica decided to refer Bill for what she called "coaching." Bill's immediate reaction to this recommendation was to make light of it; he called the referral a sham and a joke. He was not in need of "shrinking"; he countered with the suggestion that his entire work group would "profit from a series of large group hugs, followed by a large meal, followed by electroconvulsive therapy." When Veronica was clear that this was not a recommendation but a requirement for Bill's continued employment, he appeared agreeable and made no further argument.

When Bill entered the coach's office, he was his most charming self. He started by complimenting the coach on the décor of the office and then moved to making it clear that he had researched the coach and could recite the statistics of the date and title of his doctorate, his publications, his previous jobs, and his present marital status. Bill ended his recitation by stating, "See, I know all about you. In fact, there is very little I don't know. Now just who do you think you are to think that you are going to change me?" At this point, Bill's pleasant demeanor vanished and he became more inquisitorial: "What have you been told? Who told you these things? Given that you have no expertise in business just what do you think that you are going to do for me? Have you ever worked with successful people? How much money are they paying you to do this? What magic mumbo-jumbo are you going to use? Do you want a list of my toilet-training experiences? Who do you report to? What sort of report will you write, and to who?" He then sat back in his seat and stated, "I expect an answer to all of my questions."

The coach's response was to immediately address each of Bill's questions directly. Having read through the referral, the coach had developed a tentative diagnostic hypothesis that Bill had a narcissistic personality. The therapist made several statements that seemed to reduce Bill's aggressive stance.

"I'm a coach. My job is to help people perform better. For example, even Hemingway had an editor, and every major baseball team has a batting coach. Your questions are excellent. You are no different. What I can do for you is to help get all of these people off of your back so that you can do what you do best and they can continue to reap the profits of your work." (By alluding to Hemingway, a Nobel Prize winner, and major league baseball teams, the therapist put Bill in the company of high performers.)

"Regarding a report, you and I will write the final report together." (This immediately spoke to the collaboration). "Let me recommend a plan, for your approval. I recommend that we meet for no more than 10 sessions, after today, on a weekly basis. This should give us adequate time to make and implement the plans that we need to develop.

"Let's get started. Who hassles you most? What has been the nature and frequency of these experiences?" Many similar questions followed, and Bill shifted once again and became not only collaborative but almost conspiratorial. The coach laid out the plan for all 10 sessions and asked Bill for his agreement for each small part of the plan. The coach indicated that it would be to Bill's great advantage to do a number of behavioral experiments between sessions: "I don't want you to change who you are. Remember, Popeye said, 'I yam wot I yam.' We're going to talk about how to change what you do to get your work team, your boss, and anyone else around to see a new Bill." Homework involved planning a behavior that was not what people expected of him. He would then evaluate the reactions of others. As before, Bill was asked, "What do you think?" As Bill approved each step, his anxiety about being attacked, insulted, demeaned, or denigrated lessened. In subsequent sessions he would greet the therapist with, "Hey coach. What's shaking?"

At the fifth coaching session Bill reported that Veronica had called him in and complimented him on a particular interaction that she had seen. Bill's response was, "She's so *dumb*." As Bill changed what he did and was reinforced for his "new" behaviors, he was willing to continue them. There were, however, several missteps where Bill could not control his anger at the incompetence of the worker and reverted to the old Bill. With great effort he spoke to the person the next day and stated to them that he was aware that he had lost his temper. Although he did not apologize, the fact that he had approached the person and acknowledged his loss of temper was the stuff of office gossip for a week.

At the eighth session termination was begun. There was a review of basic skills and strategies. Bill made a list of specific persons at work and their likely annoying behaviors. He then added a column on how he could deal with these people.

As agreed, the final report was done collaboratively, and Bill was satisfied that no "secrets" were told and that he was not exposed in any way. In the last session Bill asked if he could contact the coach if his "batting average" started to slip. The coach informed him that that was a decision that Veronica could make, but he believed that she would agree. In fact, Veronica was pleased with the result of the therapy/coaching, agreed that Bill could come as often as he thought necessary, and referred several other executives for therapy.

Given the long-standing nature of Bill's "style," his successes over time that he (and his mentors and bosses) attributed to his style, and the reinforcement that he has garnered as a result of his successes, it was unlikely that he would alter his style (unless the consequence for maintaining it was loss of his position). Change was promoted as helping Bill get even more of the things that he cherished. The changes, however, were of necessity minimal, and some were short-lived. Furthermore, they may ultimately have been more cosmetic than internalized. The goals of the change were explicated and discussed with Bill, not euphemistically but directly. He would have to understand that the changes being requested were to help him get more of what he wanted, rather than less, but the new behaviors would have to be in line with the requirements of the organizational hierarchy, in the person of Veronica. Furthermore, in addition to working with Bill, Veronica must make clear to Bill's supervisor and organizational leadership the importance of the changes for Bill and for the organization and the ramifications of failing to change.

SUMMARY

There is a fine line between positive self-esteem and narcissism. The narcissistic individual comes by his or her style honestly: learning in the context of the family, modeling important, powerful, and credible others; and having the narcissistic style and behavior reinforced.

Narcissism cannot be viewed as a unitary phenomenon; rather, it is a collection of related behaviors and styles that are then seen to typify the individual. When these styles or modes interfere with adaptation, a disorder emerges. Stemming from early interactions with family, the direction of the narcissism reflects the culture, demands, expectations, and schematic modes of the family. When the behaviors are further reinforced by peers, teachers, school personnel, or relatives, the individual may see little reason to modify his or her narcissistic behavior.

A more reasonable approach is to help narcissistic individuals be less obvious in their narcissistic expressions, to show greater flexibility and less compulsivity, and to be willing to modulate their behavior, all in the service of getting more of what they want. In effect, the therapy must focus on using the narcissistic pathology in the service of patients' best interest.

REFERENCES

American Psychiatric Association. (2000). *Diagnostic and statistical manual of mental disorders* (4th ed., text rev.). Washington, DC: Author.

Beck, A. T., Freeman, A., & Associates. (1990). *Cognitive therapy of personality disorders*. New York, NY: Guilford Press.

Beck, A. T., Freeman, A., Davis, D. D., & Associates. (2004). *Cognitive therapy of personality disorders* (2nd ed.). New York, NY: Guilford Press.

Federn, P. (1952). *Ego psychology and the psychoses*. New York, NY: Basic Books.

Freeman, A., Pretzer, J., Fleming, B., & Simon, K. (1990). *Clinical applications of cognitive therapy*. New York, NY: Kluwer. doi:10.1007/978-1-4684-0007-6

Freeman, A., Pretzer, J., Fleming, B., & Simon, K. (2004). *Clinical applications of cognitive therapy* (2nd ed.). New York, NY: Kluwer. doi:10.1007/978-1-4419-8905-5

Freeman, A., & Rigby, A. (2003). Personality disorders among children and adolescents: Is it an unlikely diagnosis? In M. A. Reinecke, F. M. Dattilio, & A. Freeman (Eds.), *Cognitive therapy with children and adolescents* (2nd ed., pp. 434–464). New York, NY: Guilford Press.

Hamner, T. J., & Turner, P. H. (1985). *Parenting in contemporary society*. Englewood Cliffs, NJ: Prentice-Hall.

Hill, R. W., & Yousey, G. P. (1998). Adaptive and maladaptive narcissism among university faculty, clergy, politicians, and librarians. *Current Psychology, 17,* 163–169. doi:10.1007/s12144-998-1003-x

Horney, K. (1937). *The neurotic personality of our time*. New York, NY: Norton.

Kernberg, O. (1975). *Borderline conditions and pathological narcissism*. New York, NY: Jason Aronson.

Knell, S. M., & Ruma, C. D. (2003). Play therapy with a sexually abused child. In M. A. Reinecke, F. M. Dattilio, & A. Freeman (Eds.), *Cognitive therapy with children and adolescents* (2nd ed., pp. 338–368). New York, NY: Guilford Press.

Lubit, R. (2002). The long-term organizational impact of destructively narcissistic managers. *The Academy of Management Executive, 16,* 127–138. doi:10.5465/AME.2002.6640218

Mandler, G. (1984). *Mind and body: Psychology of emotions and stress*. New York, NY: Norton.

Millon, T., & Everly, G. S. (1985). *Personality and its disorders: A biosocial learning approach*. New York, NY: Wiley.

Millon, T., Millon, C. M., Meagher, S., & Grossman, S. (2004). *Personality disorders in modern life*. Hoboken, NJ: Wiley.

Rosenthal, S. A., & Pittinsky, T. L. (2006). Narcissistic leadership. *The Leadership Quarterly, 17*, 617–633. doi:10.1016/j.leaqua.2006.10.005

Taylor, S. E., & Crocker, J. (1981). Schematic bases of social information processing. In E. T. Higgens, C. P. Herman, & M. P. Zanna (Eds.), *Social cognition* (pp. 89–134). Hillsdale, NJ: Erlbaum.

Wallace H. M.. & Baumeister, R. F. (2002) The performance of narcissists rises and falls with perceived opportunity for glory. *Journal of Personality and Social Psychology, 82*, 819–834.

APPENDIX 18.1. SPECIFIC ASSESSMENT FOR NARCISSISM

1. Assess the individual's empathy skills through history and observation.
2. Are empathy skills situational or contextual?
3. What is the individual's threshold for being empathic?
4. What is the "gain" or value to the child to be empathic?
5. Has there been a "payoff" for limiting or lack of empathy?
6. Is empathy (or lack thereof) culturally related?
7. Does the individual understand the construct and purpose of empathy?
8. Are empathy and morality connected by the individual?
9. What empathy skill set is missing for the individual?
10. How can the skill(s) be taught or modeled by the therapist?
11. Does the individual understand the idea, purpose, and rationale for assuming the perspective of another?
12. How will it profit the individual to become aware of the needs, views, and feelings of another?

INDEX

Narcissistic personality disorder (NPD).
See also specific headings
and borderline personality organization, 240–242
comorbidity research on, 183–184
definitions for, 93–94
diagnostic models for, 51–54
DSM–5 proposed changes to, 54–57
DSM criteria for, 48–51
empirical data on, 29
etiology of, 133
measurement of, 93–94
as official diagnosis, 46–47
as prototype, 130
in psychodynamic tradition, 147
schema modes for, 287, 288
in self psychology, 258
suffering with, 301–302
Narcissistic Personality Inventory-21, 171
Narcissistic self, 256
Narcissistic subtypes, 29–40
arrogant/entitled, 53, 73
in case examples, 38–40
countertransference patterns with,
210–215
depressed/depleted, 53, 73
development of criteria for, 30–33
diagnostic criteria for, 33–38
empirical findings on, 51
in Greek myth, 18
in historical overview, 21–24
interpersonal problems with, 115
key features of, 210
new directions for, 34–38
in *Psychodynamic Diagnostic
Manual*, 40
treatment for, 38
Narcissistic transference, 261
Narcissistic vulnerability
features of, 168
and narcissistic grandiosity, 115
in PNI approach, 95–98, 101–105
scales for, 99–101
Narcissus, 16–22, 24
Narcissus, 18
Narcotics, 17
National Epidemiologic Survey on
Alcohol and Related Conditions
(NESARC), 184, 198–199
National narcissism, 19

Needs, unmet, 286–287
Negative self-images
as defense mechanism, 156
in intrapsychic conflict, 149–150
in short-term dynamic
psychotherapy, 277–278
Nelson-Gray, R. O., 52
NESARC (National Epidemiologic
Survey on Alcohol and Related
Conditions), 184, 198–199
Neurotic personality disorders, 66–67
Neutrality, technical, 248
Nobel Prize complex, 151
Nondeclarative memory systems
and mentalization, 132–133
regulatory solutions for, 137–141
shame in, 134–135
Nondeclarative structures, 139–141
Nonverbal behavior, 122
Nottestad, J. A., 170–171
NPD. *See* Narcissistic personality disorder

Object hunger, 152
Object relations. *See also* Selfobjects
defensive style of, 212
dyads in, 239, 250
and omnipotence, 244
and personality traits, 208
Oblivious narcissism, 211, 309
Observation, 91
Observer, excluded, 211, 214–215
Oedipal psychopathology, 272
Ogrodniczuk, J. S., 104, 209, 213
Omnipotence
as defense mechanism, 154–155
and fragmented identity, 241
in transferences, 244–246
Omnipotent control, 214–215
Only-child status, 305
"On Narcissism" (S. Freud), 19, 20
Optimal frustrations, 255–257
Others
denigration of, 138
disregard for feelings of, 114
idealization of, 156
lack of concern for, 83
observation of, 91
perceptions of, 71
rejection of, 149–150
schemata for, 86–88
as subhuman, 84

Overcompensating mode, 288, 296
Overgeneralizations, 306
Overt narcissism, 4–5, 96–97
Overvaluation, 48, 153
Ovid, 16–18

Painful states, 74–75
Paradise Lost (J. Milton), 18
Parallel process, 292–293
Parenting style
    in borderline personality
        organization, 237–238
    in child development, 47–48, 270
    conditional love in, 293–294
    in development of self, 270
    in disruption of self-
        representations, 30
    in maladaptive schemas, 286–287
    in pathological narcissism inventory,
        103–104
Parents
    disruption of self-representations
        by, 30
    idealization of, 22
    idealized imagoes of, 256, 257,
        262–263
    indulgent, 303–304
    overvaluation of child by, 48
    rejection by, 47–48
Parkin, A., 87–88
Parthenius, 16
Passive audience, 244–245
Pathogenic experiences, 270
Pathological development, 257–259
Pathological grandiose self, 240–242
Pathological grief, 272, 279
Pathological narcissism. *See also*
    Narcissistic personality
    disorder
    in affect regulation–based model,
        130–133
    and borderline personality
        disorder, 237
    construct definition of, 93–94
    core dynamics of, 271
    in short-term dynamic
        psychotherapy, 271–273
    and TFP, 240–242
    therapeutic boundaries with,
        225–232

Pathological narcissism inventory
    (PNI), 93–105
    overview of, 97–101
    phenotypic description for, 94–97
    validity of, 101–105
Pathology, 65
Pausanias, 16
PCRS (Psychodynamic Conflict Rating
    Scales), 148–149
*PDM. See Psychodynamic Diagnostic
    Manual*
Perfectionism, 271
Perlman, Itzhak, 308
Persecutory dyad, 237–238, 240n3
Personality, 18–19, 65. *See also*
    Personality traits
Personality disorders. *See also specific
    headings*
    defense hierarchies with, 153
    definition of, 65
    descriptive criteria for, 47
    diagnosis of, 63
    in *DSM–5*, 54–55
    neurotic, 66–67
    in self psychology, 258–259
Personality Disorders Workgroup, 54, 55
Personality organization. *See also*
    Borderline personality
    organization
    PDM approach to, 66–69
    in *PDM* assessment, 76–77
    reformation of, 90–91
Personality traits
    assessment of, 32–33
    in descriptive assessment, 65
    in diagnosis, 37–38
    dislocation of, 82
    externalization of, 88
    and object relations, 208
    in pathological narcissism inventory,
        101–102
Phenomenology, 51
Phenotypes, 94–97, 307
Pincus, A. L., 4, 49, 99–100, 102–104,
    121, 122, 168
PNI. *See* Pathological narcissism
    inventory
Polythetic classification, 31, 47, 49–50
Positive self-esteem, 308, 314
Power, 302–303

Svindseth, M. F., 170–171
SWAP-200 (Shedler-Westen
    Assessment Procedure 200), 32–34
SWAP-II (Shedler-Westen Assessment
    Procedure-II), 34
Symington, N., 214

Tangney, J. P., 176
Tartakoff, H., 151
Technical neutrality, 248
Teiresias, 17
Temperament, 307–308
Tension arc, 257
Termination
    with EB-STDP intervention,
        278–279
    premature, 231–232
    with vulnerable narcissism, 231
Terminology, 94–97, 168
TFP. See Transference-focused psycho
    therapy
Theoretical perspective, 46–47, 254
Therapeutic alliance
    definition of, 310
    protypical formation in, 88
    in state stabilization, 89–90
Therapeutic boundaries, 219–232
    identification and counteridentifica-
        tion in, 224–225
    maintenance of, 221–222
    and narcissism construct, 219–220
    and pathological narcissism,
        225–232
    and vulnerable narcissism, 222–223
Therapeutic relationship
    boundaries in, 222
    in cognitive behavioral perspectives,
        310–311
    emotional antennae in, 222–223
    limit setting in, 297–298
    and suicide risk, 178
Therapist
    accommodation behaviors by, 311
    boredom of, 227, 246–247
    competence of, 292–293
    countertransference responses of,
        207–208, 243
    disregard for feelings of, 114
    emotions of, 209, 212, 265–266
    fear of patient by, 247

hopelessness feelings of, 247
idealization of, 213–214
interpretations centered on, 250
as object of contempt, 212–213
as passive audience, 244–245
patient devaluation of, 244–246
in schema therapy, 291–292
self-disclosure by, 296–297
self-focus of, 227–228
as sounding board, 117, 210–212
and vulnerable narcissism, 222–223
Thomson, J. A., 51
Tolerance, 86, 138–141
Torgersen, S., 169
Transference(s). See also Selfobject
    transferences
    coldness in, 122
    contempt of therapist as, 212–213
    and countertransference, 208–209
    in EB-STDP intervention, 275–277
    exploitability in, 124–125
    idealization as, 213–214
    merger self-object, 24
    mirroring, 178, 261, 262, 265
    mutual admiration as, 215
    narcissistic, 261
    omnipotence in, 244–246
    omnipotent control as, 214–215
    and resistance, 272–273
    in self psychology, 261–263
    self-sufficient, 24
    social avoidance in, 123
    "sounding board" pattern of, 117,
        210–212
    in TFP, 244–246
    with vindictiveness, 119
Transference-focused psychotherapy
    (TFP), 235–251
    borderline personality organization
        in, 237–242
    evaluation and anamnesis in,
        242–243
    overview of, 236–237
    and pathological narcissism,
        240–242
    treatment contract for, 243–244
    treatment process in, 244–250
Transmuting internalization, 142,
    256–257
Treatment bond, 310

Treatment contract, 243–244
Treatment goals
  in cognitive behavior therapy,
    311–312
  of EB-STDP, 274–275
  of schema therapy, 291–292, 296–299
  of self psychology approach, 266–267
Treatment planning, 311–312
Treatment process
  for narcissistic subtypes, 38
  protypical formation in, 88–91
  with self psychology approach,
    259–266
  shame in, 139
  of short-term dynamic
    psychotherapy, 273–279
  with structural assessment and
    diagnosis, 69
  with TFP, 236–237, 244–250
Trial therapy, 273–274
Tritt, S. M., 102
Turner, P. H., 304
Twenge, J. M., 287
Twinship transference, 261–262

Unconditional acceptance, 229
Unethical behaviors, 75
Unmet needs, 286–287

Validation, 95
Validity, 33, 101–105
Vanity, 3
Verbal interventions, 141
Vertical split, 258–259
Vindictiveness, 117–119
Violations, boundary, 221–222
Violence. *See* Aggression
Virgil, 16
Vulnerability
  with counter-dependent conflict, 151
  and covert narcissism, 96

expression of, 4–5
of therapist, 223
Vulnerable child mode, 288, 294–295
Vulnerable narcissism. *See also*
    Narcissistic vulnerability
  and child development processes, 23
  coldness with, 121–122
  connection in, 230
  criteria for, 33
  criticism in, 227–228
  devaluation in, 227–228
  empirical data on, 121
  features of, 4
  interpersonal problems with,
    121–125
  of psychotherapist, 222–223
  responsibility taking in, 228
  and termination, 231
  therapeutic boundaries with,
    222–223
  in therapist, 220
  therapist caretaking with, 225–226
  and therapist identification, 224–225
  unconditional acceptance in, 229

Wallin, J., 170–171
Wave 1 NESARC study, 185
Wave 2 NESARC study, 184–193
Weishaar, M., 285
Westen, D., 32, 51
Widiger, T. A., 55
Wilson, J. P., 176
Withholding, 230
Wolf, E. S., 153, 156
Wright, A. G. C., 99–100

Young, J. E., 52, 285, 286

Zeigler-Hill, V., 103
Zeus, 17

ABOUT THE EDITOR

John S. Ogrodniczuk, PhD, is an associate professor and director of the Psychotherapy Program in the Department of Psychiatry, University of British Columbia. In his role as director, he coordinates the operations of Canada's second largest medically based psychotherapy training program. In addition, he has developed a psychotherapy research program that is recognized as one of the more comprehensive and productive of its kind. His research involves a variety of psychotherapies and patient populations, but he has a particular interest in studying psychodynamic psychotherapy, personality disorder, and men's mental health.

Dr. Ogrodniczuk has received regular funding to support his research and has more than 100 scientific publications. He has coauthored three previous books with the American Psychological Association. He is a recipient of the Outstanding Early Career Achievement Award presented by the Society for Psychotherapy Research. In addition to his research, he is involved with teaching medical students and psychiatry residents, serves as associate editor for the journal *Psychotherapy Research*, serves on the editorial board for three other journals (*Group Dynamics*, *Journal of Personality Disorders*, and *Psychotherapy*), provides regular reviews for more than a dozen scientific and clinical journals, and consults with mental health clinics about service provision and evaluation.